VW Transporter 1700/1800 Owners Workshop Manual

by J H Haynes
Associate Member of the Guild of Motoring Writers
and K F Kinchin

Models covered
All models based on the Transporter:
   1700 — 1972 to 1973
   1800 — 1973 to 1974

ISBN 85696 226 0

Printed in England

J H HAYNES AND COMPANY LIMITED
SPARKFORD YEOVIL SOMERSET ENGLAND

distributed in the USA by
HAYNES PUBLICATIONS INC.
9421 WINNETKA AVENUE
CHATSWORTH LOS ANGELES
CALIFORNIA 91311 USA

Acknowledgements

Special thanks are due to the VW Organisation for their assistance with technical information and the supply of certain illustrations. Castrol Limited provided lubrication details.

Car Mechanics magazine kindly supplied several of the photographs in the bodywork repair sequence of Chapter 12.

Mr Jack Hatcher of Dunnicks Mead Motors, Wedmore, Somerset, provided invaluable help; he allowed us to climb all over and photograph a 1975 model 1800 Transporter and also gave much useful advice.

Lastly, thanks are extended to all of those people at Sparkford who helped in the production of this manual. Particularly, Brian Horsfall who carried out the mechanical work; Les Brazier and Tom Grainger who took the photographs and Stanley Randolph who planned the layout of each page.

About this manual

Introduction

Whether it is a caravan providing splendid holidays, a fire tender, a station wagon, or a workhorse delivery van or pick-up the Transporter is a good tempered, hard-working, reliable vehicle which will grace any car park.

The 1700cc version introduced in 1972 complete with Automatic or Manual Transmission was followed in 1974 by the 1800cc engine version. This will cruise happily all day in the upper 70 mph bracket, if you can find a road to do it on, and then turn off and tackle rough ground just as cheerfully.

The unusual design of twin carburettor with central idling gives a smart acceleration for this type of vehicle yet retaining reasonable economy, but the adjustment is critical. For this a few special tools and meters are needed but they are not expensive and may be used on any make of vehicle.

The American versions are fitted with Exhaust Afterburn equipment and Exhaust Gas Recirculation. This is described in the text as well as the charcoal filter for the petrol tank vent.

We took an engine to pieces and rebuilt it, and did the same for a gearbox and final drive. We did not have any special jigs or fixtures so in some instances we stopped dismantling where it was considered that unless special tools were available that more damage than good would be done. Most of the remainder of the working parts were dismantled and replaced, as the photos will show.

Even the best vehicles wear out or suffer accident sometimes and should this happen it is hoped that the owner may be helped in his decision of what to do by "getting out the book".

Its use

The book is divided into twelve Chapters. Each Chapter is divided into numbered Sections which are headed in **bold** type between horizontal lines. Each section consists of serially numbered paragraphs.

Procedures, once described in the text, are not normally repeated. If it is necessary to refer to a particular paragraph in another Chapter the reference is self-explanatory (eg; 'Chapter 1/5:5'). Cross-references given without the use of the word 'Chapter' apply to a Section in the same Chapter (eg; 'See Section 8' means also 'in this Chapter').

All illustrations carry a caption. Where the illustration is designated as a Figure the reference is merely a sequence number for the Chapter. Where the illustration is not designated as a Figure (ie; photographs) the reference number pinpoints the Section and paragraph in that Chapter to which the picture refers.

When the left or right side of the vehicle is mentioned it is as if looking forward.

Whilst every care is taken to ensure that the information in this manual is correct no liability can be accepted by the authors or publishers for loss, damage or injury caused by any errors in, or omissions from, the information given.

Contents

4

1974 VW Continental - UK Specification

5

1973 VW Station Wagon - North American Specification

As this book has been written in England, it uses the appropriate English component names, phrases, and spelling. Some of these differ from those used in America. Normally, these cause no difficulty, but to make sure, a glossary is printed below. In ordering spare parts remember the parts list will probably use these words:

Glossary

English	American	English	American
Accelerator	Gas pedal	Layshaft (of gearbox)	Counter shaft
Alternator	Generator (AC)	Leading shoe (of brake)	Primary shoe
Anti-roll bar	Stabiliser or sway bar	Locks	Latches
Choke/venturi	Barrel	Motorway	Freeway, turnpike etc.
Battery	Energizer	Number plate	Licence plate
Bonnet (engine cover)	Hood	Paraffin	Kerosene
Boot lid	Trunk lid	Petrol	Gasoline
Boot (luggage compartment)	Trunk	Petrol tank	Gas tank
Bottom gear	1st gear	'Pinking'	'Pinging'
Bulkhead	Firewall	Quarter light	Quarter window
Camfollower or tappet	Valve lifter or tappet	Retread	Recap
Carburettor	Carburetor	Reverse	Back-up
Catch	Latch	Rocker cover	Valve cover
Circlip	Snap ring	Roof rack	Car-top carrier
Clearance	Lash	Saloon	Sedan
Crownwheel	Ring gear (of differential)	Seized	Frozen
Disc (brake)	Rotor/disk	Side indicator lights	Side marker lights
Driveshaft	Propellor shaft	Side light	Parking light
Drop arm	Pitman arm	Silencer	Muffler
Drop head coupe	Convertible	Spanner	Wrench
Dynamo	Generator (DC)	Sill panel (beneath doors)	Rocker panel
Earth (electrical)	Ground	Split cotter (for valve spring cap)	Lock (for valve spring retainer)
Engineer's blue	Prussion blue	Split pin	Cotter pin
Estate car	Station wagon	Steering arm	Spindle arm
Exhaust manifold	Header	Sump	Oil pan
Fast back (Coupe)	Hard top	Tab washer	Tang; lock
Fault finding/diagnosis	Trouble shooting	Tailgate	Liftgate
Float chamber	Float bowl	Tappet	Valve lifter
Free-play	Lash	Thrust bearing	Throw-out bearing
Freewheel	Coast	Top gear	High
Gudgeon pin	Piston pin or wrist pin	Trackrod (of steering)	Tie-rod (or connecting rod)
Gearchange	Shift	Trailing shoe (of brake)	Secondary shoe
Gearbox	Transmission	Transmission	Whole drive line
Halfshaft	Axle-shaft	Tyre	Tire
Handbrake	Parking brake	Van	Panel wagon/van
Hood	Soft top	Vice	Vise
Hot spot	Heat riser	Wheel nut	Lug nut
Indicator	Turn signal	Windscreen	Windshield
Interior light	Dome lamp	Wing/mudguard	Fender

Miscellaneous points

An "Oil seal" is fitted to components lubricated by grease!

A "Damper" is a "Shock absorber" it damps out bouncing, and absorbs shocks of bump impact. Both names are correct, and both are used haphazardly.

Note that British drum brakes are different from the Bendix type that is common in America, so different descriptive names result. The shoe end furthest from the hydraulic wheel cylinder is on a pivot; interconnection between the shoes as on Bendix brakes is most uncommon. Therefore the phrase "Primary" or "Secondary" shoe does not apply. A shoe is said to be Leading or Trailing. A "Leading" shoe is one on which a point on the drum, as it rotates forward, reaches the shoe at the end worked by the hydraulic cylinder before the anchor end. The opposite is a trailing shoe, and this one has no self servo from the wrapping effect of the rotating drum.

Buying spare parts and vehicle identification numbers

Buying spare parts

Spare parts are available from many sources, for example: VW garages, other garages and accessory shops, and motor factors. Our advice regarding spare part sources is as follows:

Officially appointed VW garages - This is the best source of parts which are peculiar to your vehicle and are otherwise not generally available (eg complete cylinder heads, internal gearbox components, badges, interior trim etc). It is also the only place at which you should buy parts if your car is still under warranty - non-VW components may invalidate the warranty. To be sure of obtaining the correct parts it will always be necessary to give the storeman your car's engine and chassis number, and if possible, to take the 'old' part along for positive identification. Remember that many parts are available on a factory exchange scheme - any parts returned should always be clean! It obviously makes good sense to go straight to the specialists on your car for this type of part for they are best equipped to supply you.

Other garages and accessory snops - These are often very good places to buy materials and components needed for the maintenance of your car (eg oil filters, spark plugs, bulbs, fan belts, oils and greases, touch-up paint, filler paste etc). They also sell general accessories, usually have convenient opening hours, charge lower prices and can often be found not far from home.

Motor factors - Good factors will stock all of the more important components which wear out relatively quickly (eg clutch components, pistons, valves, exhaust system, brake cylinders/pipes/hoses/seals/shoes and pads etc). Motor factors will often provide new or reconditioned components on a part exchange basis - this can save a considerable amount of money.

Gaskets - special note

With gasket sets - for both engine and gearbox - do not be alarmed if there seem to be many items included in the set you buy, which do not fit your vehicle. To save a lot of variety of kits they include in one enough to cover a variety of types over a period of time so you are certain to have some left over. However, it is a good idea to check the set before leaving the parts store. Some of the ones you may need could be omitted. Oil seals particularly are not all included - and this applies to some of the smaller ones. (Oil cooler).

Vehicle identification numbers

Although many individual parts, and in some cases, sub-assemblies such as distributors, fit a variety of VW models it is dangerous to assume that just because they look the same that they are the same. Differences are sometimes not visually detectable at all (except by serial numbers).

Components are being modified and developed all the time and do not necessarily coincide with publicly announced model changes. Make sure, therefore, that both the chassis number and the engine number are known when a part is ordered.

The chassis number is to be found on a plate fitted to the panel alongside the driver's seat (photo). The first two numbers of the chassis number denote the basic type. For example '21' is the van, '22' and '24' the Microbus in standard or de luxe versions, '23' the Kombi, '26' the pick-up range and '27' is an ambulance. The next number is the year. The new model is usually produced in August for the following year so a van with the first three figures 234 would be a deluxe Microbus year 1974. The remainder of the figures are the serial number of that particular design so '234 2000 001' would be the 1st Microbus of 1974 (the 2 denotes the type).

The chassis number is also found on the RH engine cover plate and the dashboard.

Engine numbers are stamped on the top half of the crankcase just below the breather. The letter indicates the type of engine.

Vehicle identification plate

Routine maintenance

1 A great deal is rightly said about the importance of routine maintenance, which can be divided into:

a) a test drive
b) regular renewal of filters
c) inspection of oil leaks, renewal of oil and greasing of joints
d) renewal of wearing parts (plugs, points, belts, brake pads etc) and tightening of loose bolts.

2 VW provide a computor service to diagnose the condition of your van. How often you use it will depend on the type of life your vehicle leads. It is recommended that the vehicle should be taken for diagnostic inspection every 6,000 miles, or once a year, if it does not cover that sort of mileage.

3 Every drive should be a test drive. If the vehicle is not behaving normally find out why and rectify it straight away. Oil leaks show up on the garage floor. If you find oil on the floor then find out where it is coming from and correct the fault. The old theory that if oil is coming out there is some inside is all very well, but oil coming out means something is loose or worn out and needs attention. Some faults creep in so gradually that the owner does not notice them, ageing headlamp bulbs for instance. The diagnostic service will take care of these.

4 Maintenance may be divided into two sections. Those things you **must** do if the vehicle is to continue to work, and work safely, and those things that you must do if you expect to sell it

for cash eventually. The latter is discussed at length in Chapter 12. To it we would add, keep it in a dry unheated garage, and wipe it as dry as you can when you put it away.

5 For convenience we have divided the essential maintenance into mileage intervals. However, such things as tyre pressures, engine oil level and windscreen washer fluid levels should be checked at least once a week. This applies also to the level of the battery electrolyte. Study the tyre treads for undue wear (Chapter 8) (Chapter 11) weekly.

6 LUBRICATION

Every 3,000 miles
(a) Change the engine oil and clean the oil strainer. The photograph shows the drain plug 'A' and the strainer 'B'.
(b) Check level of brake fluid.

Every 6,000 miles (in addition to above)
(a) Gearbox. Remove the filler plug on the side and check the level. Top-up if necessary.
(b) Oil door hinges and latches (Chapter 12)
Check sliding door runners and the hinge link.
(c) Automatic transmission. Check the level of oil in the final drive housing.
(d) Grease the four points on the front suspension cross-tube and steering damper.
(e) Change engine oil filter (fit new one).

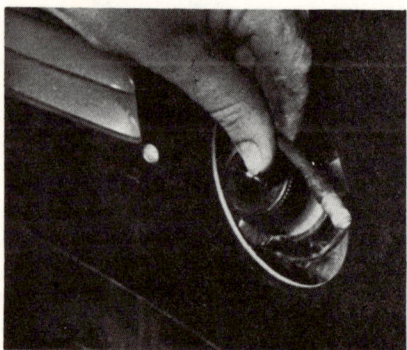
1 The windscreen washer reservoir pressure valve

2 Engine oil change. A is the drain plug, B is the strainer bolt

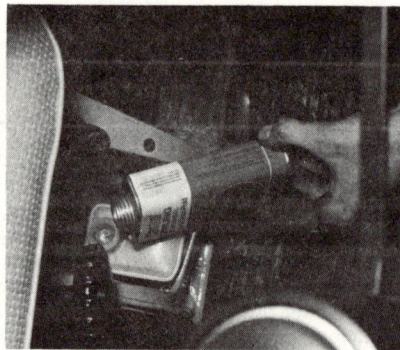
3 Filling the brake fluid reservoir under the driver's seat

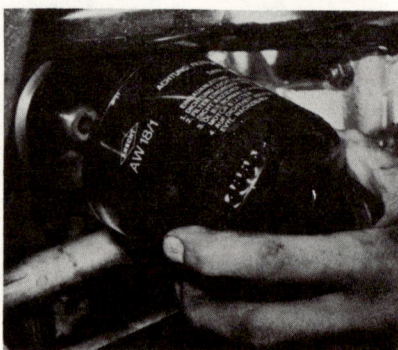
4 Removing the oil filter

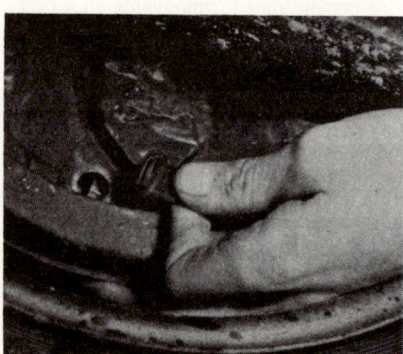
5 Removing a plug to inspect the rear brake shoes

Every 18,000 miles (in addition to above)
(a) Check lubrication of front suspension, front hubs and steering linkage.
(b) Repack constant velocity joints if necessary.
(c) Check lubrication of rear hubs.

7 ROUTINE INSPECTION

Every 6,000 miles
(a) Use VW diagnostic inspection.
(b) Check tappet clearance (Chapter 1).
(c) Check distributor points and dwell angle (Chapter 3).
(d) Adjust idling speed (Chapter 2).
(e) Inspect brake pads (Chapter 8).
(f) Inspect brake shoes (Chapter 8).
(g) Inspect steering linkage and measure free-play.
(h) Check free-travel of clutch pedal.
(j) Adjust alternator and air pump belt tension.

Every 12,000 miles (as above plus)
(a) Replace contact breaker points.
(b) Fit new plugs (or serviced ones).
(c) Check rotor cap, and leads of distributor.
(d) Test headlamp bulbs and replace if necessary.
(e) Remove battery for servicing and charging.
(f) Clean filters on fuel pump.

Every 18,000 miles (as above for 6,000 miles plus)
(a) Check starter motor brushes.
(b) Check alternator brushes and charging rate.
(c) Service air cleaner and check air flaps.
(d) Change A.T.F. fluid (where applicable).

Every 24,000 miles
(a) Change filters on air pump.
(b) Check recirculation valve (exhaust).
(c) Lubricate carburettor linkage.

8 If the points listed are attended to faithfully the van should live to a ripe old age, but remember rubber grows old too. Steering joint covers, CVJ boots, and the various rubber and plastic stops and washers will age and should be checked with increasing frequency as they grow older. If they fail the parts they protect will wear rapidly.

9 The Diagnostic Service gives a complete check of the following points. It does not include any servicing, that must be done by the owner or the mechanic at the VW agency. The manual will explain how to rectify things that are wrong, but you cannot possibly inspect your vehicle as thoroughly and expertly as this service does. Why not use it?

DIAGNOSTIC SERVICE CHECK LIST

1 Steering/ignition lock, warning lights *
2 Brake pedal pushrod, clearance
3 Brake pedal, free travel
4 Clutch pedal, clearance
5 Play at steering wheel rim
6 Handbrake, free play
7 Windscreen washer operation
8 Windscreen wiper mechanism (mechanical)
9 Windscreen wiper blade rubber
10 Windscreen wiper blade assembly
11 Low beam
12 Fog lights *
13 High beam
14 Lights operating with ignition switched on
15 Reversing lights *
16 Instrument panel illumination
17 Fuel gauge *
18 Warning lamp, emergency warning system *
19 Control lamp, brake warning system *
20 Battery voltage, engine switched off
21 Condition of battery
22 Side, rear and number plate lights
23 Brake lights
24 Battery, electrolyte level
25 Indicator (left) - control light
26 Indicator (right) - control light
27 Heated rear window (operation) *
28 Tyre pressures, adjusted
29 Spare wheel type (pressure)
30 Spare tyre for damage
31 Level of brake fluid
32 Engine oil level
33 Front wheels, total toe   + degrees/minutes
34 Front wheels, total toe   − degrees/minutes
35 Front wheel left, camber   + degrees/minutes
36 Front wheel left, camber   − degrees/minutes
37 Front wheel right, camber   + degrees/minutes
38 Front wheel right, camber   − degrees/minutes
39 Upper torsion arm axial play *
40 Brake lines, inside vehicle
41 Engine oil temperature   (°C)
42 Starter motor current   (amps)
43 Compression pressures: cylinder 1   (units)
44 Compression pressures: cylinder 2   (units)
45 Compression pressures: cylinder 3   (units)
46 Compression pressures: cylinder 4   (units)
47 Horn operation
48 Voltage control regular, function at 2,000 rpm
49 Distributor (dwell angle) degrees
50 Generator current (maximum output) amps
51 Kickdown solenoid *
52 Kickdown solenoid *
53 Coolant level, antifreeze content
54 Cooling and heating system
55 Engine, upper part
56 Pre-heating circuit and restrictor *
57 V-belt tension and condition
58 Ignition timing
59 Headlights
60 King pin and link pin, play *
61 Ball joint, axial play (upper left) *
62 Ball joint, axial play (lower left) *
63 Ball joint, axial play (upper right) *
64 Ball joint, axial play (lower right) *
65 Ball joint, dust covers and sealing plugs
66 Tie rod ends, play
67 Tie rods, mounting and dust covers
68 Steering rack bellows *
69 Steering gear
70 Brake lines and hoses (front)
71 Brake linings: thickness (front)
72 Suspension strut upper ball and dust covers *
73 Tyre (front left)
74 Tyre (front right)
75 Dust sleeve (CV joints) *
76 Final drive
77 Transmission
78 Engine lower part
79 Torque converter and lines (automatic, stick-shift) *
80 Exhaust system
81 Brake lines and hoses (rear)
82 Brake regulator valve, linkage and dust seal *
83 Intake ducts, water drain flaps
84 Shift clutch (automatic, stick-shift) play
85 Brake linings: thickness (rear)
86 Tyre (rear left)
87 Tyre (rear right)
88 Wheel bolts torque

*These test operations do not apply to all vehicles.

Recommended lubricants and fluids

Component	Grade	Castrol Grade
ENGINE	(Summer) SAE 30 or (Winter) SAE 20W - 50	CRI 30 (Summer), CRI 20 (Winter) or GTX (all seasons)
MANUAL GEARBOX	SAE 90 Hypoid oil to MIL—L—2 105A Specification	Castrol Hypoy 90
AUTOMATIC GEARBOX	Dexron R B10100	Castrol TQ Dexron R
FINAL DRIVE (Auto)	SAE 90 Hypoid to MIL—L—2105B	Castrol Hypoid B
HUBS AND CV JOINTS	Multi purpose HMP Grease. V.W. special pack	Castrol LM Grease
AIR CLEANER	For oil filled use engine oil	CRI 20, 30 or GTX
DISTRIBUTOR	SAE 30 or special V.W. satchet	CRI 20, 30 or GTX
LOCK CYLINDERS	Graphite powder	
HINGES AND LOCKS	SAE 30	Everyman Oil or CRI 20 or 30
BRAKE FLUID	Hydraulic fluid SAE 70 R3	Castrol Girling Universal Brake and Clutch Fluid
CONTACT BREAKER AND BATTERY TERMINALS	Petroleum jelly (Vaseline)	

Lubrication Chart

C.V.J's

Check & repack every 18 months

ENGINE

Weekly: Check level and if necessary replenish with Castrol

3 Months: Drain off old oil while warm and refill with fresh, clean, Castrol.
Owners are advised that more frequent sump draining periods are derivable if the operation of the car involves:-
1) Frequent start/stop driving.
2) Operation during cold weather, especially when appreciable engine idling is involved, i.e. town operating conditions.
Capacity — 4.4 pints (2.5 litres).

TRANSMISSION

6 months: Check level and if if necessary top up to the edge of the filler plug hole with Castrol Hypoy Gear Oil.

BRAKES

Check level in header tank every 3 months. Change brake fluid every 2 years

FRONT AND REAR WHEEL BEARINGS

18 months. Remove hub clean out and re-pack with Castrol LM Grease

SUSPENSION
Grease 4 points every 6 months

H. 1078

Frequencies are based on an average monthly mileage of **1000**

Chapter 1 Engine

Contents

Specifications

Engine - general

	1700 cc	1800 cc
Type	Horizontally opposed, flat, 4 cylinder, air cooled pushrod, overhead valve	
Weight (approx)	270 to 300 lbs	
Bore	3.543 in (90 mm)	3.661 in (93 mm)
Stroke	2.598 in (66 mm)	2.598 in (66 mm)
Capacity	1679 cc	1795 cc
Code letter	CB	AW
Compression ratio	7.3 : 1	7.3 : 1
Compression pressure (normal)	100 - 135 psi	85 - 135 psii
Octane rating	91	91
Horsepower:		
SAE	63 at 4800	65 at 4200
DIN	66 at 4800	68 at 4200
Torque:		
SAE	81 lb ft at 3200	92.4 lb ft at 3000
DIN	11.6 mkg at 3200	13.2 mkg at 3000
Idling speed (rpm):		
Manual	850 ± 50	850 ± 50
Automatic	950 ± 50	950 ± 50
Firing order	1−4−3−2	1−4−3−2
Oil capacity (both engines)	3.5 litres, 6.125 Imperial pints, 7.5 U.S. pints	

Essential differences between 1700 cc and 1800 cc engines

1	Valves	larger diameter
2	Cylinder heads	different shaped ports and larger combustion space
3	Pistons	larger diameter
4	Piston pins	thicker wall section
5	Clutch	stronger spring pressure
6	Ignition	different timing setting

Note: the crankcase, crankshaft and connecting rods are identical

Cooling system

Type	Radial fan on crankshaft	
Delivery volume	28.5 cu ft (800 litres) per second at 4600 rpm.	
Thermostat opening temperature	65 - 70° C (150 - 160° F)	

Lubrication system

Type	Wet sump - pressure and splash	
Filter	Full flow - replaceable cartridge	
Capacity:		
With filter change	3.5 litres/6.1 pints Imp/7.3 pints US	
Without filter change	3.0 litres/5.25 pints Imp/6.3 pints US	
Oil required to fill from the lower to upper marks of the dip-stick	1 litre/1.75 pints Imp/2.1 pints US	
Oil pressure	SAE 30 70° C at 2500 rpm/42 psi	
Oil pressure	SAE 30 70° C at minimum/28 psi	
Oil warning light comes on between	2 - 6 psi	
Oil cooler	Pressurized, multi tube, air cooled	
Oil pump	Twin gear	
Oil pump gear/body end clearance	Nil	
Oil pump gear/backlash	Nil	
Oil pressure relief valve spring	1.3 inches at 17 lbs ± 2	
Oil pressure regulating valve spring	1 inch at 4 lb ± ¼	

Crankshaft and main bearings

No of bearings	4	
Journal diameters:		
Nos 1, 2, 3	59.97 - 59.99 mm	2.3609 - 2.3617 in
No 4	39.98 - 40.00 mm	1.5739 - 1.5748 in
Undersize main bearing shells	0.25, 0.50, 0.75 mm	
Bearing shells type		
Nos 1, 3, 4	Aluminium, lead coated	
No 2	Split, 3 layer steel backed	
Bearing clearances:		
Nos. 1, 3	0.04 - 0.18 mm	0.0016 - 0.007 in
No 2	0.03 - 0.17 mm	0.0011 - 0.0066 in
No 4	0.05 - 0.19 mm	0.0019 - 0.0074 in
Crankshaft endfloat limits	0.07 - 0.15 mm	0.0027 - 0.0051 in
Journals, maximum ovality	0.03 mm	0.0011 in

Crankcase

Main bearing bore diameters		
Nos 1, 2, 3	70.00 - 70.03 mm	2.7570 in.
No 4	50.0 - 50.04 mm	1.9685 - 1.970 in
Oil seal bore diameter (flywheel end)	95.00 - 95.05 mm	3.7401 - 3.742 in
Oil seal bore diameter (fan pulley end)	62.00 - 62.05 mm	2.4410 - 2.4429 in
Camshaft bearing bore diameter	27.5 - 27.52 mm	1.0825 - 1.0834 in
Oil pump housing bore diameter	70.00 - 70.03 mm	2.7560 - 2.7570 in
Tappet (cam follower) bore diameters	24.00 - 24.05 mm	0.9448 - 0.9467 in

Camshaft and bearings

Camshaft drive	Right alloy gear from crankshaft	
Bearings	White metal steel backed shells	
Journal diameters	24.99 mm - 25.00 mm	0.9837 - 0.9842 in
Bearing radial clearance	0.02 - 0.12 mm	0.0008 - 0.0047 in
Endfloat	0.04 - 0.16 mm	0.0016 - 0.0063 in
Gear backlash	0-0.05 mm	0 - 0.0019 in

Connecting rods and bearings

Type	Forged steel	
Big-end bearings	3 layer thin wall shells	
Small end bush	Steel bush lead bronze coated	
Undersize big-end shells	0.25 mm, 0.50 mm, 0.75 mm	
Big-end clearance limits	0.02 - 0.15 mm	0.0008 - 0.006 in
Crankpin endfloat limits	0.1 - 0.7 mm	0.004 - 0.028 in
Gudgeon (wrist) pin/bush clearance	0.01 - 0.04 mm	0.0004 - 0.0016 in
Connecting rod weight:		
Brown/white	746 - 752 grams	
Grey/black	769 - 775 grams	
Crankpin, maximum ovality	0.03 mm	0.0011 in

Cylinders

Type	Single barrel, finned, cast iron	
Oversizes	0.5 mm, 1.0 mm	0.020 in, 0.040 in
Distance between centres	124.5 mm	4.9 in

Cylinder heads

Type	Aluminium alloy, 1 per pair of cylinders	
Depth of cylinder seating	5.4 - 6.5 mm	0.212 - 0.255 in

Pistons and rings

Type	Light alloy with steel inserts, domed crowns for fuel injection, flat crowns for carburettors	
Cylinder clearance limits	0.04 - 0.20 mm	0.0015 - 0.008 in
Ring/groove clearance:		
Top compression	0.06 - 0.12 mm	0.0023 - 0.0047 in
Lower compression	0.04 - 0.10 mm	0.0015 - 0.0039 in
Oil control	0.02 - 0.10 mm	0.0008 - 0.0039 in
Piston oversizes	0.05 mm, 1.0 mm	
Gudgeon (wrist) pin	Fully floating, steel tube	
Gudgeon pin diameter	22.996 - 24.00 mm	0.9052 - 0.9448 in
Top compression ring gap limit	0.35 - 0.90 mm	0.014 - 0.035 in
Lower compression ring gap limit	0.30 - 0.90 mm	0.012 - 0.035 in
Oil control ring gap limit	0.25 - 0.95 mm	0.010 - 0.037 in

Tappets (cam followers)

Type	Cylindrical, flat based	
Diameter	23.96 - 23.98	0.9433 - 0.9440 in

Pushrods and valve rockers

Pushrod type	Hollow cylindrical with hemispherical ends	
Rocker shaft diameter	19.95 - 19.97 mm	0.7854 - 0.7862 in

Valves, valve seats and timing

	1700 cc	1800 cc
Inlet:		
Head diameter	39.3 mm 1.546 in	41.0 mm 1.613 in
Stem diameter	7.94 - 7.9 mm 0.3125 - 0.3109 in	
Seat width	1.8 - 2.2 mm 0.07 - 0.086 in	
Seat angle	30°	
Guide bore diameter	8.00 - 8.06 mm 0.3149 - 0.3173 in	
Maximum rock in guide	0.9 mm 0 035 in	
Exhaust:		
Head diameter	33 mm 1.299 in	34.00 mm 1.338 in
Stem diameter	8.91 - 8.87 mm 0.3507 - 0.3491 in	
Seat width	2.0 - 2.5 mm 0.08 - 0.98 in	
Seat angle	45°	
Guide bore diameter	8.98 - 9.06 mm 0.3535 - 3566 in	
Maximum rock in guide	0.9 mm 0.035 in	
Seat width correction angle:		
Loaded length	29 mm 1.14 in	
Load	80 kg 176 lb	
Inlet (cold)	0.15 mm 0.006 in	
Exhaust (cold)	0.15 mm to chassis 2132210554 Thereafter 0.20 mm (0.008 in)	

Torque wrench settings

These are included in the text at the appropriate places

1 General description - engine

1 The Transporter was modified in August 1971 to fit the 1.7 litre engine with all options except the Pick-up models. All vehicles sent to the USA were fitted with this engine.

In effect the engine is the ''suitcase'' model as fitted to the 411/412 with some small modifications. It is supplied with fuel by twin Solex 34 PDSIT carburettors.

The code letters CA or CB for engines with exhaust control are used for this version of the engine which is fitted with recessed pistons to give a compression ratio of 7.3 to 1.

In August 1973 a further increase in power was obtained by increasing the engine capacity to 1.8 litres. Whilst basically the same engine with an increase in cylinder diameter from 90 mm to 93 mm the large engine, code letters AP, has a number of modifications to accommodate the increased power output.

Twin Solex 34 PDSIT carburettors are still fitted, but the head and valves are modified, ignition timing altered and stronger clutch springs fitted. The exhaust muffler is also modified.

Details of the various modifications are discussed in the appropiate Chapters. Neither of these engines may be fitted to earlier models of the Transporter, which was fitted with the fan type 1600 engine.

2 The four cylinder air cooled engine is bolted to the transmission unit and the whole power pack is held in the van by eight bolts. When the two drive shafts have been taken off and various air and petrol hoses disconnected and a number of electrical connections unplugged, the mounting bolts may be withdrawn and the whole unit lowered away from the rear of the van and taken away underneath.

Alternatively the engine may be taken out without moving the gearbox and thus without having to remove the drive shafts, although it is more difficult to install by this method.

With the engine comes the exhaust system and all the cooling and heating arrangements. It is not possible to discuss engine overhaul and cooling/heating/exhaust system repair separately so the whole unit is covered in this Chapter.

The detailed overhaul of the gearboxes is discussed in other Chapters, as is the fuel system, and the ignition system. These are therefore not included in this Chapter except for passing reference.

3 The engine is a flat horizontally opposed fourstroke. It is totally enclosed in sheet metal and aluminium castings in such a way that the cooling may be thermostatically controlled to small limits. The fan, mounted on the end of the crankshaft sucks air from a ducted system and blows it over the engine in a guided and variable system of ducts allowing the engine to warm up quickly and then opening flaps to provide a cooling air stream which increases in volume as the speed of the engine increases.

4 The layout of the engine is normal VW style: a split crankcase containing the crankshaft, camshaft, and oil pump; camshaft, oil pump and distributor being driven by gearing off the end of the crankshaft.

The cylinders are finned castings arranged in pairs with one cylinder head for each pair. Overhead valves (although in VW engines these are at the side!), are operated by pushrods bearing on followers activated by the camshaft, and the conventional rocker gear and valve springs.

5 Alloy pistons have steel inserts and are fitted with two compression and one spring loaded scraper ring. The gudgeon (piston) pins are fully floating and retained in place by circlips.

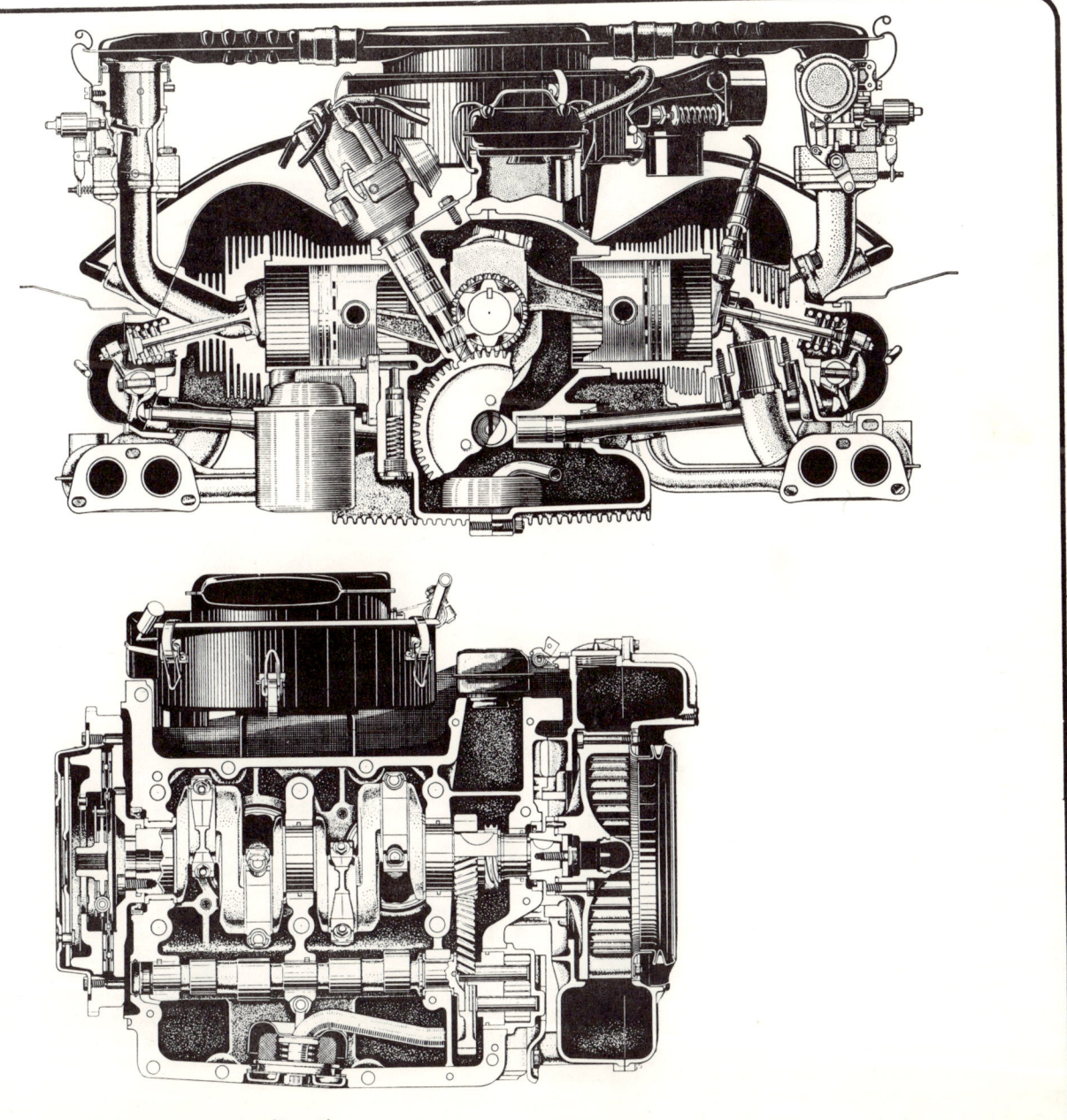

Fig. 1.1. Engine - cross section (Sec. 1)
The layout shown is a 1700cc engine with the oil element air cleaner. Later models and 1800cc engines have a paper element air The layout of the 1800cc engine is identical but with different cylinder head contour.   *cleaner.*

6 Split shell bearings are fitted to the big-ends, camshaft bearings and one of the main bearings. The other main bearings are circular shells in one piece.

7 Lubrication is by pressure feed from the pump, the pressure regulated by a relief valve at the end of the circuit. An oil cooler is fitted and a renewable filter with a bypass valve. The usual VW strainer is fitted to the pump suction. A warning light operates from a pressure switch which lights the lamp at pressures below 6 pounds/square inch.

8 The engine provides a lift for which four men are required in its unit form, so if you are thinking of moving it by yourself, think again.

9 Very little work may be carried out on the engine itself, other than routine maintenance, without removing it from the van, but this does not include those items classed as ancillaries and forming part of the electrical, ignition or fuel systems. For details of these refer to the appropriate Chapter.

The tables below give an idea of the degree of dismantling required once the engine is removed in order to renew or repair various items:

a) *Not necessary to split the crankcase.*
   Cylinder heads and valves
   Oil cooler
   Fan and cooling systems
   Oil pump
   Cylinders
   Pistons and rings
   Flywheel
   Crankshaft oil seals
b) *Necessary to split the crankcase.*
   Camshaft
   Crankshaft and main bearings
   Distributor drive gear
   Camshaft bearings
   Big-end bearings

2 Items repairable, engine in vehicle

1 The extent to which items may be removed and replaced without removing the engine is, as was stated, very limited. It is also much easier to remove and replace these items when the engine is out - for even with the new floor hatch, access is very limited and if you drop something inside then life becomes difficult for it must be located and recovered.

2 The air cleaner, carburettors and fuel pump may be removed and serviced with the engine in-situ, as may the afterburning equipment. This is all discussed in Chapter 3.

3 The coil and distributor may be removed and serviced; this is discussed in Chapter 4.

4 The alternator and the starter motor may be removed and replaced, although the latter is a grim struggle, if it is to be reinstated correctly.

5 The silencer and the heat exchangers may be removed and replaced, but the connection of the heat exchangers to the exhaust ports is not easy. This is discussed in Section 3 of this Chapter.

6 It is possible to remove the thermostat and replace it without taking the engine out. (Section 4 of this Chapter).

7 The rocker box covers are removable if the rear wheels are removed. Make sure the whole lot is clean before disturbing them. The valve clearances may be adjusted but we do **not** subscribe to the theory that the heads may be removed with the engine in-situ.

3 Exhaust system and heat exchangers - removal, overhaul and replacement (engine in vehicle)

1 The exhaust system is made of heavy gauge material which may be welded and patched if holes appear. However the effect of the exhaust gas afterburn has yet to be evaluated. Obviously if

serious combustion is taking place in the muffler and pipes the rate of scaling will increase. So, similarly with the amount of heat available to the heat exchanger.

2 The muffler and tailpipes may be removed without removing the engine from the vehicle, but the nuts are difficult to get at and will probably be very rusty. Soak them well with penetrating oil. The muffler will come away leaving the heat exchangers in position.

3 A typical muffler system is shown which gives the layout for the early 1700 cc engines. This has now been modified so that the tailpipe now comes out on the right for the 1800 cc engine and it is fitted to a flange. (Fig 1.2)

4 On 1700 cc models just prior to the 1800 cc, yet another type was fitted. A union nut connected a pipe to the muffler to supply the EGR system with exhaust gas, via a filter. This was discontinued when the exhaust gas, as it is now, was extracted from No 4 exhaust manifold.

5 In each case remove the six nuts holding the muffler and the tailpipe to the heat exchangers and pull the muffler off to the rear. It will require quite a lot of manoeuvring to ease it off the heat exchanger.

6 If you do decide to renew the silencer (muffler) renew the tailpipe as well.

7 The heat exchangers may be removed with the engine still in the vehicle but it is a difficult job to reinstall them satisfactorily. First of all remove the silencer (muffler). Now remove the two screws that hold the heat exchanger cover on the heat exchanger. This will free the heat exchanger from the fan housing. Now remove the hoses from the top of the blower ducts and then the heater ducts (connectors) by removing the screw from the tab and pulling the duct upwards.

The heat exchanger is now held only by the four studs which hold the heat exchanger pipes to the cylinder head. If you can get those undone then the exchanger may be removed downwards.

The seals must be removed from the exhaust ports and new ones fitted. When replacing the heat exchanger the nuts must be torqued to 14 lb ft. This is easier said than done but it is worth a try if you do not wish to remove the engine and there is a damaged heat exchanger. It is of course much easier to do when the engine is out of the vehicle.

8 If either heat exchanger or the silencer do become damaged to the extent that they leak the change in exhaust note will tell you and apart from the noise there will be fumes leaking into the body compartment so get the job done straight away.

4 Thermostat - removal, testing and adjustment (engine in vehicle)

1 If it is suspected that the thermostat is defective and is not operating the flaps as it should it may be removed without much trouble. Remove the right lower coverplate (you may need an impact screwdriver) and the thermostat is visible on its bracket. (photo)

2 The cable operating the flap is in the hexagon end of the thermostat. (photo) Remove the bracket and detach the cable and take the thermostat away. Heat a pan of water to 65-70°C (150-160°F) and put the thermostat in the water for a few minutes. Using a vernier or calipers measure the overall length as shown in Fig. 1.3 'A' should be 1.8" (46 mm) minimum length. If it is less you need a new thermostat.

3 When the thermostat is refitted and back to room temperature check the flap setting. Loosen the screw that holds the cooling air control cable on to the control flap shaft. Hold the flaps in the fully closed position and tighten the screw to hold the cable in that position. Replace the coverplate. This is about all that can be done without removing the engine.

5 Engine removal - preparation and tools required

1 The removal of the engine without the gearbox is a simple

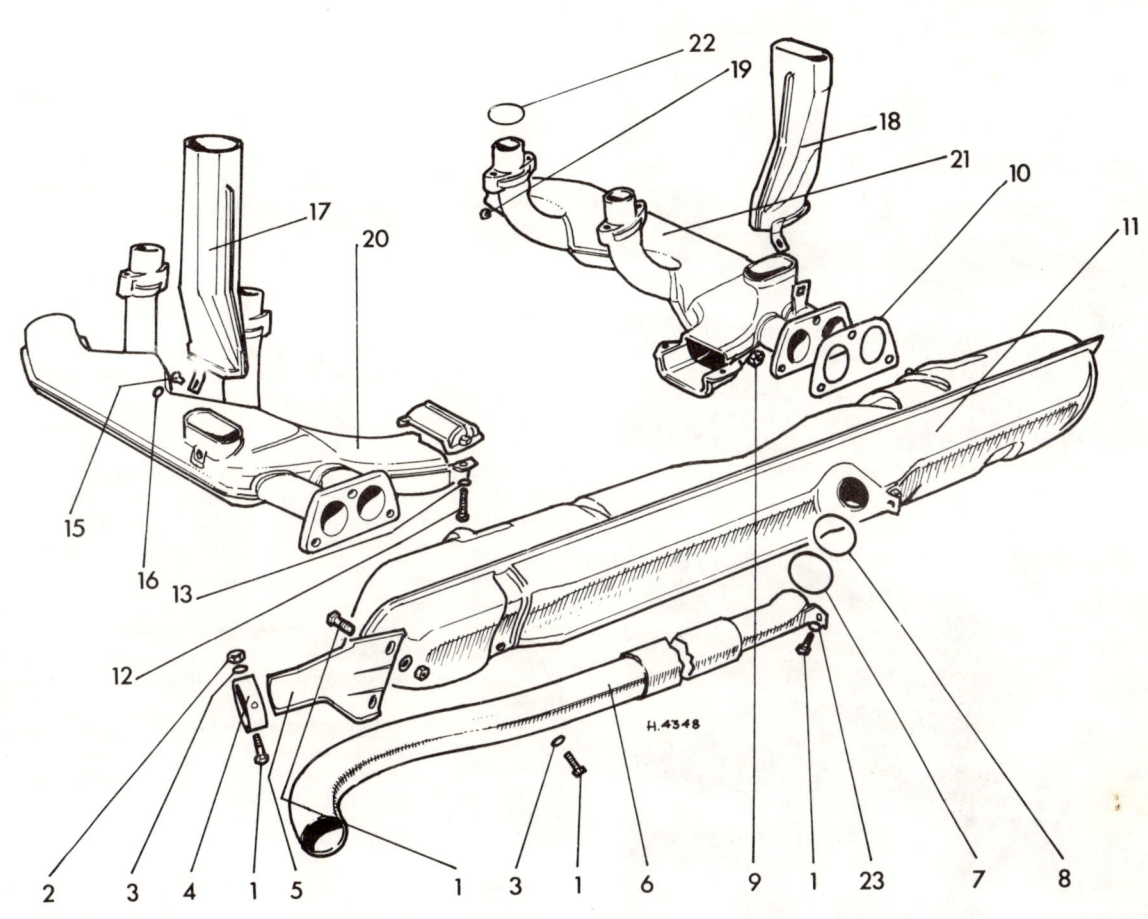

Fig. 1.2. Typical exhaust layout (Sec. 3)

1 Bolt M8
2 Nut M8
3 Washer
4 Clip
5 Bracket
6 Tail pipe
7 Conical ring
8 Gasket
9 Self locking nut
10 Gasket
11 Muffler (silencer)
12 Screw
13 Washer
14 Heat exchanger cover
15 Screw
16 Spring washer
17 Connector
18 Connector
19 Self locking nut
20 Heat exchanger (L)
21 Heat exchanger (R)
22 Sealing ring
23 Spring washer

*Note. The system has been modified
for the 1800cc engine. The tail pipe is
moved to the right. The flanges (gasket
10) are different on the later 1700cc
models*

4.1 Coverplate removed to show the position of the thermostat

4.2 Control wire shown in hexagon of thermostat

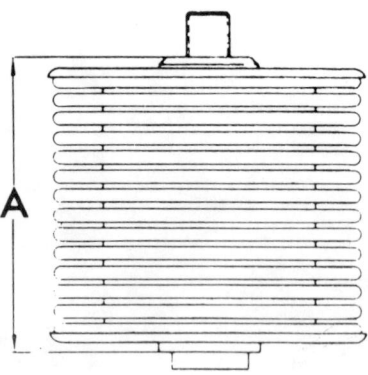

Fig. 1.3. Thermostat bellows (Sec. 4)

A = 46 mm (1.8 in)
minimum at 65 - 70°C
(149 - 158°F)

task if tackled systematically. The essential tools are a good set of metric spanners, open-ended and ring, and a set of metric socket spanners.

As you are going to work on the engine after it has been taken out an impact screwdriver will be required.

As there is no need to lift the vehicle, it can stand on its road wheels all the while, no slings are required, but a trolly jack is recommended. Failing this it is possible to lower the engine with a combination of screw jacks and a suitable wooden cradle, but remember it weights nearly 300 lbs, so make sure the lowering arrangements are adequate.

A selection of containers for nuts and bolts, paraffin or proprietary solvent for cleaning, plenty of clean non-fluffy rag, a note book and pencil, and a number of tags to tie onto wires and hoses as you disconnect them are all required.

If you do not have a trolly jack then the vehicle **must** be pushed from over the engine when the engine has been lowered, so make sure that the vehicle can move forward at least four feet after the engine removal has been done.

Finally read through the removal sequence **before** starting work, locate all the nuts, bolts, hoses and wires that have to be undone, and then follow the sequence given. Tag all wires, hoses and pipes as you undo them and keep a list of them as you disconnect them; it will save you a lot of trouble later.

6 Engine - removal

1 Remove the trapdoor over the engine and open the rear door as far as it will go. Disconnect the battery earth wire (ground strap).
2 Underneath the bumper is a gravel guard. This must be taken off. Remove the four bolts, do not lose the spring washers. Drain the sump (see paragraph 20).
3 Remove the air cleaner (see Chapter 2).
4 Remove the air heater hoses and controls.
5 Disconnect the wiring to:

  (a) the coil
  (b) the alternator regulator
  (c) oil pressure switch
  (d) carburettors (auto chokes, cut off valves)
  (e) transmission switch
  (f) back-up lights
  (g) trigger for ignition timing

and any other wires that join the engine to the frame.
6 Remove all the hose connections and tag them. Disconnect the fuel lines to the pump and clip them to stop fuel escaping. Tie them up in polythene bags to keep the dirt out.
7 Disconnect the accelerator cable from the operating arm of the carburettor system. If you are going to dismantle the engine anyway then remove the carburettors and the cross-shaft. The engine will come out with them in position, but if they are out of the way they cannot be damaged during the withdrawal process. Otherwise just remove the air hose from the top of the central idling unit (Chapter 2).
8 Remove the coil from the back of the engine where it is bolted to the fan housing.
9 If the vehicle is fitted with afterburn equipment (Chapter 2) the air pump must be removed from the top of the fan housing. The hose from the activated charcoal filter for the fuel tank should be disconnected.
10 Take the clamp off the oil filler neck and remove the filler neck. Take out the dipstick, ease the grommet off the dipstick tube. Remove the screws which hold the right rear engine coverplate and slide the coverplate up the oil filler pipe and remove it. The grommet will come with the plate. Now remove the left-hand rear side plate and the engine sideplates.

Removing all the tinware not only gives more room but it also allows you to see what the jack and packing are bearing on. A word about these fillister head screws. It seems that they are installed with a power screwdriver. They are certainly very tight and we had to use an impact screwdriver on two of them. If you cannot borrow such a tool we suggest you invest in one; they are not expensive and you can struggle for a long while with an ordinary screwdriver and only succeed in ruining the screw head.

11 On automatic transmission vehicles (see Chapter 6) there are a few more points to attend to before you can remove the engine.

(a) *The ATF filler pipe must be removed. Slacken the nuts (M6) which secure it to the casing, turn the pipe anticlockwise and pull it out.*

(b) *Disconnect the vacuum hose from the intake manifold balance pipe.*

(c) *The bolts holding the torque converter to the driveplate must be removed. There is a hole in the lower left-hand side of the converter bellhousing. You can get at these bolts, one at a time, if you rotate the engine.*

12 Disconnect the wires from the starter. This is done from underneath and mainly by feel. Note which wire goes where.

13 Remove the cables from the heater flap control arms and pull out the ducts connecting the heat exchangers with the interior of the van. Remove the two upper engine to transmission bolts.

14 Make sure the vehicle cannot move inadvertantly (chock the front wheels) and arrange a support for the gearbox to take the weight when the engine is removed. This can be a static jack with packing, or a sling made out of a piece of angle iron with chains on either side hooked up to the frame. There is a special VW tool (VW 785); perhaps the agent will let you look at one, but a small trolly jack or a screw jack will do just as well.

15 Now remove the two bolts which hold the lower part of the transmission to the engine. Get these out of the way before you put the engine jack in place. Using a movable jack and packing, take the weight of the engine. Study the angle of the engine bearer brackets. They should be vertical, and the bearer should be parallel with the fan housing. Measure the gap. It will all help when you are installing the engine if you have noted how the bearers are aligned. (photo)

Now undo the bolts which hold the engine bearer brackets to the frame. (photo)

16 The engine is now supported on the jack but the mainshaft of the gearbox is still engaged in the clutch driven plate and this must be disengaged. On automatic transmission vehicles the driveplate has to be freed from the torque converter. The engine must be drawn to the rear as far as it will come and you must be quite sure that the shaft is disengaged before the engine may be lowered. If it isn't clear then you will either bend the shaft or

something even more horribly expensive. On vehicles equipped with afterburn it will help if you remove the extension shaft and pulley from the fan (the part that drives the air pump).

Once the shaft is clear of the clutch the engine may be lowered to the ground and withdrawn to the rear. Now check the rubber seal round the engine compartment. If it is badly damaged you will need a new one.

17 It is best to have three people on the job for the removal operation. One person to be foreman, watch for possible snags or things getting entangled. One person to work the jack, and one to steady the engine if necessary through the hatch in the vehicle floor and watch for snags on the top of the engine. When drawing the engine back unless it is firmly held on the jack it may tilt as the shaft splines come out of the clutch. Watch for this as there will be trouble later when reassembly is taking place.

18 Vehicles with automatic transmission have one further problem. The torque converter will fall out when the engine is removed unless something is done to stop this. The easiest way is to drill a hole in a piece of flat bar (1'' x 1/8''), the hole ½'' diameter 2'' from one end, the bar about 12'' long, and bolt the bar to the transmission casing, using one of the top retaining bolt holes, so that the bar is fixed across the torque converter and stops it falling out.

19 Now clean the engine thoroughly. Get rid of all the grease and dirt before you move the engine to the bench where dismantling is going to take place.

20 The problem of draining the oil (3½ litres, 7½ american pints) is one which must suit your convenience. The best time to do it is an hour before you start work on dismantling the engine from the vehicle. However this has some disadvantages as it will not all drain out, and some may spill just where you want to work.

We leave it in until the engine is out of the frame, support the engine on blocks, remove the drain plug, and go and sit down to recover from the exertions of removing the engine. However, whichever way you do it there will still be some left in the engine, about which, more later.

21 Replacement, which is mostly the reverse of removal is discussed at the end of the Chapter after overhaul is complete.

22 Removal of the engine and transmission as a unit is discussed at the beginning of Chapter 5.

7 Lubrication system - general description

1 Before dismantling the engine it is important to understand how the oil is pressurized and delivered to the bearings. As the engine is taken to pieces each part containing oilways must be

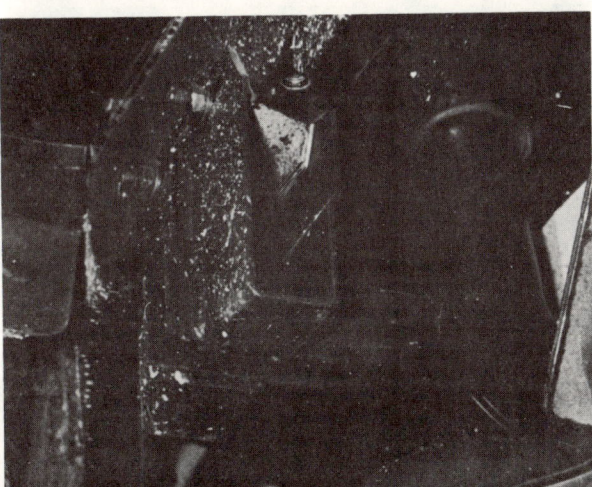

6.15a The rear engine brackets which support the engine bearer

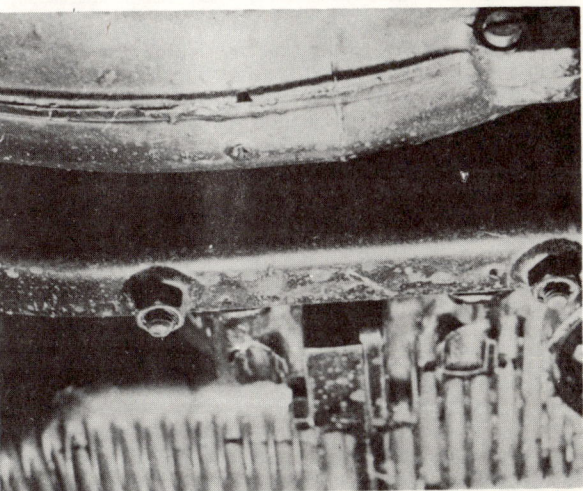

6.15b Alignment of the engine support beam with the fan casing

checked to see that passages are clear. The oil is drawn from the crankcase by the suction tube via a strainer which removes the larger impurities. Fig 1.4 refers.

2   The gear type pump delivers the oil to a filter (the first time this type of engine has had such a device) which is fitted with a spring loaded valve bypass. From the filter (or bypass) the oil goes to a cooler which again has a bypass valve, depending upon the pressure, which in turn depends on the temperature. The cold high pressure oil thus does not go through the cooler.

3   From the cooler (or bypass valve) the oil is distributed to the various bearings from which it returns to the sump. At the end of the pressure line is yet another pressure valve which controls the pressure in the bearing circuit.

4   An oil pressure switch is included in the system. For SAE 30 at 70°C (158°F) the pressure at the switch for engine revolutions of 2500 rpm should be 42 lbs per square inch. If this pressure sinks below 28 lbs sq. inch then remedial action in the bearing circuit or pump is indicated.

5   A cross section of the oil filter is given at Fig. 1.5. When changing the filter ensure that the sealing surface on the oil filter flange is clean, oil the seal lightly and screw in the filter by hand as far as it will go. (photo) For tightening further a special wrench is required, but doubtless the owner will manage to improvise. Start the engine and check for leaks, top up as required.

8   Cooling system and coverplates

1   Two illustrations are shown of the various metal plates. These fall into two categories, those which control the air flow and those which merely cover the engine to ensure that the air goes in the right direction; it is important to know what shape they are as they are referred to in the text. These plates must be in good order and do not permit significant air leaks or fumes will enter the vehicle body. The shape and contour of the various plates has been modified from time-to-time but the general layout has not. (Figs 1.6 and 1.7)

2   A further illustration is given of the fan and fan casing together with the alternator and flaps which allow air to blow round the engine for cooling when running, or close off the air circuit when the engine is cold. The flaps are actuated by the thermostat. (Fig 1.8)

3   The right-hand rear coverplate is now made in two pieces which allows the removal and installation of the alternator without disturbing the engine (see Chapter 9).

9   Engine dismantling - exhaust and cooling systems, cylinder heads, cylinders and pistons and lubrication systems

1   This Section takes up the action at the end of Section 6. The engine, clean and with all its components is sitting on the bench. The oil has been drained and the plug replaced.

2   Plenty of containers, a tray to catch surplus oil, metric spanners ring, socket, and open end are required, together with drifts, screwdrivers, a suitalbe extractor, hide and ball peen hammers, and a set of Allan keys (metric). Other useful tools are a blow lamp and a mole grip.

3   Plenty of clean non-fluffy rag and a paraffin cleaning bath are necessary.

4   If not already removed now is the time to remove the carburettors and the cross-shaft. This is all described in Chapter 3. The air cleaner must be removed.

5   Next the silencer. This requires a little patience to remove the six screws which are sure to be rusted in. (photo)

6   Now remove the right rear cover plate unscrewing four screws from underneath. (photo)

7   Using the correct tools slacken the fan adjuster nut and remove the fanbelt. If the nut is obstinate remove the stay at the back of the fan adjuster and ease the cover for the alternator away so that you can get a mole wrench on the nut.

8   Remove the right lower warm air duct (Fig 1.6) (photo).

9   Now the right-hand heat exchanger may be removed using a

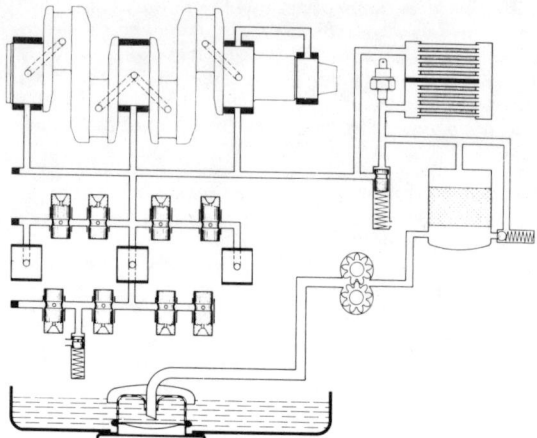

Fig. 1.4. Diagrammatic layout of the Lubrication System (Sec. 7)

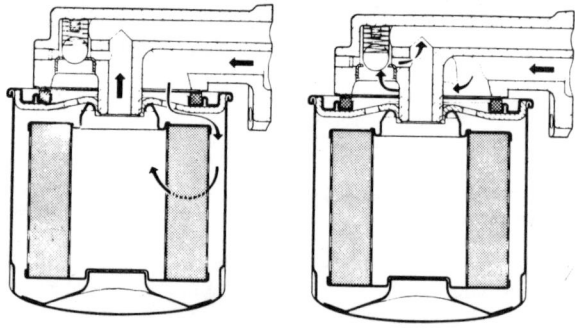

Fig. 1.5. Oil filter - cross section (Sec 7)
When the filter is blocked the ball valve in the flange opens ensuring a supply of oil (unfiltered) to the engine bearings. (Left) normal oil circuit (Right) oil circuit through bypass valve

7.5 The oil filter (the coverplate has been removed to give a better picture)

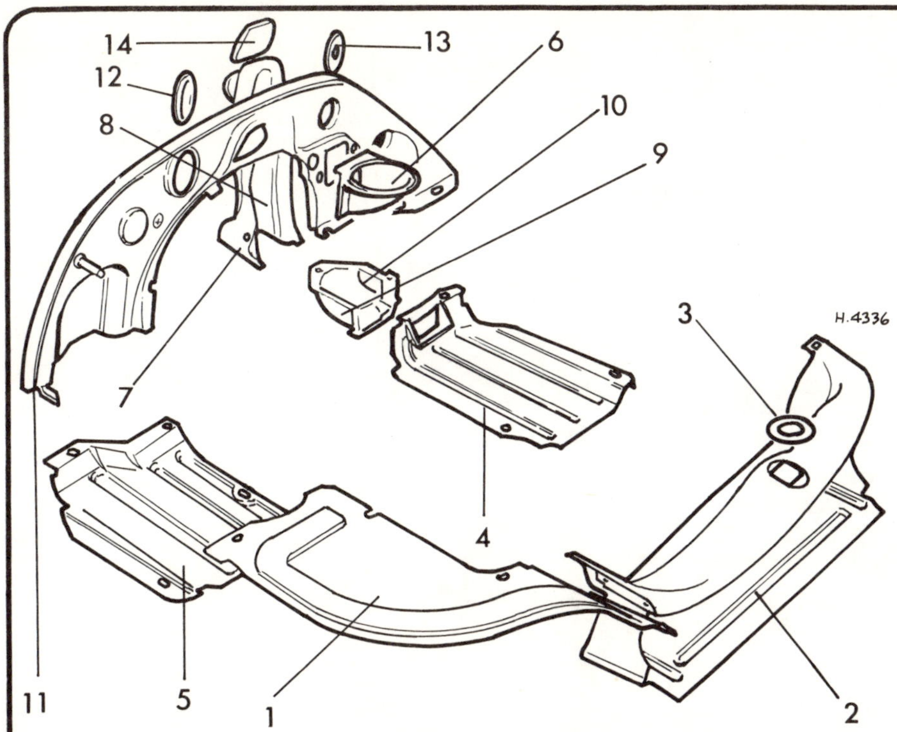

Fig. 1.6. Engine cover plates (Sec. 8)

1 Rear left cover plate
2 Rear right cover plate (2 part from August 1971)
3 Grommet for oil filter
4 Right lower warm air duct
5 Left lower warm air duct
6 Carburettor pre heat connector
7 Carburettor pre heat dust upper port
8 Insulation for top of pre heat duct
9 Pre heat duct. Lower pair
10 Insulation
11 Front cover plate
12 Dipstick grommet for convertor
13 Grommet
14 Grommet

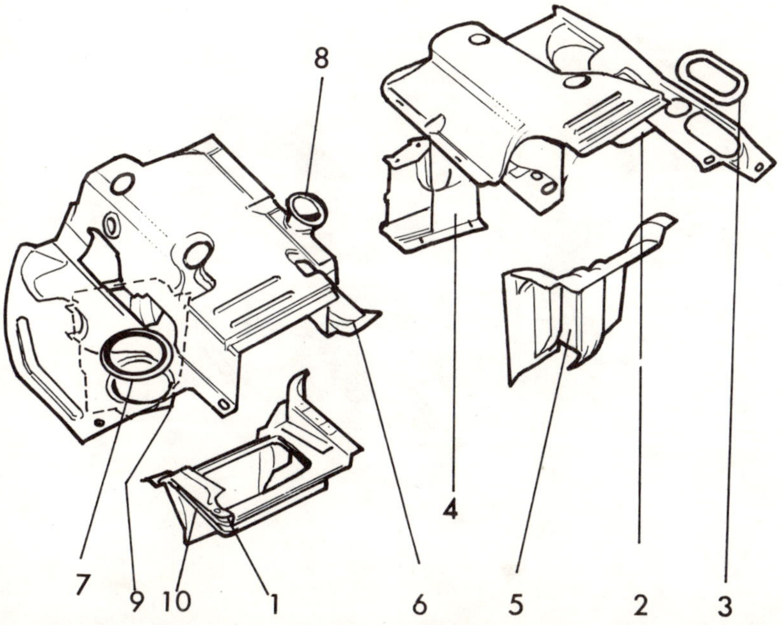

H.4336

Fig. 1.7 Engine cooling system — cover plates and ducts (Sec. 8)

1 Seal for oil cooler
2 Cylinder cover plate (R)
3 Grommet
4 Warm air duct (R front)
5 Warm air duct (R rear)
6 Cylinder cover plate (L)
7 Grommet
8 Oil pressure switch cap
9 Warm air duct (L front)
10 Warm air duct (L rear)

H.4337

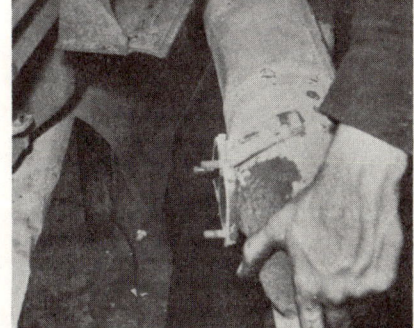

9.5 Remove the silencer ...

9.6 ... and right rear coverplate

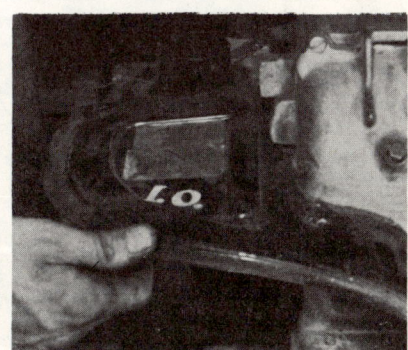

9.8 Remove the right lower warm air duct

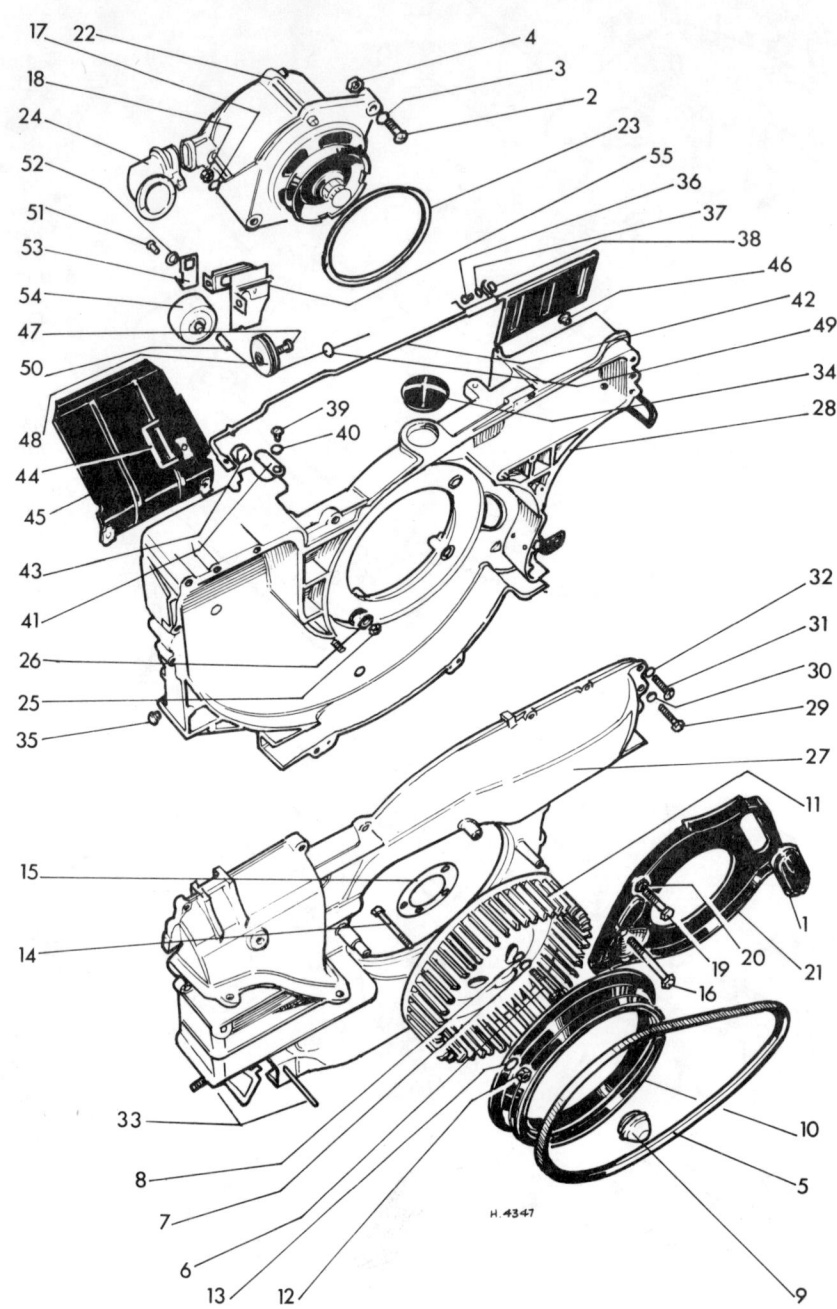

Fig. 1.8 Engine cooling system (Sec. 8)

1 Plug	15 Spacer	29 Bolt M8	42 Flap (left with shaft)
2 Screw	16 Bolt M8	30 Spring washer	43 Support
3 Spring washer	17 Spring washer	31 Screw M6	44 Flap link
4 Nut M8	18 Nut M8	32 Spring washer	45 Flap (right)
5 Alternator drivebelt	19 Bolt	33 Air non return flap	46 Flap stop
6 Screw M8 socket head	20 Spring washer	and pin	47 Bolt M6
7 Spring washer	21 Cover plate	34 Timing hole cover	48 Pulley
8 Flat washer	22 Alternaor	35 Plug	49 Washer
9 Cap	23 Sealing ring	36 Bolt M4	50 Cable
10 Pulley	24 Elbow	37 Washer	51 Bolt
11 Fan	25 Nut M8	38 Nut	52 Washer
12 Square nut M7	26 Spring washer	39 Screw M6	53 Bracket
13 Spring washer	27 Fan housing (rear)	40 Spring washer	54 Thermostat
14 Screw	28 Fan housing (front)	41 Retainer	55 Support

socket spanner from underneath. This will probably be a stiff fit and a little tapping with a hide hammer may be necessary. (photo)

10 Now remove the alternator completely. Undo the nut at the back and remove the bolt. (photo), then the alternator; (photo) and finally the coverplate. The grommet round the dipstick pipe may be stuck and require easing away. (photo)

11 The remainder of the cover plates should now be removed, noting carefully where they go and which flange goes over which. Now remove the left-hand heat exchanger and set it to one side.

12 The engine proper is now exposed. Look around and mark the cylinder heads, cylinders, crankcase etc., in such a way as to be able to reassemble them in the same place after overhaul. Use paint, centre punch marks, sticky tape, or any other method, but mark them.

13 Remove the clutch, (six bolts), which comes away in one piece (photo). Mark its exact position before removal or there may be an imbalance on reassembly.

14 Remove the three socket head screws holding the fan to the crankshaft and draw off the fan; again mark it so that it will go back the same way. (photo)

15 Remove the cable from the flap control lever. (photo)

16 Undo the four bolts holding the fan housing and wriggle the fan housing off past the oil filler tube. (photos)

17 Remove the engine carrier from the crankcase and examine the rubber mountings very carefully. The one we dismantled had a broken rubber mounting. Replace if necessary.

18 Undo the three nuts and remove the oil cooler. (photo) Preserve the seals and note carefully how they fit. The cooler pulls off sideways.

19 Now undo the five bolts from the centre of the flywheel, remove the spacer and tap the flywheel gently off the crankshaft. (photo) Take care not to damage the locating pin which remains in the crankshaft hub.

20 Start with the L.H. head. Remove the valve covers and rockers complete with rocker shaft. Pull out the pushrods, watch what you are doing because they are hollow and will be full of

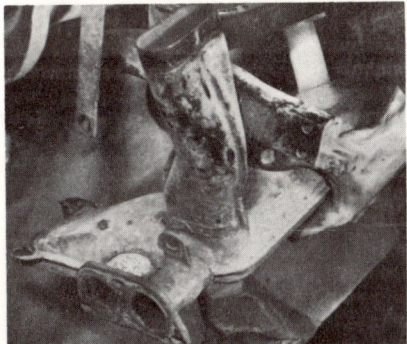
9.9 Remove the right-hand heat exchanger

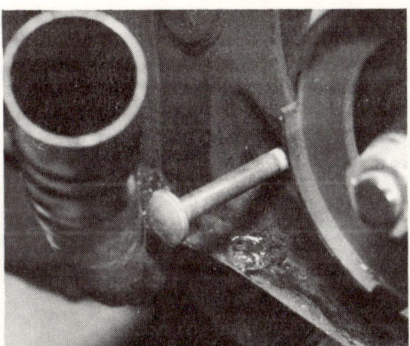
9.10a Remove the alternator bolt

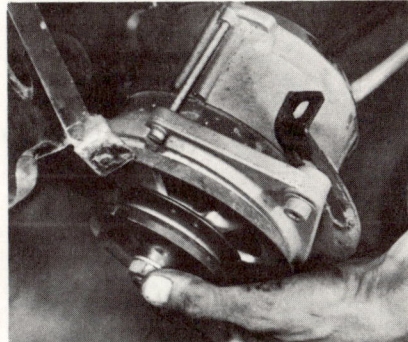
9.10b ... and then the alternator ...

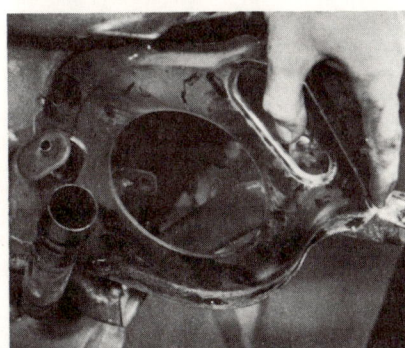
9.10c ... and finally the alternator cover plate (watch for the dipstick grommet)

9.13 Remove the clutch (six bolts). Mark its exact position so that it will go back to the same place or there may be an inbalance on reassembly

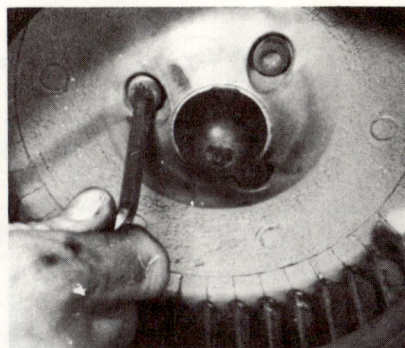
9.14 Removing the fan

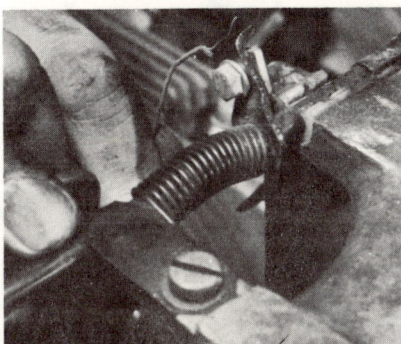
9.15 Removing the cable from the flap control lever

9.16a Remove the fan housing bolts ...

9.16b ... and wriggle the fan housing away

oil which is a trap for the unwary. Note how the spring fits under the rocker shaft.

21 Refer to Fig 1.9 for details of the cylinder heads. Refer to Fig. 1.14 which gives the tightening sequence for cylinder head bolts and using a reverse sequence slacken and remove the cylinder head nuts. Remove the screw from the deflector plate to the cylinder head; and then the two screws holding the deflector plate to the crankcase and the head may be drawn off with the deflector plate. (photos) Note the sealing rings at the top and bottom of the cylinders. Remove the gaskets from the exhaust ports. Pull out the pushrod tubes marking them to ensure correct assembly.

22 Now repeat the process for the other cylinder head.

23 If the thermostat is still in place undo the two nuts and remove it. (photo) It should be tested as in Section 4.

24 Take off the oil filler pipe and elbow and the oil filter complete with elbow. Be careful because the filter is full of oil.

25 Draw off the cylinders in turn. (photo)

26 Remove the circlips from the gudgeon pins (photo) and holding the piston firmly tap out the gudgeon pin and remove the piston from the connecting rod. If the pin will not come out easily, warm the piston to 100ºC (no more). No 4 gudgeon pin presents a little difficulty as it can be taken out only one way and the casing gets in the way.

27 Take the nut off the stud holding the distributor clamp and remove the distributor. **Do not** undo the clamp - unless you want to retime the ignition. (Chapter 4).

28 Remove the square sheet metal oil breather box from the top of the engine crankcase. It is held only by a clip.

29 Now undo the four screws holding the oil pump, and using a lever on each side, ease the pump away and set it on one side. Replace the nuts on the studs. (photo)

30 Undo the socket head screws holding the fuel pump and remove the pump, flange and pushrod.

9.18 Removing the oil cooler (it will be full of oil)

9.19 Tap the flywheel off the crankshaft

9.21a The screw holding the deflector plate to the cylinder head

9.21b Withdrawing the head with the deflector plate

9.23 Removing the thermostat

9.25 Removing the cylinders

9.26 Removing the circlips from the pistons

9.29 Removing the oil pump

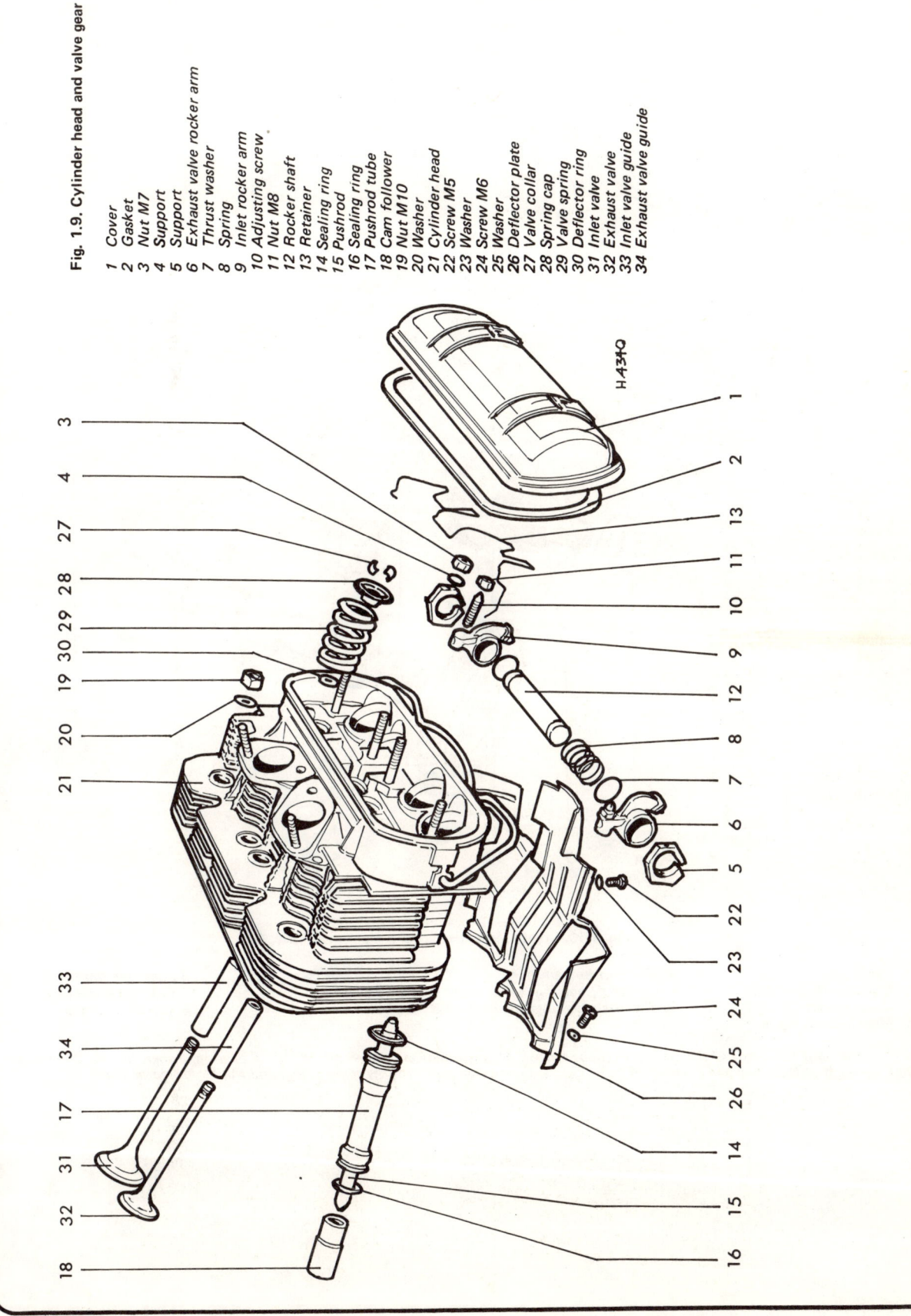

Fig. 1.9. Cylinder head and valve gear (Sec. 9)

1 Cover
2 Gasket
3 Nut M7
4 Support
5 Support
6 Exhaust valve rocker arm
7 Thrust washer
8 Spring
9 Inlet rocker arm
10 Adjusting screw
11 Nut M8
12 Rocker shaft
13 Retainer
14 Sealing ring
15 Pushrod
16 Sealing ring
17 Pushrod tube
18 Cam follower
19 Nut M10
20 Washer
21 Cylinder head
22 Screw M5
23 Washer
24 Screw M6
25 Washer
26 Deflector plate
27 Valve collar
28 Spring cap
29 Valve spring
30 Deflector ring
31 Inlet valve
32 Exhaust valve
33 Inlet valve guide
34 Exhaust valve guide

H.431Q

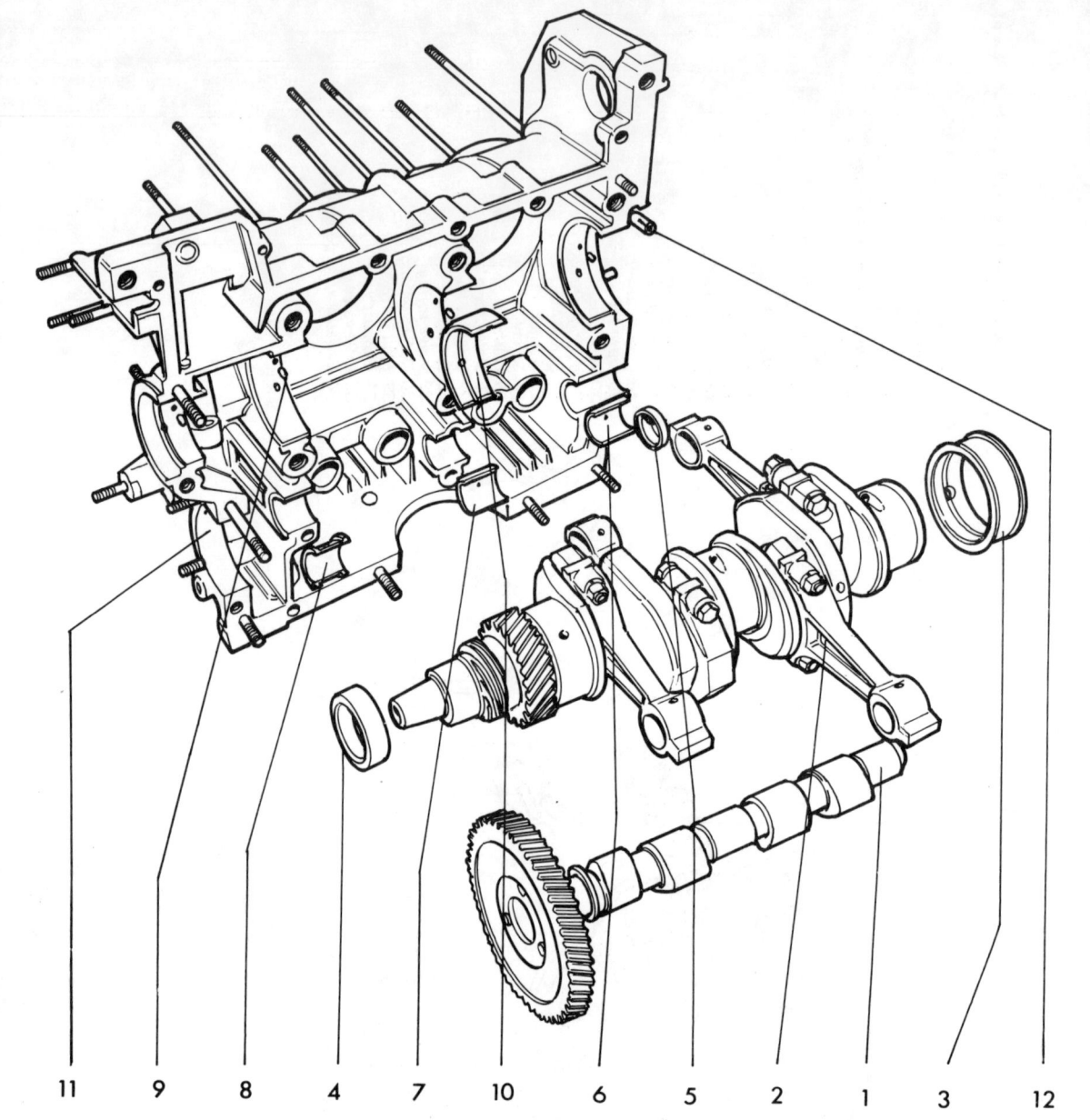

Fig. 1.10. Crankcase, camshaft and crankshaft (Sec. 10)

1 Camshaft	5 End cap for camshaft	8 Left shell for camshaft
2 Crankshaft assembly	6 Camshaft bearing No. 1	No. 3 bearing
3 Main bearing No. 1	7 Camshaft bearing No. 2	9 Dowel pin
4 Main bearing No. 4		

10 Shell bearing No. 2 main
11 Crankcase left half
12 Vibration limiter

Note — the right hand half of the crankcase is not shown. This contains the dowel pin for No. 2 bearing, a shell for No. 2 main, a shell for each of Nos. 1, 2 and 3 camshaft bearings, the oil suction pipe with its sealing ring, and the oil deflector plate.

10 Engine dismantling - splitting the crankcase, dismantling the camshaft and crankshaft

1   If it has been decided to overhaul the crankshaft and camshaft then the crankcase must be split. Two illustrations are given, one of the crankcase and bearings and the other of the crankshaft. (Figs. 1.10 and 1.11)

2   Undo the nuts and remove the bolts holding the crankcase halves together. There are 24 in all, 16 x 7 mm, 2 x 5 mm, and 6 x 10 mm. Work methodically using wooden blocks to support the crankcase while removing the bolts as there are studs sticking out in all directions.

3   Tap the halves apart, but do not tap too hard. If it will not come apart look for more studs or bolts. When all of these are out it does come easily. **Do not** push the faces apart with a wedge. Tap the right-hand half and lift it off the left-hand half leaving the crankshaft and camshaft in the lower half.

4   There will be a gentle tinkle as the cam followers fall into the lower half. Remove them, noting if possible which bore they came from.

5   Put the right-hand half of the crankcase safely away and turn to the left-hand half. Lift out the camshaft (photo), and remove the white metal shell bearings from both halves of the crankcase noting which way they came out. Unless there are signs of wear there is no need to remove the bearings for more that a careful inspection, when they may be replaced right away.

6   With camshaft removed remove the shims from the end of the crankshaft (photo), next remove the crankshaft. (photo)

7   The distributor drive shaft is still in the crankcase. It may be removed at this point if necessary. First remove the preload (anti-rattle) spring.

8   Remove the screw from the end of the crankshaft and pull off the cap (photo). The No 4 main bearing may now be removed.

9   Now using the puller remove the skew gears from the end of the crankshaft. Pull on the camshaft drive gear. Remove the circlip before starting to pull and if a lot of force seems necessary warm the distributor drive gear a little. (photo)

10   The circular main bearing (No 3) may now be removed for inspection. The Woodruff key from the camshaft drive gear should be stored safely.

11   No. 1 main bearing, the circular one at the clutch end of the crankshaft, may be removed for inspection, and of course the shell bearings of No 2 main bearing.

12   All that remains is to remove the big-ends and inspect them and the crankshaft. Mark the bearing caps so that they go back in the same place, the same way round. Remove the nuts from the connecting rod bolts and ease the cap from the rod. Remove the rod from the shaft and replace the cap on the connecting rod.

13   It is now all in pieces. The next job is inspection.

11 Crankcase, crankshaft and camshaft - inspection

1   All the parts should now be cleaned again and oiled lightly.

2   Examine the two halves of the crankcase. Look for cracks, burrs, loose studs and any sign of rotating parts fouling the crankcase. If all is well set the two halves on one side.

3   Next examine the crankshaft. If it can be run between centres the main bearing surfaces masy be checked to ensure the shaft is straight.

4   All bearing surfaces of the crankshaft must be checked for scoring or signs of overheating. Measure them accurately with a micrometer for ovality and diameter against the Specification or a replacement.

5   The connecting rods should be examined for twist and bending. Unless special tools are available this is beyond the

10.5 Removing the camshaft

10.6a Removing the shims from the end of the crankshaft

10.6b Removing the crankshaft

10.8 Removing the cap from the end of the crankshaft

10.9 Pulling the drivegears off the crankshaft. The distributor drive may require warming a little

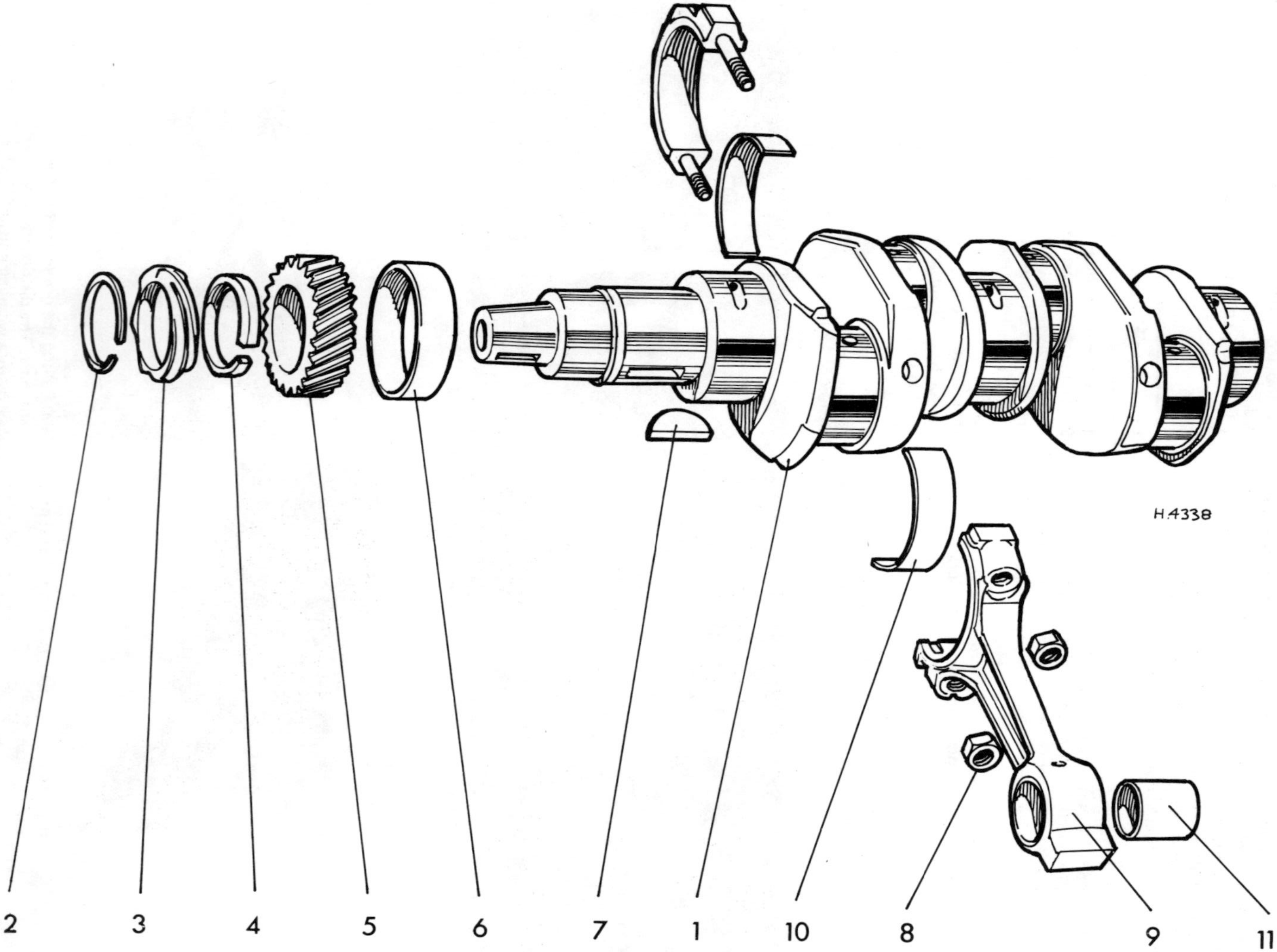

28

Fig. 1.11 Crankshaft assembly (Sec 10)

1 Crankshaft
2 Circlip
3 Distributor drive gear
4 Spacer
5 Camshaft drive gear
6 Crankshaft No. 3 bearing
7 Key
8 Nut
9 Connecting rod
10 Connecting rod shell bearing
11 Gudgeon pin bush

H.4338

scope of the keen owner driver, but unless something drastic has occured the rods will not be distorted. If it has (a seizure or a sudden stop) then take the rods along for checking. If rods are replaced they must be matched for weight. This again is a job for the agent.

6 Assuming the rods are in good order, and the shaft is satisfactory next examine the big-end shells. With the shells fitted correctly and the caps torqued to the right amount, the roundness or ovality of the bearing may be measured with an inside micrometer. Discolouration, scoring or ovality beyond the limit condemn the shells. Indeed if the shaft measures up to the standard Specification it is a false economy not to fit new big-ends right through.

7 If the shaft has to be reground then special shells must be fitted to both the big-ends and mains. Leave this job to the firm who do the grinding and make sure the shaft is assembled and runs freely when returned to you.

8 A reasonable test for a new big-end when assembled is that the rod should fall slowly under its own weight from just off top dead centre. If it doesn't it is too tight, but it must descend slowly or the clearances are too great.

9 The main bearings may only be examined and measured against Specification.

10 End play, both of mains and big-ends should be checked when the crankshaft is reassembled to the crankcase before the two halves of the crankcase are joined.

11 The camshaft must show no signs of wear or overheating on the cam surfaces. The gear must be firmly rivetted to the shaft. If either of these do not seem right the shaft must be replaced. It is not a scheduled spare as we found to our annoyance.

12 The camshaft bearings must now be checked. They are all different so make sure the right partners go together. Check them against Specifcation and for superficial damage. Again, if there is the least doubt, renew the whole lot. The cost is small compared with the total work of the job.

12 Cylinders, pistons and rings - inspection

1 It is convenient to inspect at the same time pistons, rings and cylinders.

2 Cylinders should be measured with an internal micrometer for wear and ovality. The danger point is the top of the piston stroke on the thrust side of the bore. A ridge tends to wear here. Cylinders may be reground and fitted with oversize pistons and rings.

3 However there is a snag to this. There are two sizes of oversize. For the 1700 cc the nominal size is 90 mm. The oversizes are nominally 90.5 mm and 91 mm. So that if one cylinder is reground to 91 mm and the others remain at 90 mm, the piston may be several grams different in weight with vibration and wear problems ahead. This applies to the 1800 cc as well.

   Cylinders must not be bored and installed with standard cylinders. All four must have the same dimensions. This means that if one cylinder only is scored, it should be replaced, not rebored.

   Again, if there are problems of this nature it is better for a reputable firm to sort them out and set the engine to rights rather than risk an out of balance torque.

4 Piston rings should be replaced if the engine has done 30,000 miles since the last overhaul. There are two dimensions to check. The first one is the wear in the groove. The upper ring wear limit is 0.005 ins. (0.12 mm) and the lower ring and scraper rings 0.004 ins., (0.10 mm). Piston ring gaps are (ins):

a) Top compression new 0.014 to 0.022 (wear limit 0.035)
b) Lower compression new 0.012 to 0.022 ins (wear limit 0.035)
c) Scraper ring new 0.010 to 0.016 ins (wear limit 0.037).

5 This means that the rings must be removed from the pistons for measurement. They should be placed in the bore and pushed down approximately 0.20 ins. from the **bottom** of the bore.

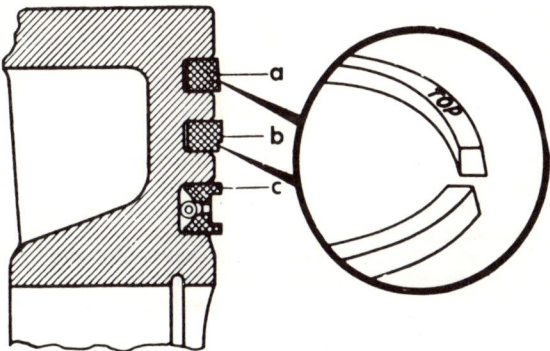

Fig. 1.12 Piston rings (Secs. 12 and 20)

(a) Top compression ring
(b) Lower compression ring with stepped lower edge
(c) Oil control ring

Make sure they are square to the bore when measured.

6 Pistons should be measured for ovality, but seldom require renewal unless the cylinder does as well. The fit of the piston pin is important. The wear limit is 0.0015 ins. (0.04 mm) in other words it should be a stiff fit or there will be small end knock.

13 Valve gear and cylinder heads - inspection

1 The cam followers should be checked for wear on the flat surfaces. Any with other than flat surfaces should be replaced. Do not attempt to grind out indentations.

2 Push rods should be checked for distortion. The maximum bend (or run out between the centres) should be 0.3 mm (0.012 ins.).

3 Valve guides seldom require replacement. As the valves work in a horizontal plane the problem of oil running down worn guides is not nearly so serious. The rock at the end of the stem is 0.45 mm (0.017 ins.) for a new valve and guide, and a wear limit of 0.900 mm (0.035 ins.) is permitted.

4 Inside diameters vary somewhat but the 'rock' test will decide whether replacement is required.

   If new guides are required this is a job for the VW agent. The old guides must be drilled out partially before removal and the new ones reamed to size after installation.

5 If the valves cannot be ground in satisfactorily by hand using the traditional method of a rubber sucker and paste, then, again the agent must be consulted. Exhaust valves may only be ground in, not refaced on a machine, inlets may be refaced but the owner is unlikely to possess a machine so the agent must again be sought. The correct loaded length for a valve spring is 29 mm (1.14 ins.) at 80 kg (176 lb).

6 Cylinder head inserts may be installed where valve seats are damaged but this is a factory job. Check the head for cracks between seats, and check the threads of the plug sockets.

7 If you have to replace exhaust valves the old ones must be destroyed. Saw through the centre of the stem and then throw the valve into a bucket of water. The valve is sodium filled. There will be a reaction, so do not stand too near. The valve may now be thrown in the scrap box.

14 Lubrication system - inspection

1 All oilways and passages should be checked carefully for blockages. An engine with a blocked oilway in the crankcase is a disheartening, expensive sight — it does happen, so check that rag, grease and sludge are absent from oilways.

2 If the oil cooler is functioning satisfactorily when the engine

is dismantled, leave it alone; if it isn't, replace it with a new one. The old cooler will be tested by the agent to a pressure of 6 kg/cm^2 on a special rig. This is 85 lbs per square inch. It is unlikely that a suspect cooler will stand up to this. If there has been a bearing failure and the bearing has broken up then it is essential to fit a new oil cooler as the oil cooler may harbour metal particles which will start the process all over again.

3   The oil pump is not easy to dismantle. An extractor (VW tool 803), is required to pull the cover off. When this is done the only inspection is a visual one of the housing and cover for scoring, particularly where the gears may rub on the housing and cover. If there is any scoring a new pump is required.

4   The two pressure valves must be inspected. The relief valve is situated alongside the oil filter, and is removed by undoing the relief valve plug. Under this there is a sealing ring, a spring and the valve. The valve must not be ridged or worn, the spring should be 1.53 inches (39 mm) long under a pressure of 17lbs ± 2lbs.

5   The regulating valve is found on the right-hand side of the block just under the oil breather. There is a similar arrangement but this time the spring should be 1 inch long under a pressure of 4lbs ± ¼lb.

6   Be careful not to get these springs and valves mixed up. Weak springs should be replaced. If the valve is stuck do not try to pry it out, you will damage the bore. Screw a 3/8" tap into the plunger and remove it that way. Be careful not to scratch the bores with the spring and **do not** use sealant on the thread of the plug or it will not come out next time.

7   The oil strainer should be checked for cleanliness and to see that the delivery pipe joint is intact.

8   Always refit a new oil filter when overhauling an engine.

---

15 Cooling system - inspection

1   There is nothing to dismantle and measure in the cooling

17.1 No 3 main bearing. The blind hole must be next to the crankshaft web

17.2a Fit the camshaft drivegear ...

17.2b ... followed by the spacer

17.3a Fit the distributor drivegear ...

17.3b ... and the circlip

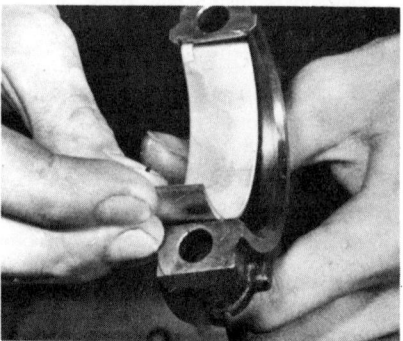

17.4a Assemble a shell bearing to the connecting rod

17.4b Assemble the rod to the shaft

17.4c Torque the nuts to 24 lb ft

17.6a Crankshaft assembly with main bearings

system other than to test the thermostat. This should be immersed in water at 70°C and the length should then be at least 46 mm measured across the bellows. (see Section 4).

2 Check that the flaps work, the pulley goes round on its axis and that the cable is in good order.

3 Finally have a look at all the 'tin ware' to check for rust, bent flanges or other damage, and that it fits together properly. The boot for the dipstick must fit tightly on both tubes.

16 Engine reassembly - general

1 Everything has been checked and rectified and it is all laid out neatly ready for reassembly. Start with a clean bench top, an oil can of light oil, all the tools clean, plenty of clean non-fluffy rag, and clean hands and overalls.

2 Gaskets, 'O' rings and seals should be replaced by new ones and the set should be laid out conveniently on a clean flat surface.

3 Finally — take your time. The engine is a well made piece of machinery which goes together in a most satisfactory way, but each job must be completed properly and checked before going on to the next one.

17 Crankcase and contents - reassembly

1 Lay the crankshaft on a clean surface and lubricate the bearing surfaces. Assemble the No.3 main bearing. The blind hole must be next to the crankshaft web. (photo)

2 Heat the camshaft drive pinion to 100°C and slide it into position, the chamfer edge of the bore leading (photo) and then

fit the spacer. (photo)

3 Now heat the distributor drive pinion to 100°C, slide it on (photo) and then fit the circlip. (photo)

4 Assemble a shell bearing to the cap, making sure that each cap goes back to its own rod the right way round. (Centre punch marks) (photos). Repeat with the other three rods and then torque the nuts to 3.3 mkg (24 lb ft) (photo). Check the centre punch marks to see that the rods and caps are in the right place.

5 Measure the axial play of the connecting rods with a feeler gauge. This should be 0.004 ins. to 0.016 ins. It must not be more than 0.028 ins. Now lock the nuts with a peening tool.

6 Now layout the crankshaft as shown in the photos with No. 1 main bearing, the two shells for No. 2 main bearing, and the No. 4 main bearing.

7 Add the two halves of the crankcase and the camshaft with its bearing, and the stage is set to assemble the crankcase.

8 Assemble the No. 2 (shell bearing) to both halves of the crankcase. (photo)

9 Fit the camshaft bearings to the crankcase, try the camshaft in position and remove it. Note that the flanged thrust bearing goes at the distributor end. (photo)

10 Oil all the bearing surfaces of the mains and the crankshaft and camshaft, lift the crankshaft by the 2nd and 4th cylinder cam rods and lower it into the crankcase, feeding No. 1 and 3 cam rods through the holes in the crankcase. (photo) Check that Nos. 1,3 and 4 mains have located properly with the dowels in place and that No. 2 shell main is in place.

11 Rotate the crankshaft so that the two punch marks on the side of the camshaft drive gear are horizontal and install the camshaft so that the pip mark on the camshaft gear fits between the two marks on the drive gear. (photo). This is all there is to

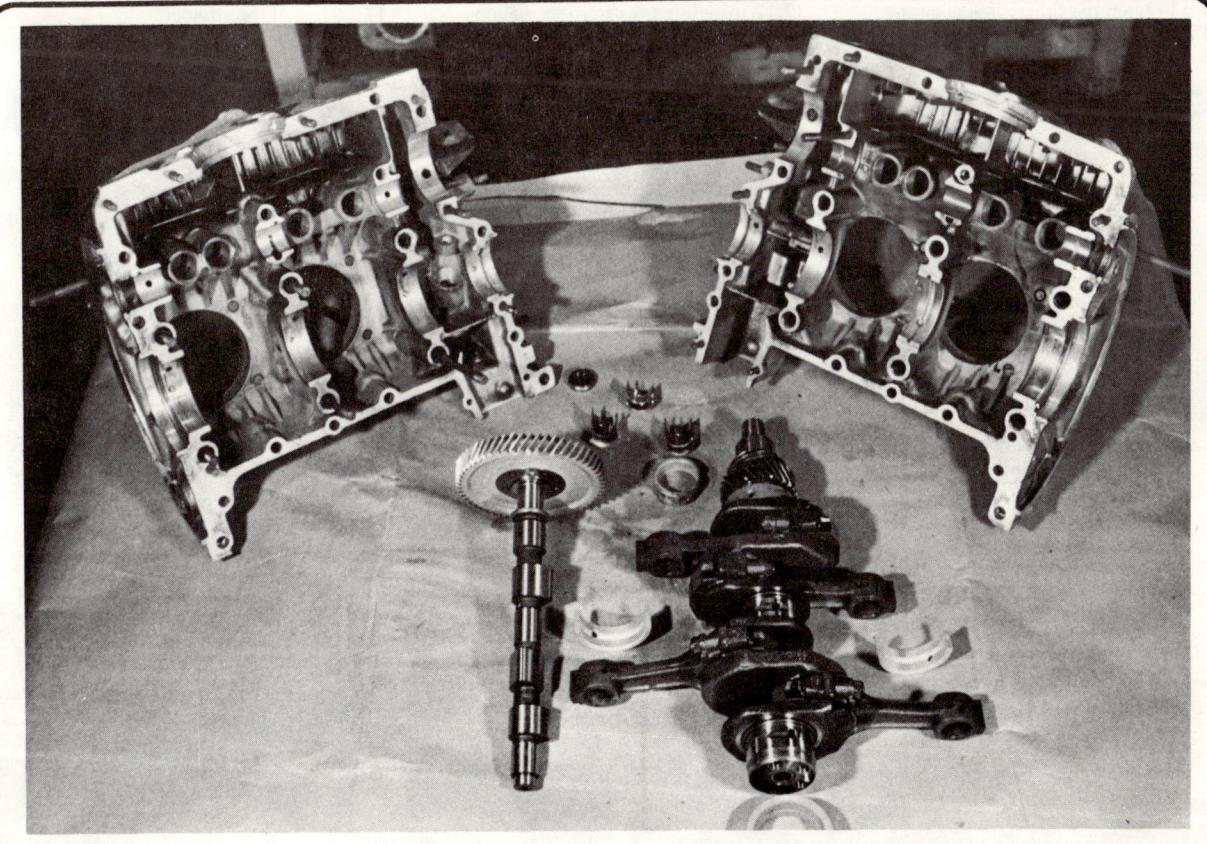

17.6b Crankcase - camshaft, crankshaft assembly and bearings laid out for assembly

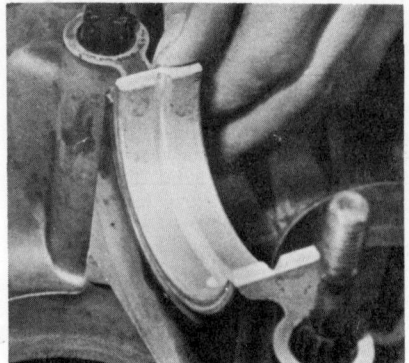
17.8 Fitting the shell (no 2) bearing to the crankcase

17.9 The flanged camshaft bearing

17.10 Lowering the crankshaft into position

17.11 Match the timing marks on the drive and driven gears for the camshaft

17.12 Installing the camshaft sealing plug

17.14 Install the strainer

17.15 Fitting the second half of the crankcase

17.19a Refit the remainder of the oil strainer ...

17.19b ... and fit the nut to the cover

17.20 Fit the oil pump

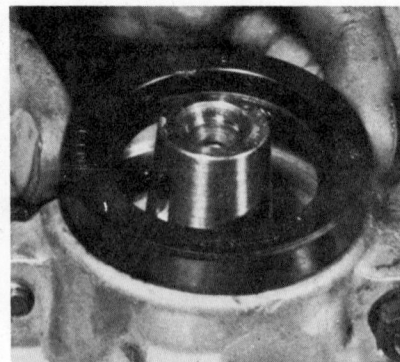
18.3a Fit the oil seal ...

18.3b ... and the sealing ring

valve timing. Check all the bearing shells again.

12 Fit the sealing plug for the end of the camshaft into position (photo). This should be coated with VW jointing compound, or with Hylomar before installation.

13 Wipe carefully round the two mating surfaces of the crankcase and coat the one in which the crankshaft is installed with jointing compound. Use this sparingly.

14 Now turn to the other half of the casing. Install the oil suction pipe and the strainer (photo). Use a new seal ring.

15 Check that the shell bearing for No. 2 main bearing is in place correctly, and that the camshaft shells are safely in position; oil the bearing surfaces, and holding the crankcase by the cylinder bolts lower it carefully into position over the crankshaft and camshaft, feeding the connecting rods through the cylinder openings as the case is lowered. (photo)

16 Install the six M.10 bolts with the washer and sealing nuts, coating the heads of the bolts with sealing compound. The sealing rings of the nuts should be outwards. Install all the other nuts and bolts and tighten them slightly. Now stop to think:

1 Are all the connecting rods protruding from their right holes?
2 Did you fit all the bearings (or are some still on the bench)?
3 Was the camshaft timing meshed correctly?
4 Is the camshaft sealing plug in position?

17 Turn the crankshaft through 360° to make sure that nothing is fouling and now tighten the M.10 nuts to 15 lb ft, working diagonally as for a cylinder head. Check the rotation of the shaft again. If it is stiff in any way undo the nuts, split the case and search for the reason. It will probably be a bearing not seating properly. It is essential to find the reason before pressing on as damage will ensue if the casing is tightened further.

18 When all is correct tighten the large (M.10) nuts to 25 ft lbs and all the smaller ones to 14 ft lbs working diagonally all the while. Check the rotation frequently (at the end of each round of tightening).

19 Now fit the rest of the oil strainer (photos) and cover to the bottom of the sump and torque the nut to 10 lb ft. Refit the oil pressure relief valve and screw home the plug. Check that the oil pressure switch is in place.

20 Reassemble the oil pump to the crankcase. Use a new gasket. The tab on the drive gear shaft should be aligned with the slot in the camshaft gear. Centre the pump by turning the crankshaft two revolutions and tighten the nuts to 15 lb ft. (photo)

18 Oil seals, fan hub and flywheel - reassembly

1 The oil seals will have been removed and the seats cleaned. It is not necessary to split the crankcase to do this job.

2 Cover the seats with a thin coat of sealing compound. If necessary make a small lead in the seat, and remove all burrs.

3 Press the oil seal and ring in at the fan end of the shaft. The seal is 2.5 ins diameter. (photos)

4 Fit the Woodruff key, then the fan hub and finally the bolt with the large washer. Torque the M8 bolt to 23 lbs ft. (photo)

5 The hub is now ready for the fan to be installed.

6 Going to the other end, install the flywheel with two shims behind it. Do not fit the seal yet.

7 Now measure the axial play of the crankshaft. If it is possible to obtain a dial gauge read the play on the dial gauge, otherwise you will have to rig up an arrangement to use feelers. The axial play should now have 0.004 in. (0.10 mm) subtracted from it and this will give the thickness of the third shim required. Shims of 6 thickness are available (ins) 0.0095, 0.0118, 0.0126, 0.0134, 0.0142 and 0.0150. Unless major repairs have been done the reinstallation of the old shims will usually meet the requirement. Having settled the shim problem remove the flywheel, install the shims (photo) with the seal and sealing ring; then refit the flywheel. (photo)

8 Be careful, the small dowel must not be damaged, it locates the flywheel correctly and ensures the correct dynamic balance of the crankshaft and flywheel. The seal must be bedded squarely in the crankcase recess. It can be driven in but it is better pressed in using VW tool 191.

9 When refitting the flywheel, first fit the spacer and then the five bolts and torque them to 80 lb ft. (11mkg) (photos).

19 Valves and valve springs - reassembly and overhaul (engine in vehicle)

1 The clean cylinder head minus all carbon and other fouling should now be assembled with the valves. The valves have been serviced, either machined or ground in and are ready for fitting (Section 13).

2 Refer to Fig. 1.13. Insert the valve into the guide, fit the oil deflector ring, slip the spring over the stem, fit the spring cap, compress the spring with a valve lifter and fit the cotters in place. (photos)

3 If the cotters are difficult hold them on the end of a screwdriver with a blob of grease and poke them into place that way.

4 When the valve is assembled compress the spring to open the valve and let it go sharply. This will indicate whether the cotters are properly seated.

5 Clean off the flange of the cylinder head, and repeat for the second cylinder head.

20 Pistons, cylinders and cylinder heads - reassembly

1 First replace the cam followers in their bores. (photo). They should go into the bore from which they came.

2 The rings should be fitted to the pistons before assembly to the connecting rod. Gapping is discussed in Section 12. Ease the rings over the piston carefully for they are brittle. Use a

18.4 ... the woodruffe key, the hub, the bolt and washer

18.7a Install the shims with the seal

18.7b and then the flywheel

18.9a Fit the spacer and five bolts

18.9b Torque to 80 lb ft

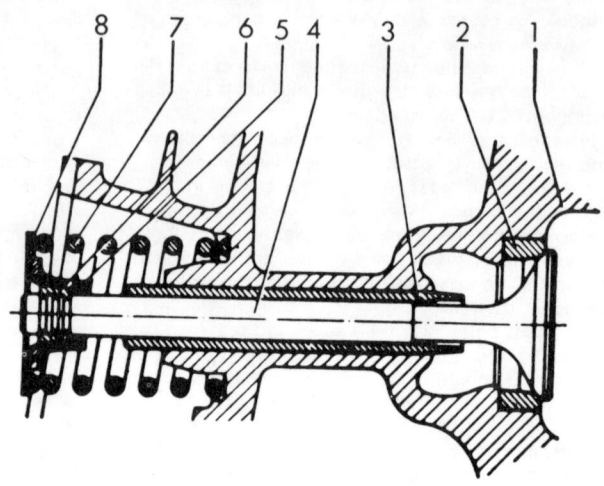

Fig 1.13 Valve assembly - cross section (Sec 19)

1 Cylinder head	4 Valve	7 Valve spring
2 Seat insert	5 Oil seal ring	8 Spring retainer
3 Guide	6 Split collar	

19.2a Install the valve ...

19.2b ... then the seal washer

19.2c ... followed by the spring and cap ...

19.2d ... and compress the spring to insert the cotter

20.1 Replace the cam followers

20.3 Fit the pistons to the connecting rods

20.4 Replace the circlips

20.6a Using a home made clamp to compress the piston rings

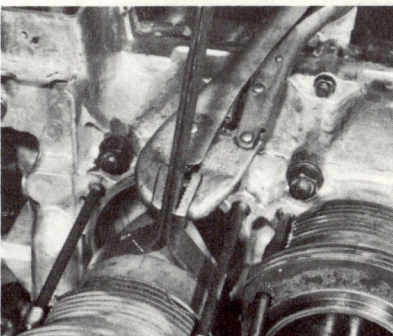
20.6b Push the clamp off the piston using the cylinder until all the rings are in the cylinder then remove the wrench and the clamp

20.7 Fitting the cylinder head

20.8 Torque the head down to 23 lbs ft

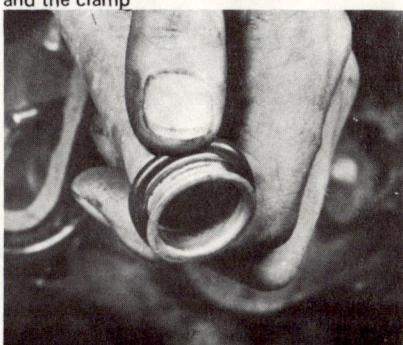
21.1a Fit a new sealing ring

piston ring expander, or slide them over a thin piece of metal wrapped round the piston. The rings are marked 'TOP' on one surface near the gap. This surface should point to the piston crown. The lower compression ring (middle of the three) has a step on the lower edge. Space the gaps 120° apart. (Fig 1.12)

3 The gudgeon pin is a push fit in the piston. Heat the piston with an electric lamp and fitting the piston over the small end bush push the gudgeon pin through the bush. (photo)

4 Install the circlips. It is advisable to use new circlips. (photo)

5 As each piston is installed to the connecting rod, slide the cylinder over the piston installing the cylinder over the studs. Do not forget the sealing ring at the bottom of the cylinder. Lightly oil the piston and the cylinder before installation.

6 Getting the piston into the cylinder is not as easy as it might be. Various methods are recommended from proprietary piston ring compressors to jubilee clips. We had none of the right size so a piece of 1'' x 1/8'' (25.4 x 3.17 mm) mild steel was bent to form a circle about 1/16'' (1.6 mm) larger than the piston and was then sawn opposite the open end to form two half circles, each with a long stem. These were clamped round the rings and held with a mole wrench. It was then simple enough to push the clamp off the piston with the cylinder until all the rings were in the cylinder, and by removing the mole wrench extract the clamp in two parts. (photos)

7 When all four cylinders are in place install the sealing rings in over the cylinders and gently ease the heads over the studs. (photo) Take care not to pinch the sealing rings.

8 Fit the M.10 nuts and washers to the studs and torque the head down using the sequence in Fig. 1.14. Tighten down progressively a little at a time to 23 lbs ft. (photo)

9 Fit the deflector plates next. The right-hand one is the smaller of the two. There is one screw in the cylinder head and two in the crankcase.

Fig 1.14 Sequence for tightening cylinder head nuts
Note - tighten first to 10 lb ft and then to 23 lb ft in easy stages (Sec 20)

21 Pushrods and rocker gear - reassembly

1 The cam followers are in place. Now install the push rod tubes; fit a new red or green sealing ring at the top and a black one at the bottom (photo) and push the tubes into place through the rocker box (photo). Make sure the seals are firmly installed (photo)

2 Now install the pushrods (photo) and assemble the rocker gear. The spring retainer for the tubes goes on first. This is a much bent piece of wire which fits round the studs and across the top of the pushrod tubes. Fit the rocker gear on top of the retainer, engaging the tops of the pushrods in the cups while so doing. (photo). Tighten the nuts on the rocker studs to 10 ft lbs (1.4 mkg)

21.1b Install the pushrod tube

21.1c The box should look like this

21.2a Install the pushrods

21.2b and fit the rocker assembly

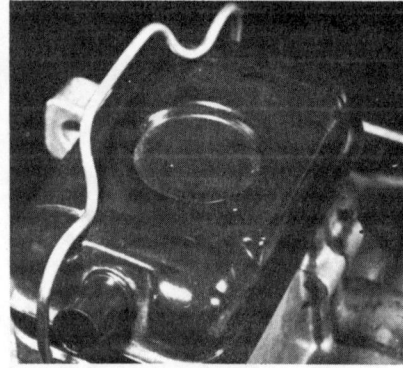
22.1 Refit the oil breather

22.2 Fitting the bracket for the oil filter

22.3 Fit new seals to the oil ports of the cooler

23.2 Fit the oil filler pipe

23.3 Fit the fan housing ...

23.4a ... the warm air duct right rear ...

23.4b ... and the warm air duct left rear

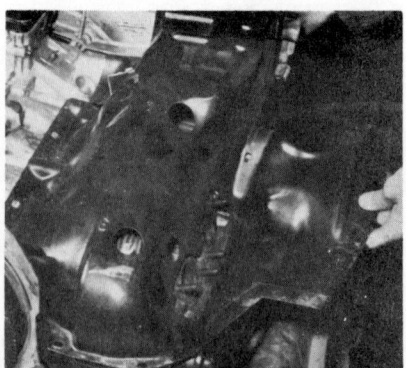
23.5a The cylinder coverplate (left) ...

22 Oil cooler and fitter - reassembly

1 Fit a new cork gasket and install the oil breather in the top of the crankcase. (photo)
2 Bolt the bracket for the oil filter to the side of the crankcase (photo). Do not forget to fit a new gasket. Install a new oil filter and tighten it.
3 Install new seals for the oil cooler (photo) and fit the oil cooler (photo 9.18). The seals should not be too soft or they will 'blow', and the engine must come down again. On the other hand do not tighten them so much that they are squashed. Do not forget the washers between the cooler and the crankcase. Watch out for residual oil if the old cooler is being replaced, it can make a mess.

23 Cooling system, fan and alternator - reassembly

1 Refit the thermostat (see photo 9.23). It goes on the two studs. The control wire should be in line with the pulley.
2 Refit the oil filler pipe. (photo)
3 Place the fan housing in position taking care to fit the boot over the dipstick housing. (photo)
4 Fit the cowl round the oil cooler (warm air duct left rear) and the counterpart on the other pair of cylinders (warm air duct right rear) but do not screw them down yet. (photos)
5 Fit the cylinder cover plate left and the cylinder cover plate right but do not bolt them down yet. (photos)
6 Manoeuvre the fan housing into position finally and tighten the nuts. Put all the screws in the tin ware and fasten it up so that it fits snugly. By doing it this way, any minor adjustments can be done with the whole cover system in place.
7 The cylinder cover plate right has a hole in it for the thermostat control wire to pass through before it connects to the flap control. Put the wire over the pulley and connect it up so that the flaps are shut when the thermostat is cold. (photo)
8 Put the warm air duct right front and the left front in position but do not tighten them yet.
9 Assemble the bracket to the back of the alternator and the sheet metal cover over the alternator. Offer it up to the fan housing. Insert the coach head type bolt at the bottom and the alternator and cover are held loosely in place. Now fit the adjusting bracket inside the cover, put your hand behind the alternator cover and fit the rubber ducting to the fan housing. Feed the wires through the top cover grommet and fit the two cheese headed screws to the alternator cover. The long one goes in the fan housing. (photos)
10 Now fit the fan spacer, and then the fan. It will only go on one way. There are three socket screws for the fan which are tightened to 15 lbs ft. (photos)
11 Fit the alternator belt set to the correct tension and lock the alternator in position with the socket head screw. Tighten the nut on the back of the coach head screw. (photo)

24 Heat exchangers and engine bearer - reassembly

1 Tip the engine so that it rests on the flywheel, support it with wooden blocks. Fit the left-hand heat exchanger (do not forget the very solid little gaskets). Slide the metal tube through the grommet in the engine cover and make sure the grommet fits snugly; there is also a clamp connecting the heat exchanger to the fan housing. Tighten all the nuts correctly. (photos)
2 Before fitting the right-hand heat exchanger fit the engine bearer. If it is not fitted before the heat exchanger it is not possible to get it in. Check that the bonded rubber mountings are in good condition, replace them if not: tighten up all the nuts and bolts. (photo)
3 Now fit the right-hand heat exchanger in the same way as the left one.

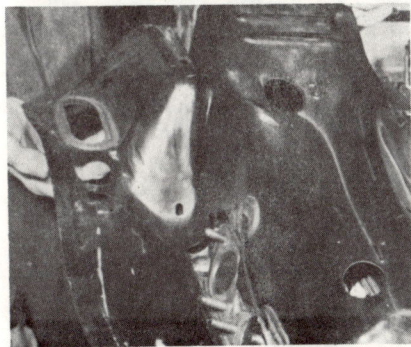

23.5b ... and the cylinder coverplate (right)

23.7 Connecting the thermostat wire to the flaps

23.9a The adjusting bracket to the alternator

23.9b Fitting the coach head bolt through the alternator cowling

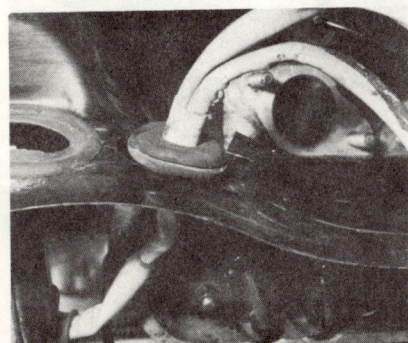

23.9c Feeding the alternator cables through the grommet

23.9d The sealing ring for the alternator

23.10a Fitting the fan spacer ...

23.10b ... and then the fan

23.11 Tighten the nut on the back of the alternator pivot

24.1a Fitting the heat exchanger

24.1b The cover for the heat exchanger

24.2 Fit the engine bearer

26.1 Adjusting valve clearances

27.2 The front plate may now be installed

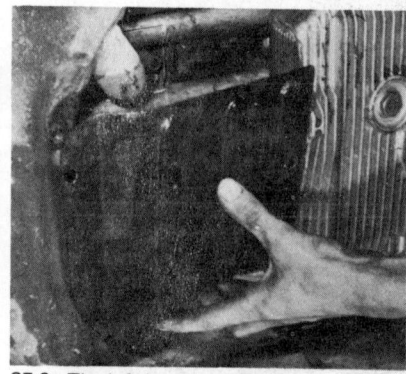
27.3a The left lower warm air duct

27.3b The right lower warm air duct

27.4 The exhaust may now be installed

28.2 The clutch correctly assembled

25 Distributor - refitting

This is discussed in detail in Chapter 4. It should be done now when reassembling the engine.

26 Valve clearance (tappets) - setting

1   It is much easier to set the valve clearances if the spark plugs are removed. (photo)
2   It was pointed out to us that nowhere do we say which is inlet and which is exhaust. The two middle ones are inlet and the two outer ones are exhaust.
3   Turn the engine until the valve to be set is completely closed (the tappet screw will be clear of the valve stem). Slacken off the locknut and fit a feeler gauge between the screw and the stem (see below for size of feeler). Tighten the screw until it just grips the feeler. Hold the screw in position and tighten the locknut. Check the fit of the feeler gauge and readjust if necessary.
4   Work in the sequence 1-2-3-4 cylinders. Settings are for the cold engine.
5   Inlet valves are set to a gap of 0.006 in (0.15 mm).
6   On earlier engines **not** fitted with sodium filled exhaust valves the gap is also 0.006 ins.
7   From chassis No. '213 2210 554' (1973) the 1700 cc engine was fitted with sodium filled exhaust valves and the gap is 0.008 in (0.20 mm). This gap also applies to all 1800 cc engines. If you are in doubt about the valves set the gap to 0.008 in; there may be some tappet clatter but you will not burn the valves.

27 Cover plates and exhaust - reassembly

1   The remainder of the 'tin-ware' may now be fitted.
2   The front cover plate may be installed. (photo)
3   Now fit the left and right lower warm air ducts. (photos)
4   The exhaust system may now be installed. Tighten the six bolts with a good nip. (photo)
5   Fit the left and right rear cover plates. Fit the large one first. Make sure the rubber grommet is in place or it will foul the alternator drive belt. Slide the cover plate over the oil filler tube after installation but before screwing the plate down. Fit the small plate (the one with the valve clearance notice on it. This may be out of date, if so cancel it). The screw at the back of the alternator belt may be a bit of a fiddle. It is fitted from the outside into a fixed nut and has to be worked past the heat exchanger. Tighten all the screws.

28 Engine reassembly - final stage before installation

1   If you have not already fitted it install the distributor drive shaft (mind those shims) and the distributor (Chapter 3 Section 10). Refit the spark plugs.
2   Refit the clutch to the flywheel. Centre the friction plate carefully, fit the clutch to the marks and torque the bolts to 18 lb ft. using a diagonal method of tightening. The long boss of the friction plate must face away from the engine or the assembly will not bolt up (see Chapter 4). (photo)
3   Install the guard grille over the fan.
4   Install the fuel pump with its intermediate flange and pushrod.
5   Install the carburettors with linkages and connect up the fuel system to the pump. If you are worried about damaging the carburettors leave them off until after the engine is in place but fit the linkages and the hoses ready for reconnection.
6   Check the rubber seal round the hole in the engine compartment. Replace it if necessary with a new one.
7   On automatic transmission do not forget you have put a clamp to hold the torque convertor in place. This must come off before the engine goes into position.

8   Wipe the clutch withdrawal race clean and smear it with molybdenum grease. Dust the splines of the mainshaft with molybdenum disulphide powder, and make sure the mating surface of the clutch housing is clean.

29 Engine - refitting

1   Position the engine on the packing and the trolley jack and ease it under the back of the vehicle.
2   The gearbox (transmission casing) is supported on a jack or with slings and the front wheels of the vehicle have chocks to prevent the vehicle moving. The handbrake is on and the vehicle in 2nd gear.
3   Raise the engine a little at a time making sure that nothing is fouling the vehicle frame. Remembering that the driveshaft has to enter the clutch driven plate and the pilot bush, keep the engine as far to the rear as possible.
4   When the engine is lined up with the transmission box move it forward gently so that the mainshaft enters the splines of the driven plate of the clutch. It will probably be necessary to rotate the crankshaft of the engine a little to get the splines to enter the clutch driven plate. Move the engine forward a little at a time, watching also the rubber seal round the engine compartment.
5   As soon as possible install the two lower engine to transmission bolts. Do not tighten them yet. Now install the top two bolts.
6   The engine bearer will have been guided into position as the engine rose to position. Install the bracket to frame bolts loosely. Now torque the engine to transmission bolts to 22 ft lbs.
7   Remove the support jack or chain from the transmission. You will have noted the postion of the engine bearers (Section 6.15) when dismantling. That is how it should seem now so move the brackets on their elongated holes until that position is restored. Torque the bracket to 14 lb ft.
8   Lower the jack, remove the packings and the engine is now ready for reconnection.
9   Check round that the engine seal is snugly fitted and adjust it if it is not.
10 Refit the coil to the fan housing, connect it up and check the ignition circuit. Refit the hoses to the vacuum advance and retard.
11 Refit the carburettors if not already in position, connect the linkages, and accelerator cable, reconnect the fuel hoses to the fuel pump and check that fuel is coming through to the carburettors (turn the engine).
12 Refit the starter leads (photo) and connect up the electrical leads to the carburettors.
13 Fit the ducts and hoses to the heat exchangers, install the air cleaner and refit the fresh air blower. Connect all the hoses to

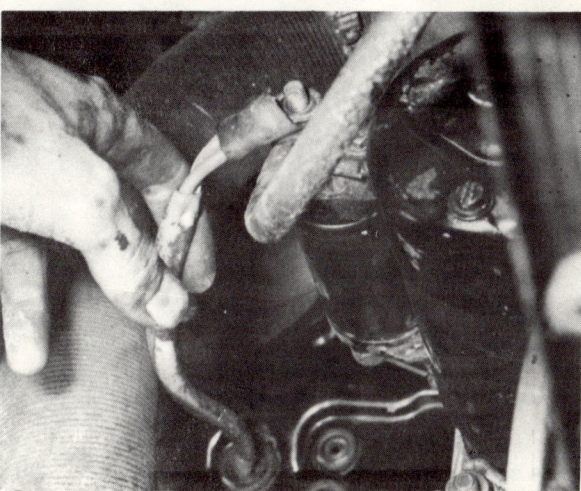
29.12 Reconnect the cables to the starter

them.

14 If you have afterburn fitted install the air pump and the extension to the fan pulley. Fit the belt and adjust the tension. Connect the hoses and leads.

15 Install the oil filler and the dipstick. Reconnect the hose from the charcoal filter. Connect the EGR hoses and leads.

16 Check the list that you made on dismantling and install any other equipment which you removed.

17 Reconnect the oil pressure switch, transmission switch, back-up lights, alternator regulator and the trigger for the flywheel ignition timing. Reconnect the alternator wiring.

18 It all sounds a lot but if you did what we said - made a list and tagged all wires and hoses - the whole thing takes about half an hour.

19 On automatic transmission vehicles the ATF fluid filler pipe and dipstick must be reinstalled and the bolts holding the torque converter to the drive plate. These should be tightened to 14 lb ft.

20 Now fill the engine with oil. It will need 7½ US pints (6 1/8 Imperial pints or 3½ litres) of the recommended type (HD).

21 Reconnect the battery ground strap (earth lead) and with the ignition disconnected spin the engine for a few turns. Reconnect and switch on and start the engine. Run it at tick over speed for a few minutes and look for air, oil, exhaust and fuel leaks. Correct if necessary. Now increase the speed to 2000 rpm for a few seconds shut down and check again.

22 If all seems well close up the flaps and road test the vehicle. If all is well then install the gravel guard under the bumper. The various tuning techniques are discussed in Chapter 2 (Fuel system) and Chapter 3 (Ignition).

30 Fault diagnosis - engine

Note:When investigating starting and uneven running faults do not be tempted into snap diagnosis. Start from the beginning of the check procedure and follow it through. It will take less time in the long run. Poor performance from an engine in terms of power and economy is not normally diagnosed quickly. In any event the ignition and fuel systems must be checked first before assuming any further investigation needs to be made.

Symptom	Reason/s	Remedy
Engine will not turn over when starter switch is operated	Flat battery Bad battery connections Bad connections at solenoid switch and/or starter motor Starter motor jammed Defective solenoid Starter motor defective	Check that battery is fully charged and that all connections are clean and tight. Rock car back and forth with a gear engaged. If ineffective remove starter. Remove starter and check solenoid. Remove starter and overhaul.
Engine turns over normally but fails to fire and run	No spark at plugs No fuel reaching engine Too much fuel reaching the engine (flooding)	Check ignition system according to procedures given in Chapter 4. Check fuel system according to procedures given in Chapters 2 and 3. Slowly depress accelerator pedal to floor and keep it there while operating starter motor until engine fires. Check fuel system if necessary as described in Chapters 2 and 3.
Engine starts but runs unevenly and misfires	Ignition and/or fuel system faults Incorrect valve clearances Burnt out valves	Check the ignition and fuel systems as though the engine had failed to start. Check and reset clearances. Remove cylinder heads and examine and overhaul as necessary.
Lack of power	Ignition and/or fuel system faults Incorrect valve clearances Burnt out valves Worn out pistons or cylinder bores	Check the ignition and fuel systems for correct ignition timing and carburettor settings. Check and reset the clearances. Remove cylinder heads and examine and overhaul as necessary. Remove cylinder heads and examine pistons and cylinder bores. Overhaul as necessary.
Excessive oil consumption	Oil leaks from crankshaft oil seal, rocker cover gasket, oil pump, oil cooler, oil strainer cover plate, or oil filter Worn piston rings or cylinder bores resulting in oil being burnt by engine (Smoky exhaust is an indication) Worn valve guides and/or defective valve stem seals	Identify source of leak and repair as appropriate. Fit new rings or rebore cylinders and fit new pistons, depending on degree of wear. Remove cylinder heads and recondition valve stem bores and valves and seals as necessary.
Excessive mechanical noise from engine	Wrong valve to rocker clearances Worn crankshaft bearings Worn cylinders (piston slap)	Adjust valve clearances. Inspect and overhaul where necessary.
Unusual vibration	Misfiring on one or more cylinders Loose mounting bolts	Check ignition system. Check tightness of bolts and condition of flexible mountings.
Engine backfires or overruns.	Faulty fuel circuit or afterburn non-return valve	Check fuel system. Replace afterburn non-return valve.

Chapter 2 Carburation; fuel and emission control systems

Contents

Specifications

Fuel tank capacity ... ...   12 gallons (imperial), 56 litres, 14½ gallons (US) (Reserve 5 gals)

Fuel pump
Type ... ...   Diaphragm, mechanically operated from front of camshaft
Minimum delivery capacity ... ...   400 cc/min at 3800 rpm (0.088 gals)
Maximum delivery pressure ... ...   5 pounds/square inch ($0.35kg\ cm^2$)
Length of pushrod ... ...   5.492 ins (139.5 mm)

Fuel gauge
Sender unit ... ...   Electro-mechanical (float on arm) in tank
Gauge unit ... ...   Balancing coil ammeter
Fuse No   11

Air cleaners
Early models ... ...   Oil bath (Use SAE 30 oil)
Later models ... ...   Paper element type

Carburettors
Type ... ...   Down draught SOLEX fitted with accelerator pump, electro-magnet cut-off valve, automatic choke and central idling system
Left-hand carburettor ... ...   SOLEX PDSIT − 2 (with central idling system)
Right-hand carburettor ... ...   SOLEX PDSIT − 3

The following dimensions are common to all carburettors fitted to 1700/1800 cc engines 1972-75
Venturi diameter ... ...   26 mm
Aux fuel jet ... ...   45 (L.H. Carb)
Aux air jet 0.7
Float needle valve diameter ... ...   1.2 mm
Washer under float needle valve (thickness) ... ...   1.0 mm except 1972 which was 0.5 mm
Fuel level measurement (flange to surface) ... ...   12 to 14 mm
Float weight ... ...   7.0 grams

The main, air correction, pilot and pilot jet air bleed varies considerably as the model and year varies. The type of transmission also affects the specification. The VW agent should be consulted for your particular model. Below is a specimen list

Transmission Engine detail & year	Main jet	Air correction jet	Pilot jet	Pilot jet air bleed
2/1700 M249 '72 Auto CE 000 001	X132.5	155	—	130
2/1700 M 157 '72 Auto CD 000 001	X132.5	155	—	130

Transmission Engine detail & year	Main jet	Air correction jet	Pilot jet	Pilot jet air bleed
2/1700 '72 CB 000 001	X137.5	155		145
2/1800 '73 Manual AP	X132.5	175	47.5	140
2/1800 '73 Auto AP	X130	175	47.5	130
2/1800 '74 AN	X130	175	52.5	120

Acceleration pump input/stroke ccs:

1972 (1700)	0.8 - 1.0
1973 (Manual)	0.7 ± 0.1
1973 (Automatic)	0.7 ± 0.5
1974 (Valve open)	0.55 - 0.85
1974 (Valve closed)	1.3 - 1.7

Torque wrench settings

	lbs ft	kgm
Carburettor to manifold (nuts)	14	2

1 General description - fuel system

1 All models are fitted with twin Solex 34 PDSIT/2/3 carburettors. The jet sizes and specifications vary. The specifications are given but generally the system falls into one of three categories, those for 1700cc engines, those for 1800cc engines, and those for vehicles fitted with automatic transmission. In addition, to comply with legal requirements there are modifications for vehicles intended for USA to restrict emission pollution. These again vary, those for California, and those for the rest of the USA.

2 Modifications are produced like autumn leaves as the restrictions become more stringent, this Chapter has tried to keep up-to-date but the author suspects that before the manual has reached the booksellers there will be yet more modifications.

3 Adjusting and tuning carburettors is now a science, not an art, and the days when the enthusiast could do this tuning by ear and instinct are over. Nowadays, instruments are required and exact measurements must be done. Unless you are prepared to buy these tools and spend a lot of time learning how to use them it will be much better to leave the tuning and adjustment of the carburettors to the VW agent.

4 Two types of air cleaner have been fitted, an oil bath until 1973 and after that a dry type, paper filter air cleaner. The air cleaner is usually modified to keep pace with intake air pre-heating and emission control modifications.

5 On most vehicles the tank is now fitted with an extensive pipework system and charcoal filters to stop raw petrol fumes being given off through the tank vent pipe. The tank may be removed only after the engine has been removed. Only on the pick-up is it accessible without this extra labour. You cannot even get at the fuel gauge transmitter without taking the tank out of the body. So if the fuel gauge will not work you are faced with a long week-end task to do a job that will take only an hour.

6 The fuel pump may be removed without taking the engine out, but it must be done from under the vehicle. It is a mechanically operated pump.

7 The system operates on 91 octane (RON) fuel. Higher octane fuel does not give improved performance, but lower octane gives decreased performance.

8 It is suggested that if you belong to a VW Club, of which there are many, that the club may decide to hold a pool of instruments and tools and thus enable the enthusiast to tune his own engine but our advice about tuning without them is the same as *Mr Punch's* advice to those about to get married: In a word - don't.

2 Routine maintenance - fuel system

1 Maintenance should be regular. It is not very extensive.

2 Service the air cleaner regularly. Replace the paper one every 18,000 miles. It should be emptied of dust weekly if you operate in very dusty conditions, until you are familiar with how much dust is filtered each week. After that adjust the period to suit. Under normal conditions a monthly clearout is sufficient

3 The Exhaust Gas Recirculation (EGR) filter (US models only) should be replaced every 24,000 miles, or once in two years if you do not reach that mileage. It is under the vehicle in front of the silencer. Remove the two nuts which hold it to the pipes and fit a new filter.

4 The air cleaner for the exhaust afterburning air pump has a pleated paper element filter. This is fitted to the inlet of the air pump. It should be replaced every 18,000 miles.

5 The filter for the vent from the fuel tank is located in the engine compartment (upper right-hand side). Detach the hoses and remove the bracket. Replace the canister every 48,000 miles or 2 years whichever comes first.

6 On US models after 1972 check the operation of the exhaust gas recirculation valves. There are two, one for each carburettor on 72 and 73 models, but only one on 74, 75 models. They should be removed from the manifold, cleaned and then tested. On 73 valves push the pin in to see that it moves freely. On 74 type valves run the engine and watch that the pin moves in and out as the revs fluctuate. This should be done every 24,000 miles.

7 Check the tension of the belt which drives the air pump. The belt is tensioned correctly when the centre of the belt may be pushed in 5 to 8 mm (0.2 to 0.3 in) with the thumb (a rough guide is ¼''); do not squeeze both sides together, just push on one leg of the belt. This should be done every 6,000 miles.

3 Air cleaners

1 The earlier 1700cc engine were fitted with an oil bath type air cleaner. Fig. 2.1 shows the layout. There are two brackets on the top of the crankcase to which the air cleaner is secured by quick release clips. The air cleaner consists of an upper and lower part which are held together by quick release clips. The lower part has an air intake elbow which contains a thermostat which operates a flap to regulate the flow of warm air from No 1 cylinder or cold air from outside depending upon the temperature of the outside air. A second flap in the elbow regulates the manifold vacuum for crankcase ventilation. At either end of the

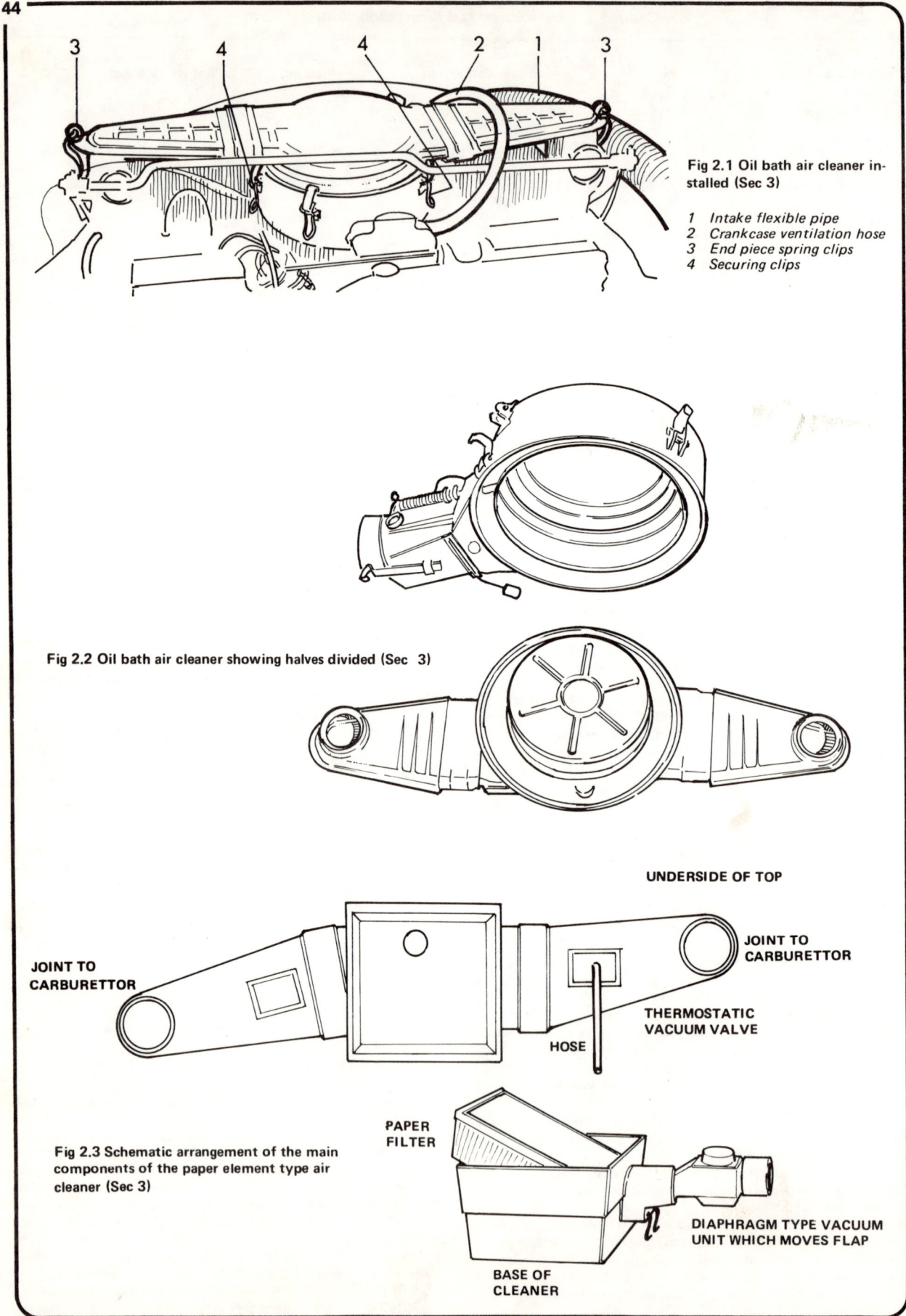

Fig 2.1 Oil bath air cleaner installed (Sec 3)

1 *Intake flexible pipe*
2 *Crankcase ventilation hose*
3 *End piece spring clips*
4 *Securing clips*

Fig 2.2 Oil bath air cleaner showing halves divided (Sec 3)

UNDERSIDE OF TOP

JOINT TO
CARBURETTOR

JOINT TO
CARBURETTOR

THERMOSTATIC
VACUUM VALVE

HOSE

Fig 2.3 Schematic arrangement of the main components of the paper element type air cleaner (Sec 3)

PAPER
FILTER

DIAPHRAGM TYPE VACUUM
UNIT WHICH MOVES FLAP

BASE OF
CLEANER

upper part the ducts terminate in bosses which fit over the carburettor intakes. These are held in position with clamping springs.

2   Refer to Figure 2.2. To remove the air cleaners pull off the flexible pipe and the crankcase ventilation hose. Release the spring clips holding the end pieces to the carburettors and lift off the end pieces. Release the clips securing the air cleaner to the bracket and lift the air cleaner away.

3   Undo the clips holding the upper and lower halves together. Lift the top away from the bottom. **Do not** place the top half on the bench upside down or dirty oil will run up into the filter.

Scrape any sludge adhering to the top half away and wipe it clean. Empty the oil and sludge from the bottom half and clean the container. Refill with 0.8 pints of SAE 30 engine oil.

4   Refitting is the reverse of removal. Make sure the embossed marks on the top and bottom coincide. Check that all seals and sleeves are correctly fitted.

5   The frequency of servicing depends largely on local conditions. In very dusty places weekly or even daily. In normal conditions monthly or even longer periods may suffice. There must be a minimum of 3/16 in (5 mm) of oil on top of the sludge for efficient working. Experience will soon dictate the time interval required but it is better to clean too often than not soon enough.

6   In 1973 the oil bath was replaced by a dry, paper element cleaner. The system is temperature and load sensitive. The cleaner has a thermostatically controlled, vacuum operated flap valve.

A schematic layout is given from which it will be seen that the thermostatic vacuum valve is in the top half of the cleaner and the diaphragm type vacuum unit that moves the flap is in the lower half. Two types of thermostatic vacuum valve have been used. Early 1972 vehicles have a valve with black plastic hose connector. The later type has a brass connector for the vacuum unit. The early type valve allows cool air to come in when the engine is under heavy load but the later type keeps the flap shut right through the warm-up period. Neither valve can be repaired and must be replaced if it goes wrong. (Fig 2.3)

7   Maintenance of the filter is simple. Remove the hoses leading to the upper part of the unit (photo), snap back the clips and lift the upper part of the unit away from the base and carburettor intakes. (photo) The filter unit is then seen in the base (photo); remove this (photo), it bends quite easily, and lift it out. Take it away from the vehicle and put it on a sheet of newspaper. Tap it gently up and down until no more dust comes out. Wipe the inside of the base to remove any dust which has settled there.

8   Reassembly is the reverse process. Make sure the carburettor intake seals are properly seated and all the hoses are firmly connected. (photo)

4   Fuel pump - removal and replacement

1   The fuel pump is mounted on the front right-hand side of the crankcase (photo). It can be worked on from underneath the vehicle without removing any other parts.

2   Clean the pump and its surrounds before undoing anything. You may either try to plug the hoses when they are undone, in which case have a bowl ready to catch any petrol that spills, or fit clamps over the hose to prevent flow of petrol and then undo the pipe at your leisure. A couple of small mole wrenches make good clamps, or if you have only one, use it as a clamp, undo and plug the pipe, and then proceed to the other one. It is a good idea to tie small plastic bags round the open ends of the hoses to prevent accidental entry of dirt.

3   Once the hoses are off the socket head screws which hold the pump to the crankcase may be removed and the pump withdrawn. The pushrod and intermediate flange may be removed carefully to check. The pushrod should be 5.492 inch (139.5 mm) long. If it varies from this length the efficiency of the pump

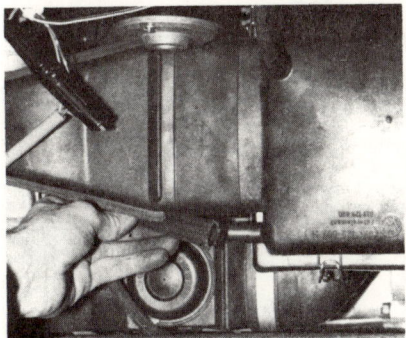

3.7a Remove the hoses from the top half of the cleaner. The diaphragm type vacuum limit cap be seen under the fitters hand

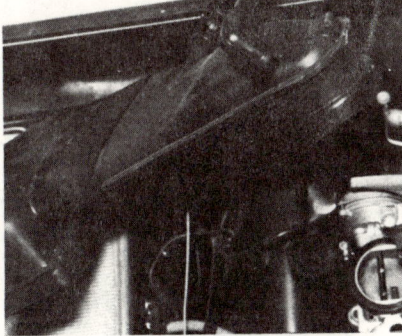

3.7b Undo the clips and lift the top half away

3.7c The filter element ....

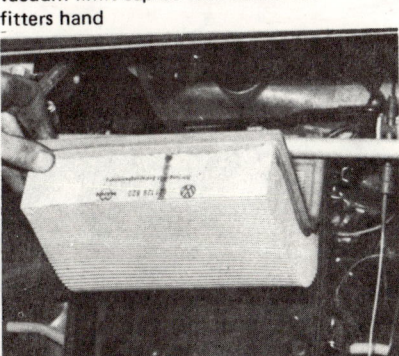

3.7d ... can be lifted out of the base and taken away for cleaning

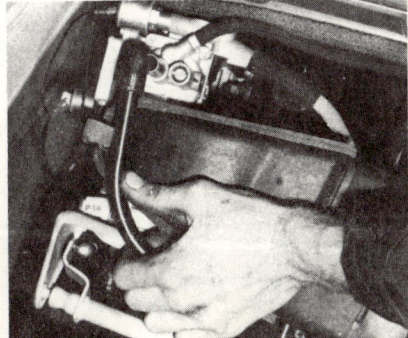

3.8 Make sure the cleaner is securely fitted to the carburettor choke tube

4.1 The pump can be serviced from below the vehicle. It is NOT necessary to remove the engine. It is on the front right hand side of the crankcase.

is affected and the rod should be replaced. Grease the ends with molybdenum sulphide before reassembly.

4   When reassembling the rod the thick end should be inserted into the intermediate flange and the two fitted together. Do not put the rod in first or it may drop inside. The inside end of the rod rests on the cam at the front end of the camshaft. Fit new gaskets on both sides of the intermediate flange.

5   The lower part of the pump should be packed with grease before reassembly. Fit the pump to the crankcase, tighten the socket screws, reconnect the hoses and the job is complete. It is as well to use new hose clips and if the hoses are frayed or damaged to replace them.

5   Fuel pump - overhaul

1   An exploded view of the pump is given at Fig. 2.4. Dismantling is straightforward but remember that absolute cleanliness is important. Wash the pump thoroughly in solvent before undoing any screws. The bottom half will be packed with grease

2   The pump should be dismantled by undoing the six screws which hold the top and bottom halves together. Mark the two halves before separating them so that they may be reassembled correctly or the petrol pipes will not fit when the pump is put back on the engine. Take the two halves apart. Push the diaphragm down with your thumb and release it from the operating lever. It will not come out of the body. Don't lose the spring. The pin may be driven out of the operating lever after the 'E' clip has been removed, and the lever removed for inspection.

3   Now look at the top half. The cut off valve may be examined by removing the four screws which hold it to the upper body, and the filter removed and cleaned.

4   It is possible to get a repair kit for the pump and we suggest this is done. Use all the parts. The diaphragms must not be stiff, hard or torn. Check the delivery and suction valves by blowing and sucking into, and out of, the intake. If either valve is faulty you need a new pump.

5   Assemble the top half first. Fit the operating lever to the bottom half and hold the bottom half in the soft jaws of a vice. Install the new diaphragm (don't forget the spring) and push it down to engage with the operating lever. Refit the top half (match up the marks you made) and tighten down the six screws carefully and evenly.

6   Pack the bottom half with grease before assembling to the vehicle.

7   If you can rig up a test arrangement, test the pump for correct operation before installation. It could save a lot of time.

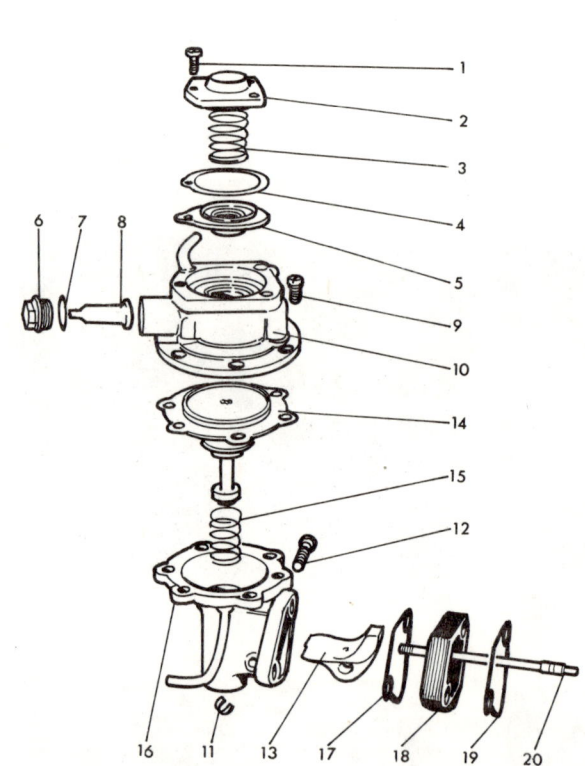

Fig 2.4 Fuel pump - exploded view (Sec 5)

1   Screw
2   Cover
3   Spring
4   Gasket
5   Cut off diaphragm
6   Plug
7   Washer
8   Filter
9   Screw (6 off)
10 Pump upper part

11 Circlip
12 Lever shaft
13 Operating lever
14 Diaphragm and spring
15 Spring
16 Pump lower casing
17 Gasket
18 Flange
19 Gasket
20 Push rod

6 Fault diagnosis - fuel pump

Symptom	Probable reason	Remedy
No delivery of fuel or insufficient delivery	1 Diaphragm split or damaged 2 Gasket between cut-off valve cover and upper body damaged 3 Valves leaking 4 Leak between two halves of body 5 Spring broken, or weak 6 Pushrod worn 7 Incorrectly installed, gaskets too thick, at intermediate flange 8 Operating lever bent or worn	1 Replace diaphragm 2 Replace gasket 3 Replace pump 4 Tighten screws 5 Fit new spring 6 Fit new pushrod 7 Fit correct gaskets 8 Fit new lever
Too much fuel pressure causing carburettor to flood	1 Spring too strong 2 Gasket at intermediate flange too thin. Pushrod extending too far*	1 Fit correct spring 2 Fit correct gasket

*Note: It is unlikely that this will cause continuous flooding, it will more likely damage the diaphragm and there will be too little fuel, but the initial trouble will be flooding

7 Fuel tank - removal, repair and replacement

1 The tank which holds 12 Imperial gallons (14½ US gallons, 56 litres) has a one gallon reserve.

2 It is very well hidden and should it need repair or cleaning then allow plenty of time for the job. On all models except the pick-up the engine must first be removed. On pick-up trucks it is not necessary to remove the engine; there are two panels at the end of the truck body which, when the eight bolts holding each one to the body have been removed, give access to the tank.

3 Assuming you do not have a pick-up and wish to remove the fuel tank, turn to Chapter 1, and following the instructions therein, remove the engine. Provide yourself with three four gallon cans and drain off the fuel from the tank as far as possible. Do not smoke, keep a fire extinguisher handy and, if possible, before starting to drain the tank - there won't be any sparks then.

4 A steel panel is now visible at the back of the engine compartment. Remove the screws holding this in place and pry the plate away from the body. The tank is now visible.

5 Loosen the hose clips which hold the hose to the filler neck and remove the hose. Depending upon the model you have there will be other smaller hoses to the emission control charcoal filter and the overflow reservoirs. (breather pipes) Disconnect these carefully and mark where each is fitted.

6 Disconnect the wire from the sender unit of the fuel gauge (you have disconnected the battery).

7 It is important to replace the tank in exactly the same spot on reassembly so now mark exactly where it sits on the floor.

8 Undo the bolts holding the straps which clamp it in position and take off the straps.

9 On pick-up trucks the tank is worked out into the truck body; on all others it comes out through the engine compartment. There is a foam cushion under it which will probably be stuck and will tear. This should be replaced with a new one.

10 Clean out the tank space, remove any rust and repaint where necessary. Do the same for the straps and the paint will dry while you deal with the tank.

11 If the tank has been leaking then there will be quite a lot of painting to do.

12 The fuel gauge sender unit is removed by undoing the five screws holding it to the top of the tank. Lift it out carefully. It will probably need a new gasket.

13 The tank fuel delivery pipe, at the bottom of the tank, may be removed by undoing the union nut and pulling out the pipe with the gauge strainer.

14 We do not recommend that you try to repair leaks, or to de-rust the tank yourself. The first is a dangerous job requiring not only skill but knowledge of safety precautions if an explosion is to be avoided. De-rusting is a specialist job if the tank is to stay de-rusted. A highly dangerous liquid is used in considerable quantity. (11 Imperial, 13 US gallons of ANTOX Extra M de-rusting phosphate agent) plus the important rinsing solution and sealing agent. If the tank requires work to be done leave it to the expert. Anyway what are you going to do with the ANTOX after you have finished? The tank should be pressure tested after repair to check for leaks.

15 Should you decide to fit a new tank be careful that you get the right one. To give greater safety when accidents happen the shape and size of the filler neck has been altered on later models and the tank may not fit your vehicle. Check with the agent. Refit the sender unit and delivery pipe with filter.

16 Replacement of the tank is the reverse of removal. The tank must go exactly where it came from. Fit the straps carefully so that the tank sits squarely on its foam seal. A full tank weighs over one hundredweight. If it moves when you go over a bump you will have to do the job again, so fasten it in securely.

17 Install the hoses with new clips and make sure no hose is strained or perished.

18 Refit the bulkhead, install the engine and battery and the job is done.

19 There is no doubt that you can save a very big bill for labour by taking the tank out yourself but, once again, do not try to de-rust or repair leaks yourself unless you have been trained to do this type of work.

8 Fuel tank - ventilation and activated carbon filter unit

1 There may be one or more vent pipes on the fuel tank to cope with expansion due to heat and to prevent spillage when the vehicle is parked at, or assumes, unusual angles.

These pipes and rising vent tubes are partially enclosed in the rear vertical body panels on the latest models.

2 Where the market calls for it there is a filter unit of activated carbon which traps hydro carbon fumes evaporating from the petrol. This filter is incorporated in the fuel tank venting system and the container is mounted in the ceiling of the engine compartment at the right. It is automatically "rinsed" when the engine is running, by air which is fed to it from the fan housing. The fumes thus driven from the filter are carried by a hose into the air cleaner where they are fed to the engine (see Fig. 2.5).

9 Fuel gauge - testing and repair

1 If the fuel gauge does not work properly the sooner it is repaired the better, if you are not to run out of petrol.

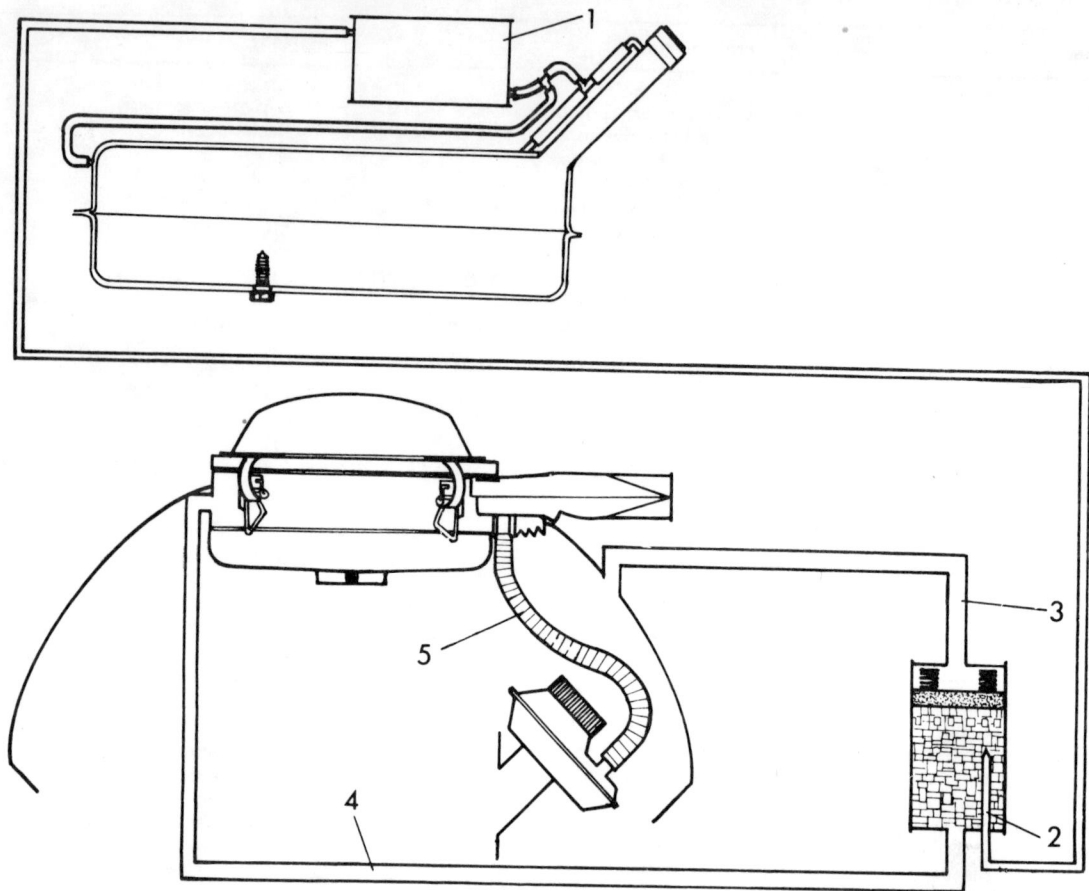

Fig 2.5 Schematic drawing of fuel tank ventilation with activated carbon filter unit (Sec 8)

1 *Expansion chamber (incorporated
  in fuel tank design)*
2 *Breather line*
3 *Pressure line from fan
  housing*
4 *Suction line from air cleaner*
5 *Crankcase breather hose*

2   There are four reasons for malfunction. The fuse (No 11) may be blown. There are other circuits on this fuse (indicators, warning lights) so clear up this business first. If all the other circuits work and the fuse is not blown then suspect the wiring. It is unlikely that the moving coil ammeter, which shows the amount of fuel, is faulty but it may be removed as in Chapter 10 and tested much more quickly than the sender unit. If the ammeter is faulty it must be replaced. The fourth offender is the sender unit. If you read the previous Section it will appal you to think how much there is to do to replace the sender unit. There are a few tests which will help you to decide. Switch on the ignition.

3   If the gauge registers full all the while (1/1) then there is a short circuit to earth somewhere either in the wiring or in the sender unit. There is a "pull-apart, in-line" connection 'T.1' located near the fuel tank (see also wiring diagram) locate this and disconnect it. If the guage now reads full (1/1) then the fault is in the wiring between the gauge and sender unit. This will have to be located. It may be quicker to run another wire. If the guage reading falls to zero then your heart will fall to because the problem is in the sender unit and the tank must come out (Section 7).

4   If the gauge refuses to register the fault may be with the meter or the sender, or the wiring, or the fuse. (That is if there is petrol in the tank).

Pull apart the connector 'T.1' Using a piece of wire connect the wire from the gauge to the vehicle body (earth) on a bright bit of the metal. If the gauge now reads 1/1 (ignition on) then the sender unit is faulty. If the gauge still does not read then it is either the wiring or the gauge unit.

5   Measure the resistance between the side of the connector 'T.1.' which goes to the sender unit and earth (ground). Use an ohmmeter to do this. If it registers infinity then the sender unit is burned out and must be replaced.

6   Refer to Section 7, remove the sender unit from the tank (several hours later) and connect it in series with a 12 volt battery and connect in a meter which will measure up to 15 volts. Do this away from the dismantled tank. Work the arm with the float up and down and check whether the needle of the voltmeter moves smoothly as the float arm moves. If it does not then the sender unit is faulty and must be replaced.

7   The moving coil ammeter on the facia board may be checked simply by measuring whether there is voltage present at the input terminal. If there is and the gauge is not reading check the earth and take it to the auto-electrician for testing and probable replacement.

10 Emission control equipment - general description

1   Before discussing the carburettors it will be as well to see the problems facing the fuel system as the laws against pollution become sticter and stricter.

2   When motor fuel burns the products of combustion are mainly Carbon monoxide, Carbon dioxide and Hydro-carbons. The air sucked into the cylinders gives up oxygen passing nearly all the remainder (Nitrogen) back to the atmosphere unchanged.

The oxygen combines with the fuel, but unless exactly the right amount of oxygen is present either the fuel does not burn completely, or the engine looses power due to weak mixture. It is even less simple than that because although all the fuel may burn, some of the carbon in it may be converted to carbon monoxide, which is a very poisonous gas. If there is enough oxygen then the carbon is converted to Carbon dioxide which is not poisonous and is absorbed by vegetation.

3   This may seem trivial but research found that in 1966, 60 million tons of pollutants where emitted from motor vehicles in the USA alone. There were another 80 million tons as well in the USA but they were from domestic and industrial sources and that problem has been tackled separately.

4   The break down of vehicle pollution was mainly carbon monoxide, nitrogen oxides, hydrocarbons and a small amount of sulphur oxides. The facts were faced and the motor industry was told to do something about it.

5   An analysis of the sources of pollution showed all the carbon monoxide, all the nitrogen oxides, all the lead compounds and half of the hydrocarbons came out of the exhaust pipe. The other half of the hydrocarbons came equally from the petrol tank breather and from crankcase blow-by. Hydrocarbons cause "smog" which while not toxic is still a killer.

6   The petrol tank vent has been treated by installing a charcoal filter. Lead is becoming less of a problem as it is being dealt with as a matter of fuel research. Crankcase blow-by is easily dealt with by extracting it from the crankcase and sending it round the cylinders again to burn any offending vapour.

7   The major problem is the exhaust gas, and that is why an exhaust gas analyser is one of the most important vehicle test instruments today.

8   The maximum permissible emission has been laid down and is becoming stricter each year. In 1970 it was 1.5% of carbon monoxide for a two litre engine. This means that to all intents and purposes the carbon monoxide and nitrogen oxides must be completely eliminated, and all the fuel correctly burned under all conditions of speed and load.

9   Everyone knows that you pull the choke out for cold starting, burn more petrol, a rich mixture with lots of white smoke. Well now you dont. No white smoke. The engine must start and warm up without undue pollution (the warm up cycle) and then it must run even more efficiently (the hot cycle). In the old days quick shut down of the throttle cut off the air but not the fuel so on overrun, the engine poured out half burned fuel. This won't do now.

10 Despite all these problems the VW fuel injection system succeeded in cutting the CO level down to 1% and the hydro-carbon to within the limit. One of the few to succeed. The transporter has never had the fuel injection system but it now has an improved type of carburettor, and in the USA two separate anti-pollution devices besides the charcoal filter in the petrol tank breather.

They are the exhaust gas recirculation system and the exhaust afterburning system.

11 Exhaust gas afterburning

1   The principle of the exhaust afterburning is simple. Air is forced under pressure into the exhaust system just behind the exhaust valve outlet in the cylinder head. This supplies more oxygen to convert the carbon monoxide to carbon dioxide and further burning of the carbon monoxide and hydrocarbons takes place in the exhaust system.

2   To do this an air pump is installed just over the engine (Fig 2.6) and an extra pulley fitted to the crankshaft between the fan and the body to drive a belt and so turn the pump. Adjustment is made by moving the pump on its bracket to tighten or slacken the belt. If the pump goes wrong it must be replaced. An air filter is fitted to the pump inlet.

3   Air goes from the pump via tubing to the cylinder heads, on early models to all four exhaust ports, and on later models to 1,2 and 3 only. A non-return valve is installed in the main pipe to stop pressure and possibly flame going into the pump in the event of a backfire in the exhaust system. This is sometimes called the "GULP" valve.

4   A further refinement is added to take care of backfiring on the overrun. Even though the carburetor is equipped to deal with overrun conditions it is possible that a rich mixture may increase the possibility of backfires and so yet further air is provided into the exhaust manifolds during overrun. This is done by bleeding air from the pump supply to a valve which is operated from the central idling system on the left-hand carburettor. From the valve the air goes to the exhaust manifold and prevents "banging" on deacceleration.

5   A schematic diagram is at Fig. 2.7. The equipment is fitted only to vehicles for USA and entails special heads and manifolds as well as the pulley mounting and pump.

12 Exhaust gas recirculation (EGR)

1   Exhaust gas recirculation is another matter. The system varies slightly for manual and automatic transmission. The manual type is described first and the variations for automatic are then discussed.

2   The principle is to extract a proportion of the burnt gas from the exhaust system and to inject it into the intake manifolds where it combines with the fuel and enters the combustion chamber. The result is to lower the flame peaks during combustion and so to lower the production of oxides of nitrogen which are a small but important part of pollution.

3   At the outset the exhaust gas was drawn from the silencer

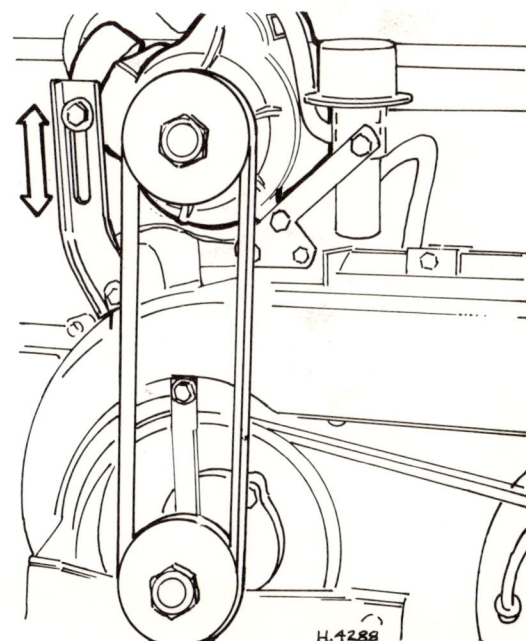

Fig 2.6 The air pump for the exhaust afterburning system is mounted on the fan case above the fan. (Sec 11)

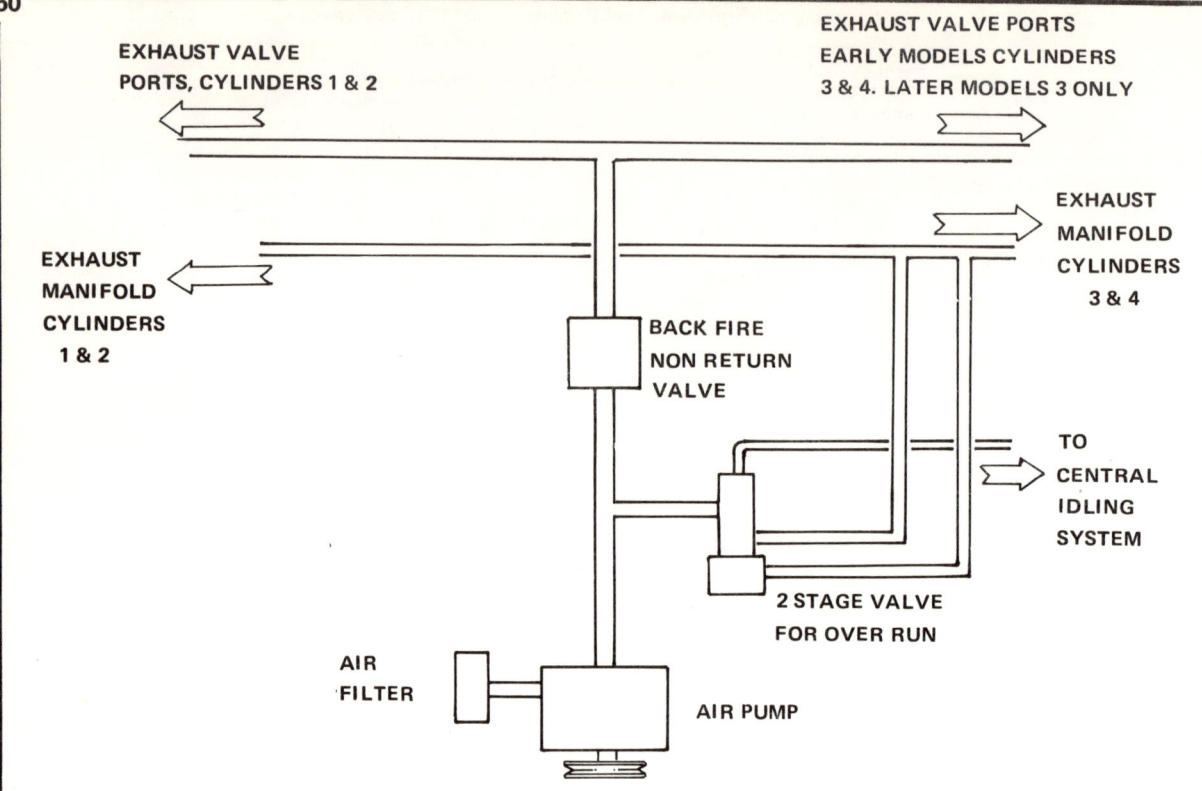

EXHAUST VALVE
PORTS, CYLINDERS 1 & 2

EXHAUST VALVE PORTS
EARLY MODELS CYLINDERS
3 & 4. LATER MODELS 3 ONLY

EXHAUST
MANIFOLD
CYLINDERS
1 & 2

EXHAUST
MANIFOLD
CYLINDERS
3 & 4

BACK FIRE
NON RETURN
VALVE

TO
CENTRAL
IDLING
SYSTEM

2 STAGE VALVE
FOR OVER RUN

AIR
FILTER

AIR PUMP

Fig 2.7 Schematic diagram of layout of Exhaust Gas Afterburning System (US only) (Sec 11)

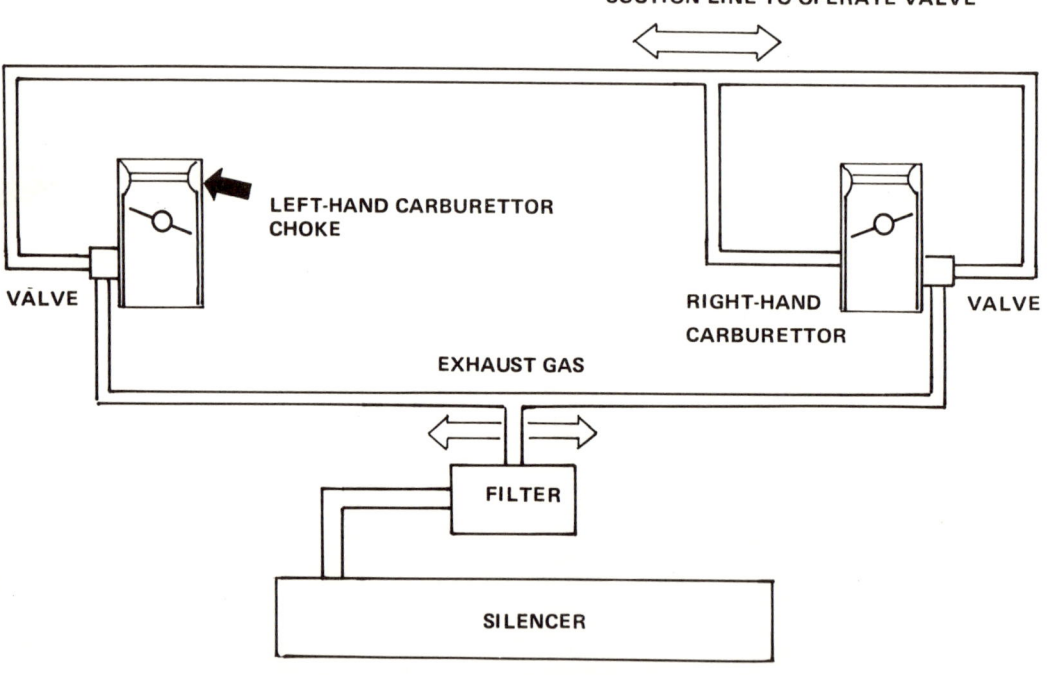

SUCTION LINE TO OPERATE VALVE

LEFT-HAND CARBURETTOR
CHOKE

VALVE

RIGHT-HAND
CARBURETTOR

VALVE

EXHAUST GAS

FILTER

SILENCER

Fig 2.8 Exhaust Gas Recirculation - manual transmission, early models (US only) (Sec 12)

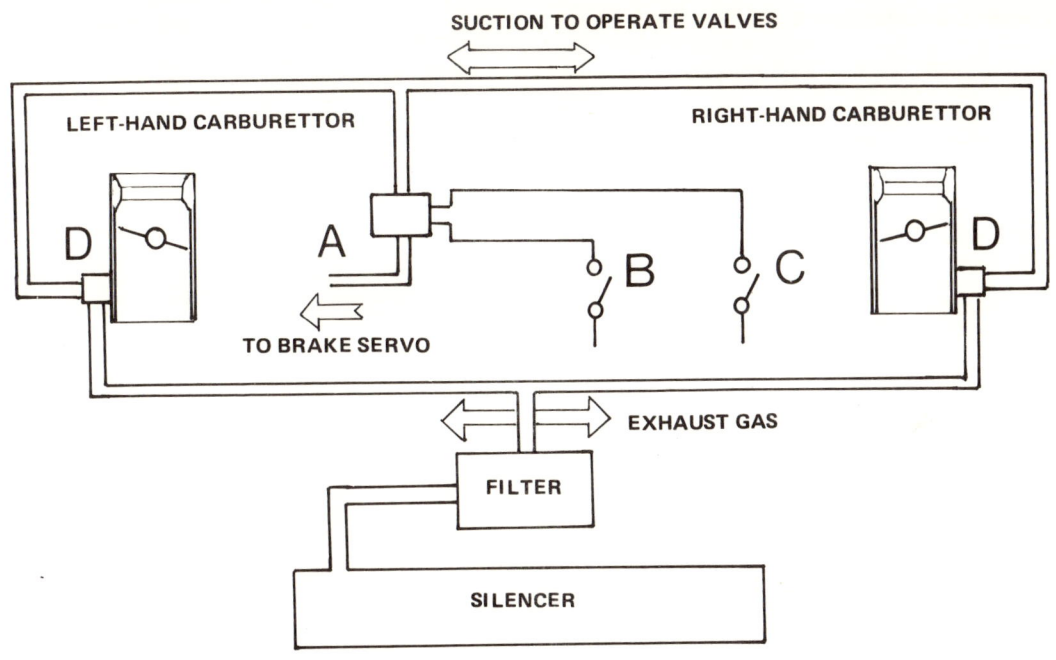

Fig 2.9 Exhaust gas recirculation automatic transmission - early models (US only) (Sec 12)

A Two way valve
C On/Off switch

B Temperature switch
D Exhaust gas recirculating valves

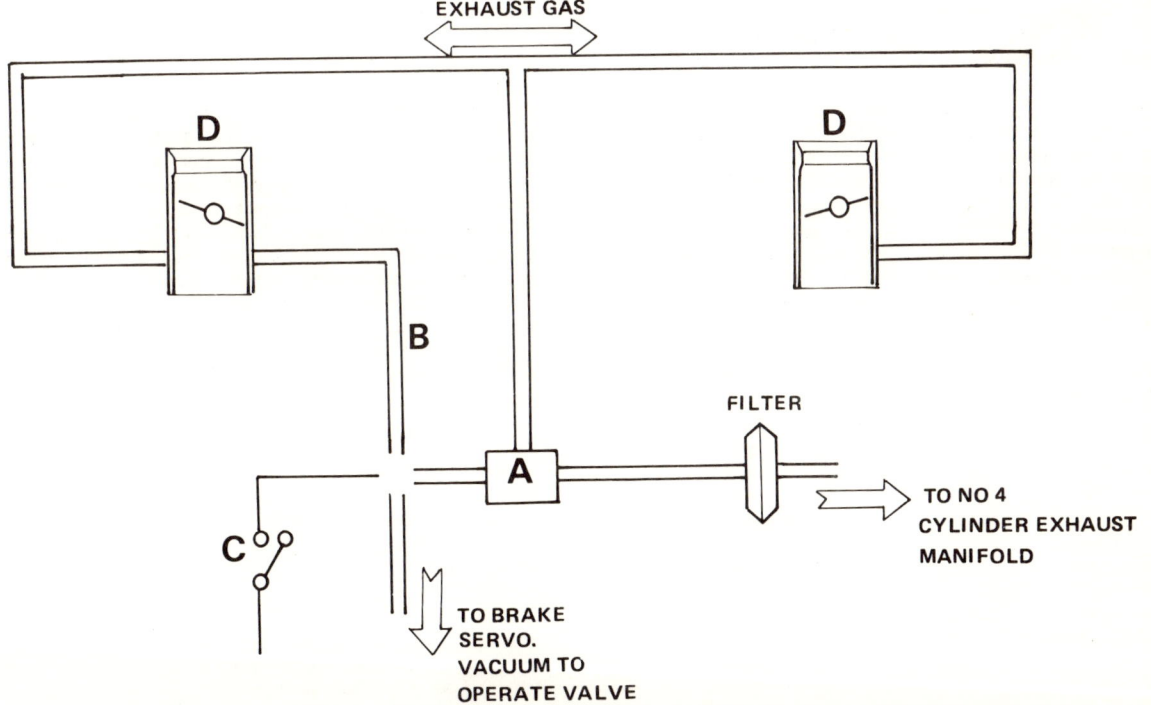

Fig 2.10 Exhaust gas recirculation Manual and Automatic transmission - later models (US only) (Sec 12)

A California only 2 stage valve rest of USA single stage valve

B Tube to supply control from choke to 4 way valve. This is fitted to California models only.

C Micro On/Off switch on auto choke ring of R.H. Carburettor

D R & L hand carburetor throttle tubes.

(muffler) and passed through a filter from whence it was fed to a valve which admitted it to the intake manifold. The valve was operated by the vacuum in the carburettor venturi and opened only to deal with partial load conditions.

This has now been altered and the exhaust gas is drawn from No 4 cylinder exhaust port instead of the silencers (hence no afterburning on No 4 exhaust) and fed, via the filter, to the intake manifolds. The control valve has been moved from the intake manifold and put in the pipe system. The one valve controls flow to both intakes and is operated by the depression in the left-hand carburettor (except in California - see paragraph 8).

4   The system for automatic transmission is identical except for the operation of the control valves. This is dependant on temperature and throttle position. On the early system this was worked as follows: The vacuum required to operate the valves was taken from the brake servo system and fed to each valve, via a central two stage valve operated by a temperature switch and an on/off switch on the automatic choke securing ring operated by the throttle valve shaft. The temperature switch operated when the outside air temperature was over 12°C (53.5^{o}F) and allowed the central two stage valve to open. It was also controlled by the on/off switch which allowed it to open from almost tick over revs to almost maximum revs, so that for the greater part of the speed range recirculation took place. The intake pipe for the emission is larger on the automatic, 4.0 mm as opposed to 2.5 mm for the manual. The temperature switch is situated above the battery (on manual transmissions there is also a switch there but it is for switching off the vacuum spark advance). The on/off switch is secured to the automatic choke securing ring and is operated by a small cam mounted on the throttle valve shaft. It switches on 10° after the throttle valve opens from the fully closed position and closes 10° before the fully open position. (Fig. 2.11).

5   The two stage valve is situated near the warm air blower. It is rather confusing because on some vehicles an identical valve is fitted in the same place on manual transmission vehicles, but this is for switching off the vacuum spark advance.

6   On later models, after June 1973, the regulations no longer allowed the temperature switch to be operated by outside air and so the switch above the battery was discontinued and temperature control was transferred to an electric switch on the left-hand end of the cooling air throttle valve shaft which controls the two way valve when the cooling air valve or cooling air thermostat opens (cooling air temperature 85°C - 185°F). As the cooling air throttle valve is closed insert a 1 mm feeler (0.04 inch) between the throttle valve shaft and the tab on the switch and you should hear a click as the switch operates. If it doesn't adjust the gap by moving the switch bracket.

7   Finally in November 1973 the 2/M/157 engine was further modified for automatic transmission by replacing the two stage valve with a single stage valve operated by the vacuum brake servo (as for the manual). The gas is drawn from the No 4 exhaust (as for the manual) and control is by the micro-switch on the throttle spindle on the right-hand carburettor.

8   The latest system for California is again modified. The system is the same for both manual and automatic and differs from the system for the rest of the USA in that the control is by on/off switch and by the depression in the venturi of the right-hand carburettor.

The valve which controls the flow of exhaust gas from cylinder 4 exhaust to both intake manifolds is a two stage valve. The first stage is operated by the carburettor depression and the second stage by the micro-switch as described in paragraph 4.

---

13   Emission control equipment - future development

1   It will be seen that determined efforts have been made to reduce pollution, and that the systems have been subject to much modification.

2   In many countries the problem either does not exist or is not taken so seriously as in the USA. Time alone will tell whether

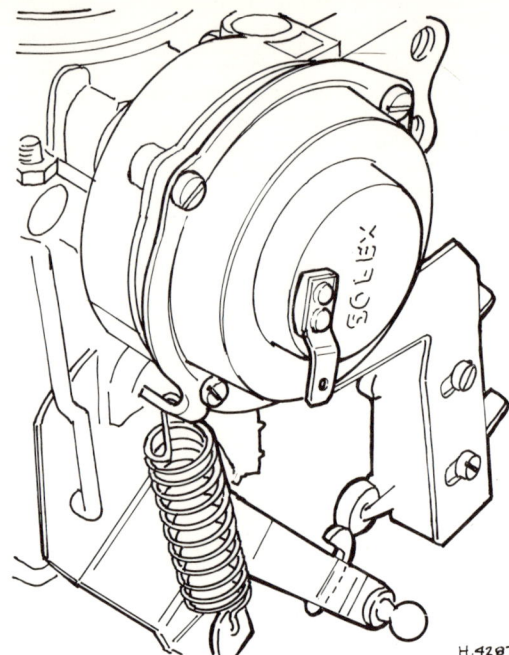

Fig 2.11 The on/off switch on the automatic choke securing ring (Automatic transmission US only) (Sec 12)

the legislation will arrive in the rest of the motoring world. Obviously, the use of smaller engines, added to the rising cost of petrol will reduce the volume of pollution. In UK the smokeless zones in large cities such as London has removed the smog, but the exhaust fumes from cars are more noticable than ever, particularly on hot windless days. It is for speculation as to how soon the equipment will become univeral.

3   The present equipment is of the "bolt on" type designed to be fitted to a standard engine. No doubt it will be subject to many modifications before it becomes a standard fitting to all engines. For this reason the owner is advised to consult regularly with his VW agent on the subject.

4   As was stated in Section 10 one of the more important items of test equipment is the exhaust gas analyser. There is no adjustment in the system, it either works or it doesn't, but the whole system can be rendered useless if the carburettor is not correctly adjusted. There can be no doubt that we have all got to go back to school to learn the rules of engine tuning all over again.

---

14   Carburettor (Solex PDSIT 34 2/3) - general description

1   Although the model is described as a twin carburettor the term is misleading. There is in fact one carburettor in two parts. The carburettor on the L.H. manifold meters the fuel to the L.H. intake manifold, controls slow running, and supplies fuel for slow running to the R.H. manifold. The carburettor on the R.H. manifold meters the fuel to the R.H. manifold as the throttle opens but does not supply all the fuel when the throttle is shut. (photos)

2   A pipe from the central slow running control goes to a distribution valve which has two further hoses going to the manifolds. This means only one adjustment for slow running and gets rid of one of the major problems of twin carburettor adjustment.

3   In all other respects it is a normal Solex PDSIT 34/2/3 but it certainly puzzled us at first.

4   Refer to Figure 2.13. The carburettor is basically a tube through which air is drawn into the engine by the action of the pistons and en route fuel is introduced into the air stream in the

tube due to the fact that the air pressure is lowered when drawn through the 'tube'.

The main fuel discharge point is situated in the 'tube' - choke is the proper name for the tube to be used from now on - between two flaps which can block off the tube. One of these is the throttle flap - operated by the accelerator pedal and positioned at the engine end of the choke tube. The other is the strangler - which is operated by an automatic device.

When the engine is warm and running normally the strangler is wide open and the throttle open partially or fully - the amount of fuel/air mixture being controlled according to the required speed.

When cold the strangler is closed - partially or fully and the suction therefore draws more fuel and less air, ie; a richer mixture to aid starting a cold engine.

At idling speeds the throttle flap is shut so that no air and fuel can get to the engine in the regular way. For this there are separate routes leading to small holes in the side of the choke tube, on the engine side of the throttle flap. These 'bleed' the requisite amounts of fuel and air to the engine for slow speeds only.

5 The fuel is held in a separate chamber alongside the choke tube and its level is governed by a float so that it is not too high or low. If too low it would only be drawn in at a higher suction than required for proper operation.

The main jet, which is simply an orifice of a particular size through which the fuel passes, is designed to let so much fuel flow at particular conditions of suction (properly called depression) in the choke tube. At idling speed the depression draws fuel from orifices below the throttle which has passed through the main jet and after that a pilot jet to reduce the quantity further.

Both main and pilot jets have air bleed jets also which let in air to assist emulsification of the eventual fuel/air mixture.

The strangler flap is controlled by an electrically operated bi-metal strip. This consists of a coiled bi-metal strip connected to the choke flap spindle. When the ignition is switched off the coiled metal strip is cold and the flap is shut. When ignition is switched on current flows through the strip which heats up and uncoils - opening the choke flap after some minutes. If anything

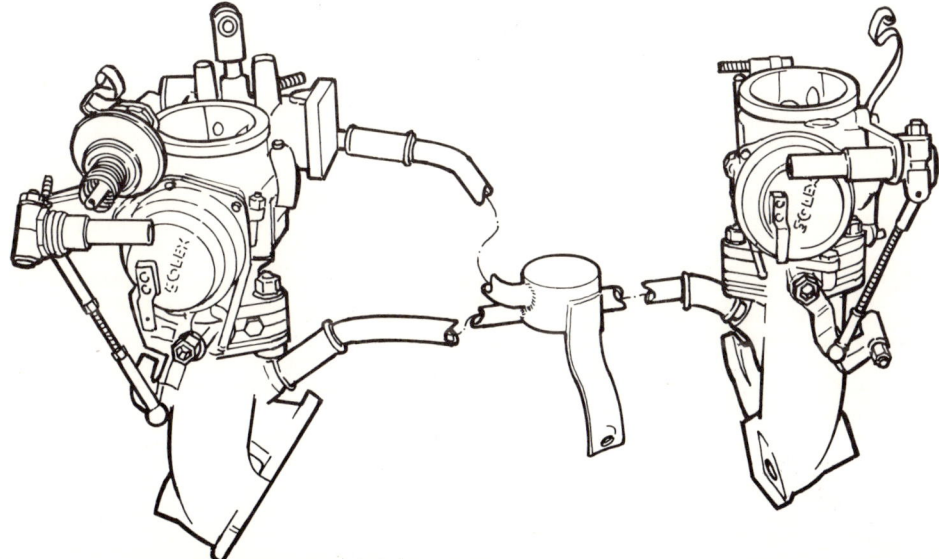

Fig. 2.12 Left and right components of the PDSIT 34, 2/3 carburettor. The idling system is in the left-hand carburettor and the distribution valve is in the centre (Sec 14)

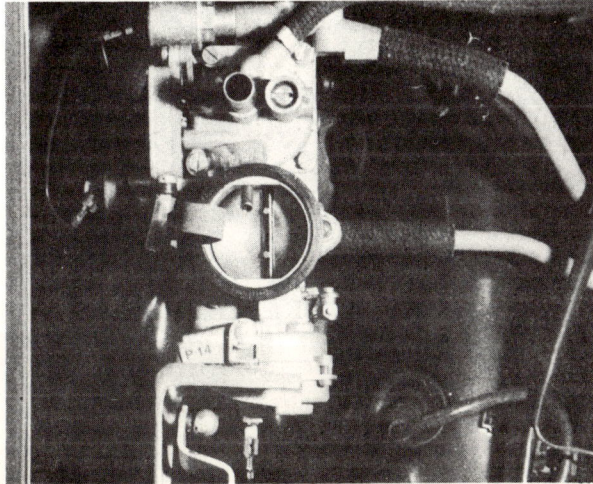

14.1a The left-hand carburettor. The central idling system can be seen above the choke tube

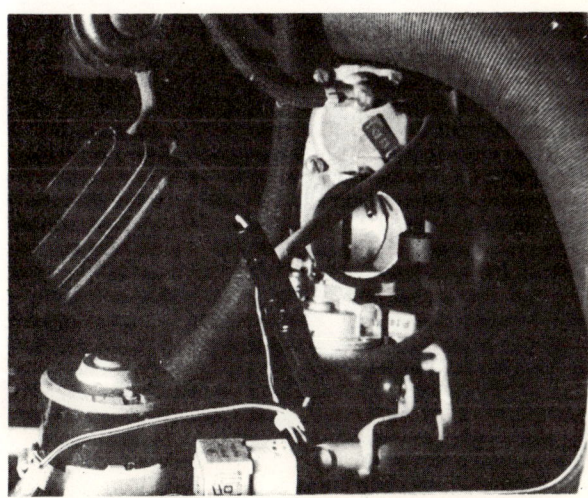

14.1b The right-hand carburettor. This does not have a idling system

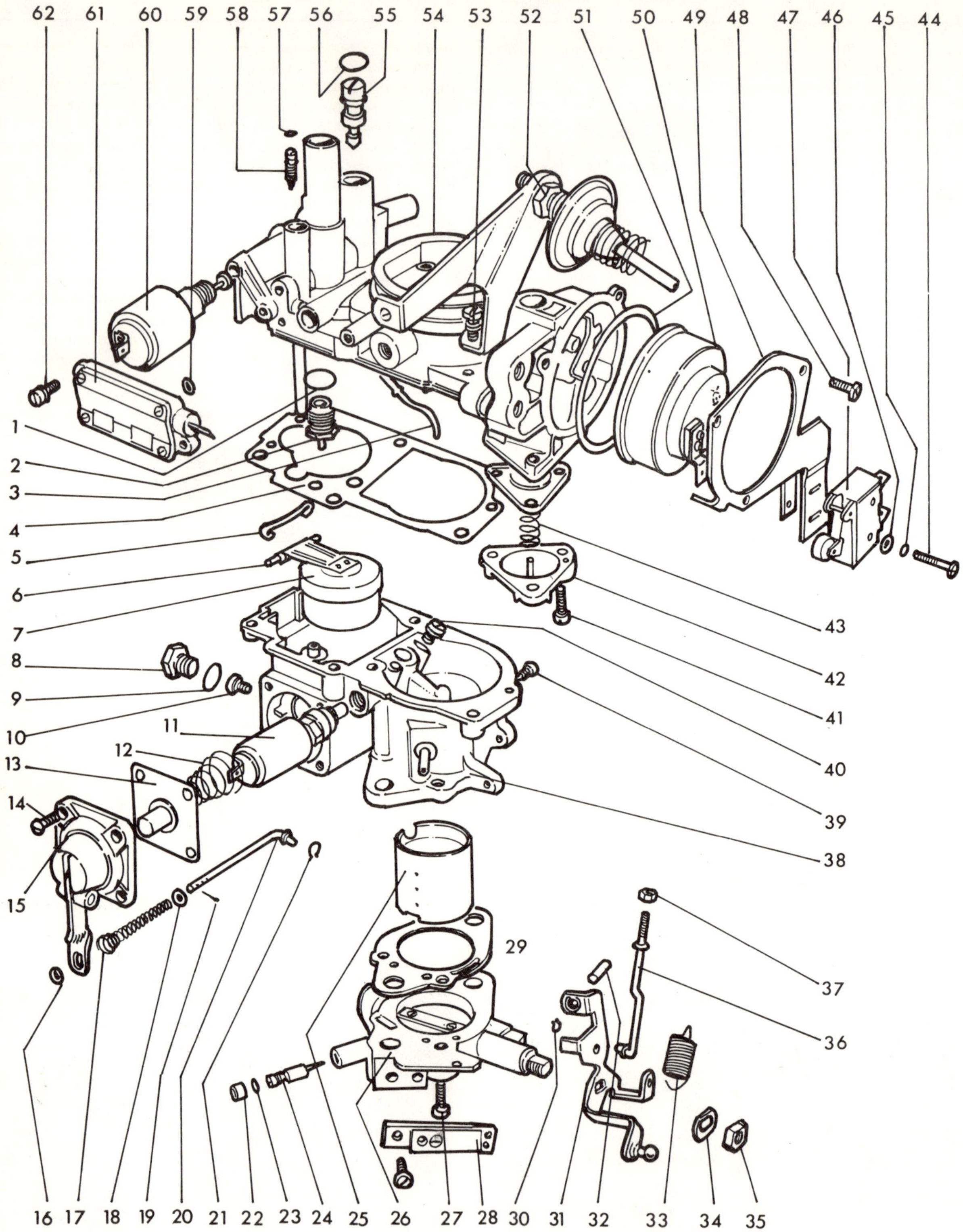

62 61 60 59 58 57 56 55 54 53 52 51 50 49 48 47 46 45 44

1
2
3
4
5
6
7
8
9
10
11
13
14
15

43
42
41
40
39
38

29

37
36

16 17 18 19 20 21 22 23 24 25 26 27 28 30 31 32 33 34 35

Fig. 2.13 Solex PDSIT 34 2/3 Carburettor - exploded view (Secs. 14 and 19)

Fig 2.13 Solex PDSIT 34 2/3 Carburettor - exploded view (Secs 14 and 19)

1 Float valve washer
2 Float valve
3 Accelerator pump injector tube
4 Gasket
5 Pin clip
6 Pin
7 Float
8 Plug
9 Seal
10 Main jet
11 Electro magnetic cut off valve, idling system
12 Pump diaphragm spring
13 Diaphragm
14 Screw
15 Cover
16 Washer
17 Connecting link spring
18 Washer
19 Split pin
20 Connecting link
21 Circlip
22 Plug
23 Sealing ring
24 Idle mixture screw (main carburettor)
25 Venturi tube
26 Throttle body
27 Screw (2)
28 Hot idling valve (automatic transmission)
29 Circlip
31 Throttle lever
32 Throttle opening adjusting screw
33 Return spring
34 Spacer
35 Nut
36 Connecting rod
37 Locknut
38 Carburettor body
39 Venturi set screw
40 Air correction jet
41 Screw
42 Vacuum diaphragm cover
43 Vacuum diaphragm spring
44 Screw
45 Spring ring
46 Washer
47 Throttle shaft switch
48 Screw
49 Cover ring
50 Choke heating element
51 Gasket
52 Dashpot
53 Screw with washer (5)
54 Carburettor (top half) body
55 Idle speed adjusting screw. (central idle system)
56 O ring
57 O ring
58 Central idle-system mixture screw
59 O ring
60 Electro magnetic cut off valve (central idle system)
61 Idle mixture enrichment
62 Screw

Fitted to models with Automatic transmission, PDSIT 34/3 only

should go wrong with this electrical arrangement the flap will return to the closed position.

With the flap closed there are two features which partially open it immediately the engine starts. The flap spindle is offset so one side tends to turn around the spindle under the depression in the choke tube. Also there is a diaphragm valve connected to another rod attached to the flap spindle. Depression in the choke tube also operates this. If these devices did not exist no air at all would get through with the fuel. This would then flood the engine.

6 Also there is the accelerator pump. This is a diaphragm operated pump which is directly linked to the accelerator controls. When sudden acceleration is required the pump is operated and delivers neat fuel into the choke tube. This overcomes the time lag that would otherwise occur in waiting for the fuel to be drawn from the main jet.

7 The fuel in the float chamber is regulated at the correct height by a float which operates a needle valve. When the level drops the needle is lowered away from the entry orifice and fuel under pressure from the pump enters. When the level rises the flow is shut off. The pump delivery potential is always greater than the maximum requirement from the carburettor. Another device fitted is an electro magnetic cut-off jet. This somewhat unhappy feature is designed to positively stop the fuel flow when the engine is stopped. Otherwise the engine tends to run on - even with the ignition switched off - when the engine is hot.

8 The central idling system on the left-hand carburettor uses the same float chamber as the main carburettor. Refer to Fig. 2.14. The idling emulsion tube extends into the float chamber and the jet is in the end of it. There is a small hole in the tube to allow the entry of air. At idling speed the depression in the intake pipes cause petrol to be drawn up the emulsion tube mixing with air as it passes the small hole and forming an emulsion. This goes up and past the mixture control screw and along the tube to the right. The small pipe protudes into the air passage, air coming in down from above and the emulsion is sprayed into this air stream.

The fuel then goes past the slow running (idle adjusting) screw and away from the carburettor. The electro magnetic cut-off valve closes the system when the ignition is switched off to prevent a hot engine 'running-on' diesel fashion.

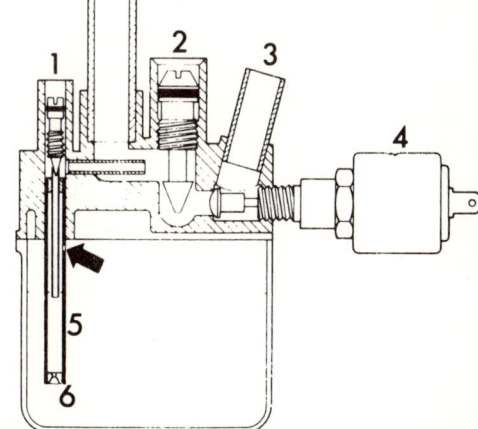

Fig 2.14 Cross section of the central idling portion of the left-hand carburetor (Sec 14)

1   Mixture control screw
2   Idle speed adjusting screw
3   Mixture outlet to central distribution valve
4   Electro-magnetic cut-off valve
5   Emulsion tube
6   Jet

Note - the arrow points to the air hole

A further refinement closes the air hole in the emulsion tube by means of a valve until the engine temperature rises to 18°C (65°F) at which point a bi-metal spring, heated by an electric heater element operated through the ignition switch, opens the valve allowing the air to enter. Thus during the colder part of starting up more petrol is drawn into the main idling air stream giving a richer mixture.

9 In late '73, on the 1.8 litre engine a valve has been fitted to the accelerator pump system to allow more petrol to go to the engine, via the accelerator pump, at temperatures below 21°C (69°F). At this temperature a thermostat operates the valve opening a passage in the carburettor which allows part of the output of the acceleration pump to go back to the float chamber. This device is fitted to all 1.8 litre engines in USA.

At cold start the pump injects about 1.5 ccs; when the valve opens the amount is halves (about 0.7 ccs).

10 On the automatic transmission engine the accelerator pump stroke capacity may be varied by moving the adjustment sleeve on engines from May '73 onwards. (Fig 2.15)

15 Carburettor adjustments - general

1 It is essential that the engine is in first class condition before the carburettors are adjusted. Contact breaker points, spark plugs, engine ignition timing, tappet adjustment and compression must all be correct before the carburettors are touched.

2 The adjustments should be done in the following order: First, the carburettor must be synchronized, and then the idle adjustment should be done. Do not reverse the order as you will have to adjust the idle screws again if you synchronize after adjusting the idle speed.

3 The dash pot will not need adjustment unless you dismantle the carburettor.

4 There are a number of other checks. The fuel level in the float chambers may be adjusted by altering the washers under the needle valve. The accelerator pump stroke may be adjusted to give more, or less fuel by moving the cotter pin in the linkage, if you have the necessary measuring equipment.

The various electrical cut-off valves must also be checked for correct operation.

5 However, remember that it is a science now, not just a case of turning screws until it sounds right and accelerates smartly. The instruments required for correct adjustment are:

(a) A thermometer to measure the temperature of the engine oil.

(b) A tachometer to measure engine speed.

(c) An exhaust gas analyser (you can get by without this but we do not recommend it).

(d) A depth gauge to set the fuel level in the float chamber.

(e) A set of feeler gauges.

(f) If you are going to check the throttle shaft switch on the automatic transmission version fitted for exhaust gas recirculation a special VW protractor is needed to measure the degrees of opening of the throttle when the switch operates.

(g) A gauge for measuring the air flow over the throat of the carburettor (UNISYN or AUTO-SYN are recommended).

(h) A measuring glass, special injection pipe and a choke valve retainer to check the output of the accelerator pump. These can easily be made at home if you cannot purchase them.

16 Carburettor (Solex PDSIT 34 2/3) - synchronization

1 Disconnect the lower ball socket joint on the relay shaft arm of the right-hand carburettor.

2 Remove the top of the air cleaner from the carburettors but prop it in position so that the hose attached to the central idling system is not disconnected. Make sure it is firm for the engine is to be run.

3 On the left-hand carburettor move the synchronizing screw until the throttle operating rod may be reconnected to the relay arm on the right-hand carburettor with both of the throttle valves in the closed position. (photo)

4 The engine should have been run to warm it up. The oil temperature should be between 50°C and 70°C (122-160°F). You can check this by inserting a thermometer down the dipstick socket, but make sure you do not drop it in, and the engine should be switched off.

5 If the oil temperature is satisfactory start the engine and run it at a steady speed of 2,500 rpm. Using a proper airflow measuring instrument measure the airflow into each carburettor. Adjust the synchronizing screw of the carburettor passing the most air until the amount of air going into each carburettor is the same. If you do not have an airflow meter there is no point in going on - best get the agent to do the job. Above all take no notice of the man who says he can judge by the hiss of the air. Leave him to adjust his own carburettor.

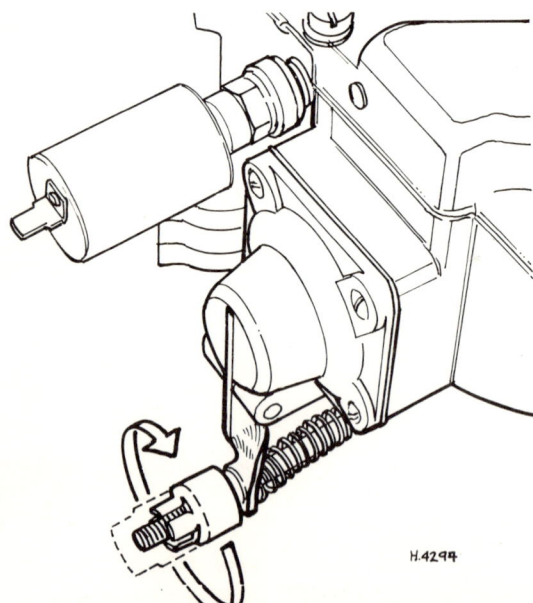

Fig 2.15 On auto-transmission carburettors after May 1973 the accelerator pump injection capacity may be varied by turning the sleeve in the direction of the arrow (Sec 14)

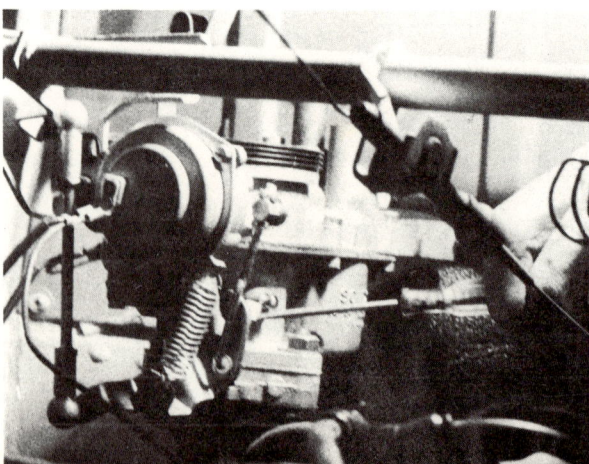

16.3 The fitter's screwdriver points to the adjusting screw on the left-hand carburettor

6 It is now necessary to adjust the idling speed (see next Section). Having done this, check the synchronization again. If you need to alter the setting you will need to readjust the idle speed again.

7 When it is finally right check the exhaust gas with an analyser. If you live in USA the CO content must be less than 1.53% and the hydrocarbon less than 400 ppm.

17 Carburettor (Solex PDSIT 34 2/3) - adjustment of idle speed

1 The following procedure is for routine adjustment. If the carburettor has been dismantled the throttle valve opening must be checked before installing the carburettor. Adjustments are given for engines equipped with full emission control. The procedure is the same for engines not so equipped but obviously some operations are left out. **Read the whole Section before doing anything,** you may not need to do all the tests.

2 This test should be carried out immediately after synchronizing the carburettors (Sec. 16). The oil temperature should be between 50°C and 70°C (120°F - 160°F). Connect in a tachometer to measure engine speed and a CO (exhaust gas analyser) meter. Paragraphs 3 to 9 should not be done if the idle speed and CO value can be got by the procedure in paragraph 10.

3 Isolate the right-hand carburettor, by taking the rod off the ball joint on the throttle relay shaft. Where applicable remove the vacuum hose on the retard side of the distributor. If the vehicle is fitted with afterburning equipment remove the left -hand hose from the air pump and put a clip on it to stop air passing through it.

4 There are two electro-magnetic cut-off valves. The one on the outside edge of the carburettor is the idle system valve. Disconnect the wire from it.

5 It is now necessary to set up both main carburettors before adjusting the central idling system. On the throttle body at the base of the carburettor (just above the flange) directly under the main carburettor electro-magnetic cut-off valve, you will find the main carburettor idle mixture screw (mixture control screw). There is one on the right-hand carburettor as well. Turn both of these screws in until they just touch the valve seating. Do not use force or you will damage the valve seating. Now screw them both out 2½ turns.

6 Start-up the engine. Turn both screws an equal amount in the same direction until the engine speed is between 500 and 700 rpm and the CO content of the exhaust gas is between 3 and 5%. You may have to experiment a bit on this but if you get lost stop the engine and reset the screws to 2½ turns and try again.

7 Disconnect the electro-magnetic cut-off valve on the left carburettor and note the drop in engine speed. Reconnect the valve and remove the wire from the valve on the right carburettor. The drop in engine speed should be the same (the engine will speed up a bit when you reconnect the left-hand valve). If it isn't then the mixture screws must be turned in opposite directions until the speed decrease is the same when each cut-off valve is disconnected. The CO valve must still be between 3 and 5%.

8 This all sounds very difficult, and if it is the first time you do it, it is best to have two people on the job. Move the screws an agreed amount each time (say 1/8 of a turn). Count the turns to arrive at the setting in paragraph 6 so that you can go back to that setting if you get lost doing paragraph 7.

9 When you are satisfied that the adjustment is correct on the main carburettors the system should be reconnected. All wires, hose and relay lever put back in place including the idle system cut-off valve.

10 You may now actually adjust the idle speed. There are two screws on the top of the central idling section of the left-hand carburettor. (photo). In the photo the screwdriver in the fitter's hand is on the idle speed adjusting screw. We have taken the air cleaner away to indicate the screw more plainly. You will still have the air cleaner on top of the engine. The other screw is the mixture control screw. Start the engine again and turn the mixture control screw until the exhaust gas analyser gives a reading of 3% (4.5% is acceptable, but **not** in USA). Now turn the

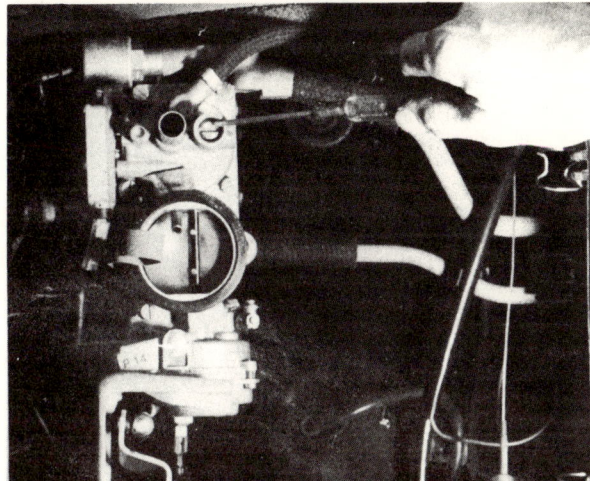

17.10 The screwdriver in the fitters hand points to the idler adjust screw on the central idling system of the L.H. carburettor. The mixture screw is the other side of the idling inlet hole

idle speed adjusting screw until the speed is $900 \overset{+}{-} 50$ rpm for manual transmission or automatic $950 \overset{+}{-} 50$ rpm automatic.

11 This has been the whole process. It is really only necessary to tune the main carburettors when you cannot get a satisfactory CO and speed reading on the idle system control. Then you must get down to it and reset the main carburettors.

12 It may be that you do not have a CO meter. The following method will give you a rough adjustment. Screw the idle mixture screw slowly until the engine speed drops, noticably, now screw it out to give maximum idle speed, note this speed and turn the screw in again to give a drop of 50 rpm. Now screw the screw out a quarter of a turn. Set the idle speed with the idle speed adjusting screw as in paragraph 10. This will give an approximate adjustment but the sooner the CO level is checked with a meter the better.

13 In some territories only certain service stations are allowed to touch the carburettor adjustments. It is as well to find out about this legal requirement. The VW agent will know. There isn't an awful lot to the tuning of carburettors but the kit is expensive and you may think it better to leave the whole job to the VW agent. It doesn't need doing all that often.

18 Carburettor (Solex PDSIT 34 2/3) - removal and replacement

1 Before starting to remove the carburettors remove the earth lead (ground strap) from the battery. Remove the air cleaner.

2 Disconnect the wires from the automatic choke heating elements and from the three electro-magnetic cut-off valves. Tag each wire as you remove it so that replacement is easier. Marking tape for the freezer is as good a colour code as any.

3 Next disconnect the accelerator operating rod ball sockets from the throttle arms. Unhook the return spring and take it off.

4 Now disconnect the hoses and pipes from the carburettors. Make a diagram of where these go and label the hoses if it is the first time you have done it.

5 The carburettors are now isolated and each one may be removed from its manifold by undoing the nuts from the studs. Do not loose the spring washers. Lift the carburettor away from the manifold. There is a gasket, which if it is damaged, must be replaced. Cover the hole in the manifold to stop dirt or foreign matter getting in while you overhaul the carburettor. It is best to overhaul one carburettor and replace it before removing the other one. This way you cannot get bits mixed up.

6 Replacement is the reverse of removal. Be particularly careful that the joint between the carburettor and the manifold is airtight. Use a new gasket but do not use gasket cement.

If replacements are required be certain that the new piece has exactly the same part number as the old one.

19 Carburettor (Solex PDSIT 34 2/3) - overhaul and adjustments

1   Clean the outside of the carburettor carefully with a suitable solvent. Provide yourself with a number of receptacles for the bits as you dismantle the carburettor. Lay out a sheet of clean paper on the bench and work with clean hands. Refer to Fig. 2.13. Do not dismantle the carburettor unless you have a good reason, and then no more than is strictly necessary.

2   Keep the diagram in front of you. The carburettor dismantles into three main sections. Disconnect the end of the automatic choke operating rod from the throttle lever. Take out the five screws which hold the top section to the body. Lift it away from the body taking care not to damage the central idling system emulsion tube or the accelerator pump injector.

3   The throttle body may be removed from the main body by removing the two screws which clamp the two together. Before this is done dismantle the accelerator pump linkage. Note how the lower end of this is connected to the throttle arm so that it goes back correctly.

4   The carburettor is now in its three main sections. Deal with the main body first. Remove the main jet cover plug and un-screw the main jet. Clean it by blowing through it. Do not poke it with wire or a pin. If it is blocked or damaged fit a new one.
Remove the air connection jet and check it. Undo the screws holding the accelerator pump cover and dismantle the pump. Check the diaphragm and replace if necessary. Check that the accelerator pump bypass valve (1800 cc engines only, at the side of the accelerator pump, a small dome screwed in at right angles to the pump) works. It should open the drilling at 21°C. Below this temperature you should not be able to blow through the drilling. (Fig. 2.16)

5   The float requires a special check. Remove the float pin re-tainer and push out the pin. Immerse the float in hot water. If any bubbles appear there is probably a hole in the float. This will cause the petrol to enter the float and the carburettor will flood. If there is a hole replace the float, do not attempt to repair it. If you do see bubbles make sure they are due to air escaping from inside the float and not from air trapped under it.

6   Assemble all the parts in the centre body and turn to the lower part. Remove the idle mixture screw. First of all screw it in until it touches the seating counting the turns so that you can replace it with the same setting. The taper on the end should not be grooved or ridged. If it is, a new screw should be fitted. Check the bearings of the throttle valve. If they are worn a new car-burettor will be needed.

7   The upper part of the carburettor should now be checked. Undo the inlet needle valve and examine the seating. If it seems in good condition replace it, hold the needle on its seat and blow into the fuel inlet, to test for leaks. A faulty valve must be replaced. Dismantle and check the automatic choke assembly.

8   The electro-magnetic cut-off valves may be checked for operation either when the carburettor is in the vehicle, or on the bench. To check in the vehicle turn on the ignition (don't start the engine), take the wire off the valve terminal and touch the wire back to the terminal. The valve should click. To test out of the vehicle connect the body of the valve to the negative terminal of a 12v battery and the terminal tag to the positive terminal. Lightly press the cut off valve head and the plunger should go into the solenoid. If the valves do not function they must be replaced.

9   It is most important that the valve clearance or gap between the throttle valve and the throttle body must not be more than 0.004 inches (0.10 mm). Check this (Fig. 2.17) and adjust the gap if necessary by moving the stop screws. When it is right cover the screws with plastic caps. If this dimension is not correct then it is unlikely that satisfactory idling will be achieved.

10   The level of the fuel in the float chamber can be checked only when the carburettor has been filled with petrol, via the inlet hose. This should be done when all other jobs are finished and only if flooding is suspected. Simply hold the assembled carburettor level, fill the float chamber through the inlet until the needle valve shuts. Remove the upper half of the carburettor and using a depth gauge measure the distance from the top of the float chamber to the surface of the fuel. Keep away from the side of the float to avoid errors due to capilliary attraction. The distance should be 0.500" ± 0.030" (12 to 14 mm). Adjustment is made by altering the thickness of the washer under the needle valve. If the fuel level is too high fit a thicker washer; if too low a thinner washer. Four thicknesses of washers are available: 0.020", 0.030", 0.040" and 0.060", (0.5, 0.8, 1.0 and 1.5 mm). This can all be done with the carburettor in the vehicle.

11   If you are patient you can check the delivery volume of the accelerator pump. The trickly bit is fitting a piece of hose to the injector. You may need a tiny mirror like dentist's mirror to see the hose down the throat of the carburettor, or of course you could take the top of the carburettor off, fit the hose and re-assemble. Open the choke valve and prop it open with a retainer. Now work the throttle smartly ten times and catch the petrol expelled down the hose in a 25 cc measuring glass. Divide the amount by ten and the answer is the delivery per stroke. It should be in accordance with the table given in the Specification at the beginning of this Chapter.
On 1974 models (1800cc) this test should be done at a temperature less than 19°C (66°F) so that the thermostatic valve is shut in the correct position.

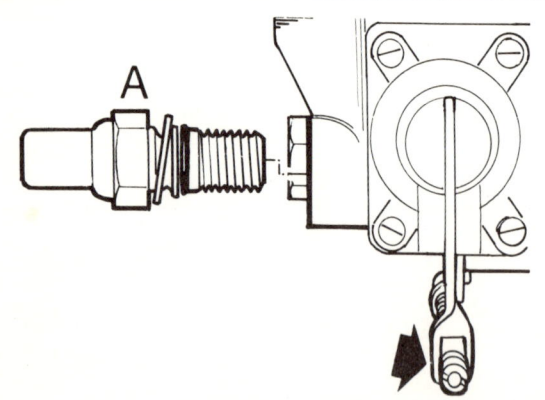

Fig 2.16 The thermostatically controlled bypass valve for the accelerator pump. 'A' is the valve. The arrow points to the thread-ed part of the link which can be turned to adjust input (Sec. 19)

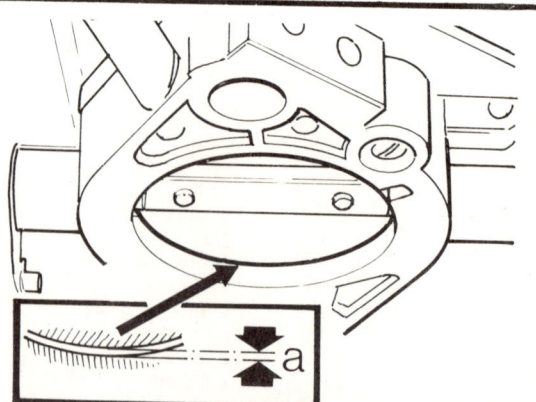

Fig 2.17 Checking the gap of the throttle valve to throttle body measurement (a) should be exactly 0.004 inches (Sec. 19)

Adjustment is by installing the cotter pin through a different hole in the connecting link or on the 1974 models by turning the threaded part on the operating rod.

On automatic transmission after May '73 the adjustment is by turning the sleeve as shown in Fig 2.15.

12 The dashpot (see Fig. 2.13) does not normally require adjustment unless it has been taken off for some reason, or the throttle linkage has been overhauled. The correct setting for it is achieved when with the plunger held fully in the clearance between the plunger and the tab on the throttle relay shaft is 0.0015". (Use a 0.002 feeler, all that is needed is that there is minimum clearance).

13 Cleaning the carburettor before reassembly is an important business. Use only a good recommended carburettor cleaning solvent, and a non-fluffy rag. Lubricate the choke and throttle valve shafts with engine oil, use molybdenum grease sparingly to lubricate the linkage, fit new hose clips and gaskets and make sure all the joints are air tight.

14 The linkage has not been disturbed in this Chapter. If the accelerator cable is disconnected and reconnected it is important that when the accelerator is pressed down fully there is no overdue strain on the operating arm of the throttle valve. There should be a clearance between the arm and the stop on the carburettor body of 0.05". Get someone to hold the pedal flat to the floor, slacken the cable clamp on the linkage and set the cable so that the clearance is correct and then retighten the cable clamp.

20 Fault diagnosis - Carburettor (Solex PDSIT 34 2/3)

Before tracing faults in the carburettor make sure the ignition settings and gaps are correct, the fuel pump is delivering fuel correctly and that there is some fuel in the tank

Symptom	Probable reason	Remedy
1 Engine will not start. (Ignition correct)	1 Choke valve stuck 2 Auto choke not working 3 Carburettor flooding	1 Dismantle and correct 2 Dismantle and test 3 Clean or replace needle valve
2 Engine will not idle correctly	1 Dirty jet in idle system 2 Throttle valve gap incorrect 3 Leaks in vacuum hoses to brake servo or automatic transmission 4 Manifold gasket leaking 5 Carburettors not synchronized 6 Automatic choke not switching off	1 Clear 2 Dismantle carburettor and reset 3 Check all hoses and servo for leaks 4 Refit gasket 5 Synchronize carburettors 6 Check heater element corrections
3 Engine idles and hunts or stalls	1 Leak in servo vacuum hose 2 Leak in EGR hoses 3 Pilot jet blocked 4 Air leaks from intake manifold	1 Check servo hoses 2 Check EGR hoses 3 Clean jet or replace 4 Check manifold gasket
4 Engine will not stop when switched off	1 Electro-magnetic cut-off valve(s) faulty 2 Idle mixture too rich	1 Test valves and replace if necessary 2 Adjust
5 Backfires in exhaust on overrun	1 Weak mixture 2 Faulty mixture control valve (Exhaust afterburn vehicles)	1 Adjust 2 Replace valve
6 "Flat spots", engine will not accelerate from idle evenly	1 Accelerator pump not working properly 2 Idle adjustment incorrect	1 Test and adjust. Repair if necessary 2 Readjust
7 Black smoke from exhaust - engine rough at low speeds - plugs fouled	1 Float chamber trouble (too much pressure) 2 Automatic choke not working properly	1 Check needle valve. Check level in float chamber. Check fuel pump delivery. Check float for puncture 2 Dismantle and repair
8 Engine accelerates but lacks power at speed	1 Fuel starvation	1 Check pump delivery 2 Dismantle and clean carburettor and do all tests and adjustments 3 Dirt in tank or pipe lines - clean filters
9 Miles per gallon too low	1 Wrong jets fitted 2 Float punctured or needle valve leaking 3 Leak in fuel hose 4 Leak in petrol tank 5 Automatic choke not working correctly	1 Check and fit correct jets 2 Test and repair or replace 3 Tighten joins or replace hose 4 Remove and service 5 Dismantle and repair

Chapter 3 Ignition system

Contents

Specifications

Spark Plugs

Type (Normal conditions)	CHAMPION N. 88
	BOSCH W 145 T2 or BERU 145/14/3
Type (Tropics)	BOSCH W 175 T2 or BERU 175/14/3
Plug thread size	14 mm (metric thread)
Spark plug electrode gap *	USA engines and early European engines 0.024'' (0.6 mm)
*Consult handbook supplied with vehicle	Later European Engines (manual) 0.028'' (0.7 mm)

Firing order ... ... 1 - 4 - 3 - 2

Coil ... ... 12v BOSCH

Distributor

One of several types may be fitted. The part number of the distributor is 021905205 followed by a suffix. The table below is representative - consult the agent if in doubt.

The timing setting varies

Country/Type	Engine	Suffix	Vacuum hose	Idle Speed	Setting
Europe	AP	P	off	900	7.5° before TDC
USA (automatic)	AW	S	on	950	10° after TDC
USA (manual)	AW	N	on	900	5° after TDC

Contact breaker points gap ... ... 0.016'' to 0.020'' (0.40 to 0.60 mm)
Dwell angle gle
New points	44° to 50°
Used points	42° to 58°

Torque wrench settings
	lbs ft	Kgm
Spark plugs to cylinder head	22	3

1 General description

1 The ignition system is conventional. The 12v supply is fed through the ignition switch to terminal 15 of the coil, thence, via the primary winding, to terminal 1 of the coil. The LT current then goes to the distributor to the moving arm of the circuit breaker.

2 When the points are closed current flows through the coil and the points. The points are opened by a cam with four lobes on the distributor shaft. Each cylinder requires one spark for two revolutions of the crankshaft so that the distributor shaft rotates at half engine speed. The distributor shaft is driven by a skew-gear on the crankshaft (see Chapter 1) not by the camshaft as on other engines.

3 A condenser is connected across the points to prevent undue sparking and to speed the collapse of the magnetic field in the coil and raise the induced voltage.

4 The HT winding of the ignition coil is connected to the input terminal of the LT coil and is wound round the same core. The other end of the winding emerges from the insulator on the top of the coil and a heavily insulated wire takes the HT to the centre of the distributor cap.

5 The wire is connected to a small carbon brush inside the cap

and the spring of the rotor arm bears against this brush as the arm rotates. The outer end of the rotor arm passes close to four segments situated in the inside of the rotor cap, each equally spaced 90° apart. As the rotor goes round the HT jumps the gap to each segment in turn and HT current is supplied, via the plug lead, to the spark plug: thus causing a spark at the plug electrodes. The plug leads have a high resistance to assist in radio interference suppression (5,000 - 10,000 ohms).

6 Although the timing is set very carefully at idle speed different degrees of advancement and retardation are required for best operation at high speeds and on light or heavy loads.

A centrifugal type governor is fitted in the distributor. As speed increases the weights of the governer move out and cause the cam to turn relative to the distributor shaft and to advance the ignition slightly. As the speed drops the springs of the governer retract the weights, returning the cam to its original position. This makes adjustment of the ignition timing for varying speeds.

The adjustment for load conditions is governed by the pressure variation (vacuum) in the carburettor. On the side of the distributor is the vacuum control bellows. According to the air pressure in the unit casing a diaphragm moves against a spring actuating a small lever which goes through the distributor body and is connected to the plate which carries the contact breaker. It is in fact the anchor for this plate which is able to rotate about the distributor shaft a few degrees as determined by the position of the lever and the bellows. Thus the horn of the contact breaker is moved relative to the cam giving advance or retard to the ignition setting according to load.

7 The VW system (except for 1974 manual transmission) is further modified. At temperatures below $12^\circ C$ ($54^\circ F$) the automatic vacuum advance operates in all gears. Above $12^\circ C$ ($54^\circ F$) it operates only in top gear. A two way cut-off valve operated by a temperature sensor in the engine space and a switch on the transmission is inserted in the vacuum hose from the carburettor to the distributor vacuum control unit. This system is discussed in detail in Section 5, of this Chapter. As will be realized the actual position of the cam and movable contact lever horn depend on the vacuum unit so that it is most important when setting the ignition timing to know whether the degrees of advance or retard relative to top-dead-centre (tdc) are given with the system operative or inoperative. (hoses "on" or hoses "off").

8 Another innovation is the top-dead-centre marker unit. This is an electronic device fitted after August '73 to enable the position of tdc to be established accurately so that during the routine computer diagnostic inspection the timing may be checked quickly and accurately. It is discussed in Section 9, of this Chapter. Its existence makes it all the more sensible to have your vehicle inspected this way. The inspection will tell right away whether the ignition is correctly set. If it is, go on your way rejoicing; if it isn't, read this Chapter and decide whether to leave the van to be serviced or to do something about it yourself. Remember, that like the fuel system, if the ignition system isn't functioning correctly you could be contravening the emission control laws in territories where they apply.

2 Contact breaker - points setting

1 The most accurate method of setting points is by measuring the dwell angle, which is the angle of revolution of the cam while the contact breaker arm is in contact with it at each lobe. If the shaft bearings are worn then the shaft can move about and setting the points on one lobe of the cam may not be accurate for the other three. A variation of 0.004 inches will alter the ignition timing about 3°.

2 However, providing there is no significant wear in the distributor shaft, it is possible to set the points using a feeler gauge. The correct setting is 0.016 to 0.020 in (0.4 mm). If there is

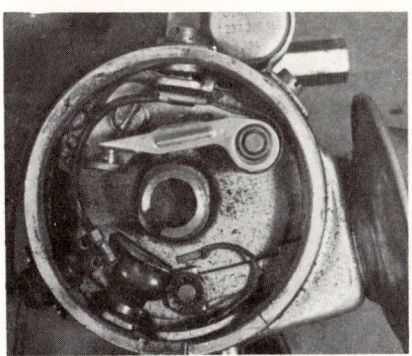

2.3a Contact breaker viewed from top, cam follower on the lower part of the cam, points closed.

2.3b Lead pulled off the terminal. Grip the spring with the pliers and pull off the spring, moving point and lead from the pivot post

2.3c Take out the securing screw and remove the fixed point for cleaning (see para 8)

2.3d Clean off old oil and grease and lubricate the cam pivot with one drop of engine oil. Put a small amount of multi-purpose grease on the cam

2.3e Assemble the clean (or new) points with the securing screw just holding the plate gently.

2.3f With the cam follower on the high portion of the cam (see paragraph 7) move the fixed point (move the plate) until the gap is 0.020". Tighten the securing screws and check the gap again on

significant wear in the shaft or bearings this state of affairs must be rectified before the points can be set satisfactorily.

3 Remove the distributor cap and the rotor arm. The wear can be checked by rocking the top of the shaft. If there is play turn to Sections 3 and 4 for rectification. If the play is negligible then all is well. Check the gap in the points. Consult photographs 2.3 (a) to (f) and adjust the points to the correct setting. Replace the rotor arm and cap.

4 If you do posses a dwell meter and a tachometer then having set the points as above connect in the dwell meter and proceed with further adjustment. The toe side of the meter is attached to the coil at terminal 1 and the other lead to earth (ground). Run the engine up to 1000 rpm and read the dwell angle.

5 Continue to adjust the points until the dwell angle agrees with the values given in the Specification at the beginning of this Chapter. It is possible to adjust the dwell angle with the cap off the distributor by spinning the engine with the starter. Widen the gap to decrease dwell, close it to increase dwell.

6 Replace the cap and check the dwell angle again at 1000 rpm. Now run the engine up to 2000 rpm. A variation of dwell angle of more than one per cent means the distributor shaft bearings are worn, and need overhaul. (see Section 4).

7 It may be difficult to get the cam follower on the high point. Turn the engine by using the alternator belt or the pulley. On manual transmissions put the vehicle in gear and move it a small amount. If it is very stiff take the plugs out to do the initial setting with a feeler gauge.

8 The examination of the points is instructive. Normal wear gives pitting and small high points with tight surfaces. The high points should be removed with a fine oil stone. Leave the pitted surface alone so long as it is clean. If the surface is grey then either the gap was too small or the spring is weak. New points are quite cheap. A blue surface means that probably the coil or condenser is defective (see Sections 7 and 8). Yellow or black surfaces are due to oil or grease. Clean them off and do not over-lubricate on reassembly.

9 After resetting the points the timing should be rechecked.

3 Distributor - removal and replacement

1 Remove the cap, release the LT lead from the coil (pull it off the coil), and pull off the vacuum hose. **Do not slacken the distributor clamp.**

2 Undo the nut from the stud holding the distributor clamp to the crankcase and pull the distributor out. (photo)

3 While the distributor is out do not move the engine, and check the position of the distributor rotor arm with reference to the body of the distributor.

4 Look down the hole and note when the dogs of the shaft engage the groove in the drive shaft. There is an offset. Cover the hole while the distributor is being examined.

5 Replacement is the reverse of removal. If the clamp bolt has not been slackened and the shaft is correctly positioned the engine timing will not have been altered.

6 Check the oil seal ring on the shaft and renew if necessary.

4 Distributor - dismantling, inspection and reassembly

1 If a dwell test has been done then the condition of the shaft and bushes will be known. If not try rocking the shaft in its bearing. There should be no appreciable play. If there is then it must be remedied.

2 The shaft can be replaced (if one is obtainable) but the bushes in the housing cannot. Axial play may be adjusted with shims (if you can get them).

3 The distributor may be dismantled by removing the driving dog from the bottom. Knock out the pin with a punch; note the position and number of washers. The breaker unit and vacuum unit are fastened with screws. Mark the position of the driving dog relative to the shaft, and the location of the centrifugal weights.

3.2 Removing the distrubutor DO NOT UNDO THE CLAMP BOLT

4 If it is necessary to remove the clamp mark its position so that it may go back in the same place. When the driving dog and washers are off stick a piece of sellotape round the shaft and mark the clamp position.

5 If the bob weights have broken adrift or the plate is rocking then the distributor has had its day. In the author's experience if there is wear in the shaft there will be wear in the bushes so that even after a new shaft is fitted the dwell angle will not conform to Specification. Beware of breakers' yards. There are a number of distributors which will fit your vehicle, but only the correct one will make it run properly.

5 Automatic advance and retard mechanisms

1 Refer to the illustration showing the exploded view of the distributor. It will be seen that the distributor shaft is in two pieces and that the top piece may rotate on the bottom piece. Its movement is controlled by the governor parts and the top piece or cam as it is called, may move a few degrees in a clockwise direction. If the whole thing has disintegrated you can try to get spares but usually the damage is extensive and repair is not worthwhile. (Fig 3.1)

2 To check that it is working correctly remove the distributor cap and grasp the shaft at the top. Turn it gently in a clockwise direction until resistance is felt. Release the shaft and it should return smoothly to its original position. If it does not then the governor is dirty or stuck. To get at it remove the rotor arm, points and the vacuum unit off the side to disconnect the vacuum control lever, then remove the mounting plate which is held in place by screws.

3 If it is necessary to overhaul the governor mechanism it will be better to remove the distributor from the engine (Section 3).

4 The principle of the automatic vacuum advance and retard mechanism is stated in Section 1.6. A diagram is given to shown the block layout. The control valve may be found by following the hose from the distributor. Make sure this hose and the one from the valve to the carburettor is in good condition. (Fig 3.2)

The temperature sensor is on the side of the engine compartment and the transmission switch on the gearbox.

5 To check whether the system is working fit a tachometer and a stroboscopic timing light into the system. Run the engine up to 2000rpm and shine the stroboscope on the crankshaft pulley timing mark. When this is steady get a helper to sit in the driving seat, depress the clutch and engage top gear. Keep the clutch down or you will be running after the vehicle. This should operate the on/off switch of the automatic vacuum advance and

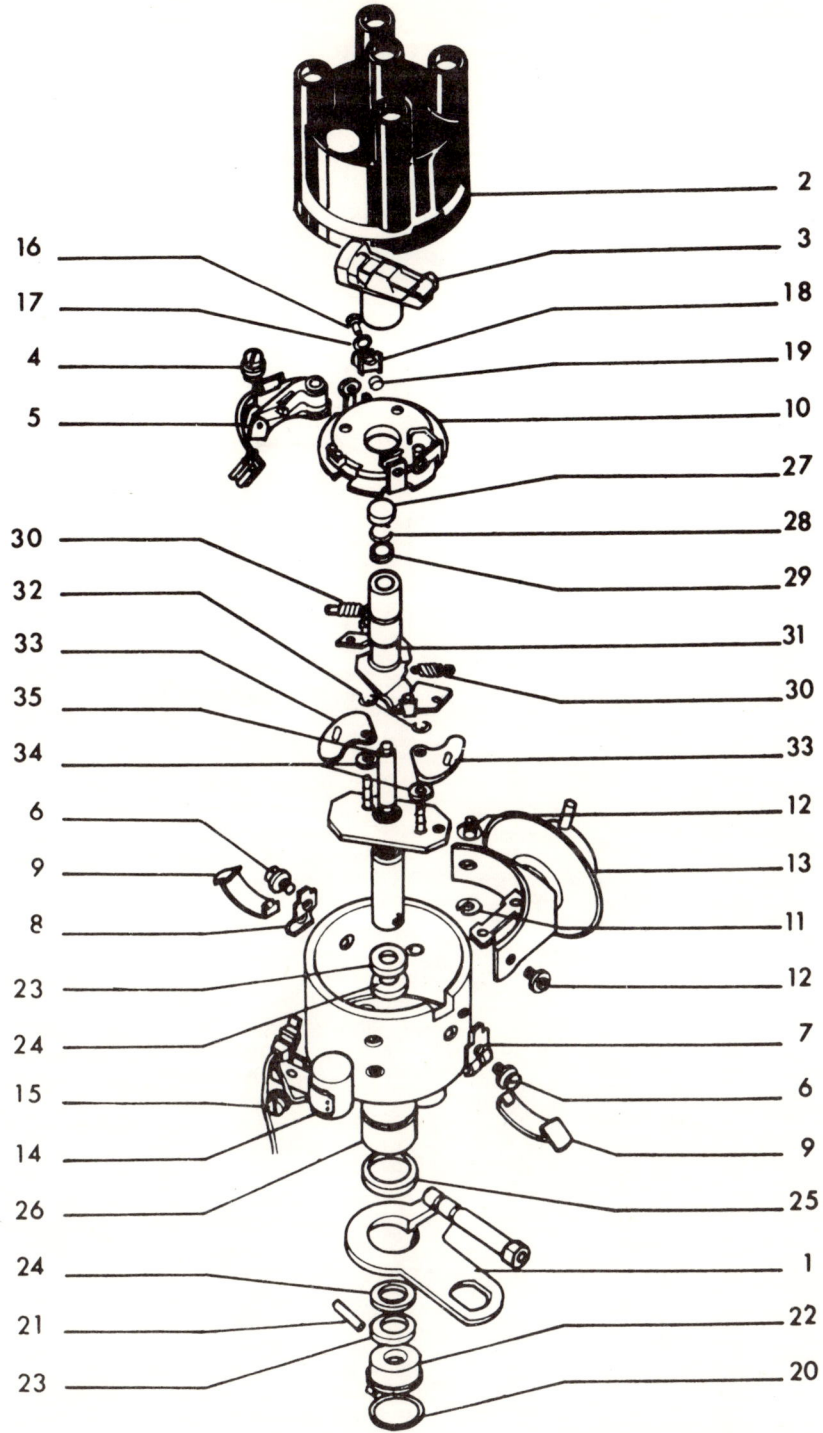

Fig 3.1 Distributor with centrifugal and vacuum advance - exploded view (carburettor engines)

1 Mounting clamp bracket	10 Contact points mounting plate	18 Retaining spring	27 Felt washer
2 Cap		19 Ball	28 Circlip
3 Rotor	11 'E' clip for pull rod	20 Circlip	29 Thrust ring
4 Contacts securing screw	12 Screw	21 Pin	30 Return spring
5 Contact points	13 Vacuum unit	22 Driving dog	31 Cam
6 Clip screw	14 Condenser	23 Shim	32 Circlip
7 Clip retainer	15 Screw	24 Fibre washer	33 Bob weights
8 Clip retainer	16 Screw	25 'O' sealing ring	34 Washer
9 Cap clip	17 Spring washer	26 Distributor body	35 Drive shaft

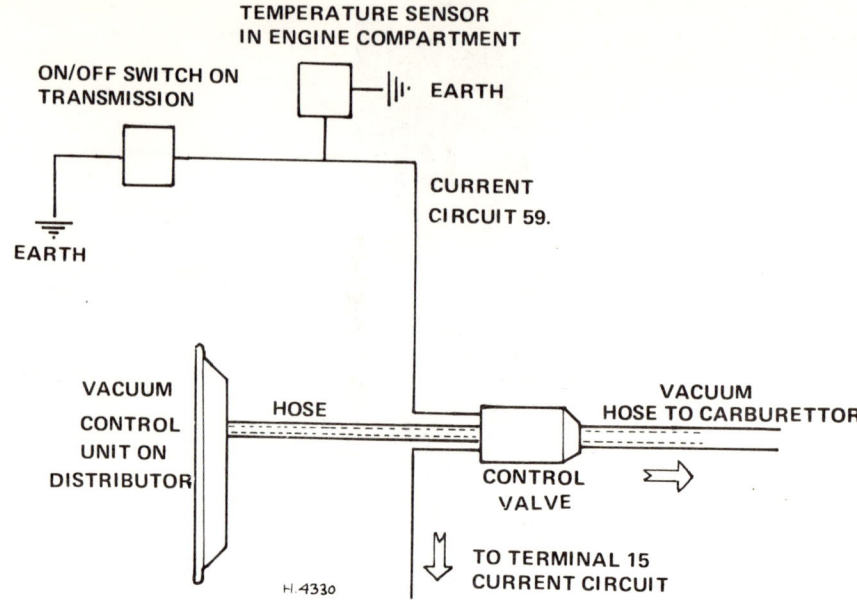

TEMPERATURE SENSOR IN ENGINE COMPARTMENT

ON/OFF SWITCH ON TRANSMISSION

EARTH

CURRENT CIRCUIT 59.

EARTH

VACUUM CONTROL UNIT ON DISTRIBUTOR

HOSE

VACUUM HOSE TO CARBURETTOR

CONTROL VALVE

TO TERMINAL 15 CURRENT CIRCUIT

H.4330

Fig 3.2 Diagram showing layout of automatic vacuum advance system (all models except 1974 manual transmission onward) (Sec 5)

the timing mark should move to the left about 1¼'' as the gear engages. If it doesn't the system is not working. Disengage the gear, stop the engine and test the system methodically.

6 Check that the wiring to the sensor is in good order and that the sensor ground contact is efficient. Check that the transmission switch does work. Take the wire off the control valve and connect in a meter. Repeat the test to operate the transmission switch. If it doesn't work then it is either the wire or the switch. Replace whichever is faulty.

7 To check the unit on the distributor, remove the cap and turn the contact breaker mounting plate counter-clockwise as far as it will go. Release it, and it should spring back to its original position. If it doesn't the unit is dirty. Pull the hose off the pipe on the unit dome. There may be two pipes for a double action unit; if there are take them both off. Turn the mounting plate counter-clockwise as far as it will go, put your finger(s) over the pipe connector(s) and remove your hold from the plate. It should not return to its original position until you remove your fingers. If it does the diaphragm is leaking and must be replaced; this will mean buying a new unit.

8 If the above tests show that the various components are good but the system still does not work it must be the two way valve. If you have access to a good one known to be working replace the unit and recheck the system. If you do not it is best to let the VW agent do the check with his special meters. He will be able to do a series of tests of both systems over the speed range and adjust matters until the vehicle conforms to Specification.

6 Condenser - testing, removal and replacement

1 Although the condenser rarely goes wrong, if it does it will cause a lot of trouble. Not only does the condenser prevent arcing at the points but its correct functioning also affects the build up of voltage in the HT circuit. This will affect starting and power output at high torque and low revolutions.

2 Fortunately the symptoms are easily recognised: the points will be badly pitted. To confirm the diagnosis pull off cable 1 of the coil connect a test lamp between terminal 15 of the coil and cable 1 (in other words put a 12v bulb in place of the coil),

switch on the ignition and open the points. The lamp must not light. If it does there is a short circuit in the condenser. If there is a short circuit then replace the condenser, clean up the points and all will be well.

3 It is unlikely but just possible to have an open circuit condenser. This would not show in the test but the effect would be similar, so if the burning of the points continues replace the condenser with a new one, or take the condenser for testing. The fault would most certainly be in the lead connection.

4 When replacing the condenser get the right one. One of the wrong capacity will not function properly, and one the wrong size will not fit. Get a new one to fit from the VW agent.

7 Coil - testing, removal and replacement

1 The coil is mounted on the fan casing on the left side of the engine (photo). To remove it undo the wires and label them so that they go back easily then undo the clip and remove the coil casing. When replacing make sure the case earth connection is made. However, it is not necessary to remove the coil in order to test it.

2 There is a lot of wire in the case; if it is faulty nothing can be done about it, so the only task with the coil is to test it, and if necessary replace. However, it is easily tested while in the car.

3 First examine the cap. It will be dirty and probably oily. Wipe this off and look for evidence of shorting or tracking: thin black lines of carbon running from the case across the cap.

4 Now pull the HT cable out of the centre of the distributor cap. With it still in the coil hold the free end about 3/8 inch (9.5 mm) from the fan housing and turn the engine over with the starter.
  There should be spark from the cable end. As the voltage is several KV use a rubber glove or a pair of insulated pliers to hold the wires or the spark may not be the only thing that jumps.

5 If there is no spark check the voltage at terminal 15. (Ignition on) It should be at least 9 volts. If it is higher then a further test is necessary.

6 Take the cap off the distributor so that with a pencil the points may be opened (turn the engine so that they are closed).

Check the voltage from coil terminal 1 to earth. There should be no reading at this terminal with the distributor points closed. Now open the points and there should be a reading on the voltmeter. If there is no reading then the coil has an open circuit and must be replaced.

7 Be sure that the connections to the coil are firmly made. A small drop in voltage in the LT circuit will mean a big one in the HT circuit and possibly hard starting or misfiring under heavy load.

8 Ignition timing - setting

1 If the distributor has been removed and the timing positon lost then follow the method given to re-install the distributor roughly in the right place.

2 Take out No 1 cylinder plug and take off the valve cover so that you can see the tappets. Turn the engine until the position in No 1 cylinder is almost at TDC and both valves are shut. The tappets will be slack when the valves are shut. You can tell when the piston is at TDC by holding your thumb over the plug hole or by bending a piece of wire and feeling the top of the piston. The timing mark on the crankshaft pulley should read zero on the scale. If the scale has not been moved do not take out the plug but just line-up the marks. The engine is now in the firing position for No. 1 cylinder.

The distributor has a mark on the rim of the body which is where the rotor should point to supply No. 1 cylinder with a spark. Turn the shaft until the rotor points to this mark.

3 If you look down the distributor shaft hole the groove in the driveshaft into which the dogs of the distributor shaft fit should form an angle of 12° to the edge of the casing. (photo)

4 Install the distributor fit the clamp nut and connect all the

hoses and wires. The engine should start. If it does then detail timing can be done.

5 Fit a tachometer and a stroboscopic timing light. The engine oil temperature should be over 30°C (86°F), measure this with a thermometer down the dipstick hole.

6 Adjust the idle speed (Chapter 2, Section 17) to 850rpm for manual transmissions and 900rpm for automatic transmissions.

7 Shine the strobe-light on the pulley marks and read the degree scale at the point the marker indicates. Refer to the table in the Specification or the vehicle handbook and check whether the timing is correct. If it is not, then stop the engine and slacken the clamp on the distributor casing until the unit may just be turned by hand. Hold the casing in position while the engine is running and shine the strobe on the pulley. Move the distributor round until the pointer comes to the correct mark. Stop the engine and tighten the clamp. Recheck the marker again in case things moved while you were tightening the clamp.

8 If the engine has a TDC marker all this is unnecessary. Take the vehicle to the agent and he can check the timing on the diagnostic computer quicker than you can walk round the vehicle. If you do it the hard way be careful not to get caught up in the alternator belt or the air pump belt.

9 Top-dead-centre (tdc) marker - description

1 On vehicles produced after August 1973 the flywheel of the manual transmission or driveplate of the auto-transmission has two small studs screwed into it. (Fig 3.3)

2 A small electronic device is inserted into the crankcase right half just below the mounting bolt and connected to the diagnostic plug (circuit 57). (Fig 3.4)

3 When the engine is working these studs rotate closely to the

7.1 The coil is mounted on the fan casing

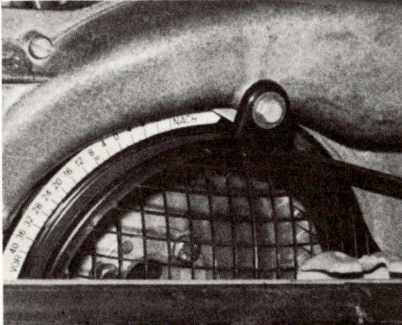

8.2 The scale on the fan casing

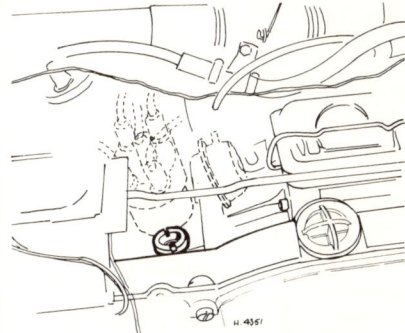

8.3 A view of the distributor driveshaft. Note the smaller segment of the drive-shaft is on the outside

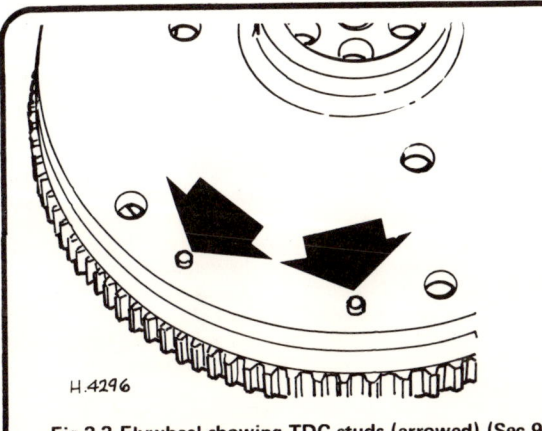

Fig 3.3 Flywheel showing TDC studs (arrowed) (Sec 9)

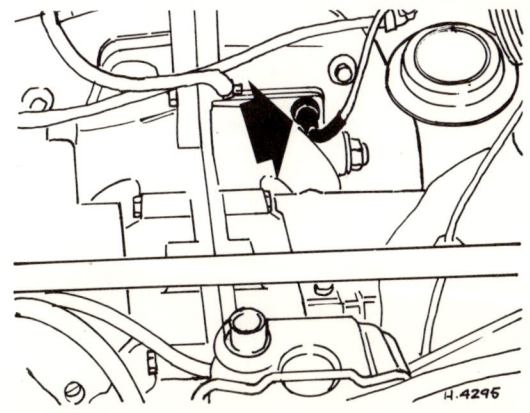

Fig 3.4 TDC electronic marker in the crankcase (arrowed) (Sec 9)

TDC marker unit and trigger off electric impulses to the computer when the diagnostic cable is connected in the test bay.
4   The studs must be inserted without damaging them and be protruding the same amount ± 0.004 in (0.10 mm). The amount isn't critical, but the difference *is* critical.
5   The electronic unit may be removed only with the engine dismantled. It is pushed out into the flywheel casing.

10 Distributor driveshaft - removal and replacement

1   Turn the engine until the pointer on the crankshaft pulley points to No. 1 cylinder firing position on the scale (Section 8.1).
2   Remove the distributor (Section 3) and the anti-rattle spring.
3   You can now see the driveshaft (photo 8.3) with the 12° angle.
4   Using either a magnet or a piece of wood tapped into the hole in the driveshaft ease it out turning it at the same time.
5   The shaft should be turned in an anticlockwise direction but make sure the engine crankshaft does not turn at the same time.
6   There may be a shim under the shaft. A magnet will be required to lift this out. **If it is dropped inside, then the engine will have to be dismantled to recover it.**
7   To reinstall is the reverse of dismantling. Make sure the crankshaft has not moved (ie; still on No. 1 cylinder firing point). When installed the offset slot in the top of the driveshaft is at an angle approximately 12° to the crankcase joint and points roughly to the rear securing screw of the air cleaner. The smaller segment is on the left. Insert the shaft so that it turns clockwise when engaging the skew gear on the crankshaft; make allowance for this when judging the angle of assembly. (photo) Do not forget the shim. Guide the shim into position on a piece of rod and **do no drop it inside the engine.**
8   The shim will stick in place better if you put a little grease on it. The shim should be smooth and undamaged. It should be 0.051 inches (1.3 mm) thick.
9   Replace the anti-rattle spring and then install the distributor.
10 There is no point in fitting a new shaft if the gear teeth are worn, for there will be equal wear on the crankshaft gear and that also must be renewed. If may be necessary to renew the shim, if there is one. On the engine dismantled by the author there was no shim fitted.
    Altogether there seems little point in taking out the shaft for curiosity and a grave danger of dropping the shim inside. Unless there has been a mishap between the drive dog of the distributor and the slot of the shaft it is thought better to leave the shaft in position until a complete engine overhaul is done.

11 Spark plugs and HT leads

1   Spark plugs should be renewed every 12000 miles. If it is not intended to fit new ones then the old ones should be taken to an agent who has the proper shot blast equipment and pressure tester, and cleaned and tested before reassembly. There is no other sensible method. A new set of plugs costs less than an oil change. The correct plug gap is 0.024 in (0.61 mm).
2   Always fit the correct grade (see Specifications) and fit them with a proper VW plug spanner, (this has an insert to hold the plug and a universal joint). Check that the washers are not flattened. Before the old plugs are taken out blow out any grit or loose dirt which may fall inside.
    Be careful not to cross the threads and do not overtighten. The torque required is 22 ft lbs (3 mkg). This is the equivalent of a "sharp nip" with the plug spanner. The cylinder head is aluminium and if the thread is stripped or overtightened causing cracks between the plug threads and the valve seat the engine will have to come out and a new head be fitted.
3   Leads should be inspected for wear and insulation cracks. The resistance of an HT lead should be between 5 and 10 thousand ohms. Terminals must be correctly fitted with proper crimping tools and the lead should be free from oil or moisture.

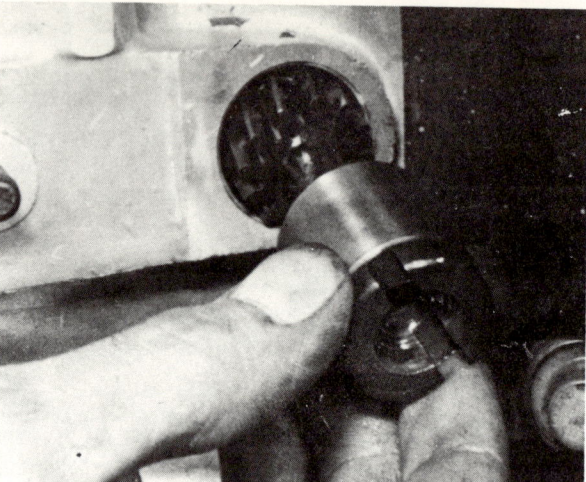

10.7 Driveshaft ready to go in. Allow for the turn of the shaft on engagement of the helical gear

Insulation tape is no use at all on HT leads. Again the cost of a new set of leads and caps is less than the cost of an oil change and the trouble that can stem from worn and faulty leads makes it a false economy not to renew them regularly.
4   The condition of the plugs will give an interesting side light on the state of tune of the engine. A diagram showing plug point conditions is included in this Chapter.

12 Fault diagnosis - ignition system

1   *Engine will not start.*

a) The engine is so enclosed that the normal wet condition after leaving the car in the open over night is not so prevalent. However before running down the battery when the car will not start after being left in the open have a look to see that everything is dry. If mist has penetrated then dry the moisture off, either with a cloth or with a proprietary type spray.
b) If the engine will not start when everything is dry, pull off a plug lead, turn back the plug cover and hold the metal end of the plug lead about 1/8 in (3.2 mm) from the crankcase. With the ignition switched on spin the engine with the starter. If there is a spark, a good fat one, then the ignition system is working. Check that the distributor body is held tight in the clamp ring, then check the timing setting. Take off the distributor cap. Set the ignition timing mark on the crankshaft pulley to the correct point on the scale (Section 8) and check that the rotor arm is pointing to No 1 cylinder plug lead. If the spark is correct and the timing has not altered then the fault is not in the ignition system.
c) If there is not a fat spark then the ignition system is at fault. Begin by checking the LT circuit in the following order:

(i)   Are the points opening correctly? Are they clean?
(ii)   Check the voltage at coil terminal 15. It should be at least 9 volts (ignition on). If no voltage then the wiring or the switch is at fault.
(iii) Check the voltage at coil terminal 1, points closed - no volts, points open - reading on the meter. If no reading on the meter with points open the coil has an open circuit.
(iv)   With the ignition switched on check the voltage across the contact breaker points; points closed - no volts, points open meter reads. Points open - no reading, then the condenser is faulty.

d) Check all the LT wiring and connections carefully and if the LT circuit is functioning correctly then proceed to the HT circuit. Check the following in the order given (ignition switched on):

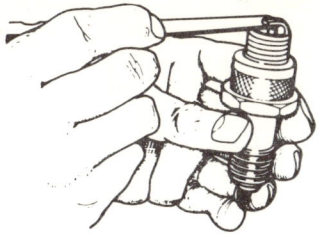

Checking plug gap with feeler gauges

Altering the plug gap. Note use of correct tool.

Spark plug maintenance

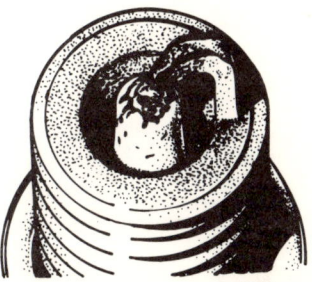

White deposits and damaged porcelain insulation indicating overheating

Broken porcelain insulation due to bent central electrode

Electrodes burnt away due to wrong heat value or chronic pre-ignition (pinking)

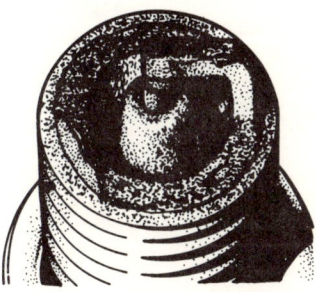

Excessive black deposits caused by over-rich mixture or wrong heat value

Mild white deposits and electrode burnt indicating too weak a fuel mixture

Plug in sound condition with light greyish brown deposits

Fig 3.5 Plug electrodes

(i) *Pull the HT lead from the centre of the distributor and hold the end 1/8 in (3.2 mm) from the crankcase. Spin the engine. There should be a spark. No spark means a faulty HT winding in the coil.*

(ii) *Turn off the ignition switch, put the lead back in the centre of the distributor cap and examine the carbon brush carefully. Is it making contact with the rotor arm spring? Examine the cap for cracks and tracking. Check that the segments are clean and that the rotor arm leading edge is not corroded. Clean these points if they are.*

(iii) *Replace the rotor arm; check the drive by turning the rotor gently. There should be a slight movement. Anything more than a slight movement means that the drive is suspect or the automatic advance and retard has disintegrated. The latter is rare but it has happened.*

e)   Finally remove a plug and check its condition. If it is oily, wet with petrol, or corroded, then clean it, and the other three. Check the gap. Oily or corroded plugs mean an engine overhaul or at least a checking of the exhaust gas composition by an expert. Wet plugs may be flooding during starting.

2 Engine runs sluggishly but does not misfire.
a) Check the contact breaker points and the plug gaps.

b) Check the ignition timing.
c) Check the octane rating of the fuel.

3 Engine misfires, runs unevenly and cuts out at low revolutions
a) Check contact breaker and plug gaps. (CB gap too large?)
b) Check the distributor shaft for wear.
c) Check the fuel system.

4 Engine misfires at high revolutions.
a) Check contact breaker and plug gaps (CB gap too small?)
b) Check the distributor shaft for wear.
c) Check the fuel system.

5 General
Ignition faults are quite often exasperating. Work steadily through the system checking all leads and connections methodically. Test the components, check the battery, and if finally the fault cannot be located then go to the expert. He has instruments specially designed to locate faults. But if his respect is to be obtained do not go about testing in a haphazard manner, that will only result in more faults being installed and the original one may never be located.

Chapter 4 Clutch

Contents

Specifications

Type

Manual transmission	Diaphragm spring operated single dry plate, pedal operates release mechanism by cable
Automatic transmission	Torque converter described in Chapter 6

Spring pressure

1700 cc	380 - 420 kg (837 - 925 lb)
1800 cc	420 - 485 kg (925 - 1070 lb)

Clutch diameter ... ... 215 mm (8.46 inches)

Lining Area ... ... 375 sq cm (58 sq ins.)

Pedal free-play

Early 1700 models with weaker diaphragm	3/8 in to ¾ in (9.5 - 19 mm)
1700 since August '73 and 1800 cc models	5/8 in to 1 in (15.8 - 25.4 mm)

Torque wrench settings

	lbs ft	Kgm
Clutch to flywheel (M 8 screws)	18	2.5
Engine to transmission (M 10 nuts)	22	3
Engine bearer to body	14	2

1 General description

1 Two types of clutch have been fitted to the transporter with a manual type gearbox. They are both diaphragm spring operated but vary in the spring pressure. The additional spring pressure has been added to cope with the extra power of the 1800cc engine.

2 The automatic transmission transporter is fitted with a torque converter in place of a clutch. This is described in Chapter 6.

3 The diaphragm clutch is a dry single plate clutch fitted to the flywheel. The withdrawal mechanism is cable operated. The clutch withdrawal mechanism, release bearing, and release shaft are mounted in the bellhousing on the end of the gearbox and remain in the vehicle when the engine is removed.

4 Maintenance is limited to checking and adjusting the free-play of the clutch pedal as the lining wears. The pedal free-play for the 1700cc model is 3/8 in to ¾ in (9.5 mm to 19 mm), the 1800cc 5/8 in to 1 in (15.8 mm to 25.4 mm). When the play becomes greater than this the adjusting wing nut must be turned to restore the limit. This is discussed in Section 2.

2 Pedal - free play adjustment

1 The clutch operating lever may be identified on the side of the gearbox bellhousing. This must be done from underneath the vehicle. The cable terminates in a threaded extension which passes through the eye in the end of the operating lever and is secured by a wing nut. (photo)

2 The operating lever is kept in the forward position by a spring.

3 Clean the lever and spring and the threaded extension with its wing nut and bushes.

4 The wing nut may now be screwed further on to the thread until the free-play of the pedal comes within the tolerance. The distance between the wing nut and the clutch lever will be 1/16 inch (1.6 mm) when the pedal free-play is correct. The nut should be turned so that it fits in the groove in the lever to stop it coming undone.

5 When the initial adjustment has been done, pump the clutch pedal hard several times and recheck. It may be necessary to adjust the nut again.

3   Clutch cable - replacement

1   Clutch cables rarely break and do not stretch significantly so if you find that the clutch is slipping and further adjustment is not possible the cause is the clutch friction plate. Do not think that the cable is at fault.

2   To remove the cable jack up the rear of the car and remove the left-hand wheel. Unscrew the cable adjusting nut from the threaded end.

3   If the cable inner only is to be removed it is not necessary to disturb the outer sheath. If the outer is being taken off as well then the mounting bracket bolted to the transmission casting should be taken off. Reassembly will then be much easier.

4   Access to the front end of the cable requires that the panel covering the underside at the front is first removed. This necessitates removing the small hexagon head screws. The front of the cable is held to the pedal lever by a clevis pin secured by a lock plate. Bend up the lock plate and remove the pin. The cable may then be drawn out from the front. If broken draw out the other piece from the rear.

5   Grease the cable thoroughly prior to replacement and make sure that the rubber sleeves are positioned correctly to seal the ends of the guide tube against the entry of water and dirt (photo). Refit the adjusting nut to the threaded end of the cable.

6   When adjusting the clutch, the pedal is the indicating factor. The top of the pedal should move forward ½ in (12.7 mm) for 1700 cc engines or ¾ in (19 mm) for 1800 cc engines before firmer resistance is felt. If it moves more than this the adjuster needs screwing up to shorten the cable. If it moves less than slacken the adjuster. When the adjustment is taken up all the way and the free play is excessive then the driven plate is in need of replacement.

7   Stiff or uneven operation of the clutch could be due to several factors. One check worth making before doing anything too drastic is on the cable outer cover at the rear end. The outer sleeve should have a bend in it and the lowest point of this bend should be between 1-1¾ inches (25-45 mm) from an imaginary straight line between the ends of the sleeve (see Fig. 4.1) The latitude is generous so the measurement is easy enough. Should there be a variation outside these limits (a most unusual occurrence unless the sleeve has been disconnected and wrongly refitted) adjustments can be made. Disconnect the inner cable from the clutch operating lever, on the transmission casing and add or remove washers to the shoulder of the sleeve as required.

8   If the rubber boot over the flexible guide tube ferrule is pushed forward against the frame crossmember a lubrication hole will be uncovered. Grease may be pumped into this with a grease gun fitted with a tapered nozzle to cure stiff, dry cables as a last resort.

4   Clutch - removal, overhaul and replacement

1   It is necessary to remove the engine from the vehicle in order to dismantle the clutch. Consult Chapter 1, for the removal of the engine from the chassis, or Chapter 5, for the removal of the engine and transmission.

2   Once the engine is removed it will be seen that the clutch assembly (diaphragm and friction plate) are bolted to the engine flywheel (photo). Shown in Figure 4.2 is an exploded view of the assembly.

3   There should be a fair amount of clutch dust but no grease or oil present. Wipe away the dust but do not at this stage attempt to remove oil or grease.

4   Mark the position of the cover relative to the flywheel with a centre punch, undo the six bolts and draw off the diaphragm spring/clutch pressure plate. The friction plate may now be removed as well.

5   Check the ends of the diaphragm springs where they make contact with the release bearing ring. Scoring up to 0.012 in (0.3 mm) can be ignored, but deeper marking means a new assembly. The one examined here had a fine coppery deposit but no scoring, even though the clutch has been abused.

6   Check the pressure plate friction surface for overheating, cracks or distortion. Put a straight edge over the pressure plate and check for warping. Taper off up to 0.012 in (0.3 mm) over the width of the pressure plate can be ignored but beyond this it is best to consult the VW agent.

7   Now examine the straps between the cover and the pressure plate for cracks. Check the rivets for tightness. The diaphragm spring is held to the clutch cover by rivets between two wire rings. If the rivets are loose or the rivet heads or wire rings show signs of wear a new clutch should be fitted. (See Fig. 4.3)

8   The friction plate should be examined for wear. If the lining has worn so that the rivet heads are less than 0.025 in (0.6 mm) below the surface then the lining requires renewal. There should be no scoring. If there is then the flywheel face on the pressure plate will most certainly have corresponding marks. The flywheel will have to be removed and serviced or replaced (see Chapter 1).

9   Scoring on the pressure plate will get worse if the damaged plate is used again so replace a damaged plate with a new one. Check also that the small springs are in good order and there are no cracks between the holes in which the springs are located. It has been known for the hub to come adrift from the rest of the plate. The springs may have been affected by overheating.

10 Overheating due to a slipping clutch will show as discolouration on the pressure plate and flywheel.

11 If oil or grease has penetrated to the friction lining the friction face will be black and shiny. The friction plate must be replaced. Equally important the source of the contamination should be found and the fault rectified (see Section 7).

12 Do not be mean about replacements. If anything is suspect it will be a very false economy to use it again.

13 Once the various parts are passed as satisfactory the reassembly is simple. Place the friction plate (right way round) (photo) on the flywheel centering it carefully so that the gearbox driveshaft will pass through it into the flywheel centre bearing. Make up a suitable spigot. Unless this is done there will be trouble when the gear is joined to the engine. (photo)

2.1 Clutch cable adjusting wing nut

3.5 Make sure the rubber dirt excluding caps are fitted

4.2 The clutch is bolted to the flywheel

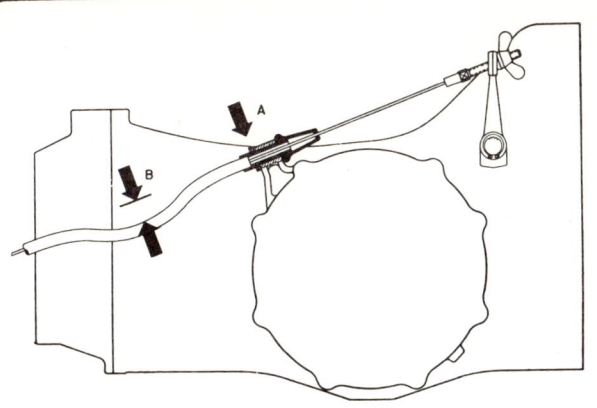

Fig 4.1 Clutch operating cable outer sleeve (Sec 3)

A *Adjustment washer location*
B *Bend measurement (1 - 1¾ in)*

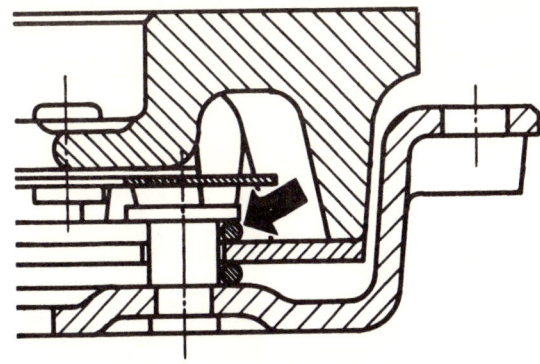

Fig 4.3 Section through diaphragm/pressure plate assembly showing rivet heads and wire rings which must be examined for wear (Secs 4 and 7)

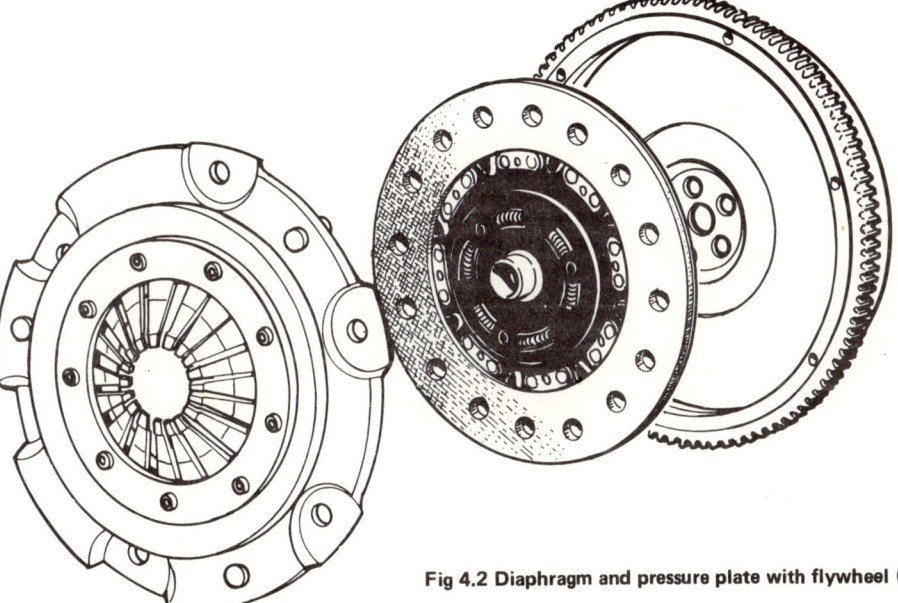

Fig 4.2 Diaphragm and pressure plate with flywheel (Sec 4)

4.13a Replacing the diaphragm/pressure plate and friction disc. Note which way round the friction disc goes

4.13b Use a suitable bar or wooden rod to centre the friction disc. If it isn't correctly centred then there will be trouble when you try to fit the gearbox

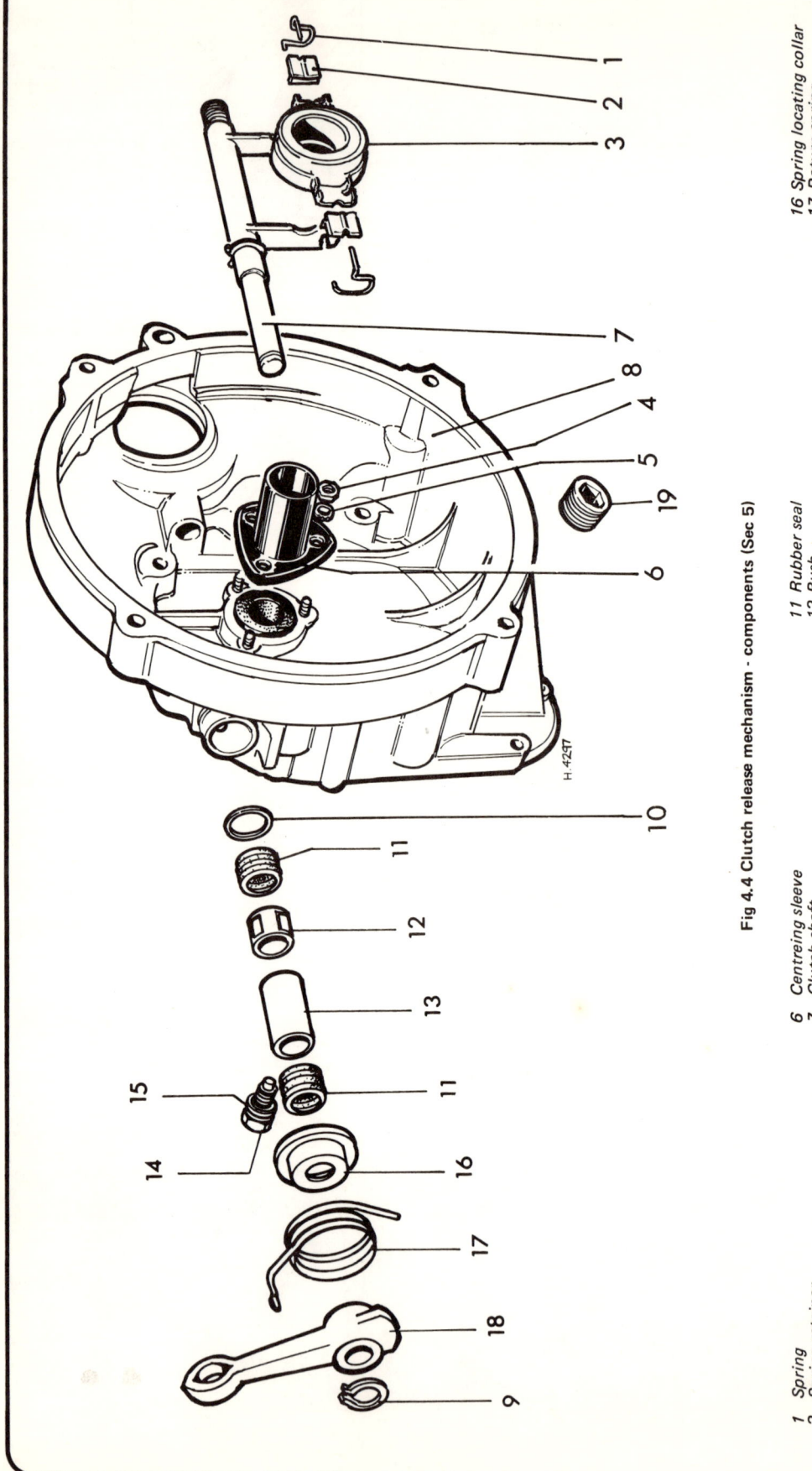

Fig 4.4 Clutch release mechanism - components (Sec 5)

1 Spring
2 Spring retainer
3 Release bearing
4 Nut M7
5 Lockwasher

6 Centreing sleeve
7 Clutch shaft
8 Clutch housing
9 Circlip
10 Washer

11 Rubber seal
12 Bush
13 Sleeve
14 Lock screw
15 Spring washer

16 Spring locating collar
17 Return spring
18 Clutch lever
19 Drain plug

H. 4297

Replace the diaphragm cover plate (with the markings made during dismantling, or you may get an imbalance), replace the six bolts and lock washer and working diagonally tighten to a torque of 18 lb ft (2.5 mkg).

5 Clutch release mechanism - removal, overhaul and replacement

1 The release mechanism is located in the bellhousing which connects the gearbox casing to the engine. To get at it the engine must first be removed. (See Chapter 1).
2 It is a very hardworked mechanism, for it has to overcome the very considerable force (480 kg) exerted by the diaphragm spring. This is done by rotating the clutch shaft so that the fingers press the release bearing against the centre part of the diaphragm. They are not in contact when the clutch is in the drive position (hence the free-play of the pedal) and each time the clutch pedal is depressed the plastic ring, which is stationary, comes in contact with the diaphragm rotating at engine speed, rotates and then is pressed by the ball race at the back of it until the clutch is disengaged. The release bearing must be in perfect order and so must the bearings of the clutch shaft or the plastic ring will not be presented squarely to the diaphragm.
3 Having removed the engine the removal of the release bearing is simple. Pry off the spring clip retainers and then the spring clips and slide the bearing off the guide tube.
4 The bearing must not be washed in solvent. It is packed with lubricant on manufacture and cannot be repacked. Spin the bearing. Any sign of wear or uneven running in the race means the race must be scrapped. If the plastic ring is worn this too means a new bearing.
5 Check the play in the clutch shaft bearings. The shaft should move easily but there should be no significant play in the bearings.

6 It will probably be easier to renew the cross-shaft bearing after taking the gearbox from the vehicle.
7 If it is necessary to renew the bushes the cross-shaft can be taken out after first taking the operating lever and return spring off the end of the shaft. Then remove the screw which locates the bush in the casing and remove all the components. When replacing the shaft lubricate well with molybdenum grease and ensure that the two concertina type grease seals are intact and properly seated inside the casing (photos). If one should come out on the inside of the casing make sure you get it put back. This bush takes considerable forces when the clutch is operated and should not be ignored.
8 When fitting a new return spring first remove the operating lever by undoing the circlip and taking it off the splined shaft. Fit the new spring so that the hooked end will eventually go round the lever and hold it back. Replace the lever and hook the spring end round it (photo).
9 Reassembly of the release bearing is the reverse of removal. Smear the guide sleeve lightly with molybdenum grease. If you are fitting a new bearing fit new clips as well. Make sure the hooked ends of the clips fit behind the operating fingers. Put a little of the grease on the thrust race and dust the mainshaft with molybdenum disulphide powder.
10 After installing the engine and gearbox back in the car remember to check the free-play of the clutch pedal.

6 Pedal assembly - removal and replacement

1 On the majority of vehicles the clutch pedal is bolted to the pedal level which is fastened to the frame.
2 Remove the bolt holding the pedal to the lever and then take out the two bolts holding the pedal unit to the frame. It will be much easier to do this if the cover plate is removed first.
3 The unit may now be eased away from the frame and the

5.7a Fitting the clutch release shaft bush ....

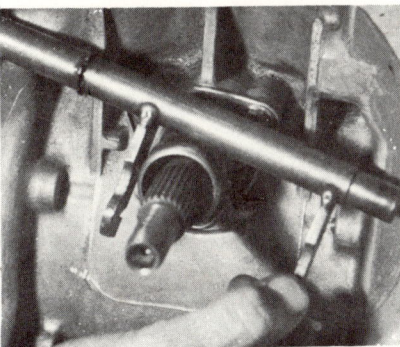
5.7b .... followed by the shaft ....

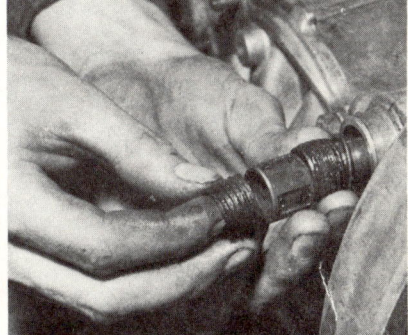
5.7c .... and bearing sleeve and seals

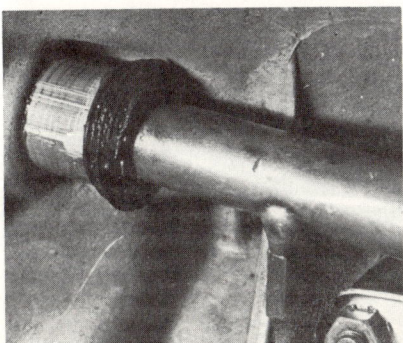
5.7d Make sure the bush and seal do not come out on the inside like this

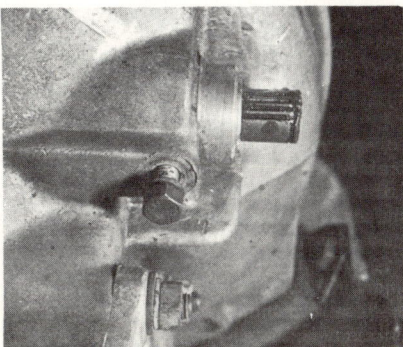
5.7e The locating screw for the bush and sleeve

5.8 The release shaft operating lever sharing circlip splines and return spring

clevis pin removed from the cable stirrup.

4   On some RHD vehicles the clutch pedal is held on a shaft which also holds the brake pedal. This is illustrated in Chapter 8, Section 21.

5   Apart from rebushing the bracket there is no repair that can be done. Do not cold straighten either the lever or the pedal after accident damage. If it is to be straightened this should be done by a smith.

6   Replacement is the reverse of removal. Do not forget the clip which holds the clevis pin. It will be necessary to adjust the clutch free-play if the pedal assembly is disturbed.

7   Oil contamination of linings - repair procedure

1   If on dismantling the engine from the car it is found that the clutch is contaminated with oil then the source from which the oil is coming must be determined and the fault rectified.

2   It will be the engine crankshaft oil seal or the gearbox input shaft oil seal (or both).

3   Oil will cause the clutch to slip and overheat. The friction plate will need renewal and a hard look at the release bearing is indicated. It all depends on how hot things have been. Oil and carbon must be removed from all the other parts very carefully.

4   To get at the crankshaft oil seal the flywheel must be removed. This is discussed in Chapter 1. It is not necessary to split the crankcase.

5   The gearbox oil seal may be removed and replaced with the transmission still in the car. This is discussed in Chapter 5, Section 7.

8   Clutch faults - general

1   A number of things can seem to go wrong with the clutch which are not actually attributable to the clutch mechanism. These points should be checked before beginning to dismantle the clutch. All the transmission mounting nuts should be checked for tightness. If any of them are loose the vehicle will vibrate excessively as the clutch is engaged - and the clutch will be blamed.

The terms used to described clutch faults are:

(a) Judder or grabbing — This condition describes the situation when the clutch engagement is rough and the vehicle vibrates or proceeds in jerks.

(b) Dragging or clutch spin - means that the clutch will not disengage and the gears cannot be engaged.

(c) Slipping — means that the engine is driving the flywheel faster than the pressure plate. It may occur only when the vehicle is accelerated quickly or going up a steep hill, it may slip all the while. It is a progressive disease and should be dealt with straight away. The physical symptom is that the engine speed increases but the vehicle speed does not. If you suspect that slip is occurring a simple test will confirm your fears. Stand the vehicle on level ground with the handbrake hard on. Start the engine and engage first gear. Rev the engine gently and let the clutch in at the same time applying the foot brake. You will need a helper to do this. The engine should stall; if it does not then the clutch is slipping. Do this test gently and do not allow the clutch to continue to slip.

A list of faults and their probable cause is in the next Section.

9   Fault diagnosis - Clutch

Symptom	Probable cause	Remedy
1 Clutch slipping	A Oil on linings	A Dismantle and replace linings. Repair oil seals.
	B Pedal not adjusted correctly due to lining wear	B Adjust pedal, to give correct free-play (Sec 2)
	C Cable sticking in sheath due to damage or rust	C Replace cable (Sec 3).
2 Clutch judder or grabbing	A Engine or transmission mountings loose	A Tighten bolts and nuts.
	B Cable incorrectly installed; bend too great or too small	B Set cable correctly (Sec 3)
	C Pressure plate bent or broken	C Replace.
	D Spring fingers distorted	D Replace diaphragm spring
3 Clutch dragging or Clutch spin	A Too much pedal free-play	A Adjust (Sec 2)
	B Cable not bent correctly	B Reset (Sec 3)
	C Pedal sticking	C Free and lubricate
	D Release bearing shaft seized	D Dismantle and repair.
	E Splines on main drive shaft damaged or rusty	E Dismantle and clean splines. Lubricate with molybdenum disulphide powder.
	F Friction plate distorted or broken.	F Replace friction plate.
	G Pilot bearing worn or seized.	G Check and replace
	H Excessive clutch (asbestos) dust on drive plate	H Dismantle and clean or replace.
4 Clutch noisy	A Pilot bearing worn.	A Replace. (See Chapter 1)
	B Release lever springs weak (diaphragm "fingers")	B Replace diaphragm assembly.
	C Release bearing defective	C Replace bearing (Sec 5)
	D Splines worn, driven plate fouling drive-plate or pressure plate	D Replace driveshaft and or driven plate.

Chapter 5 Manual transmission and final drive

Contents

Specifications

Identification code

CA	Normal up to August 1973	
CN	Normal after August 1973	
CC	With limited slip differential	

Gear ratios

	Tooth Ratio	Reduction
1	9/34	3.78
2	17/35	2.06
3	23/29	1.26
*4 November 1972	28/23	0.82
4 after November 1972	61/52	0.82
4 1973	27/24	0.89
*Reverse 1972	43/17 x 14/20	3.61
Reverse 1973	40/15 x 14/20	3.80
Reverse Chassis 2132068548 on	40/15 x 12/17	3.79

In view of the many changes consult with the agent before ordering spares.

Final drive ratios

CA	8 : 43
CN	7 : 34

Synchromesh ... ...
Baulk ring on all forward gears

Lubrication

Oil specification ... ...
SAE 80 hypoid to MIL - L - 2105 with sulphur - phosper additive

Capacity ... ...
6 1/8 Imperial pints / 7.42 American pints / 3.5 litres

If a new box is fitted drain at 600 miles and refill. Thereafter top-up only.

Torque wrench settings
These are included in the text at the appropriate place.

1 General description and extent of gearbox repair possible

1 The gearbox and final drive is a one piece composite assembly housed in a 'tunnel' type magnesium die casting. ~~ting.~~ Unlike the more orthodox design of gearbox which has an input and output shaft aligned on the same axis with a layshaft and gears below, the VW has an input shaft and output shaft only mounted alongside each other and each carrying a synchro hub. This is because the input power is at the same end of each shaft. The output shaft incorporates the pinion gear which meshes with the crownwheel. Synchromesh is fitted on all four forward speeds. The box is bolted to the engine and the engine and gearbox are supported by a carrier. An illustration is shown of

this. The front end of the box is supported on bearers attached to the cross tube. (photo 2.5)

2 The unit is a very complex piece of mechanism requiring fine adjustment and it is thought that a warning note should be sounded to potential dismantlers.

(a) *First - is the fault you wish to cure worth the time and expense. A noisy box may go on for ever, and a repaired one could be just as noisy.*

(b) *If the gearbox is in a really bad state then the cost of the spares may exceed the cost of a replacement box. When you have read the Chapter it might be as well to do some arithmetic.*

(c) *If you have not overhauled a gearbox before then this is a bad one to start on. You will need a lot of tools and know-how to get this one apart and back together again.*

(d) *You must have a good contact with the VW agent and his spares staff - we have found they are always willing to help but understandably cross if someone gets a job in a mess and expects them to put it right. Again you will not know what spares are required, and you may have to wait if you want something out of the ordinary - no agent carries 100% replacement spares.*

(e) *Even though you may have some knowledge of VW gearboxes this one requires two special tools (VW 381/4 to undo the pinion shaft bearing and VW 231/15 to undo and do up the differential adjusting nuts. Without these you will find life difficult.*

(f) *You will need access to a press.*

3 It is suggested that you read this Chapter, decide what is most likely the problem and then either go to the agent or a really experienced VW maniac and discuss the extent of repair that you can do. Then check the spares availabilty - you will need at least a set of gaskets, baulk rings and possibly bearings, mainshaft circlips and a pinion bearing retaining nut. You will not be able to dismantle the differential or remove the pinion shaft bearing - these are jobs for the man with all the special fixtures.

4 However, if you have time and patience and you really want to do the job then there is no reason why you should not succeed in saving yourself a lot of expense.

2 Transmission - removal and replacement

1 It is not possible to remove the transmission without taking out the engine as well. The best way is to take them out together, the vehicle was designed to do this and it is a quite simple job *but* the combined assembly is a very heavy one. We found it required four men to carry the combined engine and gearbox with any degree of certainty. On the other hand, provided that you can support the engine and gearbox while removing the retaining bolts and then lower it to the ground safely the vehicle may remain on its wheels and be moved away from the assembly without any trouble.

2 A study of the photo. 2.5 will show where the gearbox is supported at the front, and where the transmission carrier is located. The engine mountings at the rear are discussed in Chapter 1. They are two simple brackets. The official method is to take the transmission support bolts out of the carrier and leave the carrier in position. We tried both ways and came to the conclusion that leaving it in position was the best way but it is difficult to enter the lugs into the carrier on reassembly if you do not have it positioned exactly right. We found we could slacken the carrier locating bolts and then with the extra play ease the lugs into position. However, it is extra work and should be avoided if possible. The operation described here is based on not doing that, but it is useful to know if you are stuck.

3 First of all, remove all the wires, hoses and rods which go to the engine and gearbox. The list is formidable and we advise labelling everything as you undo it - it is so much easier to reconnect sometime later. The list is as follows but make and

keep one of your own as you go along:

(a) *disconnect the battery ground strap (earth lead).*
(b) *disconnect the wires from the:*
   (i)   *voltage regulator*
   (ii) *ignition coil*
   (iii) *carburettors (magnetic cut-offs etc)*
   (iv) *oil pressure switches*
   (v) *starter solenoid*
(c) *Disconnect all the hoses going to the engine (fuel, air, servo)*
(d) *Disconnect the throttle cable and pull the cable out forward*
(e) *Take the clutch cable away from the clutch lever, take off the bracket and guide tube that holds the cable to the gearcase*
(f) *Remove the driveshafts (Chapter 7) and tie the CJ joints away in polythene bags*
(g) *Disconnect the shift lever from the front of the gearbox. Pull back the rubber boot, with the gearshift in 3rd gear, cut the locking wire and then undo the square head screw and move the gearlever into second gear to disconnect the joint. It is suggested that you read Chapter 1, Section 3, before finally deciding what to take off the engine or leave on it.*

4 The unit should now be isolated; look round to see if there is anything else (extra emission equipment, auxiliary heaters, etc) and if you are sure all is clear then you are ready for the big lift. Take the gravel guard off te back bumper to give a little extra room. How you lift the assembly will depend on the resources you have. A garage trolley jack is ideal but an extra jack (mobile or otherwise) is also advised. We advise the use of wooden packing until you are sure the unit is balanced and ready to lower. You may find it easier if the vehicle is jacked up with solid packing under the wheels to give you more room to work, but this means more distance to lower. The VW agent has a special adapter cradle to fit on his trolley jack and he also has slings to lift up the transmission while removing the bolts. Whichever way you do it remember two golden rules. First do not drop it, and second, if it does tumble make sure you are not underneath it.

5 Having made arrangements to lower the engine, locate the bolts to be removed and work out how you are going to get spanners on them. Take the weight of the engine on the jack (use packing or you will damage the casing) and remove the two bolts that hold the transmission carrier and sump housing together. Fully support the engine and remove the two bolts holding the limiting stop to the front transmission mounting (photo). Now remove the bolts holding the engine bearer to the frame. The bearer comes away with the engine. Once all the bolts are clear lower a little, look round to see that nothing is caught up, pull

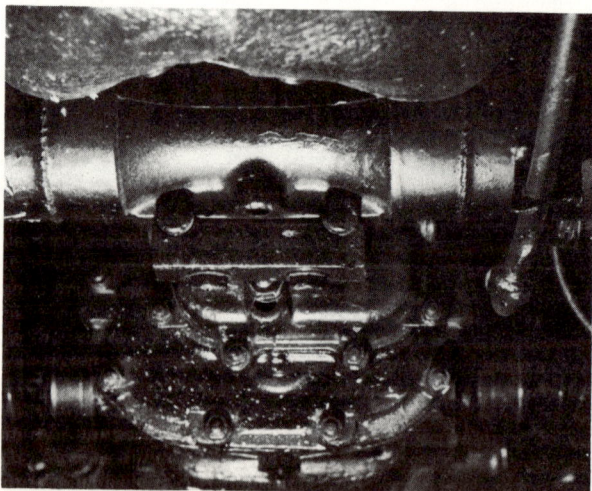

2.5 The front support for the transmission

the engine back to clean the gearshift, lower gently removing it to the rear. It is advisable to have three people at least. One to work the jack, one to steady the engine through the hatch in the body floor, and one to be foreman and check that things do not get caught up. Once the engine is down take it away to the back and with four people to lift carry it away to whereever you are going to work on the assembly.

6   Clean it all down with a proprietary solvent or paraffin, polish it well and then:

(a) *Split the engine from the transmission leaving the engine on the ground. The clutch stays on the flywheel and the withdrawal gear goes with the gearbox.*

(b) *Remove the starter motor.*

(c) *Lift the transmission up on to a clean bench and start work, dismantling, as in Section 3.*

7   Replacement is the reverse process. You will probably have taken advantage of the situation to check the clutch withdrawal race and cross-shaft (Chapter 4) and the starter motor (Chapter 9). Replace these correctly and then reassemble the transmission to the engine. Be careful not to damage the splines or shaft as the mainshaft enters the driven plate of the clutch and the pilot bush in the flywheel. Turn the engine crankshaft if necessary to pick-up the splines. It should all slide in easily and the bolts should be tightened in a diagonal pattern to 22 lbs ft.

8   Now is the time to fill the gearbox with oil (3.5 litres, 6.125 Imperial pints, 7.42 US pints) of the correct Hypoid transmission oil.

9   Position the engine and transmission on the trolley jack (or whatever means you have of lifting the assembly), check that the sleeves and rings for the transmission carrier bolts are in position in the clutch housing, line-up the clutch housing as near as possible with the carrier and lift slowly checking that nothing is fouling. Feed the accelerator cable in as the assembly comes to position and watch for the gearchange rod position.

10   When the assembly is lifted far enough install the engine bearer bolts. Do not tighten them. Go on lifting gently guiding the clutch housing into the carrier until you can install the limiting stop at the front to the cross tube. Tighten these bolts. Now lift a bit further (be careful) until the bolts will go in the transmission carrier. The amount you can lift is governed by the adjustment of the engine bearers. Do not try to lift the vehicle by raising the gearbox.

11   Check that the engine is correctly aligned, the distance from the bearer to the fan housing, should be uniform (bearer parallel to fan housing) and the engine bearer should be vertical from the side.

12   If all is correct torque all the bolts to Specification: Transmission carrier 25 lbs ft, engine carrier 18 lbs ft, front mounting 33 lbs ft.

13   Remove the jacks and fit the driveshafts (Chapter 7) reconnect the gearchange and wire up the square headed screw. Reconnect the fuel hoses, accelerator cable, electrical wires, starter cables, reconnect the clutch cable bracket, clutch cable and adjust the clutch pedal free-play (Chapter 4).

14   Check round all the items you had on your list as you disconnected them. Make sure the hoses are fitted properly.

15   Refit the gravel guard and the battery earth strap and start up the engine. Road test the vehicle and look for oil leaks.

3   Transmission - dismantling

1   The task falls into six separate operations:

(a) *Removal of the rear part of mainshaft and reverse gear.*

(b) *Remove differential and the nut which holds the pinion shaft in place. Unless you have VW tool 381/14 or an equivalent this cannot be done.*

(c) *Remove gear trains on main and pinion shafts from casing while still in the carrier.*

(d) *Remove the gear trains from the carrier.*

(e) *Dismantle main driveshaft.*

(f) *Dismantle pinion shaft.*

2   **Before commencing work read the whole Section right through** and decide whether you can do the job. The agent will not take kindly to an owner who arrives with a partially dismantled gearbox for repair. Do not throw gaskets away, they are a guide as to replacement ones. Again remember that several important modifications have been introduced so be careful when order spares. Start by referring to Fig. 5.4.

3   Remove the screws and nuts securing the clutch housing to the gear casing at the front and carefully draw it off over the input shaft.

4   Undo the circlip in part of the reverse gear and sleeve on the input shaft and draw it along the shaft so that the gear and sleeve may be drawn along behind it until it is clear of the splined part. Then unscrew the front section of the shaft which is located into the other part with a threaded stud.

5   Remove the sealing caps from the centres of the driving flanges by punching the blade of a screwdriver through them and levering them out.

6   Remove the circlips from round the splined shaft ends. The flanges can then be levered off the end of the shafts.

7   Now undo the crosshead screws which hold the lockplates and take off the lockplates.

8   The adjusting rings must now be removed. First mark them with a scriber against the casing and as you take them out count the turns so that you will be able to get them back to the same position.

9   The removal of these rings presents a problem unless you have VW Tool 231/5. We did not. By gentle tapping we managed to start the plate moving, but be very careful not to distort the serrations or the lockplate will not fit on assembly. Once the pressure was relieved we used the lockplate as a spanner. With one side free the other is not nearly so difficult to undo.

10   Label the adjusters "L" and "R" or your markings will be useless.

11   Once the adjusters are out the differential may be removed. Do not let it fall and watch for the thrust rings and lockplate seal. The thrust rings should not be moved. Put the differential in a clean safe place and now go to the other end of the box.

12   Remove the change lever end cover unit (Fig 5.9) and slacken the nine nuts that hold the carrier in place to the casing.

13   Now for the difficult bit. At the clutch end of the casing is the pinion shaft nut which holds the pinion bearing in place in the casing (Fig 5.2). This has to be removed (and later a new one put back again). As will be seen the nut has serrations round its outer edge into which VW tool 381/14 fits snugly. If you do not have a suitable tool then this is where you come to a stop. If you do then undo the nut and remove it, take out the shims and set them carefully aside. Now remove the nuts from the carrier and working it gently with pressure on the pinion face draw the carrier off its studs bringing the two gear trains with it.

14   Once removed do not dismantle anything further until the position of the selector forks has been carefully marked on the rails (photo). If this is not done and the forks are moved there is the greatest likelihood that gear selection will be upset so that the whole assembly will need repositioning in a special jig.

15   Undo and remove completely the fork clamping screws and then slide them off the rails, moving the rails as necessary (photo) in order to free them. Take note which way round the forks are fitted and which one goes on which rail because they are not the same (photo). Do not drive the rails out of the carrier.

16   The reverse selector lever is on a post clamped by a union nut. Make sure this is marked also before moving it. (photo) The brackets which support the reverse selector cross shafts are also adjustable and must be marked before the securing bolts are undone (photo).

17   The next job is to remove the two shafts from the carrier. The carrier must be supported so that the shafts hang downwards. The mainshaft is kept in place by a circlip under which there is a dished washer. Remove the circlip but watch out because the washer is under considerable pressure and the whole lot will fly out if you are not careful.

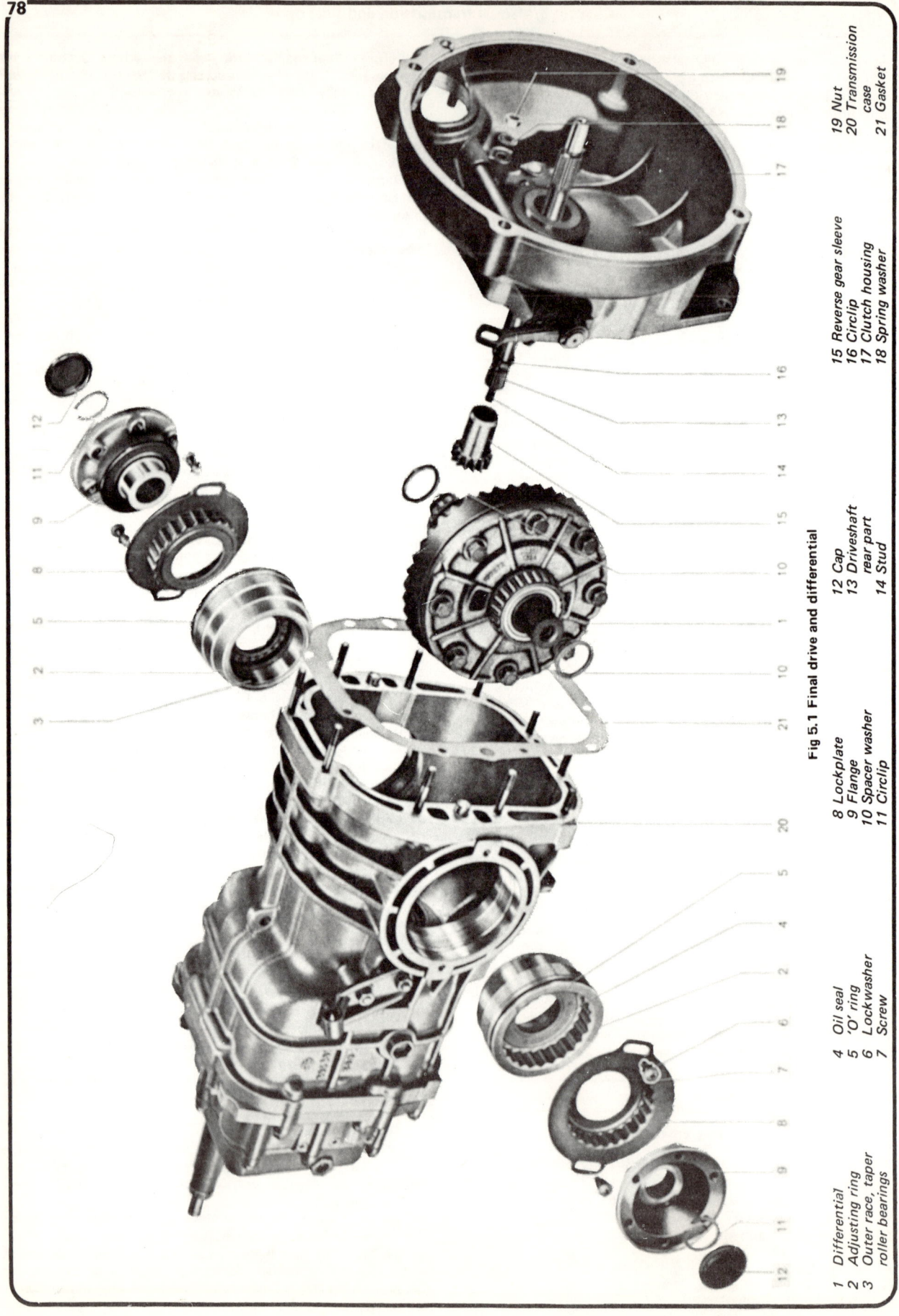

Fig 5.1 Final drive and differential

1 Differential
2 Adjusting ring
3 Outer race, taper roller bearings
4 Oil seal
5 'O' ring
6 Lockwasher
7 Screw
8 Lockplate
9 Flange
10 Spacer washer
11 Circlip
12 Cap
13 Driveshaft rear part
14 Stud
15 Reverse gear sleeve
16 Circlip
17 Clutch housing
18 Spring washer
19 Nut
20 Transmission case
21 Gasket

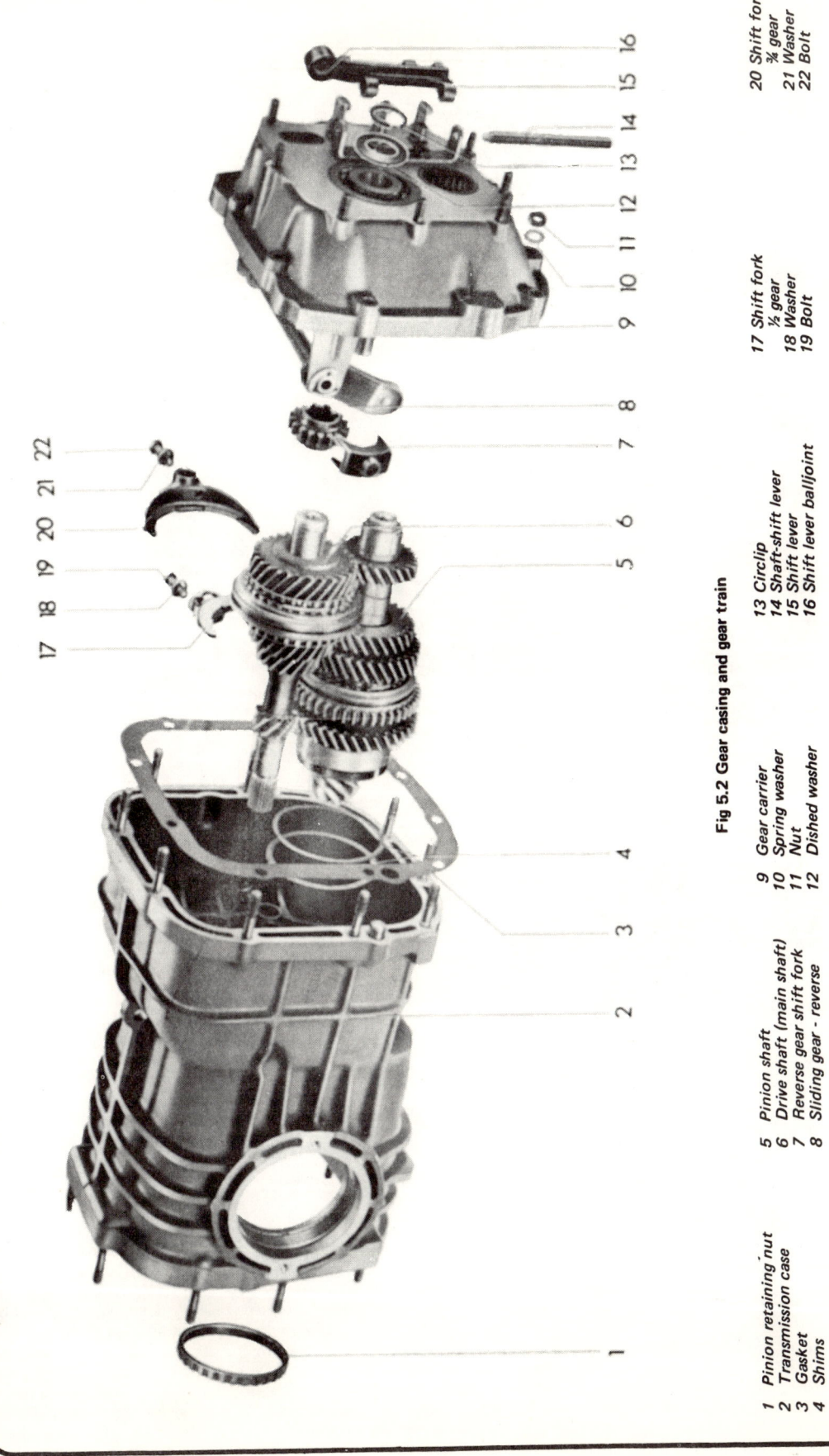

Fig 5.2 Gear casing and gear train

1 Pinion retaining nut
2 Transmission case
3 Gasket
4 Shims

5 Pinion shaft
6 Drive shaft (main shaft)
7 Reverse gear shift fork
8 Sliding gear - reverse

9 Gear carrier
10 Spring washer
11 Nut
12 Dished washer

13 Circlip
14 Shaft-shift lever
15 Shift lever
16 Shift lever balljoint

17 Shift fork ½ gear
18 Washer
19 Bolt

20 Shift fork ¾ gear
21 Washer
22 Bolt

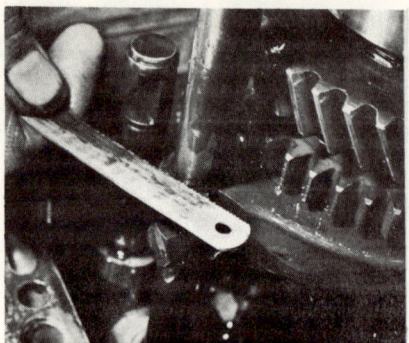
3.14 Mark the position of the selector forks

3.15a Undo the clamping screw completely and remove the selector forks

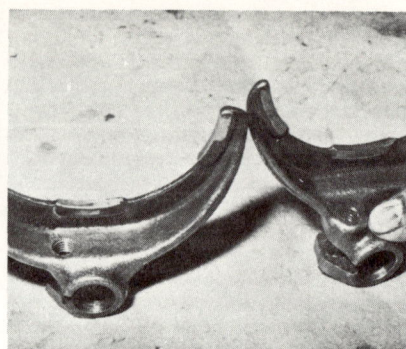
3.15b The selector forks vary in size

3.16a Note the position of the reverse selector cross-shaft before removing it

3.16b The bracket which supports the reverse selector cross-shaft is adjustable and must be marked before removal

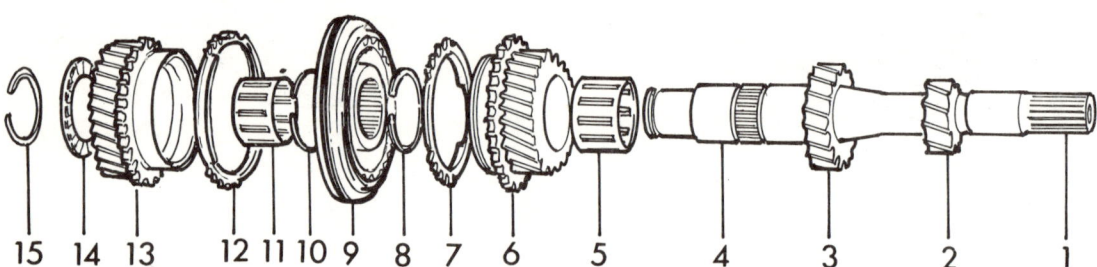

15 14 13 12 11 10 9 8 7 6 5 4 3 2 1

Fig 5.3 Main driveshaft - manual gearbox

1 Splines for reverse gear	5 Needle bearing 3rd gear	9 Synchroniser hub (complete)	3rd/4th gear
2 1st speed gear } One	6 3rd gear	10 Circlip	13 4th gear
3 2nd speed gear } piece	7 Synchronizer ring 3rd/4th	11 Needle bearing 4th	14 Thrust washer 4th
4 Driveshaft front } shaft	gear	gear	gear
	8 Circlip	12 Synchronizer ring	15 Circlip

18 The shafts may now be pressed out of the carrier by pressing on the mainshaft. We do urge that this is done in a press. It can be driven out with a drift but the chances are you will do some damage. **Do not** let the shafts fall or you will chip the gears. It is best to have someone work the press while you lower the gears as the shafts come free.

19 The bearings will remain in the carrier and should not be removed unless suspect. Press out the mainshaft bearing from the inside, using pressure on the outer race only. The pinion shaft bearing is held by a lock bolt, remove this and the bearing may be pressed out from the inside.

20 To dismantle the main driveshaft refer to Fig 5.3. Remove the circlip and slide off the thrust washer, 4th gear, the needle bearing and synchronising ring. Now remove the circlip. This presents problems and it is necessary to fit a new one on re-assembly. VW have a special tool but it can be done with a pair of long-nosed pliers and a little care. Tape the bulk rings and hub together and remove them. Watch which way they go round. There is now another circlip. A new one will be required. Remove the circlip and remove 3rd gear. Expand the split needle cage sufficiently to ease it over the splines if you wish to remove it. Examine the synchro hub and replace if necessary. Consult with the VW storeman if you are in doubt. The larger spring rings 3.071 ins are for the 1/2nd gear clutch assembly, the other

2.913 in diameter are for the 3/4th gear clutch assembly. Do not remove the inner race for 1st gear needle bearing unless necessary. It will need to be warmed to 100°C (212°F) to get it

off and to replace it or replace a new one.
21 Refer to Fig 5.5 and examine the pinion driveshaft. The output (pinion) shaft should only be dismantled to a limited

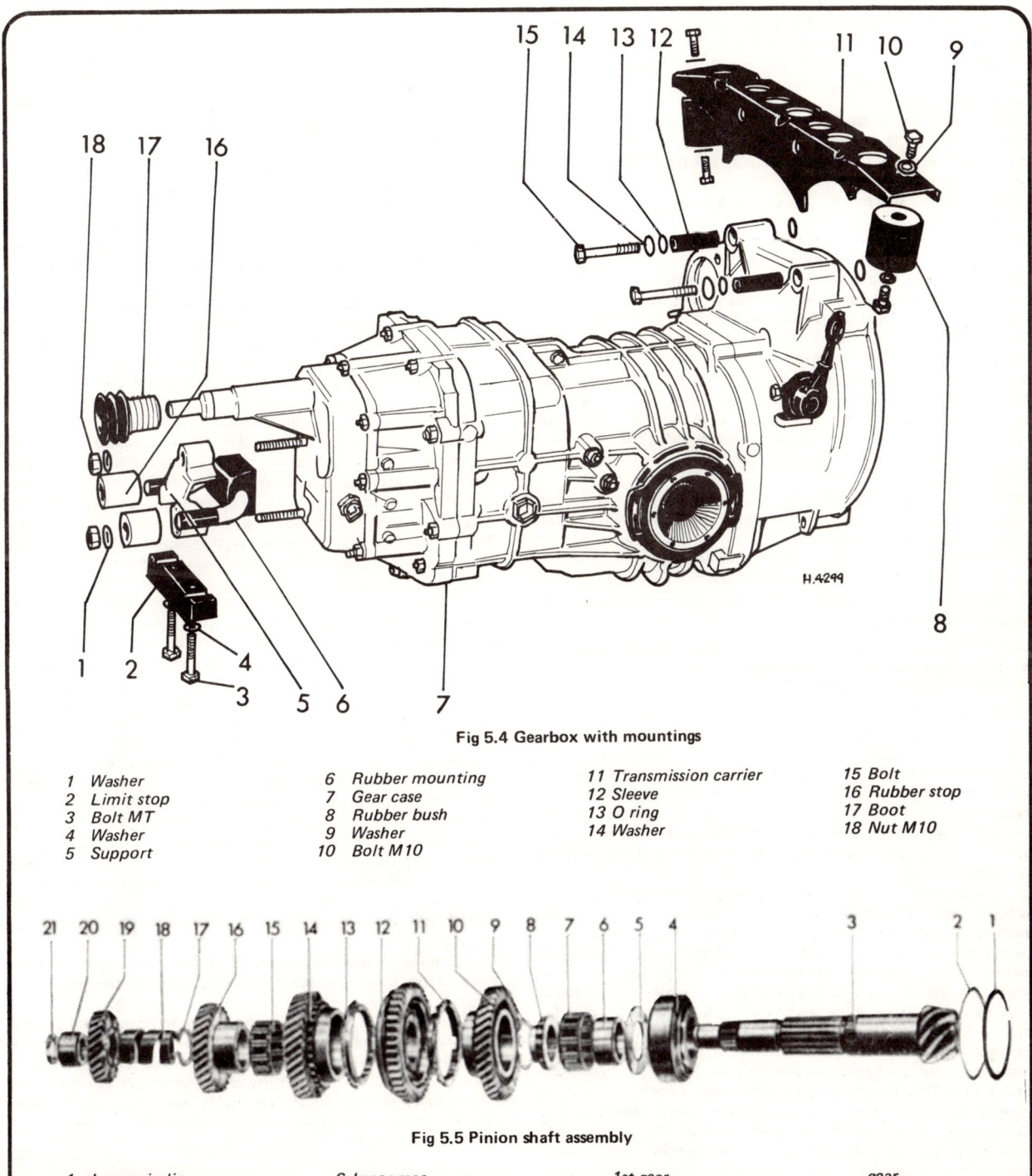

Fig 5.4 Gearbox with mountings

1 Washer	6 Rubber mounting	11 Transmission carrier	15 Bolt
2 Limit stop	7 Gear case	12 Sleeve	16 Rubber stop
3 Bolt MT	8 Rubber bush	13 O ring	17 Boot
4 Washer	9 Washer	14 Washer	18 Nut M10
5 Support	10 Bolt M10		

Fig 5.5 Pinion shaft assembly

1 Large circlip	6 Inner race	1st gear	gear
2 Shim S_3	7 Needle cage 1st gear	12 Synchronizer hub ½ gear	16 3rd gear
3 Pinion	8 Round nut	13 Synchronizer ring 2nd gear	17 Circlip 3rd gear
4 Double tape roller bearing	9 Spacer	14 2nd gear	18 Spacer spring
5 Thrust washer 1st gear	10 1st gear	15 Needle cage 2nd	19 4th gear
	11 Synchronizer ring		20 Inner gear
			21 Circlip

extent - which is sufficient to remove the gears, synchro hub and baulk rings. The pinion double taper roller bearing which is held by the notched locking nut should be left intact as this requires the use of more special tools to which we do not feel most owners will have ready access. The services of a press may be required in order to carry out the partial dismantling necessary to remove the baulk rings although if properly supported to the shaft may be driven out of the synchro hub with a heavy soft faced mallet.

22 First remove the circlip from the end of the shaft. The inner race of the needle bearing together with 4th gear may then be driven or pressed off together. Support the gear and then press or drive out the shaft.

23 Remove the spacer spring and then take off the other circlip round the shaft.

24 Third gear, the roller bearing, 2nd gears and 1st/2nd gear synchro hub and baulk rings may then be taken off in that order.

25 The synchro hub assemblies should be handled with care to prevent them coming apart inadvertently. It is important that if the centre hub and outer sleeve are separated that they be re-fitted in the same relative position. Some hubs have marks etched on each part to aid reassembly, so before anything else examine them on both sides for such marks. If none can be found make some of your own with a small dab of paint to ensure reassembly in the same position. To dismantle the hubs first lift out the spring retaining clip on each side. Then carefully slide the sleeve from the hub taking care not to drop and lose the three sliding keys.

26 Do not remove the selector fork rails from the gear carrier casing unless inspection indicates that there is something wrong with the detent balls and springs.

27 Do not attempt to dismantle the double taper roller from the shaft. If it is faulty then it should be taken to the agent for an exchange shaft. It needs a 3 ton press and a special fixture, among other things.

---

4 Inspection for wear in transmission components

1 As mentioned in the introduction to this Chapter the degree of wear in the components will to a large extent dictate the economics of repair or replacement with a new unit. If the crownwheel and pinion is obviously badly worn, resulting in noise and significant backlash, then it is possible that this may be repaired alone for approximately half the cost of a new unit provided that is the only major complaint. Such work is not within the competence of the average owner and this manual does not cover it.

2 It is possible to remove all baulk rings for examination. The grooved taper face of the ring provides the braking action on the mating face of the gear wheel cone and if the ridges are worn the braking or synchro action will be less effective. The only way to determine the condition effectively is by comparison with new parts. As the parts are relatively cheap it is considered foolish not to renew them all anyway once the gearbox is fully dismantled. As a guide, when a baulk ring is fitted over its cone on the gear wheel there should be a minimum gap of 0.6 mm (0.024 inch) between the baulk ring and the gear teeth. The normal gap is 1.1 mm (0.043 inch) so it is obvious that if the gap is near the lowest limit new rings should be fitted. When obtaining new baulk rings make sure that you get the Parts Store to identify and mark each one according to its appropriate gear. Modifications have taken place and although the new ones will still fit and work they are not necessarily identical to the ones you take out. So if you muddle them up you could get problems. They are also not all the same in the set - some have wider cut-outs for example. So mark the new ones you get carefully.

3 Two types of bearings are fitted - ball and needle roller. As a rule needle roller bearings wear very little, not being subject to end thrust of any sort. Check them in position and if there are signs of roughness then they should be renewed. If any bearing should feel the slightest bit rough or show any sign of drag or slackness when revolved then it should be renewed. The double

taper roller bearing should be similarly checked. If there is any sign of roughness or endfloat then this is a task for a specialist. If this bearing is needing renewal the condition of the pinion gear and crownwheel must be very carefully examined. Once these need renewal then the setting of the whole box is altered and clearances and shims have to be recalculated and changed.

4 The teeth of all gears should be examined for signs of pitted mating surfaces, chips or scoring. It must be appreciated that if one gear is damaged then its mate on the other shaft will probably be as bad and that one way or another a new pair of gears will be required.

5 The synchro hubs should be assembled for checking. It is important that there is no rock or backlash on the splines between the inner hub and outer sleeve. When the baulk rings are being renewed it is good policy to renew the three sliding keys and their locating spring rings as well. The keys fit into the cut-outs in the baulk rings and are subject to wear and the springs weaken with time (see also Section 6).

6 One of the most critical parts of the Volkswagen gearbox is the operation of the selector forks. The two forks run in grooves in the outer sleeves of the synchro hubs and if the clearance of the forks in the grooves is excessive then there is a likelihood of certain gears jumping out. The clearance of the fork in the groove should not exceed 0.3 mm (0.012 inch) (photo). Clearance in excess of the maximum could be due to wear on the fork or in the groove or both. It is best therefore first of all to take the forks along to the spares supplier and ask him to compare their thickness with new ones. If the difference in thickness is not enough to compensate for the excess gap between fork and hub groove then the hub assembly will need replacement as well. This is an expensive item but as the gap is somewhat critical there is no alternative. Much depends on the total degree of wear.

7 The selector rails on which the forks are mounted need not be removed from the casing. A certain force is needed in order that they overcome the pressure of the spring loaded ball in the groove. This can be measured with a spring balance hooked on to the end of each selector rod. If the required pull is significantly outside the range of 15 - 20 kgs (33 - 44 lbs) then it is advisable to check the detent springs and balls. To do this push the selector rods right out of the casing. This will release the ball and spring but to get the springs out it is necessary to prise out the plastic plugs from the drillings opposite. Before doing this make sure you obtain some new plugs to drive in when reassembling. Check the spring free length which should be 25 mm (1 inch). If less than 22 mm they should be changed. The balls should be free from pitting and grooves and the selector rods themselves should not be a sloppy fit in the bores. The detent grooves in the rails should not be worn. When the rails are removed do not lose the interlock plungers which fit between the selector rod grooves.

8 Examine all parts of the casing for signs of cracks or damage, particularly near the bearing housings and on the mating surfaces.

9 It should not normally be necessary to completely wash all the gearbox components in fluid. Wipe components on clean cloth for examination. In this way the likelihood of dry spots during the first moments of use after reassembly are minimised. The casing itself should be thoroughly washed out with paraffin and flushed afterwards with water. Do not leave the needle roller bearings in position when doing this.

---

5 Transmission - assembly - general notes

1 With all the parts cleaned and where necessary new ones obtained it is now time for the good bit. Everything is clear and laid out in an orderly fashion. Plenty of clean non-fluffy rag and an oil can full of clean oil. A clear space on the bench with a clean bench top. Last, but not least, clean hands.

2 Do not hurry, work methodically and as each stage is complete stop and check it over.

3 First of all assemble the mainshaft; set it on one side and

assemble the pinion shaft. Next assemble the bearings and reverse gear to the main casing. Fit the bearings to the carrier and then the two shafts and selector forks to the carrier.

4 The carrier and shafts must now be installed in the main casing and secured. Then comes the selector levers and cover.

5 When this is all done the differential must be installed and the bearings secured. The flanges are then fitted. Finally the reverse gear and the other half of the driveshaft and the clutch housing.

6 It sounds an awful lot but we did it in a morning and we stopped to argue and take pictures. But against that, it wasn't the first VW box we had assembled.

5A Input shaft - assembly

1 Refer to Figure 5.3. Lay the shaft and gears on the bench in the correct order. Install the needle roller cage for 3rd gear then 3rd gear with its matching synchro ring onto the bearings with the cone towards the front end of the shaft.

2 Next install a new circlip and squeeze it so that there is no radial play.

3 The 3rd/4th gear synchro hub goes on next. This has to line-up with the key on the shaft. There are three very important points to note when doing this. Make sure that the hub is on the right way round - some models have a groove in the outer sleeve 1 mm deep and this must be towards the 4th gear. If there is no indication then you may put the hub on either way round. Secondly, make sure that you only drive the centre part of the hub. Otherwise it will come apart and have to be reassembled. Thirdly, the slots in the baulk ring must be lined up with the keys in the hub. This is best done by someone holding the baulk ring in position with the keys whilst the hub is driven on the final amount. Be careful not to trap any fingers!

4 Now fit the second circlip and then needle race for fourth gear and the baulk ring and 4th gear; finally the thrust washer, and then set the shaft aside in a clean safe place.

5B Pinion shaft - assembly

1 As pointed out earlier, the pinion shaft has been dismantled only as far as the pinion bearing which has been left in position (photo). If this bearing has been renewed then the gearbox and final drive will need resetting and this is a skilled job requiring special equipment and a selection of special shims to hand from which the necessary requirements are available.

2 The first 'loose' item therefore which goes behind the pinion is the shim (if any) controlling endfloat. The endfloat is measured by a feeler gauge after the 1st gear and synchro hub have been fitted. The measurement is between the face of the gear and the thrust washer which is locked in front of the pinion taper roller bearing. The measurement range is from 0.10 - 0.25

mm (0.004 - 0.010 ins).

3 If the gap is outside this range then the shims must be altered to suit.

4 Now put 1st gear (the largest one with helically cut teeth) in position on the needle roller bearings with the cone face of the synchro pointing away from the pinion gear. (photo)

5 Select the 1st gear baulk ring and place it over 1st gear and then replace the 1st and 2nd gear hub over the splines on the shaft with the selector fork groove of the outer sleeve facing towards the front end of the shaft (photo). Make sure that the three cut-outs in the synchro ring engage with the sliding keys in the hub before pushing the hub fully home. Remember that the baulk rings for 1st and 2nd gears are slightly different. The 1st gear ring has narrower cut-outs than those in the 2nd gear ring.

6 Now check the 1st gear endfloat as mentioned in paragraph 2.

7 Put the 2nd gear baulk ring in position in the hub so that the slots engage with the sliding keys.

8 Replace 2nd gear with the cone towards the hub (photo).

9 Third gear, which has a large bearing boss integral with it, should now be replaced with the needle roller bearing which fits together with 3rd gear, inside 2nd gear. (photo)

10 Next fit the circlip on the shaft retaining third gear in position. (photo)

11 The clearance between this gear and the circlip should be 0.10 - 0.25 mm (0.004 - 0.010 ins.) If the gap is outside this range then a circlip of different thickness is necessary to correct it.

12 Next fit the spacer spring, 4th gear and the inner race of the roller bearing. (photo)

13 It may be necessary to heat the inner race in boiling water to get it to slide on easily. Drive it down against the drive pinion.

14 When the race is nearly in position put the circlip in place and drive that on with the race until it fits in its groove. (photo)

5C Main casing - installing bearings and reverse gearshaft

1 There have been two modifications to the reverse gear shaft since the 1700cc engine was fitted. Both are illustrated (Figs. 5.7 and 5.8). The new parts may be installed in vehicles built with the 1700/1800 cc engine if the occasion demands.

2 To assemble the main casing components first drive in the mainshaft roller bearing and fit two new circlips one at each end. Be careful to drive only on the outer part of the bearing.

3 Fit a circlip (lock-ring) to the end of the reverse shaft bearing and drive the clip and bearing into the casing until the clip touches the transmission casing. Now install the other circlip.

4 Fit the shaft and gear, install the concave washer and fit the circlip in place. (photos)

5 The pinion shaft bearing is on the pinion shaft and is fitted with the shaft (Section 5F).

4.6 Checking the clearance of the fork in the groove

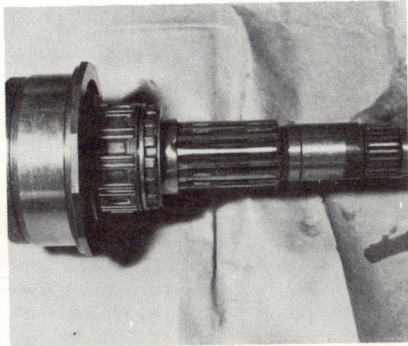
5.B1 The pinion shaft assembly

5.B4 Fitting 1st gear on the pinion shaft

5B.5 Fitting 1/2nd gear clutch hub

5B.8 Fitting 2nd gear and baulk ring

5B.9 Fitting 3rd gear and roller bearing

5B.10 Fit 3rd gear retaining circlip

5B.12 Fit the spacer ring, 4th gear and the inner bearing race

5B.14 Driving on the bearing race and circlip

Fig 5.6 Main casing - bearing and reverse gear shaft (Sec 5c)

1 Casing
2 Circlip
3 Reverse drive gear
4 Needle bearing driveshaft
5 Circlip
6 Needle bearing reverse shaft
7 Spacer sleeve
8 Locking screw
9 Thrust washer
10 Woodruff key
11 Reverse gear shaft
12 Oil filler and level plug

Note. Two different types of reverse gear have been fitted and the one shown above discontinued. See Figs 5.7 and 5.8

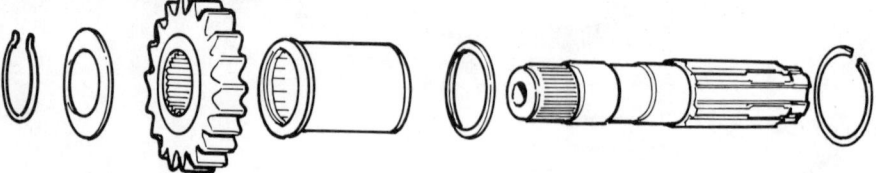

Fig 5.7 Reverse gear - 1972 (Sec 5c)

H.4300

The gear and spacer have been modified as shown. This has been superceded again in 1973 (See Figs 5.6 and 5.8)

5D Gear carrier - fitting bearings

1 The needle roller bearing for the front end of the pinion shaft should be fitted first. Line-up the recess in the bearing (photo) so that the locking screw will engage in it, tap the bearing into position and fit the locking screw, torque it to 11 lb ft.
2 The mainshaft bearing has a flange on it. Press this into the carrier, using pressure on the outer race only, until the flange fits onto the carrier. (photo)

5E Gear carrier - fitting shafts and selector forks

1 It is assumed that the selector rails are in order (see Section 4, paragraph 7) and the forks are a correct fit in the hub sleeve grooves (Section 4, paragraph 6).
2 Holding both shafts together put them into the bearings. (photos)
3 The pinion shaft will once again be the problem as it is a tight fit in the bearing and will require driving on with a suitable tubular drift.
4 When both shafts are in position the dished washer and circlip should be refitted to the pinion shaft using another suitable tubular drift to drive the circlip on. Make sure it seats completely in its groove. (photos)
5 Next assemble the selector forks to the correct rails making sure that they are lined up with the marks made (photo 3.14). The flats on the rails should also be in line with the clamp bolt holes. (photo).
6 Reassemble the cross-shaft brackets and the relay lever and post for reverse gear selector (photo). Do not omit the wave

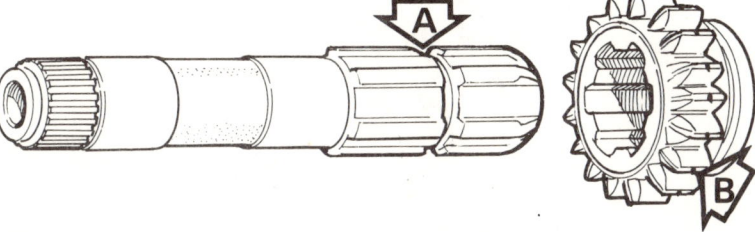

Fig 5.8 Reverse gear - 1973 Onwards

The gear has been modified by cutting a trapeze shaped groove (A). The modified gear and shaft may be fitted to models built since November 1972. The new gear has a groove in the teeth (B).

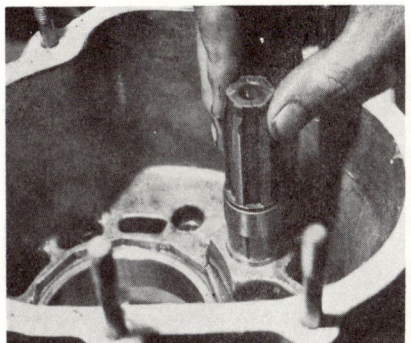

5C.4a Installing reverse gear driveshaft

5C.4b Fitting the gear and circlip

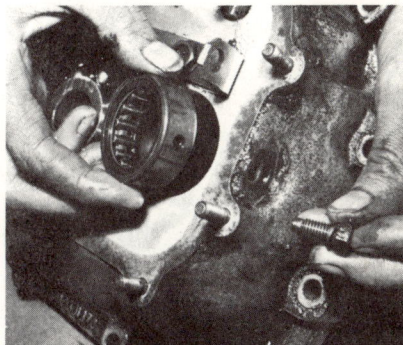

5D.1 Fitting the needle bearing and lock bolt for the pinion shaft

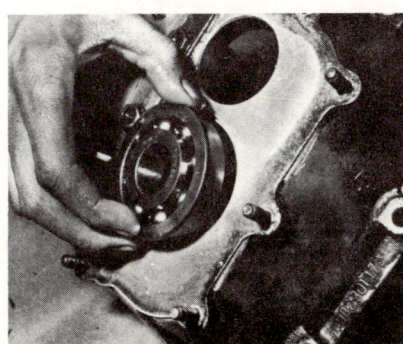

5D.2 Fitting the ball bearing with flange for the mainshaft

5E.2a Replacing the shafts in the bearings

5E.2b The shafts in position

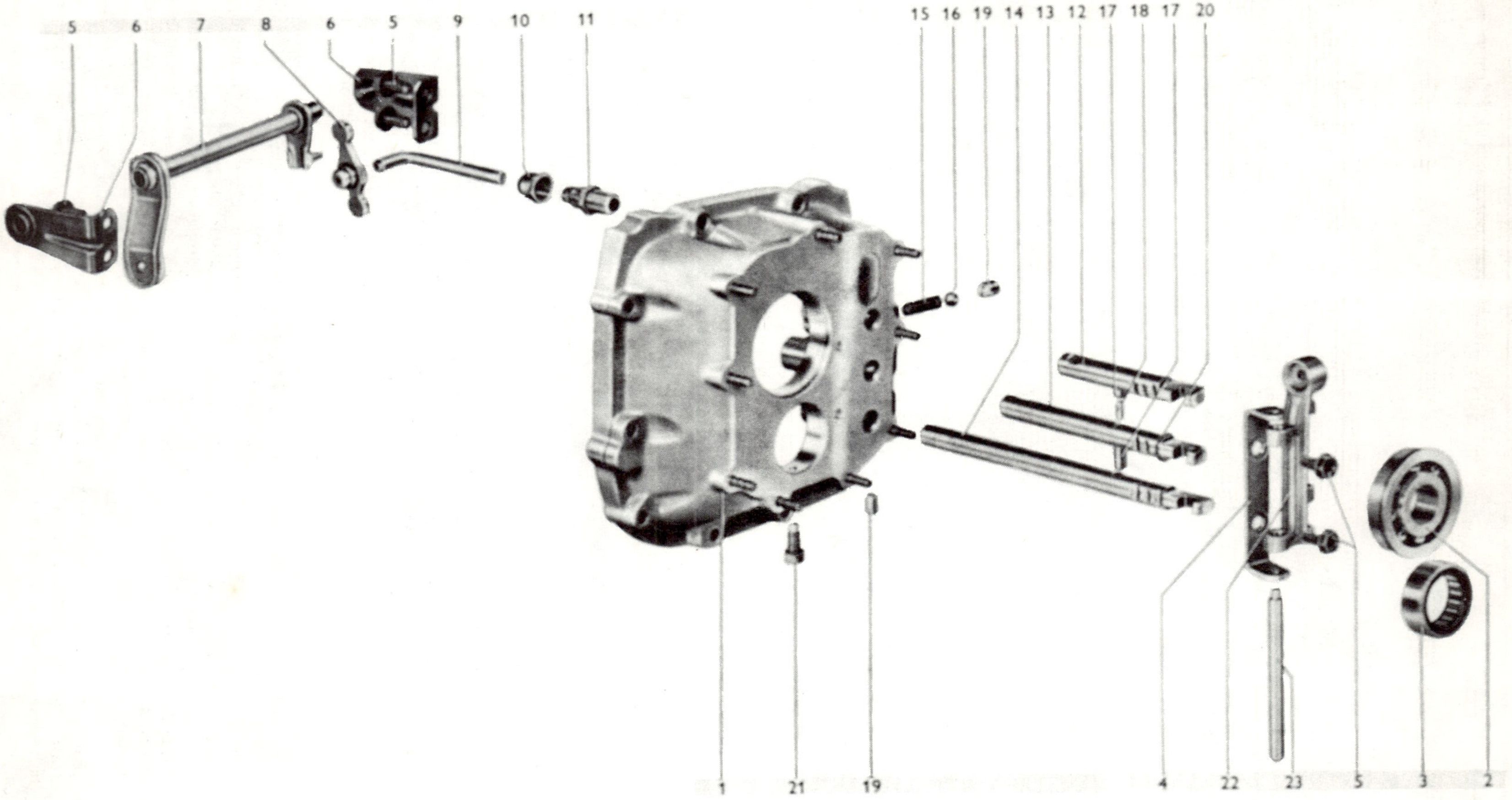

Fig 5.9 Gear carrier and selector levers - components

1 Gear carrier
2 Bearing driveshaft
3 Needle bearing -
  pinion shaft
4 Support - shift lever

5 Screw
6 Bracket - relay shaft
7 Relay shaft
8 Reverse lever
9 Support

10 Union nut
11 Clamp sleeve
12 Selector rail -
   3rd/4th gear

13 Selector rail - reverse
14 Selector rail -
   1st/2nd gear
15 Detent spring

16 Detent ball
17 Interlock plunger
18 Intermediate plunger
19 Plug

20 Circlip
21 Lock bolt
22 Shift lever
23 Shift lever spindle

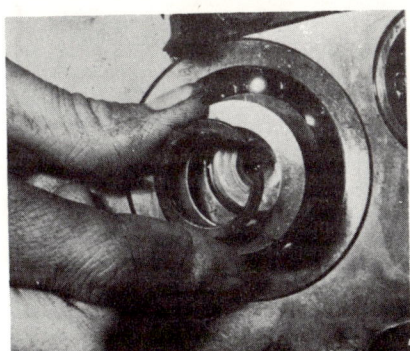

5E.4a Fit the dished washer and circlip

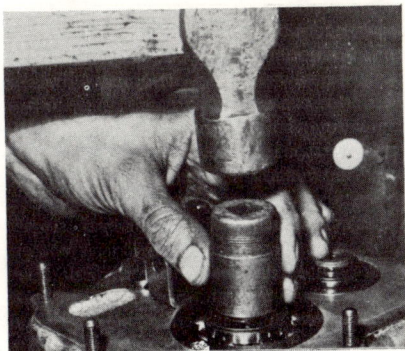

5E.4b Drive home the circlip onto the pinion shaft

5E.5 Assemble the forks to the correct rails

5E.6a The cross shaft brackets, relay lever and posts for reverse gear

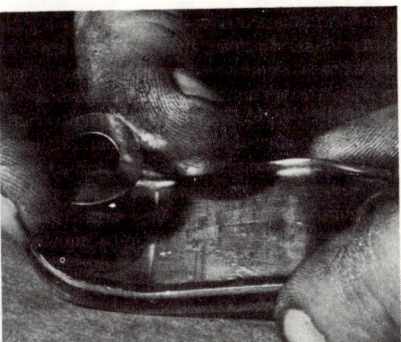

5E.6b Do not omit the wave washer on the bracket

5E.11a Assemble reverse gear sliding yoke and gear

washer on the bracket (photo). Once again the line up marks must be correctly set.

7 The selector forks setting is critical. If the wear between the fork and groove is outside the limit the possibility of a gear not being fully engaged and jumping out is increased. If you can get the unit set up in a Volkswagen agent's jig you would be well advised to do so.

8 Provided you have clearly marked the fork positions on the rails there need be no difficulty either although if new forks or hubs have been fitted the markings may no longer apply.

9 If you have no marks and no jig facility handy proceed as follows: Start with the forks loose on the rails. Set all three selector rails in the neutral position, which is when the cut-outs in their ends all line up, and set the synchro hub outer sleeves also in neutral with the forks in position. Then tighten the fork clamp bolts sufficiently to prevent them slipping. Now push each selector in turn so that each gear is fully engaged. The outer sleeve of the appropriate synchro hub must move fully over the dogs of the baulk ring and gear in question. In each gear selected the fork must not bind in the groove. If difficulty is experienced in engaging a gear slacken the fork clamp nut and get the synchro hub sleeve fully into mesh and then retighten the fork clamp in position. Then move the selector back to neutral and into the opposite gear position. In all three positions there must be no semblance of pressure in either direction from the fork on to the groove in which it runs. When both forward speed selector forks have been correctly set tighten the clamp bolts to 18 ft lbs/2.5 mkg.

10 The sliding reverse gear and yoke can be attached to the relay lever next for setting purposes. It will tend to fall out of position because it is finally held by the reverse gear shaft in the main transmission casing.

11 To set this pinion first engage 2nd gear. Hold the pinion square and in this position; it should be lined up midway between the straight cut teeth on the synchro sleeve and the helical teeth

of 2nd gear on the input shaft (photo). Then move out of 2nd gear and shift into reverse. The reverse gears should mesh completely. Adjustment for this setting is by moving the relay lever post up or down. (photo)

5F Gear carrier and shafts - assembly into casing

1 The main casing already has the mainshaft bearing and the reverse gear in place (Section 5C).

2 Set the casing in a vertical position and finally clean off all traces of the old gasket making sure none of the bits drop inside. Smear the joint face with a thin film of jointing compound and fit a new gasket. (photos)

3 The reverse sliding gear is a loose fit in its yoke and must be checked carefully. The chamfered ends of the teeth must face the square cut teeth ends of the gear hub and the gear must sit squarely in position. (photo)

4 It is best to have two people for the next operation. Lift the carrier and shafts and lower it carefully onto the main casing (photo). Guide the reverse sliding gear over the shaft in the casing. It may be necessary to hold the shafts and juggle the gear with a screwdriver to do this (photo).

5 Once the carrier is firmly on the studs and seated replace the nuts hand-tight. Unless the twelve sided bearing is seated this cannot be done, so do not force things. The purpose of the twelve sided flange is to hold the bearing while the nut is being tightened from outside to anchor the pinion shaft. Once you are satisfied all is in the correct place turn the casing so that the whole sits on the carrier. You will need packing to make things firm.

6 Once again we come to the hard bit. If you have VW Tool 381/14 then all is well; if you have not then you will have to use the method you used to get the pinion bearing nut undone, only this time a torque wrench must be used as well.

5E.11b Adjustment by moving the relay lever post up and down

5F.2a Smear a thin film of jointing compound on the casing mating face ...

5F.2b .. and fit a new gasket

5F.3 Fit reverse gear sliding gear firmly in its yoke

5F.4a Lower the shafts and carrier into the main casing

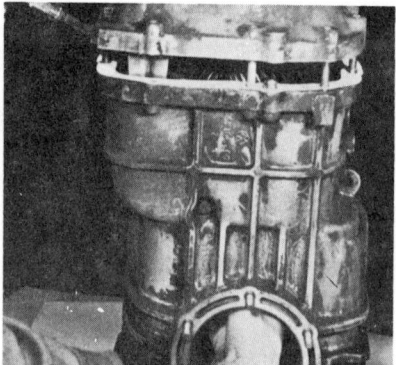
5F.4b It may be necessary to juggle the gear with a screwdriver to get reverse gear onto its shaft

5G.1a Reassemble the selector bar and pin

5G.1b Fit a new gasket to the carrier facing

5G.2a Engage the change lever into the balljoint of the selector bars and ...

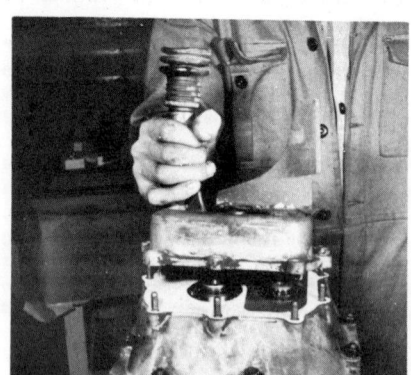
5G.2b ... fit the selector cover into position

5H.2a Fit the oil seal to the adjusting ring and ...

5H.2b ... the oil ring

7 Install the same thickness of shims as were taken out. Fig. 5.2 shows the shims inside the casing. They are, of course between the nut and the bearing. If these are not fitted correctly the mesh of the crownwheel and pinion will be altered. If a new bearing has been fitted then the mesh will not be correct and the box must be taken to the agent to get this job done properly.

8 Fit a new nut, using VW tool 381/14 torque the nut to 160 ft lb, back the nut off a little and re-torque it to 160 ft lbs to make sure the bearing is seated, then using a peening tool with a 40° vee edge, peen the nut into the recess in the bearing thread.

9 Reverse the box and tighten the carrier nuts to 14 lb ft.

5G Gear selector levers and cover - reassembly

1 Reassemble the selector bar and pin (photo), (it will only fit one way round) and place a new gasket in position on the carrier casing (photo).

2 Engage the change lever into the ball joint in the selector bar and fit the selector cover in position (photos).

3 It is a good idea at this stage to select all gears in turn and make sure that the shafts turn freely in all gears.

5H Final Drive and bearings - replacement

1 The adjusting rings should have been marked 'L' or 'R' and the number of turns they go in noted. It is assumed that the differential has not been dismantled. If this has been done then the resetting of the pinion and crownwheel is beyond the scope of the owner because he does not have the necessary gauges and the whole box must go to the agent to be set correctly. However, if the differential has not been dismantled the job can be done.

2 Prise out the old oil seal from the adjusting ring and fit a new one (photo). Do not drive it right home, it should be flush with the inner surface of the adjusting ring. Fit also a new oil ring to the adjusting ring (photo). Repeat for the other adjusting ring.

3 Fit the differential into the housing. This is a tricky job so mind your fingers. It will only go one way. There are thrust rings on the shafts between the bearing and the adjusting ring; see that they go back correctly.

there are thrust rings on the shafts between the bearing and the adjusting ring see that they go back correctly.

4 Screw in one adjusting ring to the exact position it was in before it was taken out (count the turns and set the marks). If you do not have VW tool 231/15 use the lockplate as a spanner. Coat the thread for the amount it goes into the casing with moly kote or a suitable substitute. (photo)

5 Now ease the differential taper roller into the adjusting ring and holding it in position turn the casing so that the differential sits in the adjusting ring squarely.

6 Coat the thread of the other adjusting ring and screw it in so that it takes up the taper roller of the differential. Screw it home until the right number of turns have gone in and the markings on the ring and housing coincide. This all sounds very easy, and it is if you have Tool 231/15, but it isn't if you do not.

We tried all sorts of improvisation. The locking plate pushed securely into the adjusting ring will act as a spanner until the preloading is felt. After that things become hard. We even used a pair of round nosed tinsnips pushed into the serrations and held open, and of course it can always be tapped with a soft drift.

It is a good idea to screw both adjusting rings in and out before you put the differential in place. This will tell you whether the thread is damaged or dirty and suitable remedies may be applied before you struggle.

However, it can be coaxed home even without the special tool but it is much easier with the tool. Once both rings are home check the marking again and then fit the rubber washer, nylon piece (if there is one) the locking flange and bolt. Fit the flange and the circlip and finally the plastic cap. (photos) Do this for both sides.

7 Replace the reverse gear/sleeve onto the input shaft. (photo) The input shaft extension section should have the circlip in position behind the groove and the threaded stud should be

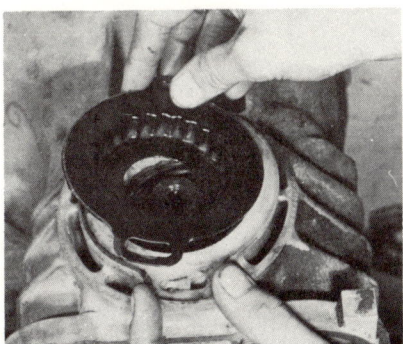
5H.4 Screw it into the housing

5H.6a Fit the rubber washer ..

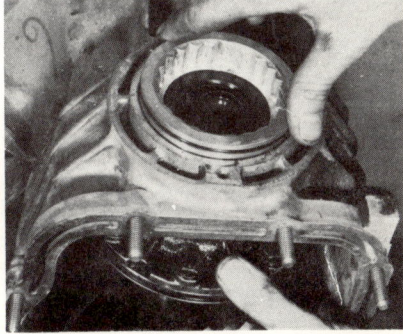
5H.6b ... the nylon packing piece and the locking flange

5H.6c Fit the flange ...

5H.6d ... and circlip

5H.6e ... and the plastic cap

screwed into the end.

8   Line up the extension shaft with the gear/sleeve (photo) and draw the sleeve back on to the extension. (You cannot get the extension and gear in position any other way).

9   Screw the extension shaft home and then back it off a fraction until the gear slides forward.

10 Refit the retaining circlip in its groove. (photo)

11 Replace the clutch housing using a new seal and torque the bolts to 14 lb ft (photos).

6   Synchromesh hub assemblies - dismantling, inspection, renewal reassembly

1   Unless the transmission is the victim of neglect or misuse, or has covered very high mileages, the synchro hub assemblies do not normally need replacement. Until recently they could only be replaced as complete assemblies but it should be possible to obtain the inner or outer section as required.

2   When synchro baulk rings are being renewed it is advisable to fit new blocker bars (sliding keys) and retaining springs in the hubs as this will ensure that full advantage is taken of the new, unworn cut-outs in the rings.

3   When a synchro hub is dismantled, intentionally or accidentally, there are some basic essentials to remember:

a) The splines of both parts wear into each other and provided neither is worn too far they should be kept matched if possible.

b) Where the three sliding keys fit there is a recess in the centre of the spline on the outer sleeve (photo). It is essential, for correct operation, that these be lined up.

c) Make sure that the sliding key retainer clips overlap on each side so that no key has the ends of both clips over it.

4   When examining for wear there are two important features to look at:

a) The fit of the splines. With the keys removed, the inner and outer sections of the hub should slide easily with minimum backlash or axial rock. The degree of permissible wear is difficult to describe in absolute terms. No movement at all is exceptional yet excessive 'stop' would affect operation and cause jumping out of gear. Ask someone with experience for advice. If a new part is being fitted to a worn part check the fit in each of the possible positions radially and also either way round to find the point of minimum play.

b) Selector fork grooves and selector forks should not exceed the maximum permissible clearance of 0.3 mm (0.012 inch). The wear can be on either the fork or groove so it is best to try a new fork in the existing sleeve first to see if the gap is reduced adequately. If not, then a new sleeve is needed. Too much slack between fork and groove induces jumping out of gear. Where a hub also carries gear teeth on the outer sleeve these should, of course, be in good condition - unbroken and not pitted or scored.

7   Input shaft oil seal - renewal

1   It is possible that clutch contamination may be caused by failure of the oil seal that goes round the input shaft in the clutch housing. During the course of transmission overhaul it would be automatically renewed but it is possible to fit a new one with the transmission installed. The engine must be removed first.

2   With the engine removed detach the clutch release bearing from the operating forks and remove the sleeve from round the input shaft by undoing the three nuts.

3   The seal surrounds the input shaft where it goes through the casing. It can be dug out with a sharp pointed instrument provided care is taken to avoid damaging the surrounding part of the transmission casing.

4   Behind the seal is a further detachable sleeve with an oil

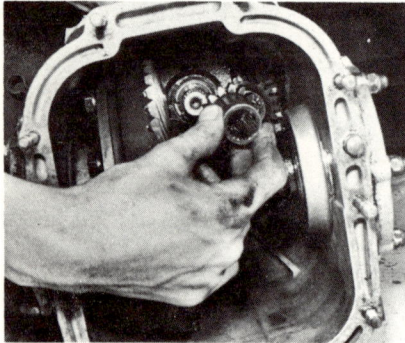
5H.7 Replace the reverse gear sleeve onto the input shaft

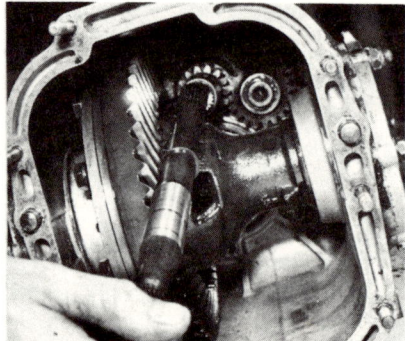
5H.8 Fit the extension shaft

5H.10 Refit the circlip

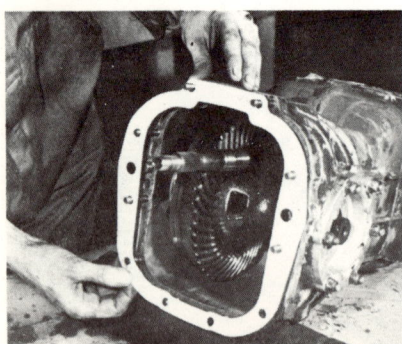
5H.11a Fit a new gasket

5H.11b and replace the clutch housing

6.3b The indented splines in the sleeve must line up with the sliding keys.

return scroll in it and this too should be renewed.

5 Fit the new oil return sleeve and then the seal. Be careful not to damage the lip when passing it over the splines of the shaft and make sure it does not turn back when it reaches the part of the shaft on which it bears.

6 It should be driven into position squarely and a piece of tube is ideal for this put round the shaft (photo). If the seal should tip in the early stages of being driven in take it out and start again. Otherwise it may be badly distorted and its life will be shortened considerably.

7 The seal should be driven in until the outer shoulder abuts the casing.

8 Differential

1 The differential gear contained in the differential casing is not normally a do-it-yourself repair job. This is because failure is extremely rare and in circumstances of extreme wear as a result

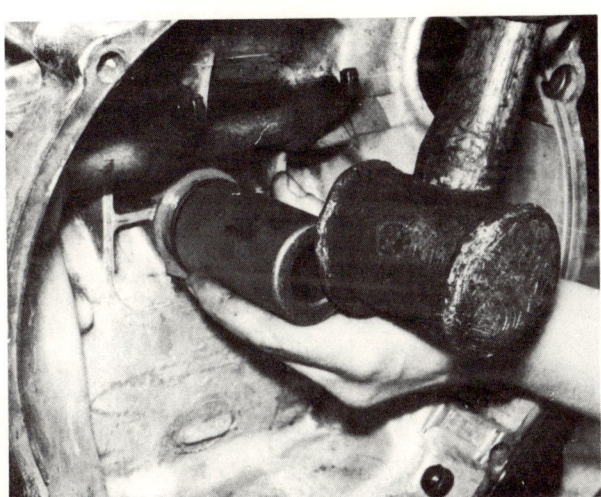

7.6 Driving a new seal into position

of either neglect or high mileages the whole assembly would need to be renewed anyway.

2 The function of the differential is to enable the driven wheels of the vehicle to rotate at different speeds when the car is turning and the outer wheel is obliged to travel in a wider arc than the inner wheel. Each drive shaft has a bevel gear at the inner end and these are meshed constantly together with two bevel pinions. The shaft on which both pinions are mounted is fixed into the differential casing.

3 The crownwheel, which takes the drive from the gearbox, is bolted to the differential casing. When the drive rotates the differential casing, the pinion shaft is carried round with it and the pinion gears therefore rotate the drive shaft gears.

4 If either drive shaft is slowed down, or stopped completely, the differential pinions rotate on their own shaft due to the speed difference between the drive shafts.

5 Under such circumstances the power must be transmitted through the shaft offering least resistance. In cornering this would be the outer wheel. When you have one wheel in a ditch the power always goes to that wheel!

9 Limited slip differential (plate type)

A limited slip differential is fitted to vehicles where the terrain they have to cover requires both drive wheels to be able to give simultaneous traction.

The side gears are connected by a friction type 'clutch' to the casing under moderate spring pressure. When the differential is called upon to function, such as when going round a corner on normal roads, the 'clutch' will slip and permit the normal differential operation between the two drive shafts. This is not the case however, if power is applied. When the differential is in operation and power is imparted, there is a tendency for the pinion and side gears to separate. This forces the covers tighter onto the casing and locks the differential. On the plate type there are two sets of pinion gears. The shafts of these are located in grooves between pressure rings. When the differential forces occur the shafts ride up in the grooves and apply the pressure without reducing the mesh depth of the pinion and side gear teeth as happens on the cone type.

It should be understood that vehicles fitted with limited slip differential have unusual handling characteristics on hard surfaced roads and their cornering reactions take some getting used

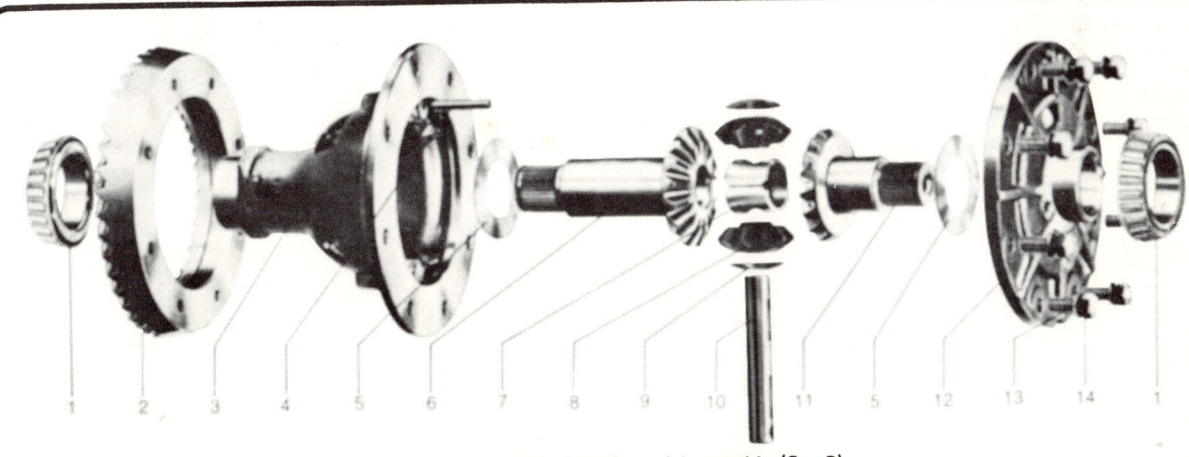

Fig 5.10 Differential assembly (Sec 8)

1 Taper roller side bearing	4 Shaft retaining pin	7 Spacer sleeve	drive shaft, short
2 Crown wheel (ring gear)	5 Thrust washer	8 Differential pinion	12 Housing end cover
3 Differential housing	6 Differential gear and driveshaft	9 Thrust washer	13 Bolt with spring washer
		10 Pinion shaft	
		11 Differential gear and	

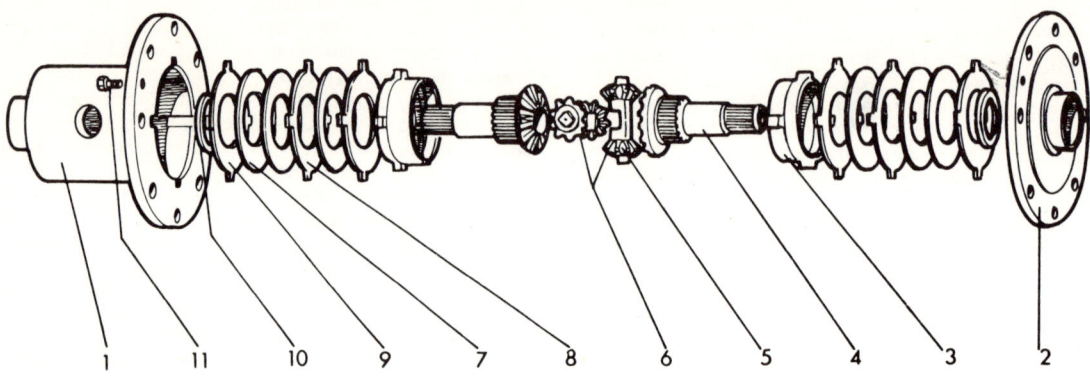

Fig 5.11 Limited-slip differential - plate type (Sec 9)

1 *Housing*
2 *Housing end plate*
3 *Pressure ring*
4 *Differential side gear*
5 *Pinion spindle*
6 *Differential pinions*
7 *Inner splined plates*
8 *Outer splined plates*
9 *Dished outer splined plates*
10 *Thrust washer*
11 *Socket head cap screw*

to. The locking mechanism will operate on sharp turns if much power is used and this can have disconcerting effects.

A further point regarding vehicles fitted with limited slip differentials is that the differentials wear out more quickly. In all conditions where there is a difference between the driving wheel speeds the friction plates are working against each other to a certain extent. Thus their surfaces are subject to frictional wear.

Special oil is required for transmissions fitted with limited slip differential.

10 Gearchange lever and linkage

1 The change lever and connecting rods are of necessity long. The rod joints and bushes may wear after considerable mileage and when they become sloppy the changing of gears may be difficult as a result.

2 The gear lever can be adjusted to provide the proper engagement of gears after either the transmission or change lever mechanism has been disturbed.

When the lever is in 2nd gear position it should be exactly vertical with the cranked upper section inclined at about 30° to the rear.

Sideways movement measured at the lever knob, with a gear engaged should not exceed 35 mm. In neutral it should not exceed 70 mm. If it is more than this it indicates that there is excessive wear in the linkage somewhere.

3 Adjustments can be made to the gear lever position by slackening the two bolts in the mounting bracket at its base. Engage second gear first and then loosen the bolts. Depress the clutch pedal and then align the lever into the correct position. Under the bracket there is a stop plate (for reverse gear). Push this to the left until it touches the shoulder on the lever but does not move the lever. Tighten the mounting bolts. Move the lever to first gear. The line of movement should be exactly longitudinal, without any tendency to move diagonally. If there is diagonal movement loosen the bolts again and turn the stop plate a little to correct it. Later models have lugs on the stop plate to avoid this misalignment possibility.

4 To remove the front section of the shift rod is not difficult but the rear section requires the gearbox to be removed first because the rod can only be taken out from the rear.

To remove the front section remove the under tray, undo the square headed locking screw on the muff coupling and then draw the muff back. The front section of rod can then be drawn off

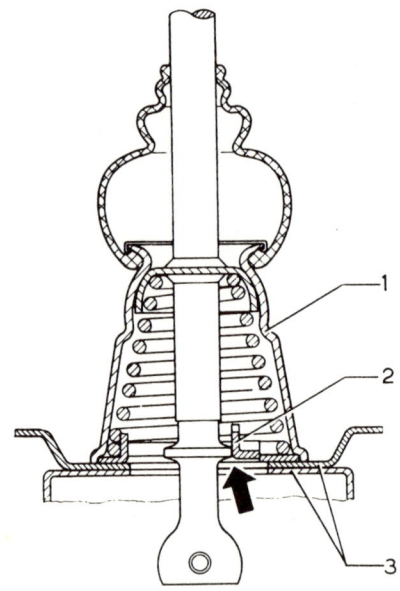

Fig 5.12 Gear lever - lateral cross section (Sec 10)

1 *Mounting bracket*
2 *Stop plate*
3 *Floor panel*
Arrow indicates lever shoulder against the stop plate in 2nd gear position

the front mounting pin. The guide sleeve at the front end can be renewed. Use molybdenum grease (Castrol MS3) for lubrication. With the gearbox removed the rear section can be drawn out complete with the coupling once the front bellows have been taken off and both couplings disconnected. The bushes on the rod and the inserts in the coupling can be renewed as required.

5 From chassis No. '211 2041 707' a new stop-plate with lugs is fitted and a cutout in the bracket slides into the lugs to provide more positive location.

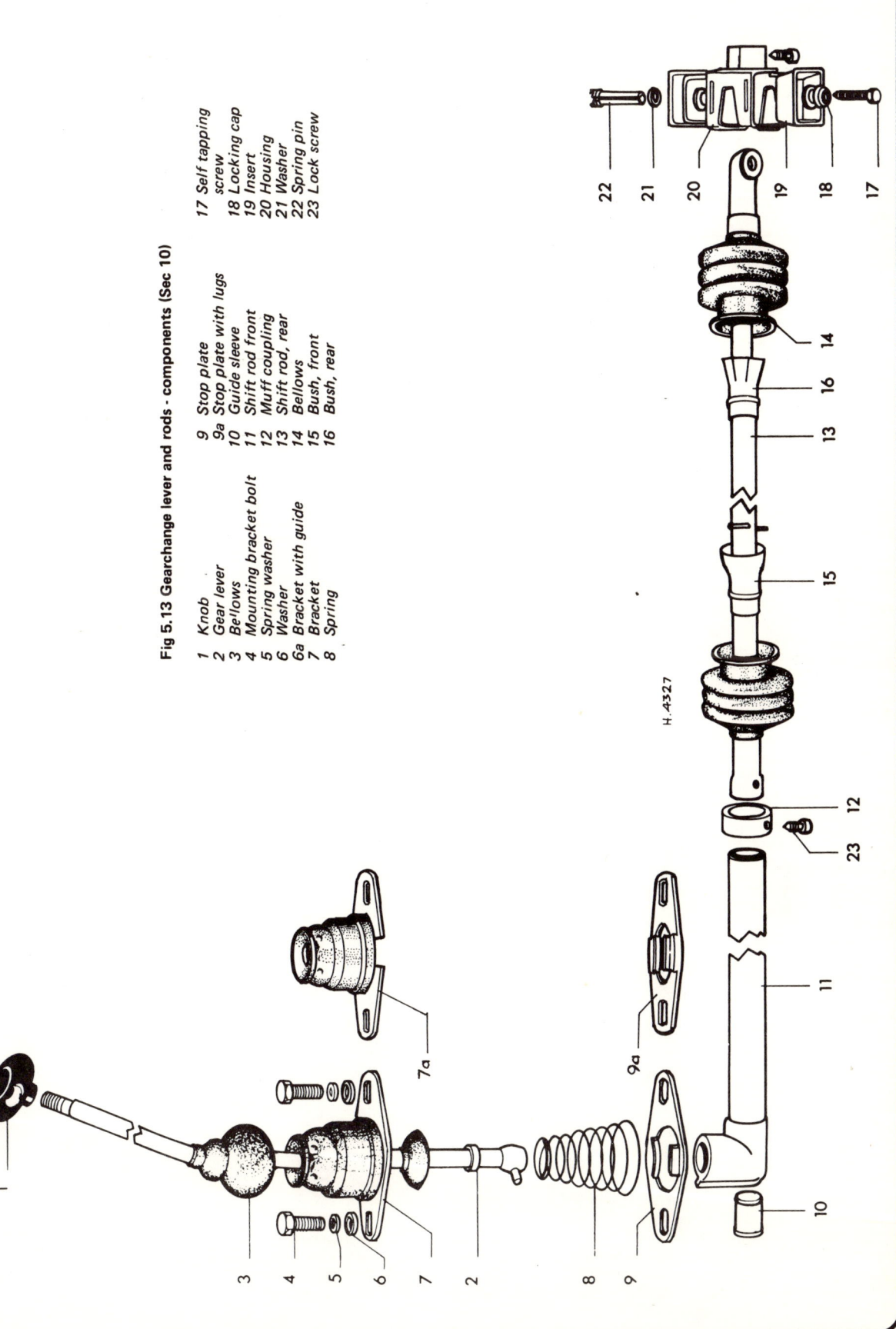

Fig 5.13 Gearchange lever and rods - components (Sec 10)

1	Knob	9	Stop plate
2	Gear lever	9a	Stop plate with lugs
3	Bellows	10	Guide sleeve
4	Mounting bracket bolt	11	Shift rod front
5	Spring washer	12	Muff coupling
6	Washer	13	Shift rod, rear
6a	Bracket with guide	14	Bellows
7	Bracket	15	Bush, front
8	Spring	16	Bush, rear

17 Self tapping screw
18 Locking cap
19 Insert
20 Housing
21 Washer
22 Spring pin
23 Lock screw

H.4327

11 Fault diagnosis - manual gearbox

It is sometimes difficult to decide whether it is worthwhile removing and dismantling the gearbox for a fault which may be nothing more than a minor irritant. Gearboxes which howl, or where the synchromesh can be 'beaten' by a quick gearchange, may continue to perform for a long time in this state. A worn gearbox usually needs a complete rebuild to eliminate noise because the various gears, if re-aligned on new bearings, will continue to howl when different wearing surfaces are presented to each other.

The decision to overhaul therefore, must be considered with regard to time and money available, relative to the degree of noise or malfunction that the driver has to suffer.

Symptom	Reason/s	Remedy
Ineffective synchromesh	Worn baulk rings or synchro hubs	Remedy.
Jumps out of one or more gears (on drive or over-run)	Weak detent springs, worn selector forks, worn synchro hubs or all three	Dismantle and renew.
Noisy, rough, whining and vibration	Worn bearings, (initially) resulting in extended wear generally due to play and backlash	Dismantle and renew.
Noisy and difficult engagement of gear	Clutch fault	Examine clutch operation.

Chapter 6 Automatic transmission

Contents

Specifications

Type	... ...	Torque converter driving a shaft which operates an oil pump and planetary 3 speed and reverse epicyclic gear train. The final drive (differential) is between the geartrain and the torque converter.

Gear Ratios

	1700 cc Engine	1800 cc Engine
Final drive ratios:		
Teeth	11 : 49	11 : 48
Ratio	1 : 4.45	1 : 4.36
Gear Ratios:		
1st	1 : 2.65	1 : 2.65
2nd	1 : 1.59	1 : 1.59
3rd	1 : 1	1 : 1
Reverse	1 : 1.80	1 : 1.80

Gearshift speeds:

	Full throttle		'Kick-down'		Full throttle		'Kick-down'	
	mph	Kph	mph	Kph	mph	Kph	mph	Kph
1 - 2	18-25	29-40	27-34	43-54	19-26	30-41	27-34	44-54
2 - 3	42-46	67-74	47-52	76-82	43-48	69-76	49-53	77-83
3 - 2*	29-26	47-41	48-44	77-71	31-26	50-41	50-45	78-72
2 - 1*	16-14	26-23	31-24	49-38	17-14	27-23	32-24	50-39

*Note: The down shift CAN occur below the larger figure but it MUST occur before the smaller one

Torque converter
Maximum torque multiplication	2.5
Stall speed (rpm)	1900 - 2100

Final drive shafts (transmission to hubs)
dimensions (length):
Automatic Left side	18" (456 mm)
Right side	19,7/8" (504 mm)
Manual L & R	18¾"

Auto shafts have a ridge in the middle

Oil capacities:

	Litres	Imperial pints	US pints
Torque converter and gearbox (ATF):			
Initial amount	6	10.5	13
Refill (oil change)	3	5.25	6.5
Final drive (SAE 90)	1.4	2.50	2.75

Torque wrench settings

	lb ft	Kgm
Torque converter to drive plate bolts	14	2
Differential housing to transmission case	14	2

1 General description

1 Refer to Fig 6.1. The unit consists of three parts and is contained in two castings which are bolted together and then attached to the engine casing at the rear. They, together with the engine, form an integral power unit which may be removed in one piece.

2 The torque converter casing is bolted to the engine flywheel. Inside the casing are two turbine discs, one (the middle one) is mounted on a one way catch (freewheel) so that it may turn only in the same direction as the engine, and the other may rotate independently but is mounted on a shaft which is splined to the drive-gear in the automatic gearbox. On the inside face of the casing next to the flywheel are turbine vanes (the impeller). The middle one is called the stator and the third one the turbine.

3 The drive goes from the turbine to the planetary gear system contained in the transmission box. Here by means of a number of epicyclic gear trains with brakes and clutches operated by hydraulic pressure through a complicated valve chest the necessary reduction in rpm is determined for the load and speed of the vehicle. Three main control devices provide the correct combination, the manual valve operated by the gearshift cable and lever by the driver, the second primary valve operated by vacuum from the engine intake manifold which makes the gearbox sensitive to engine load and speed, and the third control is the governor which controls ATF pressure and is sensitive to the road speed.

   Thus it will be appreciated that the setting of the various springs and plungers in the valve chest is critical, as is the adjustment of clutches and brake bands, and for that reason we do not recommend that the unit be dismantled. A cross-sectional diagram of the unit is included for those who must know.

4 The drive is carried from the epicyclic system through the pinion shaft which is splined into the output gear of the train. The pinion shaft is supported at the rear end by a taper roller bearing in the second casting which also houses the differential and carries the driveshaft flanges. The bellhousing at the end houses the torque converter round which it goes and is bolted to the engine casing.

5 The pinion shaft is hollow and through it goes yet another hollow shaft which is driven by the torque converter primary rotor and takes power to the ATF pump which is situated at the extreme end of the epicyclic box.

6 The transmission case of the epicyclic box is fitted with ATF, as is the torque converter and the ATF is pumped round both of them providing lubrication, cooling and a means of transmitting power in the torque converter. The final drive casing is isolated from the ATF circuit and contains Hypoid oil. Oddly enough, the governor is mounted on the final drive casing, driven by a helical gear from the pinion shaft, and is in the ATF circuit. It will be appreciated that the governor shaft seal is an important item.

7 When the engine is started the torque converter casing commences to rotate with the flywheel and the ATF pump is driven supplying ATF under pressure to the torque converter and the valve chest.

   As speed builds up the ATF is driven by centrifugal force out of the ends of the impeller into the vanes of the turbine (the one connected to the epicyclic system). It causes the turbine to turn and throw the oil back towards the impeller. At this point it meets the centre disc (stator) which is turning with the primary rotor (impeller) because of its one way clutch. This impedes the flow of the oil increasing the pressure of the flow through the secondary rotor (turbine) and speeds up the turbine by multiplying the torque. The maximum multiplication factor is 2½. As the speed of the turbine approaches the speed of the impeller the oil flows easily through the stator and the multiplication factor decreases until the speed ratio between the two wheels is 0.84:1. At this point the engine torque and the turbine torque are the same and the torque converter ceases to act as a torque converter and acts as a fluid coupling only.

8 What happens to the torque depends upon the position of the manual selector valve. If the gearlever is in 'N' or 'P' then the epicyclic rotates freely and no power is transmitted to the wheels. When the lever is moved to '1', '2', '3' or 'R' the various valves in the chest operate and move the controls of the clutches and brake bands so that the epicyclic train produces the correct ratio to the final drive. The second primary valve operates as the vehicle goes along according to engine load, causing the gear to change to suit the load, and the governor presides over the whole operation regulating the pressure of the ATF delivered by the pump according to the road speed of the vehicle.

9 It will be seen now why we suggest you leave well alone. It will also be appreciated that if the engine is not running the pump will not circulate the ATF so the vehicle cannot be push started because the turbine will not work. Furthermore if the ATF is not circulating the oil will get hot and since the lubrication is done by the ATF if the vehicle is towed for any length of time the oil will boil and the bearings suffer accordingly. For this reason a special ATF oil cooler should be fitted if the towing of a caravan or trailer is intended, and if the van itself is to be towed over 20 miles a suspended tow for the rear wheels is indicated. If this is not possible then remove the driveshafts.

2 Operation

   The six positions of the selector are described below.

1 'P' Park: Engine running or stopped, no gears 'engaged' and the gearbox output shaft mechanically locked. This in turn locks the rear wheels and immobilises the car. To select 'P' the selector lever must be lifted. Do not select 'P' while the car is in motion, the resultant damage will be horribly expensive.

2 'R' Reverse: To go backwards lift the gear lever, while the car is stationary and move the lever to 'R'. While the brakes are on the car will not move but when they are released and the engine accelerated the car will move in reverse. Lift the foot off the accelerator and the engine acts as a brake, but at low revolutions with the car brakes off the car may roll either way as the slope dictates. Again, do not engage reverse while the car is moving.

3 'N' Neutral: Gearbox positions the same as 'P' parking except that the output shaft is not mechanically locked. This is the only position in which the engine can be started.

4 'D' Drive: The normal driving position, Engages low gear, as the engine accelerates the car moves and the gears change up at the stated speed or down according to the throttle position. The engine acts as a brake in all three speeds.

5 '2' Intermediate: Used in traffic or hilly country to stop the gearbox selecting top. Will change the gear from top to second or even first when selected but should not be selected at speeds over 60 mph.

6 '1' Low: Used in heavy traffic, when climbing a long hill slowly or as a brake on steep downhill roads. Should not be selected when the speed is over 35 mph. Changes automatically up and down between 2nd and 1st gear.

7 There are six more points to be clear about:

(a) *It is not possible to push or tow start the car as the transmission oil pump works only when the engine is running.*

b) *If the car is towed the selector should be in 'N', and a limit of 30 miles of towing should not be exceeded as lubrication of the transmission is inadequate when the engine is not running and overheating and seizure may occur.*

c) *If there is a fault in the transmission the car must be towed with the driving wheels clear of the road; ie: a rear suspended tow.*

d) *If '2' or '1' are selected for overrun braking when on a slippery surface the gear will change and there may be a skid you did not expect. Do not change down at high speeds in these conditions.*

e) *The cooling fins and areas must be kept clean. The transmission fluid heats up and on long climbs can get very*

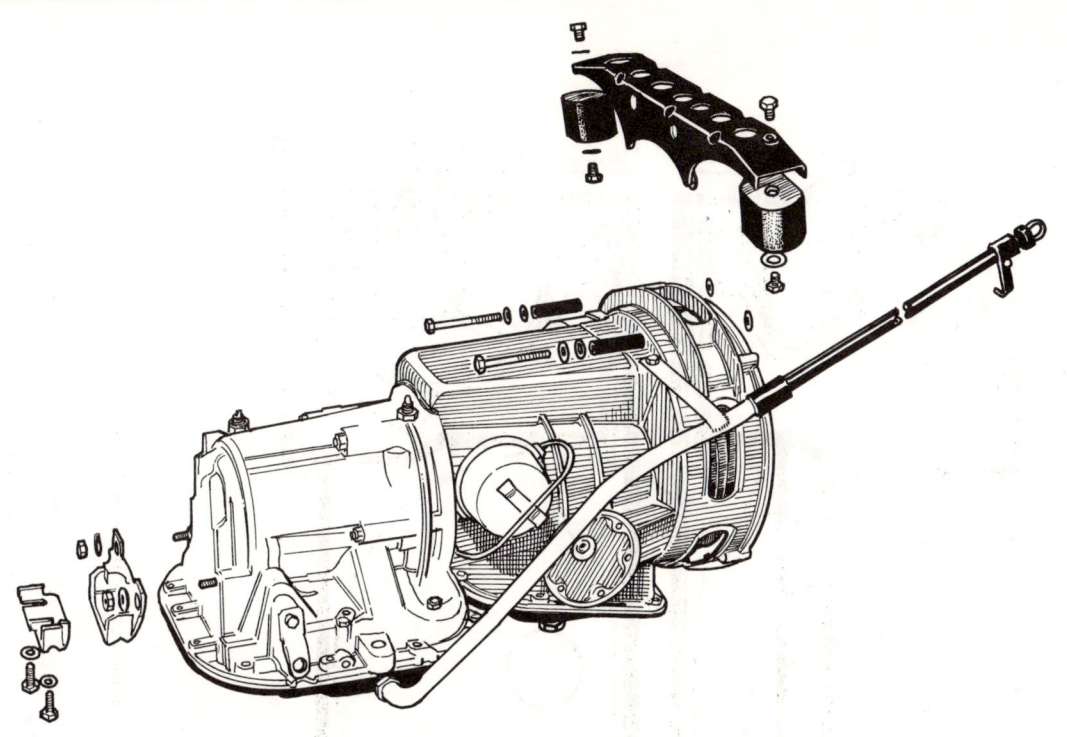

Fig. 6.1 Automatic gearbox and final drive (Sec 1)

The epicyclic train and ATF pump are in the casting on the left. The darker casting is the final drive. The torque converter (which is not shown) is in the bellhousing. The long pipe is the ATF filler pipe

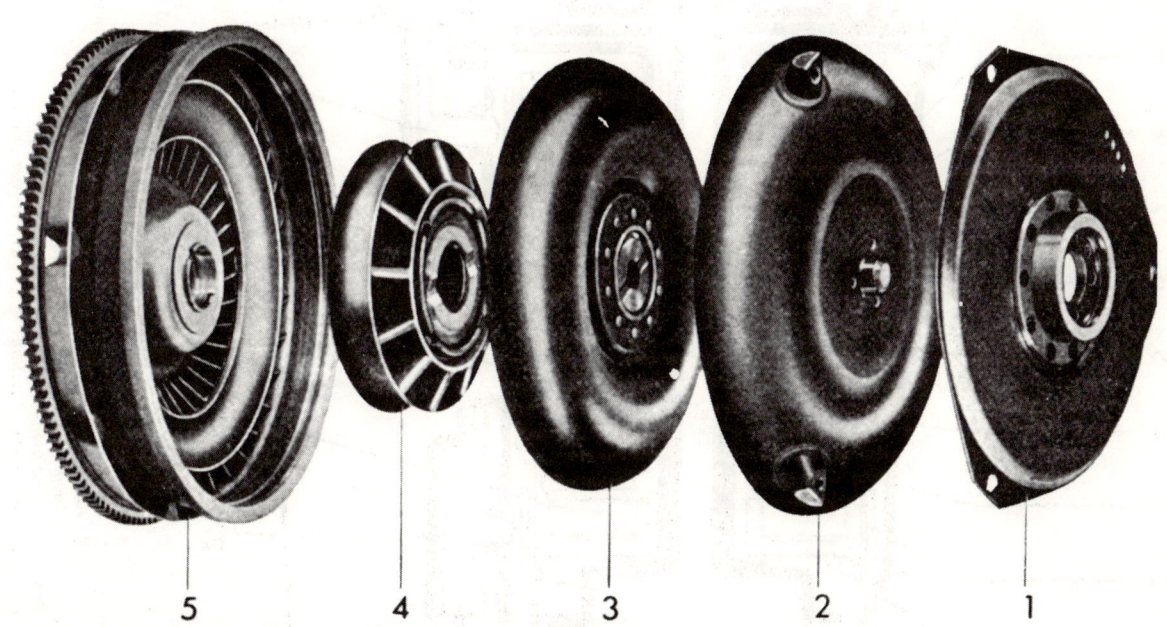

Fig. 6.2 The torque converter (Sec 1)

1 Driveplate	3 Turbine	5 Impeller and converter
2 Casing cover	4 Stator	

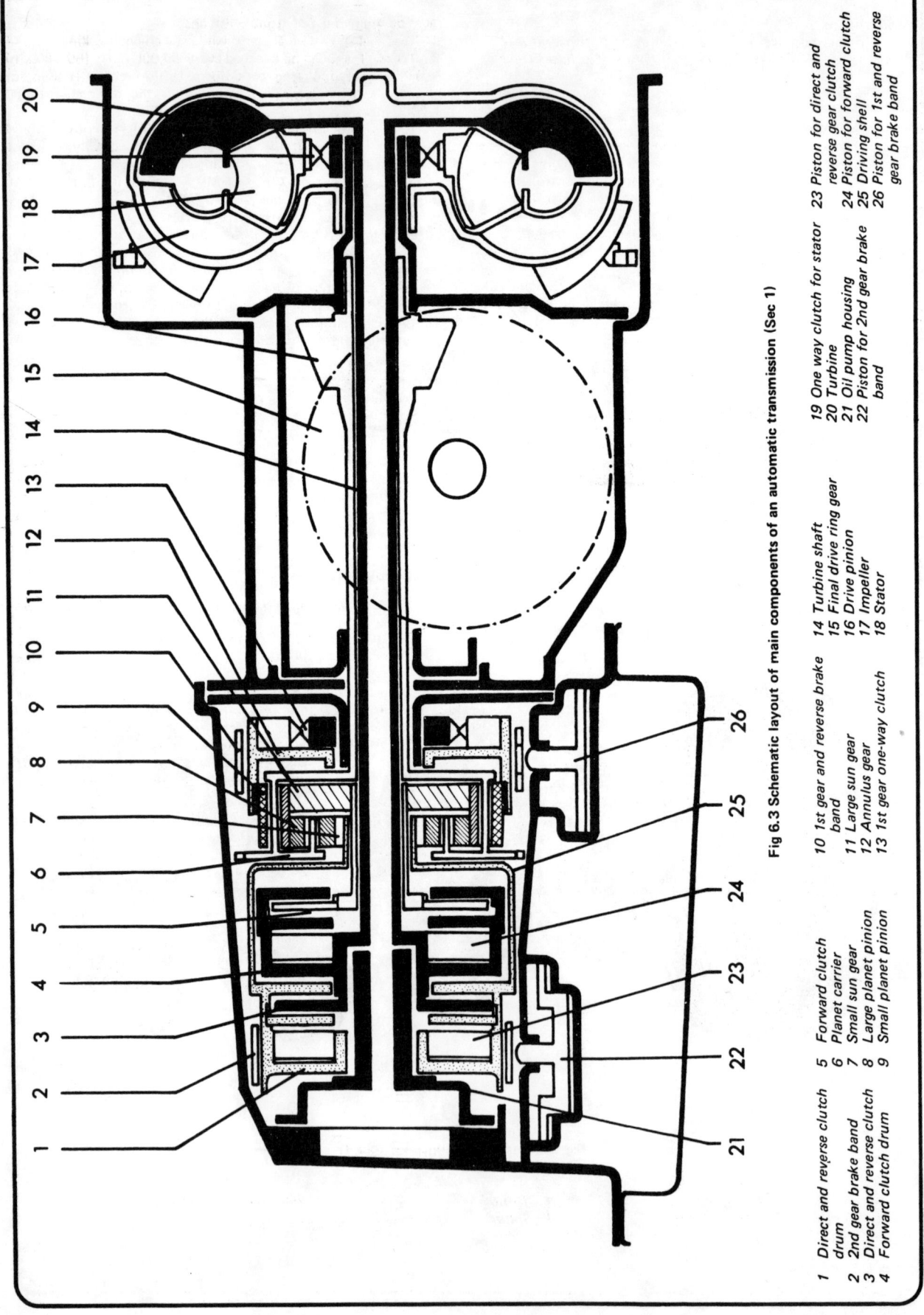

Fig 6.3 Schematic layout of main components of an automatic transmission (Sec 1)

1 Direct and reverse clutch
   drum
2 2nd gear brake band
3 Direct and reverse clutch
4 Forward clutch drum
5 Forward clutch
6 Planet carrier
7 Small sun gear
8 Large planet pinion
9 Small planet pinion
10 1st gear and reverse brake
   band
11 Large sun gear
12 Annulus gear
13 1st gear one-way clutch
14 Turbine shaft
15 Final drive ring gear
16 Drive pinion
17 Impeller
18 Stator
19 One way clutch for stator
20 Turbine
21 Oil pump housing
22 Piston for 2nd gear brake
   band
23 Piston for direct and
   reverse gear clutch
24 Piston for forward clutch
25 Driving shell
26 Piston for 1st and reverse
   gear brake band

hot indeed.

*f) There is a modification to be done to the converter if it is
wished to tow a caravan; consult a VW agent before fitting
a tow bar.*

3 'Kickdown' position

1 When the accelerator pedal is pressed right down past the
'hard spot' to the kickdown position yet another control valve is
brought into the system. Its effect is to move the gearshift points
of first and second gears to correspond with maximum engine
revolutions. The valve is operated by a solenoid controlled by a
switch under the acceleration pedal.

2 So if you are in a hurry and stamp on the pedal when you are
in top gear, the gearbox will change into second, the engine will
move up to maximum revolutions, the vehicle will accelerate
very quickly and then change back into top with the engine at
maximum power with the speedometer needle climbing rapidly.
Be careful where this is done for it can cause wheel spin and
possibly skidding.

3 When the pedal is lifted back through the "hard spot" normal
gearchange points are resumed.

4 Maintenance and fluid level

1 Apart from keeping the cooling surfaces clean and seeing that
nuts and bolts are tight, electrical connections correct and
hydraulic joints in order there is no maintenance other than that
of the correct fluid level in the transmission.

2 ATF (Automatic Transmission Fluid) is a special oil and
although suitable grades are available from most mineral oil firms
it is a wise thing to consult the VW agent as to the best one to
use.

3 The torque converter and the transmission are both operated
and lubricated with the same ATF Fluid.

4 The oil level should be checked every 6,000 miles (10,000
km). To do this, warm-up the transmission by running the engine
with the selector lever at 'N' and the handbrake applied, open up
the engine compartment, and withdraw the transmission oil
dipstick. This is at the forward edge of the engine compartment
(Fig. 6.4). Wipe the dipstick and check the level. There are two
marks and the level **must** be maintained between these marks.
The capacity difference between the marks is only 0.7 pints (0.4
litres). Make sure the dipstick handle is vertical when checking
and be careful not to overfill.

5 Use a plastic funnel with about 24 in (600 mm) of plastic
tubing and pour in a little at a time. If it is overfilled the excess

must be drained off or trouble will ensue.

6 The level should be checked while the engine is idling.

7 The ATF should be changed every 30,000 miles (50,000 km)
under normal operating conditions. If the vehicle is used for
towing, or other heavy load conditions the interval becomes
18,000 miles.

8 Take out the drain plug and allow the oil to run out. Remove
the oil pan and the strainer and clean them thoroughly. Reinstall
the oil pan and the strainer using a new gasket. Tighten the
screws to a torque of 7 lb ft (1 Mkg). Retighten after about 10
minutes to the same torque. (Fig. 6.5)

9 Fill with 5 to 7 pints (3 to 4 litres) of ATF and start the
engine. Move the selector to each position in turn to allow the
oil to circulate. Check the dipstick level with the selector at 'N'.
Top-up, if necessary, until oil just shows on the tip of the
dipstick. Drive the vehicle a short way to warm the transmission
and then check the oil level and if necessary correct it.

10 Under no circumstances start the engine, or tow the vehicle,
when there is no ATF in the transmission.

5 Tests, adjustments and repairs possible

1 The unit is made up of three major portions:

*a) The torque converter which is of welded construction and
apart from replacing the oil seal and bush if it is leaking no
further repair can be done other than draining it
(Section 7).*

*(b) The final drive. This is an alloy casting containing the
differential. Although it is different in shape it functions
like the manual final drive. In this case however the
differential is removed through the bottom, which is
closed by a pressed steel pan fixed with bolts. The pinion
drive is entirely different. As with the manual box no
repairs can be done by the owner if the differential goes
wrong but the oil seals for the drive flange may be replaced
with the box in-situ. This is discussed later (Section 8).*

*c) The third unit, the transmission box is bolted to the final
drive case. It may be removed only when the engine and
transmission are out of the vehicle. The most probable
cause of damage will be burnt out brake linings, but what
ever it is, it is thought that the dismantling and overhaul of
this item is beyond the scope of the owner driver.*

2 If things go wrong the only thing the owner driver can do is
to locate as accurately as possible what the trouble is, remove
the transmission and split it, taking the defective item to the VW
agent for overhaul. We do not doubt the ability of the owner to

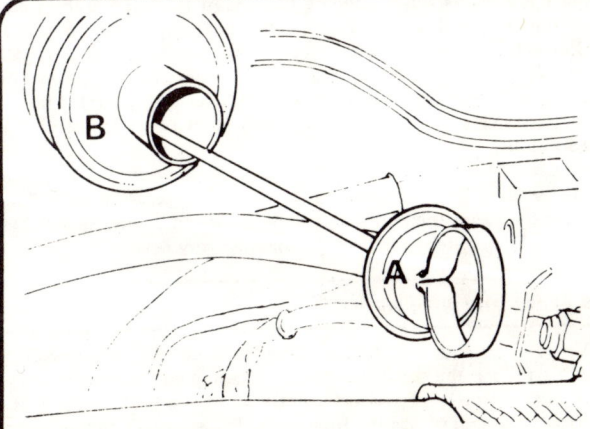

Fig 6.4 The transmission oil dipstick located at the front edge of
the engine compartment. Top-up every 6000 miles A is the dipstick B is the filler neck. (Sec 4)

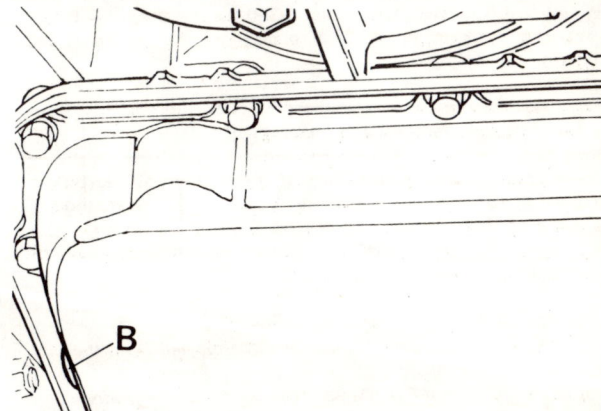

Fig 6.5 Oil pan and drain plug B (Sec 4)

*(Drain every 30,000 miles or 18000 miles under heavy load con-
ditions)*

do the job, but without the gauges, fixtures and special tools the job cannot be done properly. There are a number of tests which can be carried out to trace the trouble. The first, and most obvious is to examine the casing for external damage, leaks of ATF from the transmission or Hypoid oil from the final drive and for loose nuts. Check that the units are fastened together securely, and fastened firmly to the engine. Check the tightness of the bolts which hold the driveplate to the flywheel. They can be got at through the aperature in the left lower side of the converter housing. There are three and they may be reached one at a time by turning the engine. They should be torqued to 14 lb ft. If you are satisfied that all is secure then look elsewhere.

3 Check the oil level. If this is incorrect then correct it and maybe the trouble will disappear. Sample the ATF; if it is dirty replace it and retest. Again the trouble may go - but the dirt has come from somewhere. Sniff the oil sample, there may be a smell of burnt friction linings. If there is then the box must be overhauled.

4 The engine settings and performance should have been checked. If the power unit is not adjusted correctly the transmission will reflect its roughness.

5 Adjust the kickdown switch. To set it first depress the accelerator pedal as far as it will go and keep it there with a heavy weight. Now move the accelerator cable at the bellcrank against the pressure of the spring until it touches the stop of the lever. The accelerator cable should be locked in this position. Switch on the ignition and connect one wire of a test lamp to the terminal on the switch which has the cable leading to the transmission. Then slowly allow the accelerator pedal to return until there is a gap of 0.020 - 0.040 ins (0.50 - 1.016 mm) between the accelerator cable lever and the stop on the end of the lever. At this point the switch should operate and the lamp will go out. Adjustment may be made by loosening the screws and moving the switch.

6 Check the adjustment of the selector cable lever.

7 When all these points have been checked try another road test. Check the shift speeds against the Specification.

8 The next test is a stall speed test. For this it is necessary to measure the engine speed accurately. With the engine warmed up, brakes hard on and the wheels chocked engage drive range '3' and press the accelerator to the floor. The engine speed should be steady between 1900 and 2100 rpm. Allow only 10 seconds for this test or the ATF will overheat. If the engine rpm is too high then either the torque converter oil supply or the low band servo in the transmission are suspect. If the rpm are too low then the torque converter unit is suspect. Either way the unit requires expert attention.

9 At this point the owner drive must accept that the box has a serious fault. The car should be taken to the VW agent for confirmation of the foregoing tests and for a pressure test. The VW test involves two gauges (one 0-350 psi and the other 0-140 psi) and a complicated routine to diagnose the nature of the problem.

6 Transmission - removal and replacement

1 The removal and replacement of the engine and gearbox is discussed at some length in Chapter 5, Section 2. The method is the same so read the detail given leaving out the obvious bits about the clutch and gearchange. There are some more points to note specially for the automatic box:

   (a) *The driveshafts are of different lengths.*
   (b) *The kickdown switch must be disconnected from the side of the transmission.*
   (c) *The clamp nut for the selector cable must be undone and the cable removed from the box. The selector cable bracket must also be removed. The bolt that holds this also locates the ground strap.*

2 The combined unit will be lowered in this manner. It is very heavy (300 lbs) so if you are worried about that remove the engine first (Chapter 1) and then remove the transmission carrier bolts and the bolts from the front and lower the transmission separately. You are going to separate them anyway and with the automatic you do not have to fuss about disengaging the driveshaft from the clutch.

3 Replacement is the reversal. Both methods are discussed in Chapters 1 and 5.

4 If you removed the engine and transmission together, disconnect the driveplate from the flywheel, undo the bolts holding the casing to the bellhousing and remove the transmission from the engine. At this stage drain off the ATF from the transmission box and the oil from the final drive.

5 Pull out the torque converter, keep it level or you will do some damage, and pull out the pump driveshaft. Now undo the four bolts holding the transmission unit to the final drive housing and draw them apart. **Do not** lift the transmission by the filler pipe, it will bend and possibly break off. There will still be some oil about so be prepared to catch it.

6 The assembly is now in three parts and may be dealt with as necessary. If the epicyclic box is at fault we recommend that it should be taken to the VW agent for overhaul.

7 Torque converter - repairs

1 If only the torque converter is faulty then it may be removed once the engine has been removed without removing the rest of the transmission.

2 The usual problem is a leak from the seal in the support tube on the final drive housing. The seal is a soft one and is damaged if soaked with petrol or paraffin. It will leak too if the bushing in the hub is worn. It is best to replace them together. The seal can be extracted using a sharp pointed instrument but the bush requires an expandable extractor to remove it. When replacing the bush make sure it is pushed in squarely. The inside diameter after installation should be 1.342" + 0.002". The seal may be pressed in but remember it is soft and requires a mandrel. You can make a wooden one quite easily.

3 If the transmission has overheated so much that the ATF is polluted with carbon or other debris then the converter must be drained of the contaminated fluid. It is possible to siphon this out. From the home-brewers shop or somewhere similar get a rubber bung 1 3/8 in (34.9 mm) diameter. Bore two holes to fit 1/8 in (3.17 mm) diameter tube. Insert two pieces of tube into the bung, one about 6 in (150 mm) and the other 8 in (205 mm) long. Bend the tubes so that the top piece is a right-angle bend about 2 in (50 mm) radius., and the outlet is horizontal. Fit the bung in the converter bushing (the converter should be flat with the starter ring upwards) and adjust the tubes so that the end of the short one is flush with the bottom of the bung and the end of the longer one just touches the bottom of the converter. Connect a piece of plastic tube to the long tube and arrange a siphon. Now blow down the shorter tube to start the siphon going and leave the converter to drain for at least eight hours. Blow, don't suck, the fluid not only does not taste nice, **it is poisonous.**

4 Check the starter ring for burrs, look carefully for cracks in the welding. If the converter is noisy in operation or leaking from the welds then nothing can be done and a new one must be fitted. Fortunately this does not happen very often.

8 Final drive unit - repairs

1 Refer to Fig. 6.6, and to Chapter 5, Section 5H. It will be that although the construction of the casing and the arrangement of the pinion shaft is different the method of locating the differential and fitting the final drive flanges is very similar.

2 If oil is leaking from the flanges the job can be done without removing the transmission from the vehicle. Remove the driveshaft (Chapter 7 Section 2), take out the socket head screw from the centre of the flange and flange with shaft may be withdrawn from the casing. The oil seal and the 'O' ring may

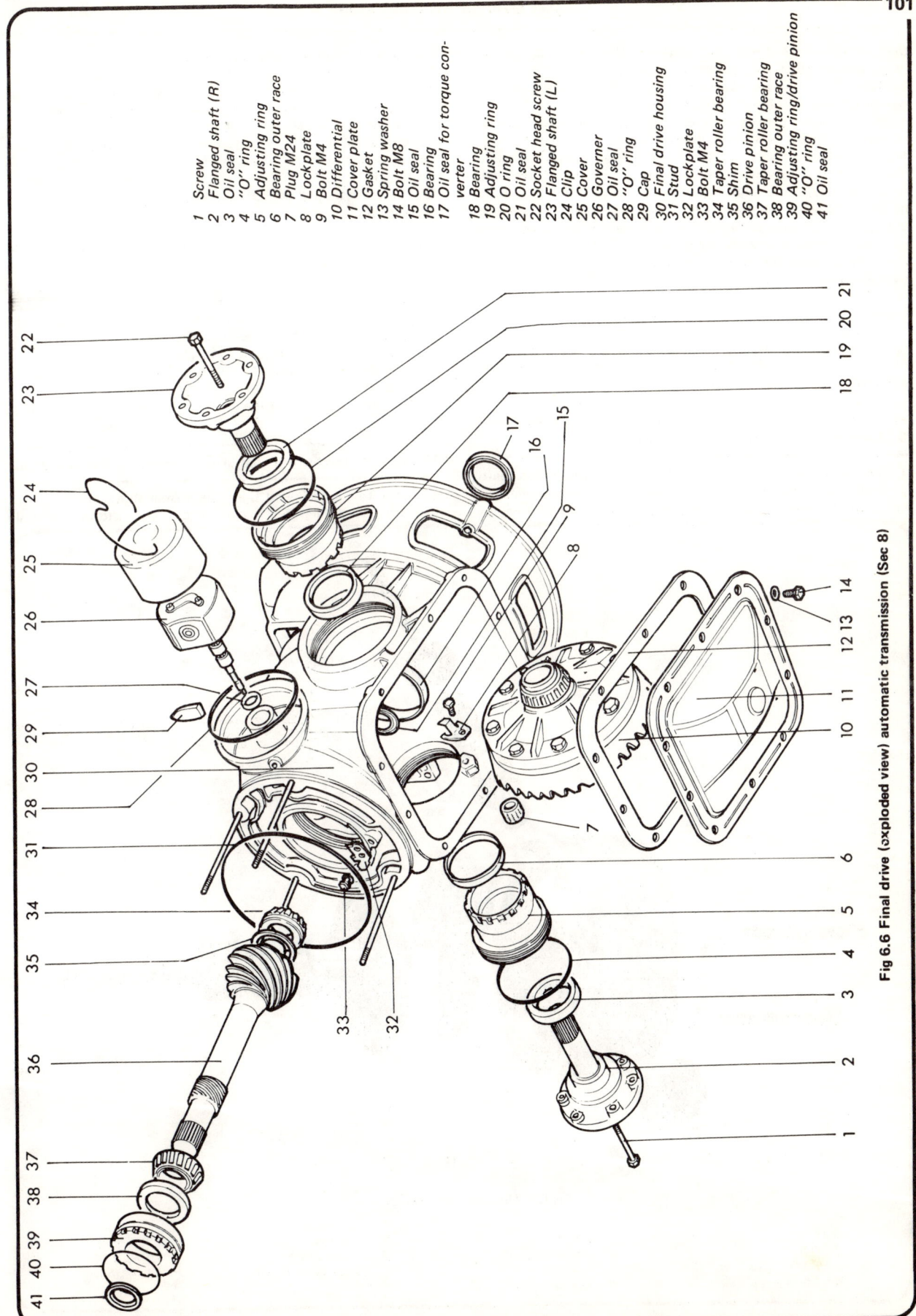

1 Screw
2 Flanged shaft (R)
3 Oil seal
4 "O" ring
5 Adjusting ring
6 Bearing outer race
7 Plug M24
8 Lockplate
9 Bolt M4
10 Differential
11 Cover plate
12 Gasket
13 Spring washer
14 Bolt M8
15 Oil seal
16 Bearing
17 Oil seal for torque converter
18 Bearing
19 Adjusting ring
20 O ring
21 Oil seal
22 Socket head screw
23 Flanged shaft (L)
24 Clip
25 Cover
26 Governer
27 Oil seal
28 "O" ring
29 Cap
30 Final drive housing
31 Stud
32 Lockplate
33 Bolt M4
34 Taper roller bearing
35 Shim
36 Drive pinion
37 Taper roller bearing
38 Bearing outer race
39 Adjusting ring/drive pinion
40 "O" ring
41 Oil seal

Fig 6.6 Final drive (exploded view) automatic transmission (Sec 8)

101

then be removed and new ones installed, after which the flange, screw and driveshaft may be reassembled.

3   The governor may be removed and serviced without removing the transmission. This is discussed in Section 9.

4   If you wish to examine the differential the cover may be removed from the bottom of the box. Drain the Hypoid oil out first. It is not necessary to drain the ATF from the transmission. The differential may be removed by taking off the driveshafts, flanges and adjusting rings. You can do this with the engine still in the vehicle if you have VW Tool '182' and you work as described in Chapter 5, Section 5H to ensure that the adjusting rings are refitted to exactly the same place, but there is no point in so doing, for if the differential is dismantled it must be reset to the pinion, as they are a mated pair and must mesh exactly. It is necessary to remove the box to dismantle the pinion and we suggest that should there be anything wrong with the differential the casing should be taken to the VW agent for overhaul and resetting. You will save a great deal of money if you do the rest of the work yourself but you cannot set the gears in mesh without the right tools and fixtures.

9   Governor - dismantling and reassembly

1   The governor is driven by the helical gear on the pinion shaft.
2   If the transmission has failed due to burning of the brake bands or clutches then as well as draining the converter it will be

necessary to clean the governor. Refer to Fig. 6.7.

3   Remove it from the casing by undoing the clip and taking off the cover. The governor may now be extracted. Look at the thrust-plate and the shaft for wear. The shaft may be replaced by a new one if it is damaged but the new shaft must be fitted to the old governor. If a new governor is to be fitted the whole transmission must go to the agent for the governor to be reset on the test rig.

4   The seals should be replaced with new ones (lip toward the governor body).

5   To clean the governor it is necessary to dismantle it. Remove the two screws from the thrust plate and take off the thrust plate and housing. The weight and the transfer plate will fall out. Remove the circlips from the pin and the remainder of the parts may be dismantled.

6   Wash it all carefully and dry it thoroughly. Reassembly is the reverse process. Dip the parts in ATF as you assemble them. The transfer plate drillings should have the narrow end of the taper next to the weight, and the thrust plate apex must be at the centre of the housing.

7   Refit the shaft, install the governor and refit the cap and clip.

10 Gearshift mechanism - adjustment, removal and reassembly

1   Refer to Fig. 6.8 and 6.9. The former shows the layout of the selector lever and cable. The latter shows the only

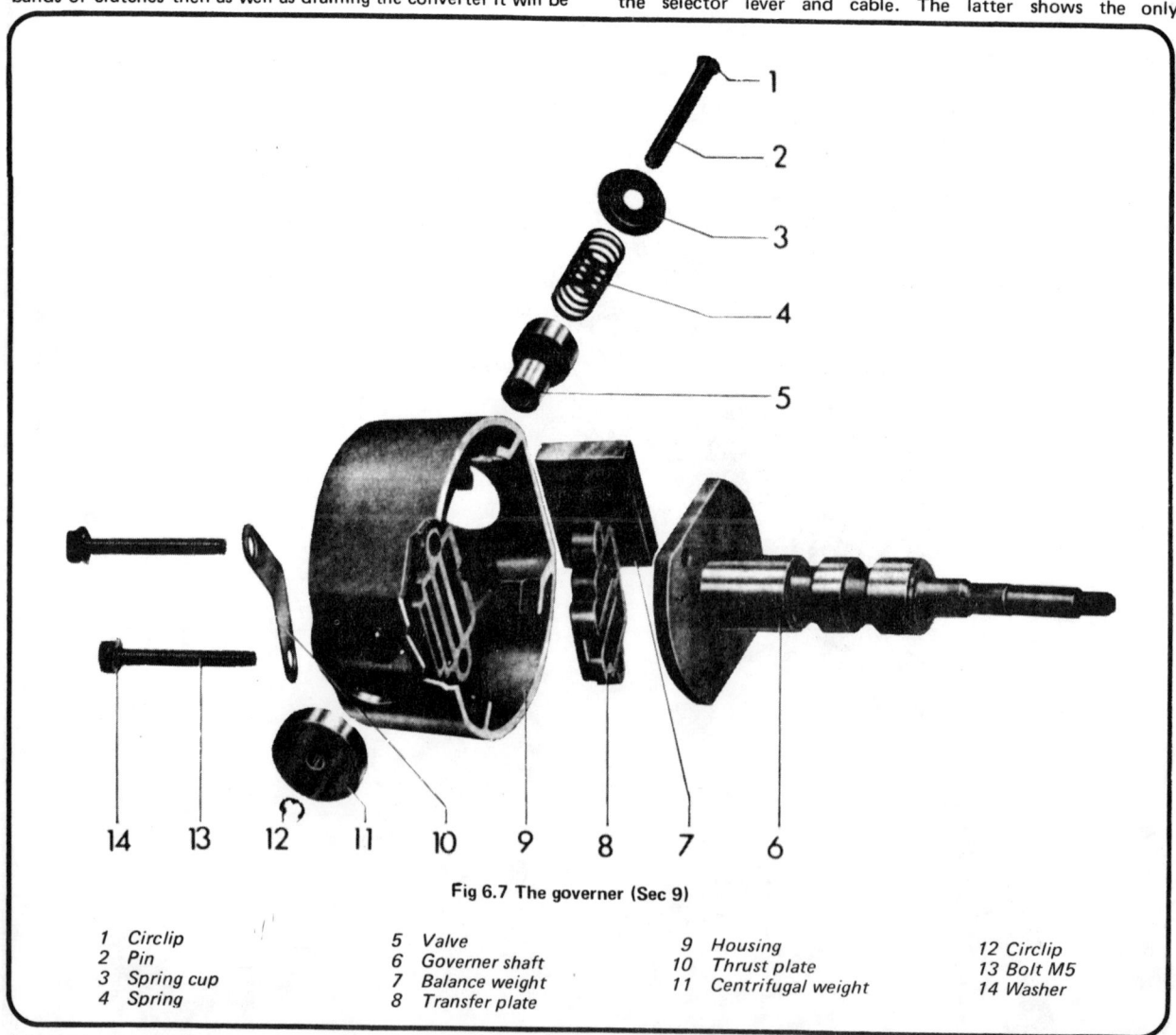

Fig 6.7 The governer (Sec 9)

1 *Circlip*	5 *Valve*	9 *Housing*	12 *Circlip*
2 *Pin*	6 *Governer shaft*	10 *Thrust plate*	13 *Bolt M5*
3 *Spring cup*	7 *Balance weight*	11 *Centrifugal weight*	14 *Washer*
4 *Spring*	8 *Transfer plate*		

103

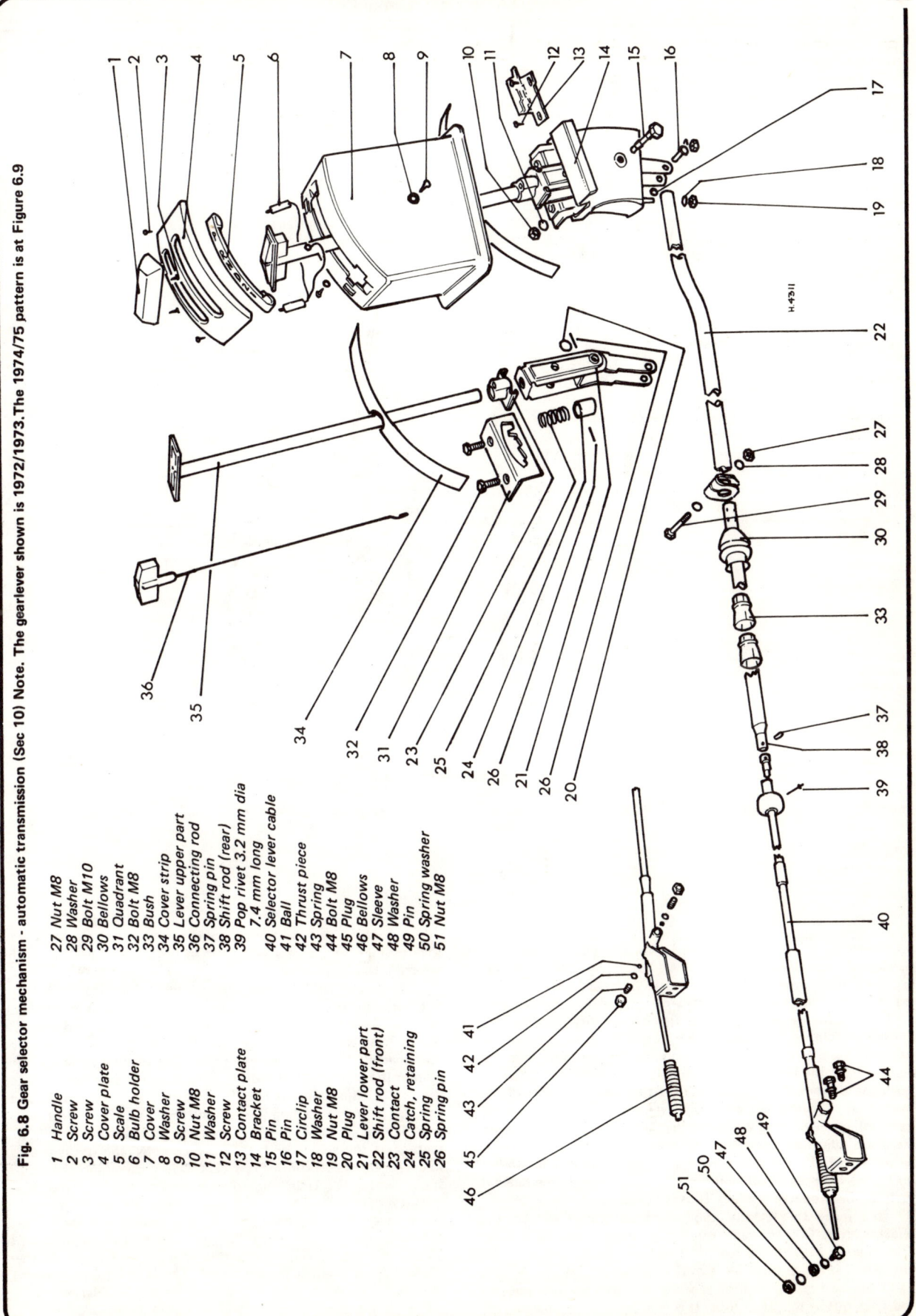

Fig. 6.8 Gear selector mechanism - automatic transmission (Sec 10) Note. The gearlever shown is 1972/1973. The 1974/75 pattern is at Figure 6.9

1 Handle
2 Screw
3 Screw
4 Cover plate
5 Scale
6 Bulb holder
7 Cover
8 Washer
9 Screw
10 Nut M8
11 Washer
12 Screw
13 Contact plate
14 Bracket
15 Pin
16 Pin
17 Circlip
18 Washer
19 Nut M8
20 Plug
21 Lever lower part
22 Shift rod (front)
23 Contact
24 Catch, retaining
25 Spring
26 Spring pin
27 Nut M8
28 Washer
29 Bolt M10
30 Bellows
31 Quadrant
32 Bolt M8
33 Bush
34 Cover strip
35 Lever upper part
36 Connecting rod
37 Spring pin
38 Shift rod (rear)
39 Pop rivet 3.2 mm dia 7.4 mm long
40 Selector lever cable
41 Ball
42 Thrust piece
43 Spring
44 Bolt M8
45 Plug
46 Bellows
47 Sleeve
48 Washer
49 Pin
50 Spring washer
51 Nut M8

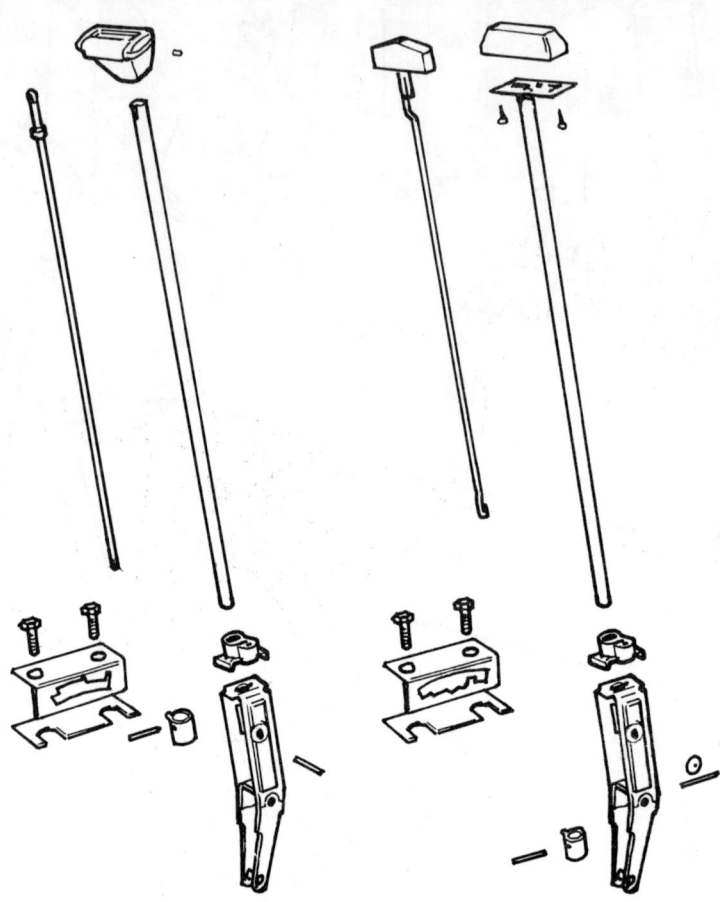

Fig 6.9 Gear lever (Sec 10)

The lever on the right was fitted up to 1973. Later models have a new type (left) which has a press button on the side instead of a pull lever.

modification so far, a gearlever with a push button stop instead of the draw-up type. This was introduced in 1974. In both types there are two small bulbs which light up the indicator plate when the lights are switched on.

2 To remove the selector levers and console first, from under the vehicle remove the cover plate beneath the lever. Remove the circlip and pin holding the lever to the connecting rod, undo the bracket from the floor, lift the assembly up, disconnect the wires from the illuminating lamps (pull off the tabs) and remove the lever. You may now dismantle the lever and repair the offending item. When reinstalling take care that the quadrant and contact plate are adjusted correctly. The engine must be able to start when 'N' or 'P' are selected. If necessary put a thin washer under the quadrant so that the catch will engage on the tapered surface of the quadrant when 'R' is selected.

3 To remove the selector cable, first disconnect it from the selector lever. Take the cable bracket off the transmission casing. The cable is held to the rear shift rod by a pop rivet, drill this out or cut it off and punch it out. Now slacken the clip holding the front and rear shift rods together and pull the rear selector rod back out of the guide tube. It is now possible to take out the spring pin and disconnect the cable from the rod. Installation is

the reverse - use a new pop rivet to hold the cable cap on the selecting rod guide tube.

4 Adjustment of the selectors is most important. Put the selector lever in 'Park'. Check that the cam engages in the latch notch. Undo the clip holding the rods together and separate them. Press the cable lever on the transmission fully towards the rear against the spring pressure so that the manual valve is on the stop in the valve body. Hold the lever in this position and tighten the nut on the clamp to 7 lbs ft. Now push the front shift rod to the rear shift rod holding the rear shift rod stationary, fit the clip and tighten it. Now chock the wheels and get into the driving seat. Start the engine with the selector in 'N' and run it at a fast idle (1000 - 1200 rpm). Press on the footbrake and then move the lever to 'R'. There should be a drop in engine speed. Move the lever to 'P'. The speed should rise denoting reverse is disengaged. Pull the lever towards 'R' against the stop. There should be no drop in speed. Engage 'R' once again then move to 'N'. The engine speed should rise. Move the lever to 'D' there should be a drop in engine speed. The lever should move to 1 without having to overcome any resistance. Adjustment of the cable must be redone until these tests are satisfactory.

11 Fault diagnosis - automatic transmission

This list is by no means complete but it contains all that the owner can rectify. The VW agent is the best person to consult about a faulty automatic transmission

Symptom	Reason/s	Remedy
No drive in any gear	ATF fluid level low Transmission box defective	Fill. VW agent.
Drive in some gears but not all	Transmission box defective	VW agent.
Power output unsteady engine surges on upshift	ATF fluid level incorrect Selector mechanism out of adjustment Oil strainer requires cleaning.	Measure and correct. Adjust. Remove pan and clean.
Speed shifts at too low speed	Governer dirty Primary throttle valve needs setting Valve body assembly dirty	Remove and clean. VW agent. VW agent.
Speed shifts at too high speed	Vacuum hose leaking Kickdown lever distorted Kickdown solenoid defective ATF pressure too low	Replace. Repair. Repair. VW agent.
Kickdown will not operate	Lever distorted, solenoid defective, wiring open circuit switch broken	Trace and correct. Replace switch/solenoid.
Heavy leakage of ATF on floor and vehicle	Torque converter seal casing defective or cracked	Replace seal. Fit new converter.
Heavy leakage of ATF NONE on floor or vehicle. Smoky exhaust	Leaking vacuum chamber or primary throttle	VW agent.
Parking lock will not hold vehicle	Selector lever out of adjustment Parking lock linkage defective	Adjust. Repair.
ATF dirty and smells of carbon and burning	Brake bands or clutches wearing in Auto Transmission box	Dismantle and take box to VW agent (check with him first). Replace oil in converter.
Oil leaks from final drive flanges	Seals in flanges worn out	Replace.
Differential noisy	Differential or pinion bearings worn	Remove final drive unit and take to VW agent.

Chapter 7 Rear suspension, wheel bearings and driveshafts

Contents

Specifications

Driveshafts

Length   ...   .   476 mm (18¾ ins)

Rear suspension

Type   ...   .   Independent trailing arms (spring plates) with locating diagonal arms. Spring plates splined to a transverse torsion bar.

Torsion Bar and Spring plate details (spring plates unloaded)

Body Type	Body Name	Transmission type	Chassis Number	Torsion Bar diameter	length	Spring setting
21. 21F 23 26	Fire truck Delivery van, Kombi, Campmobile, Pick-up	Manual	218000 002 onwards	28.10 mm (1.106 in)	610 mm (24 1/64 in)	21°10' +50'
22. 24 27. 28	Microbus, Ambulance	Manual	218000 002 onwards	26.20 mm (1.031 in)	610 mm (24 1/64 in)	23° + 50'
21. 23. 26	Delivery van Kombi Campmobile	Manual Automatic (for Campmobile only)	212 2000 001	28.9 mm 1.138 in)	610 mm (24 1/64) in)	20° + 50'
22. 24. 27	Microbus Ambulance	Manual and Automatic	212 2000 001	26.90 mm (1.059 in)	610 mm (24 1/64 in)	23° + 50'

Shock absorbers

Type   ...   .   hydraulic telescopic double acting

Camber angle (after 500 miles, spring plates correctly set)

All models (except 21F & 27)   ...   .   −50' ± 30'
Fire truck - 21F   ...   .   −2° ± 30' Maximum permissible difference between sides 30'
Ambulance - 27   ...   .   −1° 30' ± 30'

Toe-in

All models (except 21F)   ...   .   +10' ± 20'
Fire truck. 21F   ...   .   −10' ± 20'
Maximum permissible deviation in wheel alignment   ...   ...   10'

Torque wrench settings

	lb ft	kgm
Diagonal arm to rear wheel bearing housing (bolt)	94	13
Diagonal arm to frame (bolt)	58	8
Shock absorber to frame and rear wheel housing (bolt) ...	43	6
Spring plate bearing cover (bolt)	32	4.5

	lb/ft	k/gm
Rear wheel hub to rear wheel shaft (castellated nut)	253	35
Wheel nuts	94	13
Drive shaft socket head screws	25	3.5
Brake backing plate to housing M. 8 bolt	18	2.5
M. 10 bolt	25	3.5

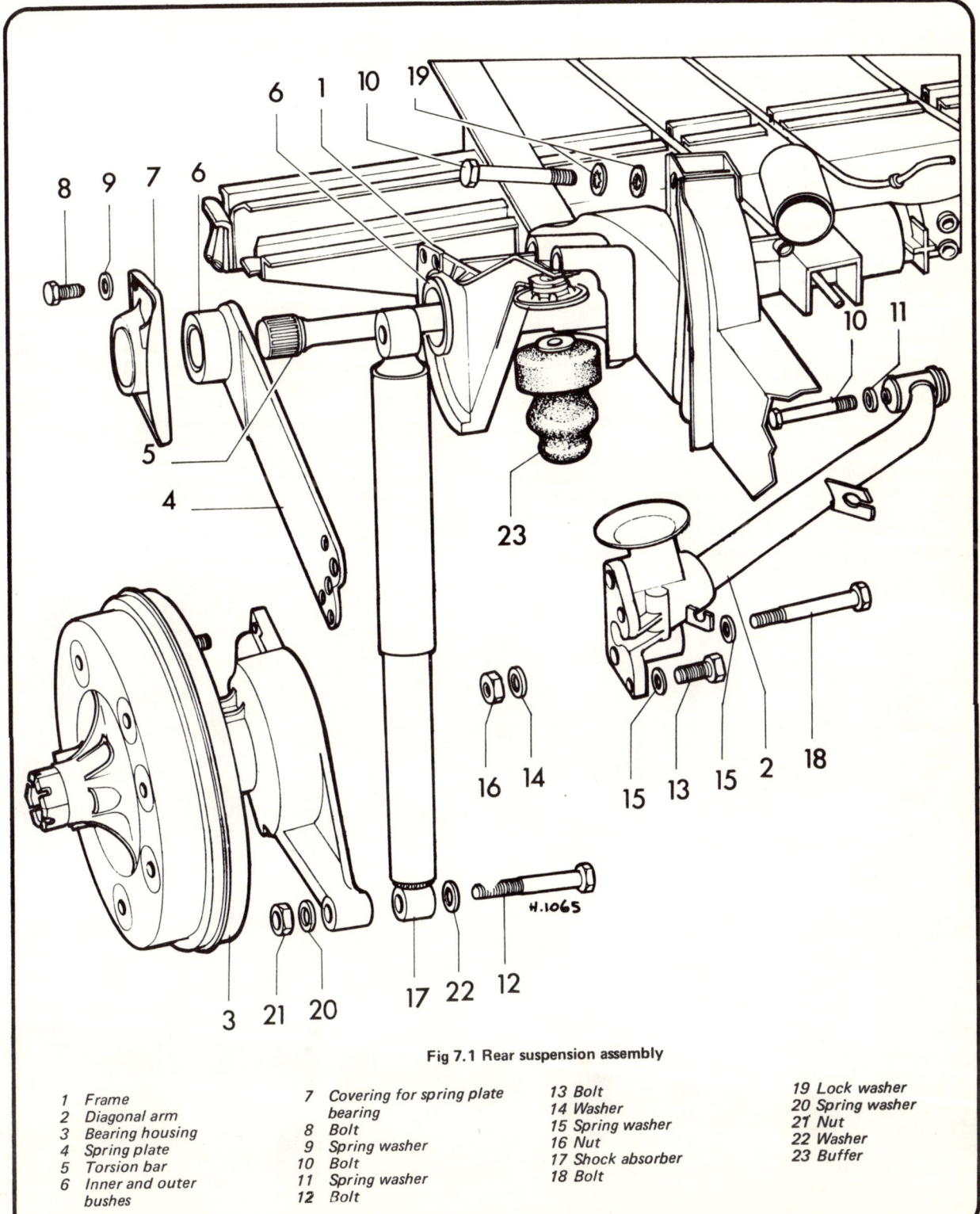

H.1065

Fig 7.1 Rear suspension assembly

1 Frame
2 Diagonal arm
3 Bearing housing
4 Spring plate
5 Torsion bar
6 Inner and outer
    bushes

7 Covering for spring plate
    bearing
8 Bolt
9 Spring washer
10 Bolt
11 Spring washer
12 Bolt

13 Bolt
14 Washer
15 Spring washer
16 Nut
17 Shock absorber
18 Bolt

19 Lock washer
20 Spring washer
21 Nut
22 Washer
23 Buffer

1   General description - spares - maintenance

1   Rear suspension is by diagonal arm, spring plate (trailing arm) and torsion bar. The drive is carried from the differential flange to the wheel hub by driveshafts which have a constant velocity joint at each end. This is known as the double jointed driveshaft and the suspension is usually called torsion bar trailing arm.

2   Refer to Fig. 7.1. The engine and gearbox are mounted to the frame and also integral with the frame is the cross tube in which the torsion arm is mounted. The torsion arm is held securely at its inner end but the outer end is free to rotate. Splined to the outer end is the spring plate, which because it points to the rear of the vehicle is sometimes called the trailing arm.

The diagonal arm is fastened to the frame at its inner end by a bolt which passes through a rubber bush. The diagonal arm is able to pivot about this bolt. At the outer end the diagonal arm is bolted to the spring plate. Thus, if pressure is exerted to the outer end of the diagonal arm in a vertical plane the spring plate will twist the torsion bar and the outer end of the diagonal arm will move in a vertical plane until the torque set up in the torsion bar balances the force exerted in the vertical plane.

The wheel hub and bearing is bolted to the outer end of the diagonal arm by the same bolts which attach the spring plate (photo). Thus as the vehicle goes along the road shocks are ironed out by twisting the torsion bar. A telescopic hydraulic shock absorber is fitted between the wheel hub and the body frame and a large rubber buffer mounted on the frame meets a cup on the diagonal arm at the extreme limit of its upward movement.

As the driveshaft has two constant velocity joints provision is made for the variation in length required by fitting the CVJs on splines. Thus the wheel is able to move in a vertical plane and not along the radius of a circle as it did with the old swing axle. This gives much better road holding and cornering, and since each wheel has its own suspension system a smooth ride.

3   In order to ensure that the body of the vehicle is in a horizontal plane it is necessary to set the spring plates in such a way on assembly to the torsion bars that they twist the torsion bars a given amount when the load of the vehicle is taken up. This is known as the setting angle (see Section 7) and must be observed carefully. Obviously the setting angle will vary for different types of body. These are given in the Specifications.

4   There have been few modifications to the suspension but considerable variation in the method of securing the rubber boot to the CVJ. It is suggested you take advice from the VW storeman before dismantling the driveshaft as to which spares you can get.

5   Driveshafts vary in length, and torsion bars in diameter so again be sure before replacing them that you get the right one.

6   Maintenance is minimal. Inspect the CVJ covers for tears or deterioration once a month. Check the tightness of the socket head bolts securing the driveshaft flanges.

The lubricant of the rear wheel bearings and the CVJs should be renewed every 18,000 miles.

2   Driveshafts - removal and replacement

1   The driveshaft cap screws have either a splined or hexagonal socket. Whichever is used make sure that the key used to undo them is a perfect fit and of good quality hard steel (photo). If the sockets are damaged the greatest difficulty will be experienced in getting them out with any sort of key.

2   Before removing all the screws make sure that there are no accumulations of dirt nearby which could get into the joints. If any dirt gets in it will have to be cleaned out and the joints repacked with special molybdenum grease.

3   With all the screws removed the shafts may be taken away (photos).

4   Replacement is the reverse of removal. Replace the hub

1.2 The driveshaft with the rubber boot attached to the wheel hub, which is supported by the diagonal arm and the trailing arm. The shock absorber is on the right

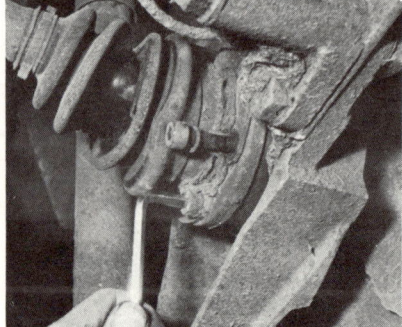

2.1 Undoing the driveshaft cap screw. Note split rubber boot

2.3a Removing the shaft from the gearbox

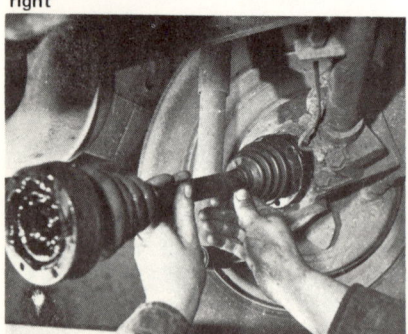

2.3b Removing the shaft from the wheel hub

3.1a A split boot (this is from a VW 411) shown to demonstrate how large the split may be without being obvious

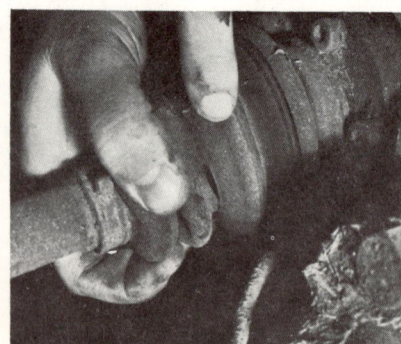

3.1b Examining a split boot

flange first and then the transmission flange.

5   If a new driveshaft is fitted make sure you have the right one. The driveshafts for the manual transmission are a different length to those on the automatic version.

---

3   Constant velocity joints - removal, inspection and replacement

---

1   If the CVJ cover is split (photos) then it is probable that mud and water have entered the joint and unless it is removed the expensive joint will be ruined. There is no repair to a CVJ, if it is damaged a complete new assembly is required, and is sold as such, no other parts being stocked.

2   It must therefore be removed from the shaft, carefully washed, inspected, and if in good order replaced with a new rubber boot.

3   However, it isn't quite as easy as that. Four different types of joint have been used.

  a)   *The earliest ones have the boot secured with a clip to the shaft and a hose clip to the joint. The end cap is a press fit and is located in a groove on the inside of the outer ring. These are not now available as spares.*

  b)   *The next version has a milled recess in the outer edge of the joint. The recess should face towards the driveshaft*

rubber boot on reassembly.

  c)   *Yet another type has a fine groove all round the outer ring near one edge. This ring goes toward the flange coupling.*

  d)   *The latest version is different again, the cap being made of plastic (Fig. 7.2).*

4   The rubber boot is fitted without the hose clips on later models. The boot is rolled into the cap, so a replacement boot will mean a new cap as well. (Fig. 7.3)

5   To separate the joint from the shaft if the boot is split either undo the hose clip (early models) and pull the boot away from the protecting cap or just ease the boot back as you tap off the protecting cap. Unless the boot is split there is no need to separate the cap from the boot, just tap the cap away from the body of the CVJ and remove cap and boot down the shaft.

6   Now support the joint across the jaws of a vice with the shaft hanging down and (if there is one) prise out the end cap (photo), remove the circlip (photo) and tap the shaft down out of the joint. There will be a concave washer behind the joint. Remove this. (photo)

7   Flush out the joint thoroughly and dismantle it by pushing the ball hub and ball cage out of the outer ring. There are six balls. Remove these carefully and do not drop them. The tracks in which the balls run should not be grooved or damaged at the edges in any way. The cage slots should not be wider than the

3.6a Prise out the end cap (if fitted)

3.6b Remove the circlip

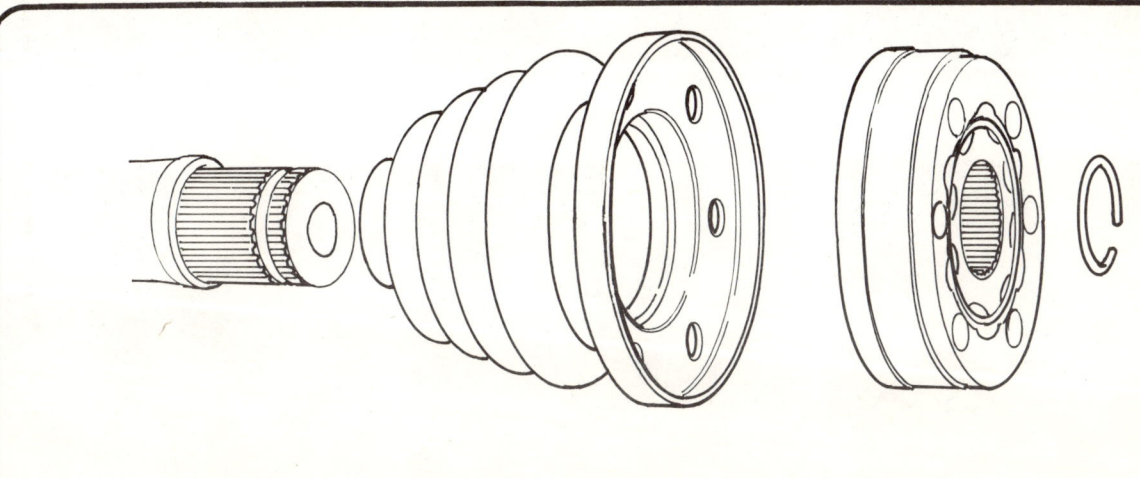
Fig 7.2 The latest version of the CVJ - note the plastic cap. The concave washer should be discarded

steel balls. The balls themselves must be quite spherical and not pitted. If split boots are not rectified without delay and the proper lubrication of the joint is diminished damage soon occurs (photos). New joints are expensive.

8 If the inner cage of the joint is dismantled or falls apart it must be correctly reassembled. First fit the splined hub inside the ball cage — it will only go in if two grooves are lined up (photo).

9 Then press the balls into the cage. They should be a snap fit unless the cage is worn badly (photo).

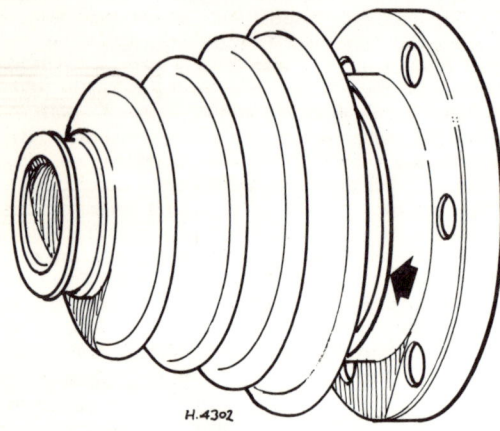

H.4302

Fig 7.3 The later type of boot and cap. This is now the only type obtainable as a replacement

10 Place the ball and hub assembly into the outer cage so that the chamfered edge of the hub splines will be in a position towards the shaft shoulder when the joint is eventually replaced on the shaft (photo). This means that it has to be the right way round in the outer cage because the outer cage goes on so that the protective boot assembly can be tapped back in position on the side away from the outer ring groove.

11 The latest VW instructions are that the concave washer should be discarded when overhauls to CVJs are done on all models. Check with the agent that this instruction still applies, and discard it.

12 Refit the new boot and cap if you have replaced the old one and then refit the joint to the shaft (photo).

13 Refit the circlip (photo) and drive it home. (photo)

14 Repack the joint with 3.2 ozs (90 grams) of molybdenum grease. Put two thirds in the joint between the joint and the cap, replace the cap and boot and then squeeze the rest of the grease in from the front of the joint. Line up the holes in the cap with those in the joint. (photo)

15 If there was an end cap refit it to the outer face of the joint.

4 Rear wheel shafts and bearings - removal and replacement

1 Remove the hubcap and bearing dust cover from the wheel. Refer to Fig. 7.4 and then take out the split pin from the axle-shaft nut. The handbrake should be on firmly. With a socket and long bar slacken the large axle-shaft nut. It is very tight.

2 Remove the driveshaft as described in Section 2.

3 Jack-up the vehicle, remove the axle-shaft nut and pull the wheel off the shaft complete with brake drum.

4 Three screws hold the back plate assembly to the bearing housing flange. If the bearings (one roller, one ball) are to be flushed out or renewed then the handbrake cable and hydraulic brake fluid line should be disconnected and the back plate

3.6c Remove the concave washer

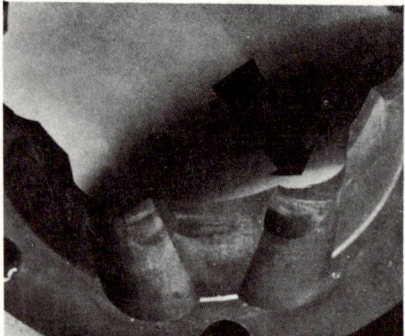

3.7a Damage to the joint outer ring (arrow)

3.7b Damage to joint hub (arrow)

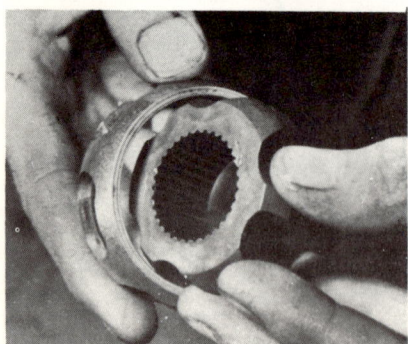

3.8 Placing the hub section into the cage

3.9 Fitting the balls to the cage

3.10 Fitting the hub, balls and cage to the outer section

3.12 Replace the joint on the shaft

3.13a Fit the circlip over the end of the shaft ....

3.13b ... and drive it home

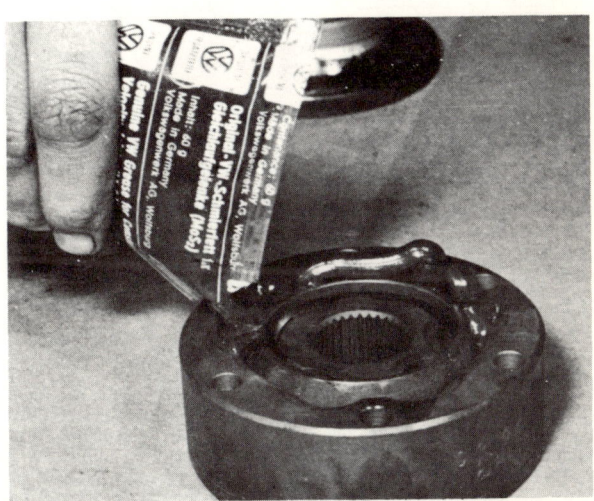

3.14 Repack the CVJ with grease

assembly taken off. Other than to add grease there is little of value to be done by merely driving the wheel shaft out without being able to get to the bearings properly. New seals should be fitted and the roller bearing outer races cannot be removed without destroying the outer race so get a new one first if you intend to remove the complete roller race. Lever out the oil seals after pressing out the wheel shaft.

5   On some models the roller race is retained by circlips; on later versions the race is a press fit on the shaft. Remove the circlips and take out the roller bearing inner race and the spacer sleeve. If the bearings are renewed the spacer should be renewed. The new spacer will have a larger outside diameter.

6   Remove the ball race using a drift on the outside diameter only.

7   If you are only going to repack the bearings with grease leave the outer race of the roller bearing in position.

8   Reassembly is a reversal of the removal procedure. The hub should be packed with 70 grams of multi-purpose grease such as Castrol LM. Work some of this well into the bearings first.

When replacing one of the later types of roller bearing it is very easy to distort the outer race if it is not driven (or pulled)

squarely into the housing. Do not forget to fit the spacer between the bearings and, where necessary replace the circlip for the early type roller bearing outer race.

The later type roller bearing has a rounded edge to one side of the cage and this side goes inwards.

When refitting the back plate, use sealing compound between it and the bearing housing to keep water from seeping into the brakes.

The oil seals themselves should be driven in squarely to each side of the bearing housing after the circlips have been fitted. See that the lips and open sides of the seals face inwards.

9   Reconnect the handbrake cable and the hydraulic fluid line and bleed the hydraulic system.

10 The axle wheel shaft unit has to be tightened to 250 lbs ft torque. This needs a proper socket and an extension on the handle. It should not be necessary to use a torque wrench because it will be simply a question of re-aligning the split pin holes with the castellations as before. The actual movement of the nut to increase the torque from, say, 150 lb ft to 250 lb ft is very little indeed. Always refit a new split pin and spread the split ends correctly.

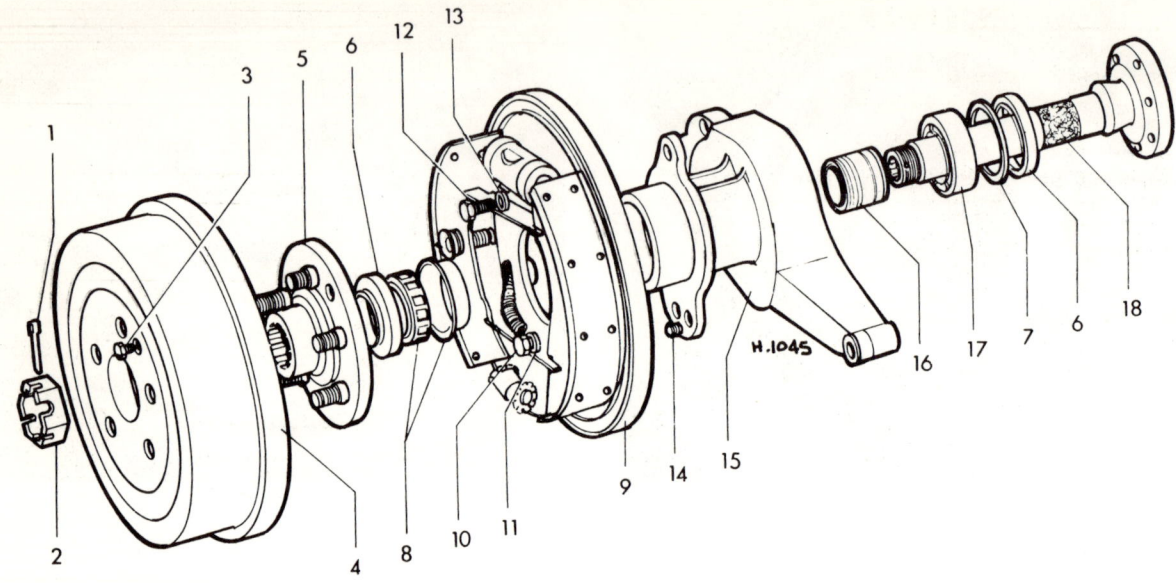

Fig 7.4 Rear wheel shaft and bearings (Sec 4)

1 Split pin	*6 Grease seal*	*11 Spring washer*	*15 Bearing housing*
2 Nut	*7 Circlip*	*12 Bolt*	*16 Spacer sleeve*
3 Bolt	*8 Roller bearing*	*13 Lock washer*	*17 Ball bearing*
4 Brake drum	*9 Backplate assembly*	*14 Dowel pin*	*18 Wheel shaft*
5 Wheel hub	*10 Bolt*		

5 Shock absorbers - removal, testing and replacement

1 If the back of the vehicle seems to bounce or sway unduly, and a knock is heard when you go over a bump the trouble is usually with the shock absorbers.

2 A simple but effective test is as follows: With the vehicle on level ground push down hard on one side of the rear bumper and hold the bumper down as far as it will go. Now let it go suddenly and the body will spring up and then it should settle without any rocking. If the van rocks or wobbles then the shock absorbers are not working correctly.

3 Inspect the shock absorber visually. If there is a lot of oil leaking from it then the seals have perished. A small leak does not matter as the shock absorber is overfilled on manufacture to allow for this.

4 However, whatever is wrong with it, the assembly must be removed. It is held by two bolts, and these will be rusty. Soak them well with penetrating oil.

5 Jack-up the vehicle, remove the rear wheel and secure the van on an axle stand. The jack is not enough support if you are going to crawl underneath with the wheel off the vehicle.

6 Take the nut off the top bolt securing the upper half of the shock absorber to the frame. It is an M12 nut. Then remove the bottom nut and tap out the bolts, top one first, so that the shock absorber may be removed from the vehicle.

7 Put the bottom bushing in a vice and pull the top up to its full extent of travel; push it down to the lower limit. Repeat this several times. The pressure should be even and uniform throughout the whole stroke. If possible get the agent to compare it with a new one.

8 The shock absorber is not repairable but the rubber bushes may be pressed out and new ones installed if you have a big enough vice or access to a press. The metal sleeve and rubber bushing come out together.

9 Now clean up the bore in the shock absorber eye, coat the new rubber bush with a silicone spray or some talcum powder and press it into the shock absorber until the shoulder on the bush meets the shock absorber eye. Then press in the metal

sleeve from the same side.

10 A word of advice about replacing shock absorbers. It is not necessary to replace them in pairs, but if one has failed and you have the time it is as well to remove the other and test it while you have the tools available. The important thing is that they should both work at the same pressure. It is not even necessary to have the two from the same manufacturer but they must damp the vehicle oscillation with the same characteristic.

  If the van is used a lot on rough ground and the shock absorbers give trouble continually it is worth considering the use of heavy duty shock absorbers, but they do make for a harsh ride on smooth roads.

  Shock absorbers for the 1600 cc version of the Transporter **do not** fit the 1700/1800 cc.

11 Re-installation is the reverse of removal. Fit the bottom bolt first and torque it to the correct amount. Pull the top half up until the top bolt may be fitted and install the bolt to the correct torque.

12 Refit the wheel, lower the vehicle to the ground, and go through the test again.

6 Rear suspension - removal and reassembly (general)

1 The rear suspension of the 1700/1800 cc is slightly different from the 1600 cc version. The rear cross tube has been moved forward about 1 inch (25.4 mm), the diagonal arm is different, the torsion bar is different, the splines are now 48/52 and the spring plate is longer. Be careful therefore when buying new parts. The 1600 version torsion bar splines are 44/48.

2 The hub may be removed separately and the spring plate may then be removed without taking off the diagonal arm (and vice-versa). The spring plate must be removed before the torsion bar can be extracted.

3 If the torsion bar is to be removed be careful not to scratch the protective covering. Torsion bars are prestressed in their working direction, be careful that they are fitted to the correct sides, the marks 'L' and 'R' are on the outer face. If they are put in the wrong way they will fracture under load.

4 When working on the rear suspension with the wheels removed it should be a golden rule that the vehicle is supported firmly on stands and the front wheels chocked to prevent the vehicle moving. The van weight is over one ton. The insurance company will probably regard it as a self-inflicted injury if the van descends on you (not that you will be all that interested).

7 Rear suspension diagonal arm - removal and replacement

1 To remove the diagonal arm first jack-up the vehicle and disconnect the outer end of the driveshaft from the wheel shaft. The rear brakes may be removed with the arm and wheel shaft if wished in which case the hydraulic pipe connection should be undone. Otherwise the wheel shaft nut should be slackened whilst the car is still on its wheels. The brake drum and backplate complete with shoes may then be taken off (see Chapter 8).
2 Before undoing the bolts securing the spring plate to the diagonal arm it is important to mark both the arm and plates with a chisel before moving their relative positions. The rear wheel geometry can be upset if this setting is lost.
3 Unclip the brake pipes from the arm.
4 The inner end of the diagonal arm pivots on a bolt. Once this is undone the arm may be taken out. The bushes on the diagonal arm are not renewable - they are vulcanised to the arm. A complete new arm must therefore be fitted.
5 When replacing the pivot bolt it must be tightened to the correct torque.
6 When clamping the spring plates back to the diagonal arm the line up marks made on dismantling must correspond.
7 If extensive repairs are being made (due to damage) which call for renewal of the arm it is important to have the suspension checked on a VW alignment jig after assembly.

8 Rear torsion bars and spring plates - removal, replacement and setting

1 Before the nuts and bolts attaching the spring plates to the diagonal arm are loosened the relative positions of the arm and the plates must be marked with a chisel.
2 The spring plate rests on a lug in the frame casing along its lower edge and to relieve residual tension in the torsion bar it must be sprung out so that it rides over the lug. This can be done quite easily with a tyre lever.
3 At this stage the setting of the suspension can be checked. The angle of the plate in this unstressed position should be as indicated in the Specifications according to the models from the horizontal line of the vehicle body. From this measurement

therefore a spirit level and protractor are needed. The horizontal line of the vehicle is taken from the bottom of the door opening in the bodyshell. Using a level and protractor work out how far this deviates from the true horizontal.
4 Measure the angle of the spring plate from the true horizontal in the same way, eliminating any play there may be by lifting the plate while the measurement is taken.
5 Depending on which way the body deviates, the angle is added or subtracted to the plate angle to give the differences between the two. Reference to Fig. 10.5 will illustrate the examples given below.

Body deviation angle	*4º*
Plate deviation angle	*20º*
Plate/body angle (AA)	*16º*
Plate/body angle (BB)	*24º*

If the correct plate/body angle is 21º 10' then in situation 'AA' the plate angle needs increasing by 5º 10'. In 'BB' it needs decreasing by 2º 50'.
6 The torsion bars are splined at each end. The inner end anchors to a splined bracket fixed in the centre of the cross tube. The outer end is splined to the spring plate. The inner end has 48 splines (7º 30' per spline) and the outer end has 52 splines (6º 55' per spline) affording an alteration possibility in graduations of 35' (7º 30' - 6º 55').
   In example 'AA' if the inner end of the torsion bar is rotated 8 splines (60º) in an anticlockwise direction and the spring plate rotated 8 splines (55º 20') in a clockwise direction round the outer end of the torsion bar the net increase in angle will be 4º 40' (60º - 55º 20') which is as near to the 5º 10' as possible (½ a degree).
   In example 'BB' the inner end of the bar is rotated clockwise 5 splines (37º 30') and the spring plate anticlockwise round the outer end 5 splines (34º 35') the difference will then be a decrease of 2º 55' which is only 5 minutes from the correct angle (2º 50').
7 To withdraw the torsion bar sufficiently to rotate the splines for adjustment first remove the four screws which secure the cover clamping the rubber cushion mounting. The spring plate can now be pulled off the torsion bar and at the same time the inner end of the bar may be drawn out of the centre splined location. (Note that torsion bars are not interchangeable side for side).
8 Having reset the torsion bar so that the plate angle is correct make sure that the rubber mounting bushes are in good condition. Renew if in doubt. Cover with flake graphite (to prevent squeaking) and make sure the inner one is installed the proper way up. (The top edge is marked 'Oben'). Before the cover is reinstalled over the rubber bush it will be necessary to

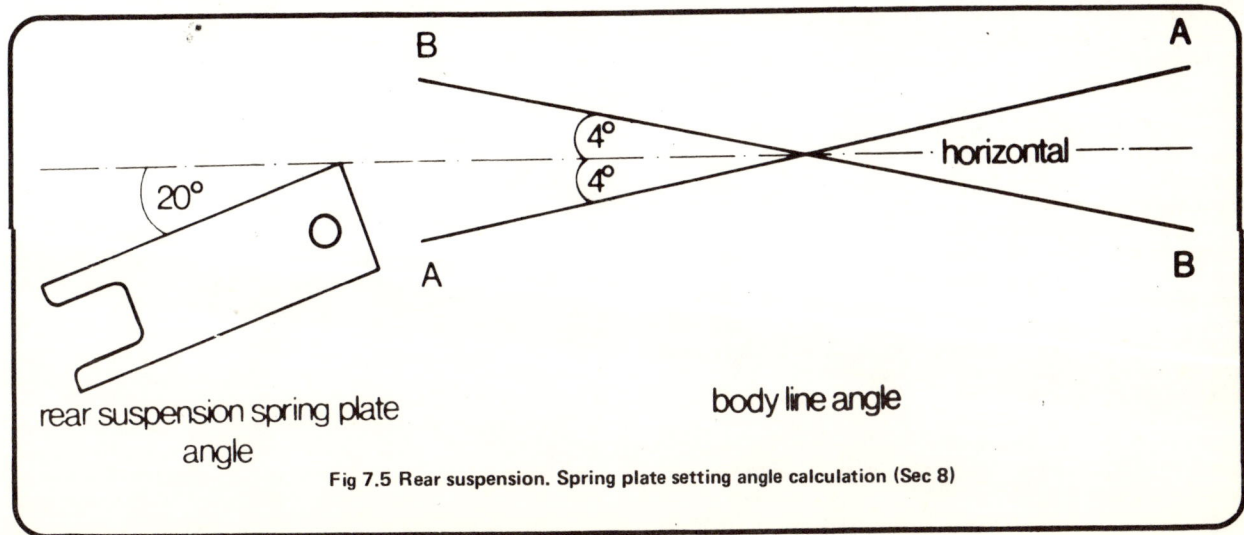

Fig 7.5 Rear suspension. Spring plate setting angle calculation (Sec 8)

raise the plate above the stop lug on the frame casting. If this is not done now the preloading of the rubber bushing will be all wrong when the cover is put back. It will also be very nearly impossible to move the plate. To lift the plate put a jack under the end. If it looks as though the vehicle is going to lift before the plate is up in position get some people to sit in the back for a minute or two. With the plate held in position replace the cover plate and setscrews.

9 It may be difficult to get the four plate securing screws to pick up their threads on replacement - particularly with a new bush. In such instances two longer screws will have to be obtained and used diagonally so that the plate may be drawn down enough to refit the shorter screws. (The short screws must be used finally otherwise the cover plate will not pull down far enough to stress the rubber bush properly.

10 With the cover tightened down the diagonal arm may be reassembled to the spring plate.

11 The angle adjustment of the spring plates must be the same on both sides of the car.

12 If the spring plates have been renewed or any other work has been carried out on the rear suspension which could affect the alignment then it is important that the camber and toe settings be checked with alignment equipment. It would also be timely to mention here that if the rear suspension spring plate settings are purposely altered to give an increased or reduced ground clearance then the effects on handling under certain circumstances are, to say the least, unusual. Tyre wear is also greatly increased if the rear wheel alignment is incorrect.

9 Rear wheel alignment

1 If for some reason the spring plate angle has been altered, or the vehicle has been in an accident then the rear wheel toe and camber (yes! - rear wheel) must be checked and if necessary reset.

2 This is done by shifting the whole axle assembly and is thought to be beyond the scope of the owner driver. It requires expensive optical measuring instruments to set the angles.

3 It should be left to the VW agent who has the necessary tools and equipment. However, if the angles are not correct vehicle handling may be difficult and there will be rapid wear on the rear tyres.

Chapter 8 Braking system, wheels and tyres

Contents

Specifications

Type	Hydraulic, dual circuit layout, with equalizer valve on rear circuit. Front brakes discs; rear brakes, drums. Some models are fitted with self-adjusting brakes on the rear wheels.	

Front brakes

Disc measurements

Diameter	278.2 mm	(11 in)
Thickness:		
New	13 mm	(0.582 in)
After machining (min)	12 mm	(0.472 in)
Maximum thickness machining allowance	0.50 mm	(0.020 in)
Maximum permissive thickness variation	0.02 mm	(0.0008 in)
Maximum allowable runout of true	0.10 mm	(0.004 in)
Wear limit	11.5 mm	(0.452 in)

Friction pads

Thickness:		
From Chassis '2112000 001'	10 mm	(0.393 in)
From Chassis '213 2000 001'	14 mm	(0.551 in)
Minimum thickness	2 mm	(0.079 in)

Rear brakes

Brake drums inside diameter:		
From chassis '218 000 001'	250.00 + 0.20 mm	(9.842 + 0.008 in)
From chassis '211 2000 001'	252 + 0.20 mm	(9.921 + 0.008 in)
Lateral runout	0.25 mm	(0.010 in)
Ovality	0.10 mm	(0.004 in)
Brake linings:		
Width:		
From chassis no '218 000 001'	45 mm	(1.770 in)
From chassis no '211 2000 001'	55 mm	(2.165 in)
Thickness:		
From chassis no '218 000 001'	5 - 4.8 mm	(0.200 - 0.190 in)
oversize from chassis no '218 000 007'	5.5 - 5.3 mm	(0.220 - 0.210 in)
thickness from chassis no '211 2000 001'	6 - 5.8 mm	(0.235 - 0.230 in)

Master cylinder

Diameter	22.20 mm	(0.874 in)
Front circuit stroke:		
From chassis '218 000 001'	24 mm	(0.944 in)
From chassis '211 200 001'	19 mm	(0.748 in)
Rear circuit stroke:		
From chassis '218 000 001'	14 mm	(0.551 in)
From chassis '211 200 001'	13 mm	(0.512 in)
Clearance piston/pushrod	1 mm	(0.04 in)

Wheel cylinders

Front caliper	25.40 mm	(1 in)
Rear wheel:		
Pre 1971 (Chassis '218 000 001')	22.20 mm	(0.874 in)
1971 onwards (Chassis '212 2000 001')	23.81 ,,	(0.937 in)

Brake pressure regulator

Type	Deacceleration sensitive inertia ball type

Servo boosting factor

... ...	2.05

Tyres

Size:	
Campmobile, 1972 on	185 SR 14 Reinforced
Delivery Van and Station Wagon 1972 on	185 R x 14C
Pressures (Radials):	
Front (all loads)	30 p.s.i.
Rear:	
Campmobile (¾ loaded)	37 p.s.i.
Campmobile (fully loaded)	40 p.s.i.
Delivery van and station wagon (¾ loaded)	40 p.s.i.
Delivery van and station wagon (fully loaded)	44 p.s.i.

Wheels

Type	5JK x 14
Offset*	41.0 mm (1 5/8 ins)

Offset is the measurement from the centre of the rim width to the mounting face that bolts to the brake drum or disc.

Torque wrench settings

	ft lbs	kgm
Master cylinder		
Stop screw in housing	3.5 - 7	0.5 - 1.0
Residual pressure valve	14	2.0
Brake light switch	14	2.0
Brake line union	11	1.5
Pushrod locknut	11	1.5
Master cylinder to servo (max)	9.4	1.3
Front brakes		
Caliper to steering knuckle (1972)	72	10
Caliper to steering knuckle (1973 on)	116	16
Bleeder valve (max)	3.5	0.5
Flexible hose to caliper	14	2.0
Disc to hub	18	2.5
Caliper halves	25	3.5
Splash shield to steering knuckles	7	1.0
Rear brakes		
Backing plate on bearing housing M.8.	14	2.0
M.10.	29	4.0
Cover to bearing housing (max)	29	4.0
Wheel cylinder to backing plate	14	2.0
Brake drum to shaft	253	35
Castellated nut	253	35
Brake drum to hub	13	1.8
Wheels		
Wheel nuts to drum	94	13

Pedals							**ft lbs**	**kgm**
Brake pedal on pin	...	...	...	...	...	...	29	4.0
Brake pedal to pushrod	...	...	...	...	...	...	14	2
Clutch pedal on pin	...	...	...	...	...	...	18	2.5
Clutch pedal support on frame		...	...	...	...	...	14	2
Servo								
Brake servo to front axle	...	...	...	...	...	...	9.4	1.3
Brake balancing valve to sidemember	...	...	...	...	...	11	1.5
Output adapter in regulator	...	...	...	...	...	16	2.2
Brake pressure regulator								
Regulator to sideframe	...	...	...	...	...	...	11	1.5
Output adapter (old type only)	...	...	...	...	...	14	2.0
Pipe unions (input and output)	...	...	...	...	...	14	2.0

1 General description

1 As the engine power of the Transporter has increased so has the effectiveness of the brakes been improved.

A tandem master cylinder supplies hydraulic pressure to two separate circuits, one for the disc brakes on the front wheels and one for the drum brakes on the rear wheels. A hydraulically operated electric switch on the master cylinder gives warning, via a lamp on the dashboard, should the systems fail.

The rear brakes are fitted with a pressure regulator to prevent the back wheels being locked in the event of emergency braking.

The system is servo-assisted utilizing the induction manifold vacuum to increase the total pressure in the master cylinder.

The handbrake operates on the rear wheels, via a mechanical linkage; an equalizing bar has been fitted since 1972 and adjustment of the cables is now done on the equalizing bar.

The area of the rear shoes has been increased and larger calipers are fitted to the front brakes, as shown in the Specification.

Export models, particularly to USA, are fitted with self-adjusting rear brakes.

Wheels, tyres, wheel balancing, and brake bleeding are all covered in this Chapter.

2 Braking system - inspection and adjustment

1 The braking system is such a tribute to design that most drivers are taken by surprise when it goes wrong. The way to avoid this unpleasant happening is by regular inspection and by understanding the symptoms of ailing brakes.

2 Many vehicles are fitted with self-adjusting rear brakes - which means that no active maintenance is required. For the few not so fitted a regular inspection of the shoes and adjustment as necessary is imperative. The handbrake will tell you when excessive wear is taking place. This is discussed in the Section on rear brakes.

3 The front discs are self-adjusting but again regular inspection does not entrail much hard labour and may save not only a lot of money but also heartache. This operation is explained in the Section on front brakes.

4 The maintenance of pipes and hoses is also gone into at some length.

5 At the conclusion of this Chapter a fault diagnosis chart is included, but this only diagnoses trouble when it has happened, the smart operator gets busy before then.

6 The brakes should operate smoothly and consistently. Any variation in performance must be investigated and cured right away.

7 Pulling to one side, or the other, however slight, means that all four brakes must be checked for adjustment forthwith. It only means jacking-up the vehicle and spinning each wheel in turn. Get someone to apply the footbrake gently and it is easy to find which wheel is at fault.

8 Loss of fluid from the header tank is serious. It is going somewhere it shouldn't and it is no use just topping-up and carrying on. Leaks at the front calipers or the various pipes can be spotted by just looking underneath the van. Leaks in the rear wheel cylinders may require removal of the drums before they can be located.

9 If the pedal goes much further down than usual when there are no leaks in the system and the brakes are properly adjusted then the trouble is at the master cylinder. **Do not** wait until it goes right down to the floor, there will not be any braking force at all then.

10 If the brakes drag, get hot, or even lock on then the trouble is probably either maladjustment of the connecting rod, or foreign matter clogging the compensating ports in the master cylinder. It may be as simple as something stopping the foot brake pedal from returning to its stop, a broken return spring for instance, or mud. It may be a problem in the servo which will not allow the master cylinder pushrod to return fully and so it is closing the compensating ports when they ought to be open.

If only one brake gets hot then that one should be dismantled checked and readjusted. If both rear brakes get hot then the handbrake may be malfunctioning (or you may have left it on of course, this happens to everyone at sometime or other).

Generally speaking slight overheating will not do too much damage, but it will eventually melt grease and cause oil seals to fail. It can crack discs or even drums if left too long.

11 Although the servo gives very little trouble, when it does it can be difficult to track down the problem. If the pedal does not go right down but very high pressure is needed to operate the brakes then the servo vacuum has failed. This is discussed in Section 16, and should be tackled right away.

12 Adjustment of rear brakes is discussed in Section 7; adjustment of the handbrake (parking brake) in Section 22. There is no adjustment for the front brakes.

13 Finally the question of "sponginess" in the pedal. This is nearly always air in the system. It can easily be cured by bleeding the brakes as discussed later on, but the worry is how did it get here. If having checked all the unions for leaks (and fluid at 800 lbs per square inch will come out of any leak), and having bled the brakes satisfactorily once, the sponginess returns then the next port of call is the VW agent. A ton of transporter travelling at sixty miles an hour is no device to be in when the brakes do not work.

3 Front disc brakes - general description

1 Refer to Fig. 8.1 and Fig. 8.2.

2 The disc brakes are bolted to the front suspension in such a way that the disc rotates with the front wheel and the caliper is fixed to the steering knuckle. Behind the disc is the splash-guard which is also bolted to the steering knuckle so that the disc is sheltered on both sides from the elements, the outer cover being the wheel. It is however open to the atmosphere which assists in cooling.

3 The caliper has two pistons, which actuate the brake pads

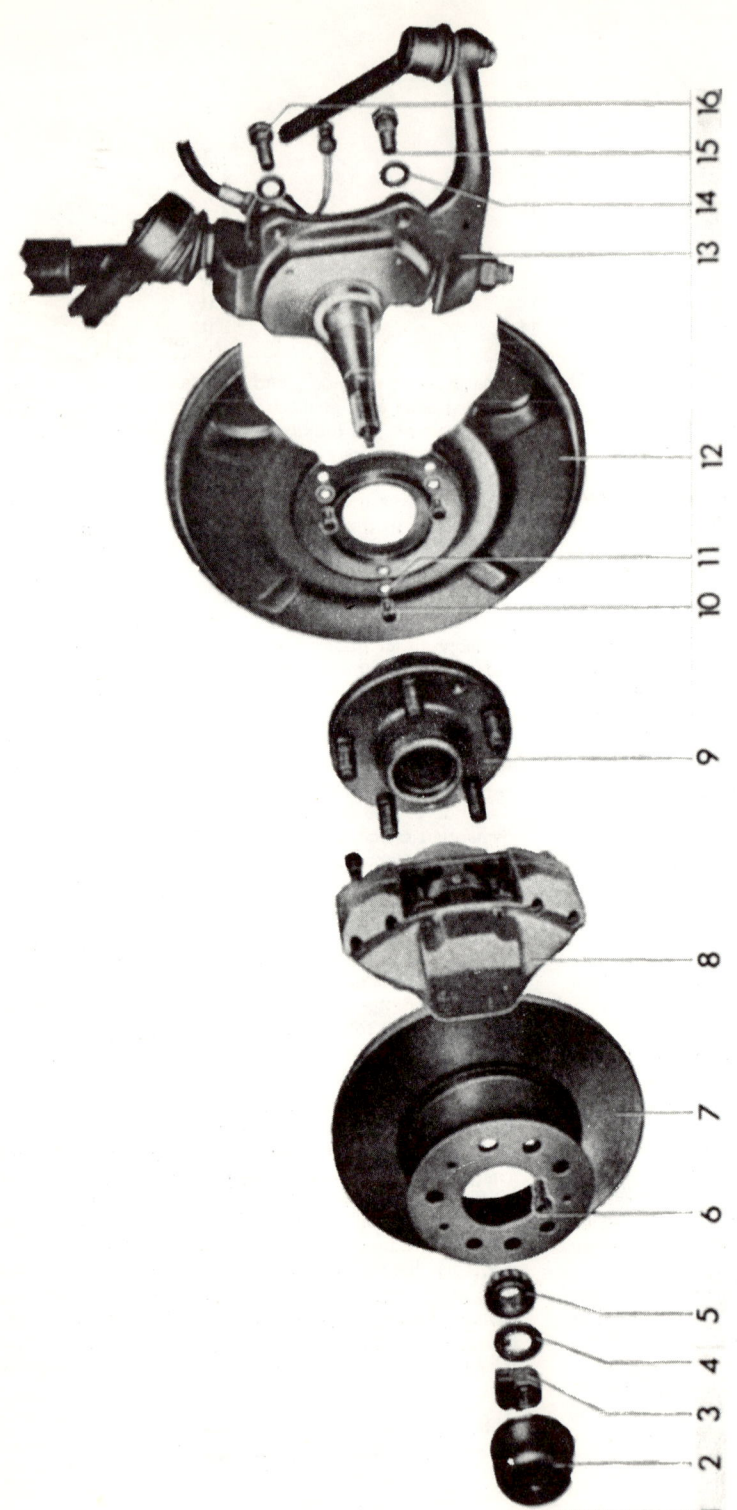

Fig 8.1 Front brake and hub assembly (Sec 3)

1	C washer	5	Wheel bearing
2	Hub cap	6	Screw
3	Clamp nut	7	Brake disc
4	Thrust washer	8	Brake caliper

9	Front wheel hub	13	Shield
10	Bolt	14	Spring washer
11	Lockwasher	15	Locating bolt
12	Shield	16	Bolt

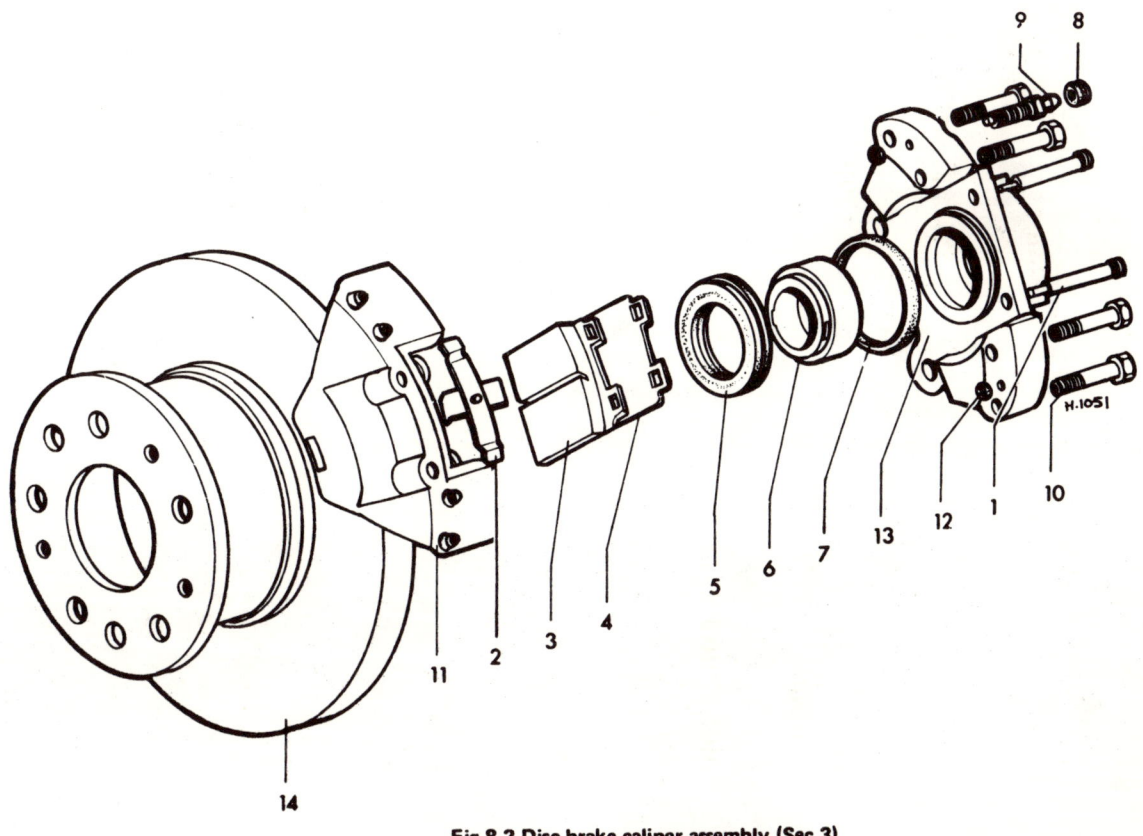

Fig 8.2 Disc brake caliper assembly (Sec 3)

1 Pad retaining pin	5 Dust seal	9 Bleed valve	13 Caliper inner half
2 Spreader spring	6 Piston	10 Screw	14 Brake disc
3 Friction pad	7 Fluid seal	11 Caliper outer half	
4 Piston retaining plate	8 Dust cap	12 Sealing ring	

pressing them against the disc when the brake pedal is depressed rather like gripping the disc in a clamp. The type used is the "Fixed caliper".

4 The calipers are split in the middle and are bolted together by six bolts, two of which extend through the steering knuckle to anchor the caliper housing.

5 The disc hub is separate from the front assembly amd may be replaced without a new hub assembly if necessary.

6 Two types of caliper may be found. Whilst to a certain extent, they are interchangeable, should a later type be used instead of the earlier one, both calipers must be changed. At the same time new steering knuckles must be fitted as the bolt sizes have been increased from M12 to M14, the fitted bolt is at the top and the tightening torque increased by 3 mkg (21 lbs ft). The splash guard is also modified.

An illustration is given of the two calipers. It will be seen that the new one is larger, the pads are longer by 0.15 in (4 mm) and 0.15 in (4 mm) thicker. (Fig 8.3)

The pistons are 5/32 in (3.96 mm) longer and the two types of piston **are not** interchangeable.

4 Disc pads - inspection and renewal

1 Remove the front wheel.

2 There are two visual examinations to be made before dismantling anything. These are the thickness of the friction pad and the gap between the pad and disc.

3 Pad friction material thickness must not be less than 2 mm otherwise the pads should be renewed.

4 The residual clearance should not be more than 0.2 mm (0.008 inch) between disc and pad. This can be measured with a feeler gauge.

5 If the gap is greater it is probably due to a sticking piston. A simple remedy is given later on in this Section.

6 If the pads are to be used again mark where they came from beforehand so they may be put back in the same position. Drive out the retaining pins from the outside with a long nosed punch. Lift off the spring plate. (photos)

7 Before removing the old pads it is best to force them away from the disc carefully, with a suitable flat metal lever. This will push the pistons back. Before doing this it will be necessary to remove some hydraulic fluid from the reservoir to prevent it overflowing when the pistons are pushed back. Do this with a suitable suction device such as an empty flexible plastic bottle.

8 Once the pistons are pushed back remove the pads. Do not disturb the piston retaining plate. If it does come out note the reassembly details in Section 5. (photos).

9 Blow out the apterature in the caliper and examine the seal which should show no signs of cracking or brittleness. If it does it should be renewed (see Section 5).

10 Fit the new pads. New pad retaining spring plates are normally provided with the pads and these should be used. When replacing the retaining pins (from the inside) do not use a punch

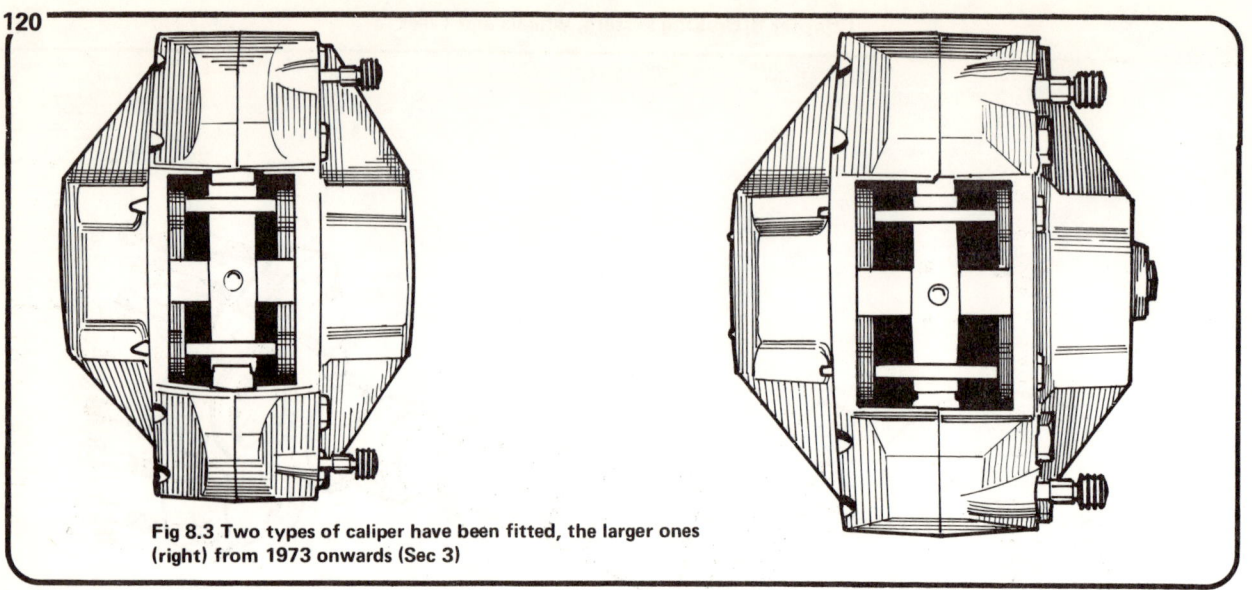

Fig 8.3 Two types of caliper have been fitted, the larger ones (right) from 1973 onwards (Sec 3)

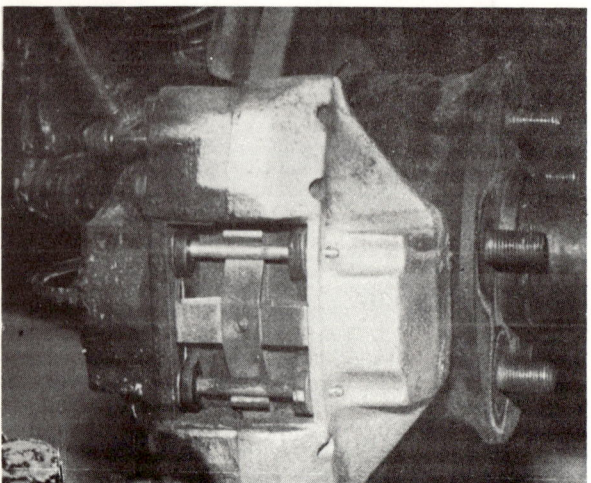

4.6a The wheel has been removed and the caliper is ready to be dismantled

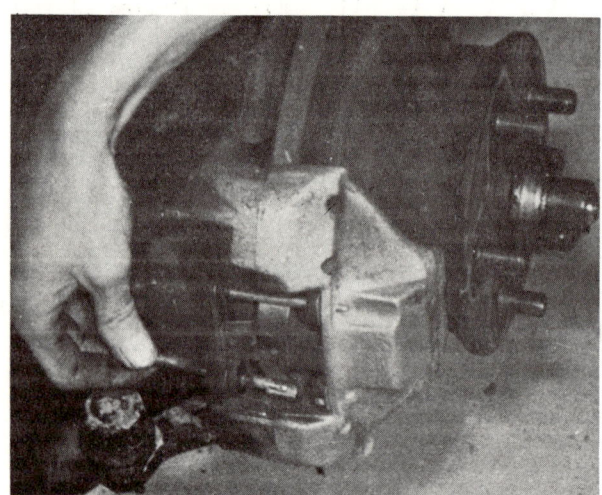

4.6b Remove the pins. Use a thin punch

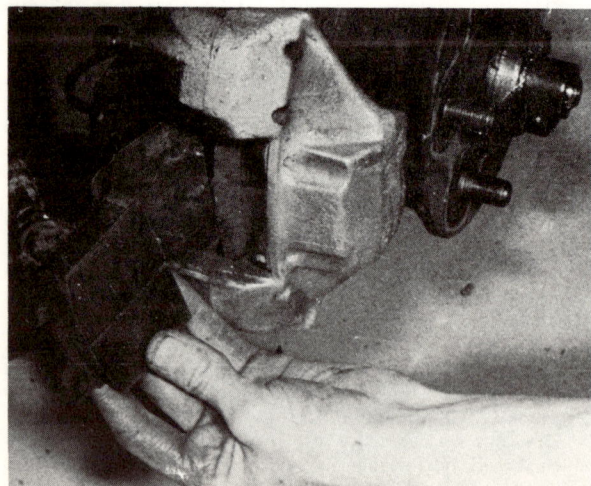

4.8a Remove the pads. These were nearly new and came out easily by hand. Well worn ones may require tongs to extract them

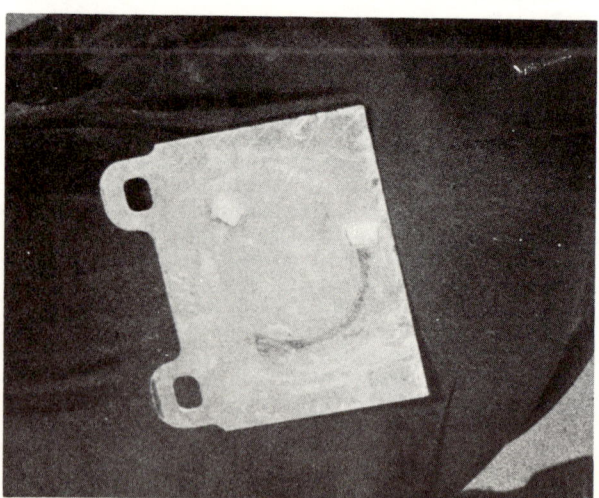

4.8b A slightly marked retaining plate

smaller in diameter than the pin. Preferably, use no punch at all otherwise there is a possibility of shearing the shoulder off against the split clamping bush.

11 Pump the brake pedal to bring the pads up to the disc and check the level of hydraulic fluid in the reservoir.

12 If the clearance between the disc and pad is too great after brake operation then this is an indication that the inner piston rubber seal is sticking somewhat and distorting more than normally. This retracts the piston more than usual when the pressure is taken off. Movement of the piston can usually cure this. Remove a brake pad and put in a block of wood no less than 6 mm thick. Pump the brakes to force the piston further out and then force it back again. Do this a few times and the problem should disappear. If not it will be necessary to check the piston seals and caliper cylinders thoroughly as described in Section 5.

5 Disc caliper pistons and seals - inspection and renewal

1 Before assuming that anything is wrong which requires removal of the caliper pistons make sure that the checks in connection with renewal of the friction pads as described in Section 4 have been carried out.

2 Discs may deteriorate, if left unused, due to corrosion. If this happens it is best to let a VW agent repolish them with special blocks which can be inserted in place of the friction pads. Discs which are badly scored or distorted must be renewed. It is possible to have them re-machined but the economics of this against fitting new parts should be examined.

The run-out of the disc can be checked only with a clock gauge micrometer. With the bearing properly adjusted the run-out should not exceed 0.2 mm (0.008 inch).

3 To renew a disc or repair piston seals, the caliper assembly must first be removed. It is held by two bolts from the back of the steering knuckle. (If the disc only is to be removed it is not necessary to disconnect the hydraulic fluid hose. The whole assembly should be tied up onto the bodywork to prevent any strain on the hose). If the pistons are to be removed from the caliper thought must first be given as to how pressure can be applied to force them out. Only one piston can be worked on at a time as the other piston must be installed and clamped in position so as to maintain pressure to force the other out. Pressure can be applied from a foot pump if you rig up a spare hydraulic pipe union and short length of pipe to which the pump connector will fit. One piston will have to be clamped in such a way that there will still be room enough for the other to come right out. Here again a tong-like clamp may have to be made up from some 1½ x 1/8 inch (40 x 3.2 mm) flat steel bar if you are unable to obtain a suitable tool.

4 Mount the caliper assembly in the vice padding the jaws suitably so that the flange of the caliper will not be scored or marked. The friction pads and retaining plates should be removed (see Section 4).

5 Prise out the outer seal using a blunt plastic or wooden tool. Do not use sharp tools for fear of scoring the piston or cylinder.

6 Using a clamp to hold one piston force the other out under pressure as described in paragraph 3. To prevent damage in case the piston should come out with force put some cloth in the caliper to prevent it striking the piston and clamp opposite.

7 With the piston out the rubber sealing ring can be taken out of its groove in the cylinder; once again use only a blunt article to get it out.

8 With methylated spirits or hydraulic fluid, clean the piston and cylinder thoroughly. If there are any signs of severe scoring or pitting then renewal will be necessary. With the cylinder this involves renewing the whole caliper unit.

9 When renewing seals the piston retaining plate must also be renewed. The VW service kit includes all the items needed. Use them. Before reassembly it is advantageous to coat the piston and new rubber seal with VW cylinder paste specially formulated for this job. Otherwise make sure they are thoroughly lubricated with clean hydraulic fluid. On no account use

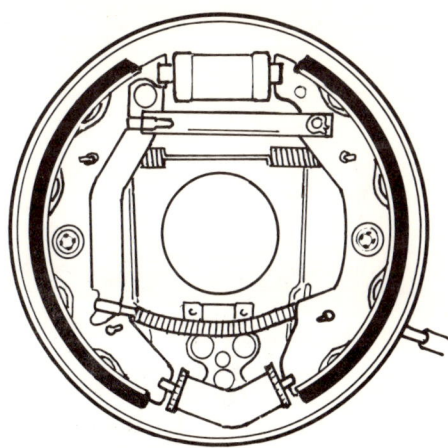

Fig 8.4 Rear drum brake assembly - drum removed (Sec 6)

anything else.

10 Fit the rubber seal in the cylinder groove and then fit the piston into the seal. Great care must be taken to avoid misaligning the seal when doing this and the piston must be kept square while it is pushed in. The cut-out portion of the piston should lie facing in to the centre of the disc and against the direction of forward disc rotation.

6 Rear wheel brakes - general description

1 Drum brakes worked hydraulically by the footbrake and mechanically by the handbrake are fitted to all models. Most vans are fitted with self-adjusting brakes, but some may not have this refinement. Fig. 8.5 refers to the layout of the hub, and Fig. 8.4 shows the brake with the drum take off.

2 The wheel cylinder was modified in 1971 and the shoes slightly altered - so if you are buying spares, be careful.

3 The brake has one leading and one trailing shoe. The hydraulic cylinder has two pistons which work opposed to one another and press the shoes against the drum when the brake pedal is depressed. The shoes pivot about the adjusters at the bottom of the drum and initial setting is obtained by lengthening or shortening the position of these pivots.

4 All adjustment is done to suit the hyraulic circuit and the handbrake circuit is then adjusted at the equalizing bar at the front of the vehicle.

5 The hydraulic cylinder and the pivots are bolted to the backplate which in turn is bolted to the suspension arm. Because the brake moves with the wheel as the suspension operates it is necessary to have a flexible hose coupling from the wheel cylinder to the brake lines carried on the frame.

6 The handbrake cable is passed through a bracket on the backplate, through a plastic hose and hooked onto the bottom of the operating lever. The cable is threaded through a spring which is compressed as the handbrake is applied and returns the operating lever to the off position when the brake is released.

The operating lever is fastened by a pivot pin to the secondary shoe at the top end. A connecting link goes from the brake lever to the other shoe, being pivoted on the lever about a quarter of the way from the pivot pin to the cable. When the cable is pulled the lever moves pivoted thrusting the connecting rod against the trailing shoe which is forced against the drum. Further pressure on the cable causes the leading shoe to pivot against the drum.

7 The shoes are pulled away from the drum in both operations when the foot or handbrake is released by two powerful return springs.

8 Adjustment of the shoes can be carried out through holes in the backplate.

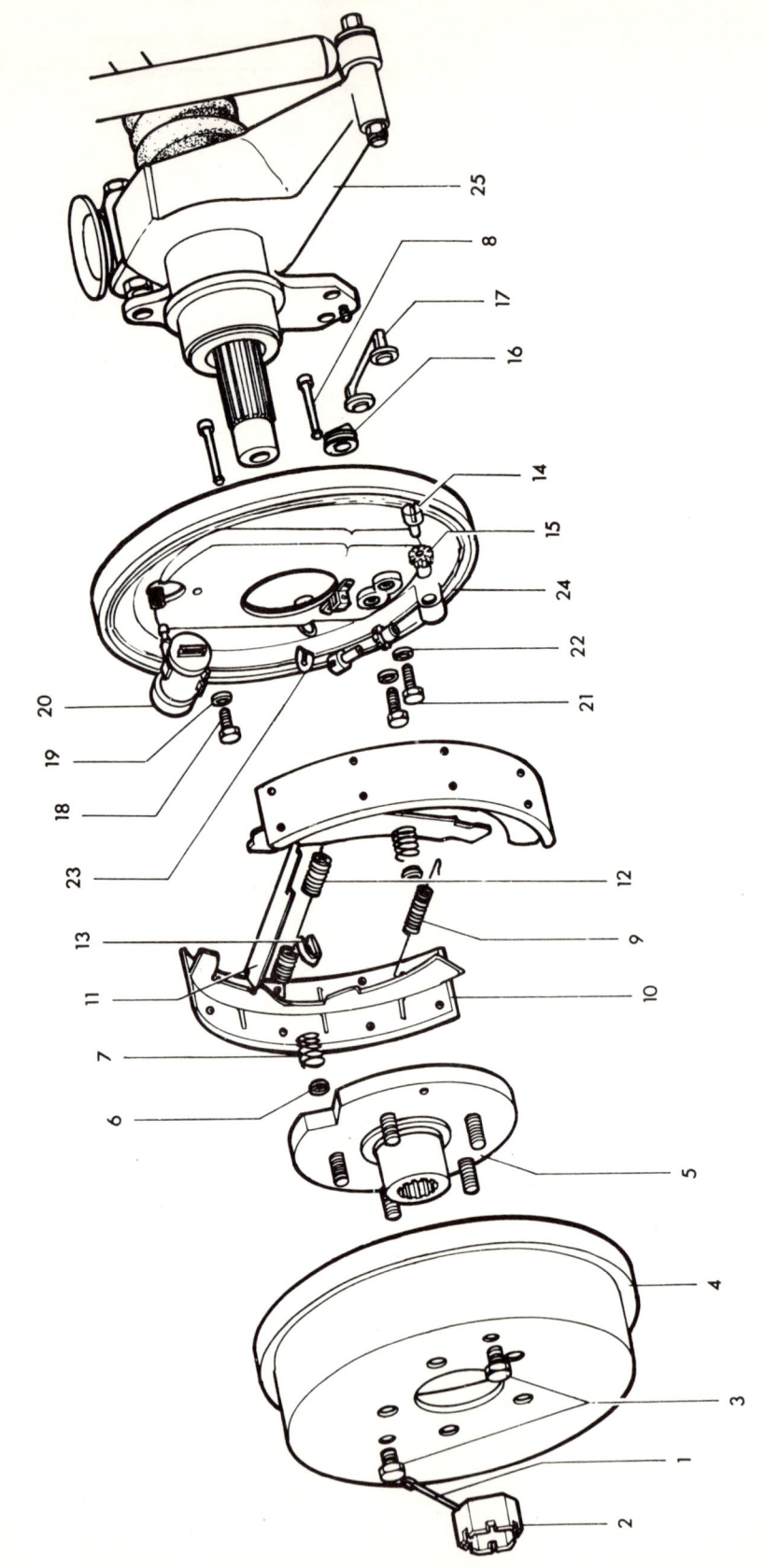

Fig 8.5 Rear wheel brake assembly (Secs. 6 and 8)

1	Split pin	7	Spring	13	Locating clip	20	Wheel cylinder
2	Nut	8	Steady pin	14	Adjuster screw	21	Back plate retaining bolt
3	Socket head screw	9	Return spring	15	Knurled adjuster	22	Spring washer
4	Brake drum	10	Brake shoe	16	Plug	23	Hose circlip
5	Wheel hub	11	Distance piece	17	Retaining pin	24	Backplate
6	Slotted cup washer	12	Return spring	18	Wheel cylinder bolt	25	Suspension arm
				19	Spring washer		

Note: On more recent models part 13 has been replaced by a horseshoe clip and the pin is grooved to fit it

7 Rear brakes - adjustment

1 The shoes must be clear of the drums for normal running or heat will be generated resulting in damage. However, this clearance is minimal or long pedal travel will result.

2 As the shoes and drums wear this clearance must be adjusted. This is effected by turning the adjuster wheels.

3 Jack-up the rear wheels so that they may rotate freely. Chock the front wheels and make sure the handbrake is in the off position. Push down the brake pedal several times to centre the shoes.

4 Remove the rubber plugs from the back of the brake backing plate (photo). It will be possible to see the adjuster wheels.

5 A screwdriver may be used to turn these, one click at a time. The one nearer the front is turned *down* to put the shoe nearer the drum and the other one *up.*

Turn one wheel three clicks and then turn the other an equal amount. Alternate the adjustment in this way until the shoes are hard against the drum.

Now slacken off each adjuster four clicks, or until the wheel turns without the brake shoe binding.

6 If a large adjustment is necessary depress the brake pedal after each wheel has turned six clicks to centre the shoes again.

7 Repeat for the other wheel.

8 Now adjust the handbrake at the equalizing bar.

9 Replace the plugs and road test the car to confirm satisfactory operation.

8 Rear wheel brakes - dismantling, overhaul and reassembly

1 Remove the nave plates, slacken the nuts on the rear roadwheels, chock the front wheels and jack-up the rear wheels. Remove the roadwheel on the side to be worked on. Arrange axle stands or substantial wooden blocks under the vehicle frame before continuing further. Vehicle jacks are a means of lifting but should not be used to support the vehicle when work is being done underneath it. Lower the frame onto the support. Refer to Figure 8.5.

2 Undo the socket headed bolts which hold the drum to the wheel hub. Tap the drum gently with a mallet and draw it off the shoes. There are two problems here. It may be necessary to back off the adjustment if the drum is fouling the shoes, and there may be some burrs on the wheel hub. Remove these with a fine file but do not use excessive force on the drum. It will come off easily if you are patient.

3 It will now be possible to inspect the shoes and other working parts.

4 If the shoes are worn beyond Specification, there must be at least 0.100 inch (2.50 mm) of lining remaining and the rivet heads must be 0.020 ins (0.4 mm) below the surface of the linings, or if the linings are scored or oil soaked, then they must be replaced with new ones. If the linings on one rear wheel are renewed then the linings on the other one must also be renewed.

5 Removal of the linings is a simple business but before removing them have a helper depress the brake pedal gently to see whether the hydraulic cylinders work properly. Once the linings are off the brake pedal must not be touched or the pistons will come out of the wheel cylinder. Make sure both pistons work, if necessary hold one piston in place to make the other work.

6 Remove the spring cups and springs from the steady pins by pressing in the cup and rotating it 90°. When released it will spring off; so ease it out gently. Push the retaining pins through the backplates and remove them. Store all the small parts together in a suitable receptacle. (photo 8.17).

7 Now remove the return springs. There is a proper tool to do this but it can be done without it. **Do not** try to force the spring out from the front or you will break it. With the springs removed the shoes may now be lifted out after the parking brake cable has been disconnected from its lever. Push the lever forward and pull the cable eye downwards.

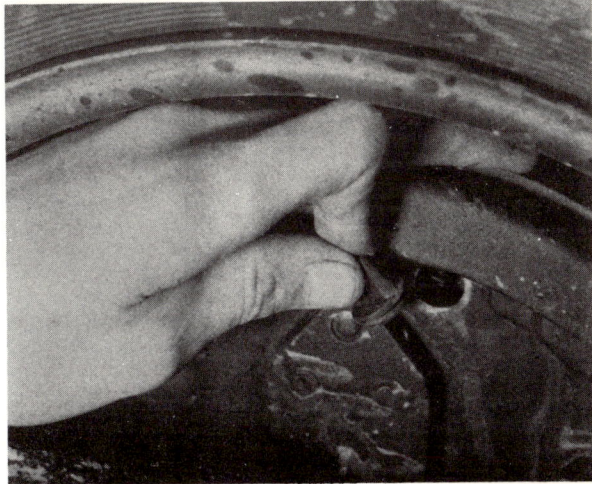

7.4 Remove the rubber plug from the backplate

8 As soon as the shoes are off fasten a clamp or similar device over the wheel cylinder pistons to prevent them from coming out.

9 Clean the drum carefully and look at the surface on which the shoes make contact. This should be smooth and not discoloured. Look for small cracks or pitting. Minor scoring or blemishes may be removed with fine emery paper. Deep scoring must be machined away, or it may be cheaper to obtain a second-hand drum. Cracked drums must be discarded. Check the drum for ovality. This is not an easy task as the drum should be set up in a lathe chuck and checked with a dial gauge. There are limits for run-out, maximum thickness variation, and a 0.020 inch maximum machining allowance.

If the drum is not scored it will be unlikely to be worn much, and machining out 0.020 inches (0.50 mm) on an 11 inch (280 mm) diameter is something which requires either jigs and fixtures or a very good operator, so if it isn't scored unless it is worn with a deep trough in its surface it may be used again.

10 The brake shoes present no problem. If they are worn, oil soaked, or scored then scrap them. A few pence may be saved by stripping off the linings from the shoes and rivetting on new ones but this is not recommended. Factory fitted shoes are rivetted on in jigs and are concentric. They are also clean on the friction surfaces. The obvious answer is to buy four exchange shoes from the VW agent and forget the d-i-y fitting of linings to shoes.

If the drums have been machined then oversize linings are needed so again consult the VW agent.

Again, if the linings are replaced, remember to remove the handbrake lever from the leading shoe and fit it to the new shoe.

11 Springs should be cleaned and checked for distortion. Dismantle the pivot adjusters and clean them. Lubricate them only with a lithium based grease; other lubricants melt and ruin the linings.

12 The wheel cylinder may now be examined. If when it was checked for operation either piston did not work properly then the cylinder must be removed and serviced. Details of this are given in the next Section. Assuming they both did work it is still necessary to check the rubber seals for damage and there must be no sign of fluid leakage.

13 Brush off all dust and foreign matter from the inside of the backplate. **Do not** use solvents of any kind. If the backplate is distorted it must be replaced as the shoes will not pivot correctly if the plate is damaged. To remove the plate first remove the wheel cylinder and then unbolt the parking brake cable from the backing plate. Soak the bolt securing the bracket with easing oil and make sure the bracket does not turn or it will damage the flexible housing for the cable.

14 The backplate may now be removed by undoing the remaining securing bolts.

15 Installation of the plate presents no problem, but be sure the hub is clean before bolting the plate to it. Reassemble the adjusters and the wheel cylinder. Torque the bolts to the correct pressure.

16 Re-install the handbrake cable. Check that the handbrake lever is on the leading shoe. Fit the connecting link. Now fit the upper return spring and wedge the spring in position in the holes with wooden pegs. Fit the shoes to the backing plate. Check that the adjusters are the right way up and fully slackened off. Now for the hard bit. Refit the bottom spring. This is the one with only one coil. When it is in position remove the wooden plugs from the upper spring.

17 Insert the steady pins from the back of the drum and then the spring cup, and spring. Hold the steady pin from the rear, push the cup over the end of the pin and turn it through 90º. (photo)

18 Check around that all is seating properly, the clip has been removed from the pistons, then hook the parking brake cable over the lever. (photo)

19 Get a helper to depress the brake pedal gently and check that everything is working. Check also the operation of the handbrake.

20 Refit the drum and the socket screws and adjust the shoes until they bear on the drum. Turn each adjuster three clicks at a time, alternately or the shoes will not centre on the drum. When they both bear on the drum back them both off three clicks and the drum should rotate. Install the rubber plugs in the adjuster holes.

21 Refit the roadwheel and lower the vehicle to the ground. Check the adjustment of the parking brake at the equalizer bar. If the wheel cylinder was removed the brake line must be bled.

22 On later models the handbrake lever is secured to the shoe by a horseshoe clip and the pin is grooved to suit. Always refit a new clip if the lever is removed from the shoe and be careful not to distort the clip when fitting it.

9 Rear brake hydraulic cylinder - removal, overhaul and reassembly

1 Dismantle the rear brake as described in the previous Section removing the drum and shoes.

2 Soak the union between the flexible hose and the hydraulic cylinder with a little easing oil, slacken the union nut a little, and wipe off all dirt and oil before disconnecting the union. Block the pipe, and do not let the brake fluid remain on the brake drum. A brake bleeder nipple cap will seal the pipe.

3 From behind the backplate remove the wheel cylinder securing bolts and take the cylinder off from the front.

4 If the cylinder is seized or leaking badly it is better to replace it as a unit. However, you may be able to get a repair kit if you wish to try to repair it.

5 There have been several types of cylinder fitted so take the old one to the store when you buy a new unit or a kit. A typical layout is shown at Fig. 8.6.

6 To dismantle the cylinder first pull off the rubber caps. The remaining parts may then pushed out. If the cylinder is scored or damaged the whole unit must be replaced. If a new piston seal is required make sure the piston is perfectly clean and fit the seal with the lip facing in to the cylinder. Lubricate the parts with brake fluid before reassembly, and finally wipe the cylinder clean and fit the rubber caps.

7 Refit the cylinder to the backplate, reconnect the hose connection and reassemble the brake complete. When the vehicle once more stands on four wheels bleed the brake line.

10 Self-adjusting rear brakes

1 Refer to Figure 8.7.

2 In general construction the brake is similar to the adjustable brake. It differs only in the method of adjusting the shoes. Instead of the adjusting tappets at the bottom the brake shoes are mounted in slots in a fixed bracket.

3 The handbrake lever is fitted to the shoe as in the adjustable type but has a different curvature. The connecting link or pushrod which connects the handbrake lever to the other shoe is now adjustable with an adjusting gear operated by an adjusting lever also pivotted and held by a spring which is attached at the other end to the handbrake lever.

4 When the brakes are operated this spring is stretched and moves the adjusting lever which, moving in a vertical plane turns the adjusting wheel which in turn rotates the one portion of the connecting link. This causes the rod to unscrew itself slightly so increasing its length fractionally and adjusting the brake by moving the shoes nearer to the drum by a very small amount.

5 Basic setting is only done when new shoes are fitted. The shoes and brake gear are fitted as normal. Then lift the adjusting lever away from the adjusting rod and lengthen the connecting rod by turning the adjusting wheel until it is only just possible to install the brake drum. Now fit the drum and then press down the brake pedal slowly about ten times. The drum should rotate easily with the brake off and grip as soon as the pedal is depressed. Adjust the handbrake in the normal way.

6 It does however have disadvantages. It is not possible to slacken off the shoes in the normal manner when removing the drum by moving them away from the drum with the tappet type adjusters.

To slacken off the shoes it is necessary to slacken off the handbrake cable. If this does not give sufficient adjustment poke a screwdriver through the inspection hole in the backplate and push the lever further towards the brake lining lifting it over the stop on the shoe. This will permit the return springs to contract the linings further and the drum should come away easily.

7 Should so much wear have taken place that the drum is grooved to such an extent that the shoes will not contract enough to clear the ridge then you are in real trouble because you cannot get at the adjusting gear to slacken if off further.

8 It is therefore necessary to drill a 0.55 in (14 mm) hole in the drum to get at the gear. Make a centre punch mark in the centre of the head of each of the two bolts securing the drum to the hub. Now using these as centres scribe an arc of radius 3.54 inches (92 mm) on the drum. The point where the two arcs intersect is the centre of the hole to be drilled. Centre punch the mark and drill the hole. The adjusting gear may be turned by using a screwdriver through this hole.

9 The drum will be scrap of course, but if it was so badly grooved it would be scrap in any case.

10 For this reason it is essential to check the state of the secondary lining more often. This can be done through the inspection hole in the backplate. It is also a good case for removing the drum at least every 30,000 miles to check the state of things before it becomes necessary to drill holes.

11 Brake fluid reservoirs - removal and replacement

1 The header tank is under the driver's seat. A small window in the front of it shows the correct level for the brake fluid. There is a vent hole in the cap which must be kept clean.

2 If for some reason the header tank is damaged it should be replaced. Using a pump remove all the fluid from it but do not empty the twin chamber reservoir. Then undo the screw which holds the tank in position, remove the output pipe and lift the tank out from under the seat.

3 Be careful not to spill brake fluid as it removes paint and spoils upholstery.

4 When reinstalling the tank refit the outlet pipe first and test the joint before fitting the tank securing screw.

5 The twin chamber reservoir is mounted directly on top of the master cylinder. To get at it the coverplate under the brake pedal must be removed. This is done from underneath the vehicle.

6 It is virtually impossible to get all the fluid out of the twin chambers so that arrangements must be made to catch the fluid

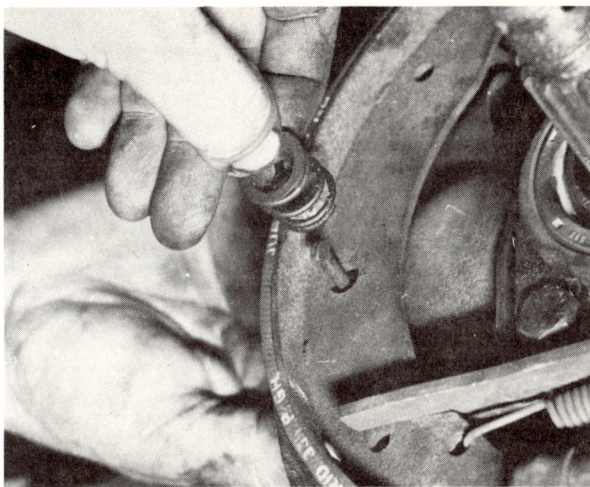

8.17 Fitting the steady pin, spring and washer whilst assembling the right rear brake shoe assembly

8.18 Hooking the handbrake cable onto the lever

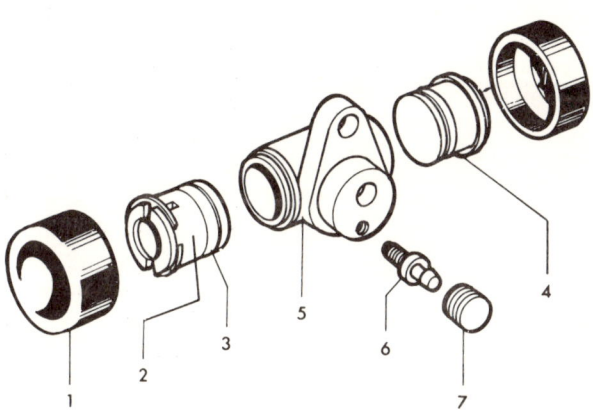

Fig 8.6 Rear wheel hydraulic brake cylinder (Sec 9)

1 Boot	5 Housing
2 Piston	6 Bleed valve
3 Seal	7 Dust cap
4 Circlip	

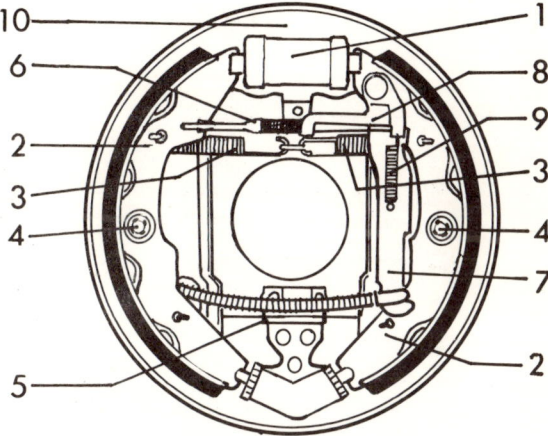

Fig 8.7 Self adjusting drum brakes (Sec 10)

1 Wheel cylinder	with wheel and sleeve
2 Brake shoe	7 Brake lever
3 Upper return spring	8 Adjusting lever
4 Spring with cup and pin	9 Return spring for
with wheel and sleeve	adjusting lever
5 Lower return spring	10 Back plate
6 Adjustable connecting link	

as the chambers are removed.

7 Empty the header tank and pull out the twin chamber reservoir from the master cylinder. Ease out the rear circuit chamber first and then the front circuit one. Now pull the reservoir to the rear and disconnect the refill pipe. This pulls out of the rubber seal.

8 When re-installing first connect the refill line and then press the front circuit plug into the master cylinder followed by the rear one.

9 When refilling make sure the reservoir is full and that no air bubbles are in the pipe.

10 After removing the reservoir it is necessary to bleed all four brakes (see Section 23).

---

12 Tandem master cylinder and servo mechanism - general description

---

1 The master cylinder has two pistons, one operating the rear brake circuit and the other the front brake circuit. A twin chambered reservoir is mounted on the top of the cylinder casting and supplies both circuits. An exploded view is shown at Fig. 8.8. Fig. 8.9 shows the layout of the servo unit and master cylinder. Fig. 8.10 shows a cross-section of the servo unit.

2 When the brake pedal is depressed it revolves about the centre pin of the bracket holding it to the sidemember and the lower arm of the pedal moves to push the connecting rod to the rear. The connecting rod operates the servo pushrod which in turn operates the servo piston, the servo valve operates and the resultant pressure moves the pushrod into the tandem master cylinder bearing on the cup face of the rear brake circuit piston.

3 The rear brake circuit piston moves forward and the primary cup covers the compensating port so that pressure now builds up in the rear brake circuit pressure chamber. This causes the front brake system piston to move forward too and cover the front braking system compensating port with the primary cup thus sealing off the reservoir and allowing pressure to build up in the front brake circuit.

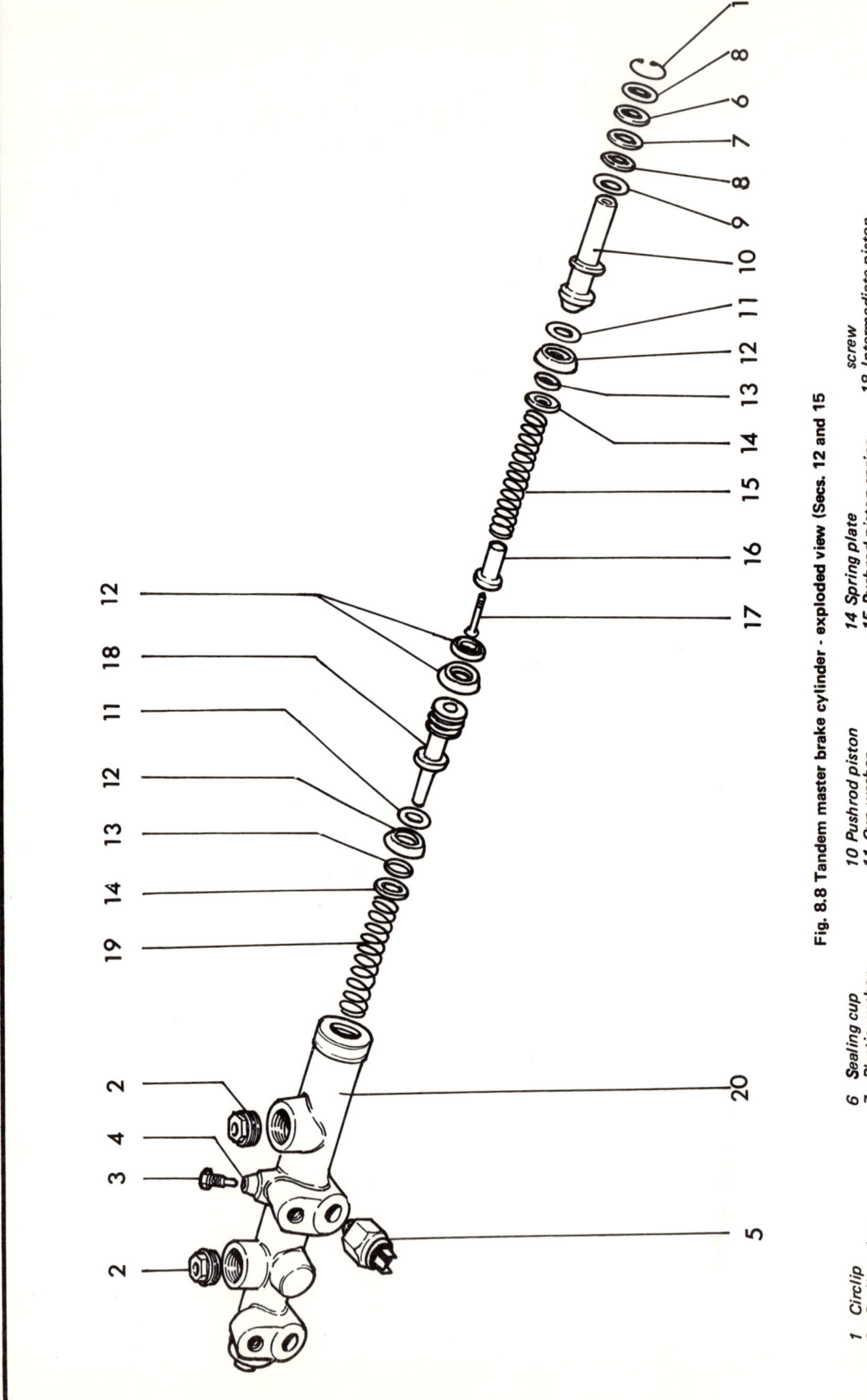

Fig. 8.8 Tandem master brake cylinder - exploded view (Secs. 12 and 15

1 Circlip
2 Sealing plug
3 Stop screw
4 Seal
5 Brake light switch

6 Sealing cup
7 Plastic washer
8 Plain washer
9 Plain washer

10 Pushrod piston
11 Cup washer
12 Primary cup
13 Support washer

14 Spring plate
15 Pushrod piston spring
16 Stop sleeve
17 Stroke limiting

18 Intermediate piston
19 Intermediate piston spring
20 Master cylinder housing

screw

Note: Master cylinders are supplied either by Teves (Ate) or Schafer ("S"). The complete master cylinders are interchangeable but the individual parts are NOT. A repair kit must be matched with the master cylinder

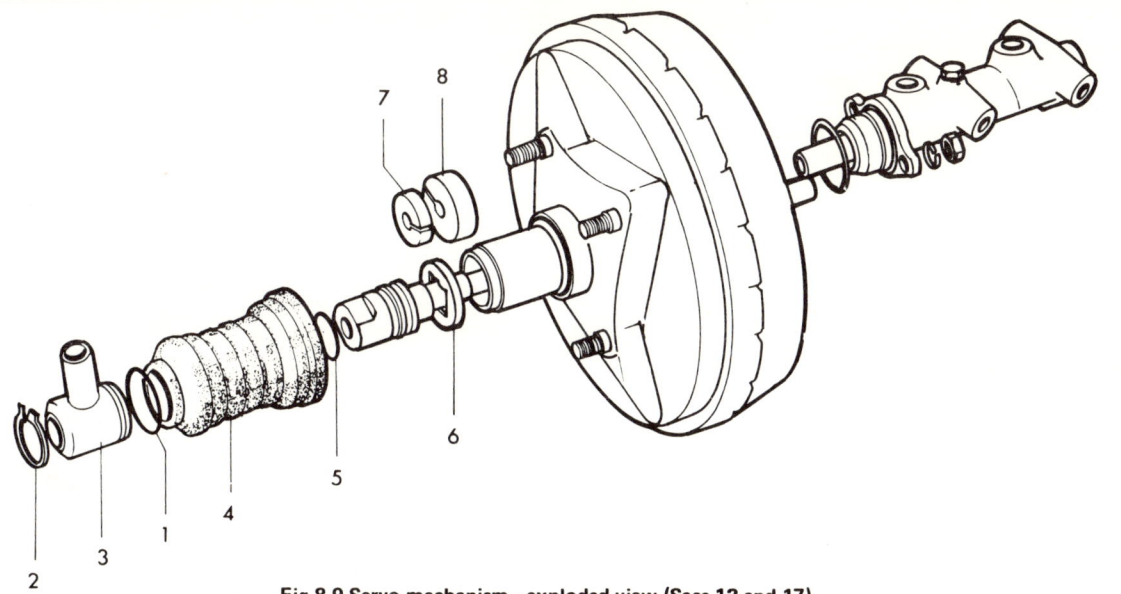

Fig 8.9 Servo mechanism - exploded view (Secs 12 and 17)

1 Retaining ring	3 Air connection	5 Seal	7 Damping ring
2 Circlip	4 Rubber dust excluder	6 Cap	8 Filter

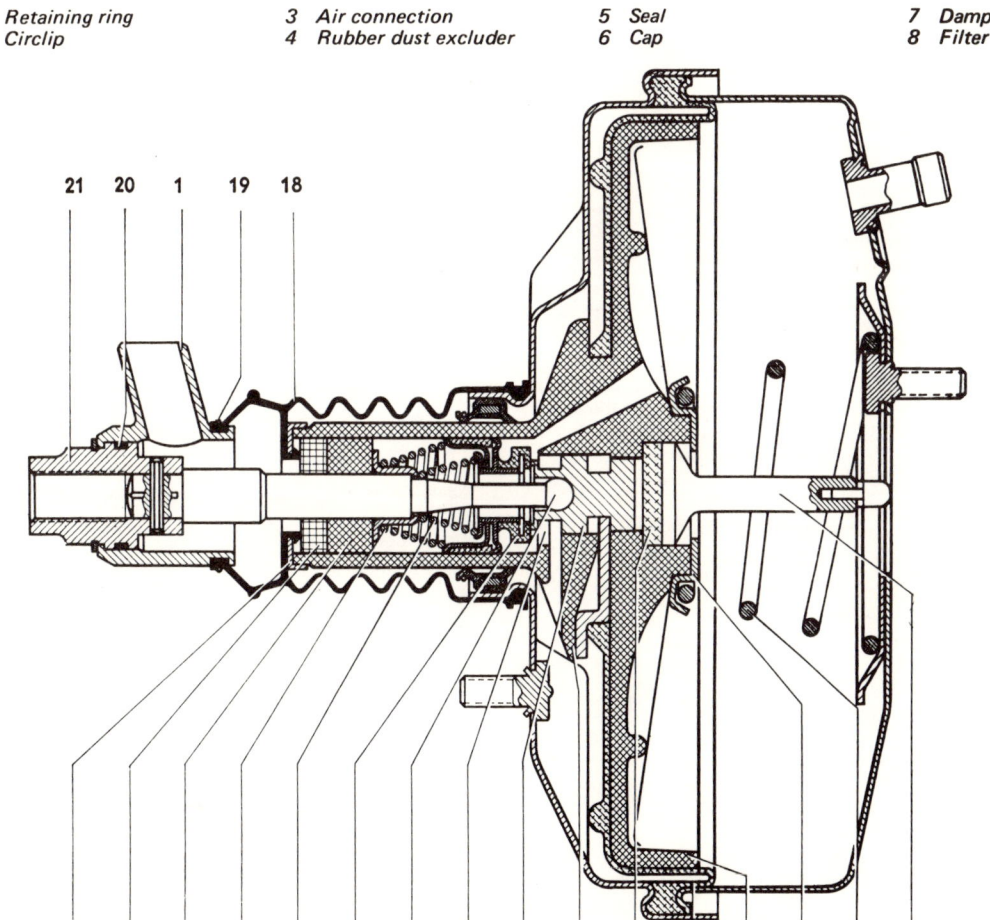

Fig 8.10 Servo mechanism - cross section (Sec 12)

1 Air connector	6 Spring plate	12 Spring	17 Cap
2 Damping washer	7 Diaphragm body support	13 Spring	18 Rubber boot
3 Filter	8 Diaphragm	14 Valve	19 Clip
4 Master cylinder push-rod	9 Valve housing	15 Reaction pad	20 Sealing ring
5 Spring	10 Piston	16 Vacuum cylinder air passage	21 Connector rod adapter
	11 Servo pushrod		

4   Failure of the front brake system (broken pipe or faulty caliper pistons) will remove the pressure from the front brake piston and it will move to the end of the brake cylinder compressing the return spring but providing a pressure seal for the rear brake circuit which will continue to operate.

5   Failure of the rear brake circuit will cause the rear brake circuit piston to move against the stop sleeve and further pressure on the pedal will increase the servo action and operate the front brake system piston by pressing the stop sleeve against it.

6   Should the servo fail the servo pushrod actuated by the connecting rod from the pedal will bear against the servo piston which will in turn push the reaction disc onto the brake cylinder piston rod. The line will be solid and of course much more pressure is required to operate the brakes. It is for this reason that the servo boost factor is kept as small as 2.05 to 1 for were it higher the pressure required on the brake pedal if the servo failed would be more than the average motorist could supply.

7   For good reasons VW have changed the design of the master cylinder several times over the last five years.

In 1969 a separate boring in the cylinder contained a piston which actuated a switch should either of the circuits fail. This was discontinued after 1969. In 1970 the servo was fitted as an optional extra, and in 1971 the servo was introduced to all Type 2 vehicles in USA, a practice followed shortly by all vehicles.

In addition VW obtain master cylinders from ATE and from SCHAFER, which although they seem similar and fit the vehicle are different inside in minor details.

Again, in 1972 only one brake light warning switch was fitted and the one for the front circuit discontinued. In this case there may be a casting with one hole only, or the second hole may have been blanked off with a screw. If a new master cylinder is fitted to a vehicle which previously had two switches, and the new master cylinder has only one switch then the wires which went to the second switch should be cut and insulated.

As will be seen from the photograph the later models have yet another variation. However, the method of operation is the same and the difference in connections is obvious. (photo)

The layout of the interior with the two pistons, springs cups and seals, remains the same. It is a good thing to discuss the matter with the VW spares storeman if overhaul of the master cylinder is contemplated, as he will be able to tell you by consulting the Parts List armed with the chassis number of your vehicle exactly which type of cylinder you have, and which spare you need.

8   The master cylinder is fastened to the servo unit with two studs and nuts, and the servo to the front axle frame by a bracket having four bolts.

---

13 Tandem master cylinder - adjustment of pushrod clearance

1   The compensating ports of the master cylinder must be open when the brake pedal is not depressed. Unless they are open brake fluid cannot return to the reservoir and the hydraulic cylinders in the brakes will not release the pads and shoes from the discs and drums. It is essential therefore that there is a small clearance between the pushrod and the rear brake circuit piston in the "rest" position.

2   In the older, non-servo type it was possible to adjust this and measure it. With the servo type it is not, so other means must be used to ensure this clearance.

3   The brake cylinder pushrod is a one piece, non-adjustable item which, if the brake servo is fully retracted will allow the necessary rearward movement of the pistons to uncover the compensating ports. The problem is therefore to be certain that the servo pushrod is pushed right back by the spring and does not operate the servo valve in the "rest" position. This is achieved by adjusting the length of the connecting rod. There is some consolation in the fact that if the master cylinder only is removed for servicing then it can be re-installed without further adjustment.

4   To adjust the length of the connecting rod first go under the

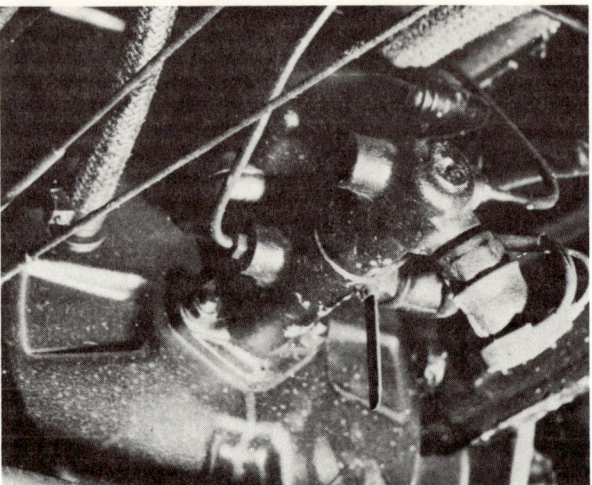

12.7 The latest version of the master cylinder and servo unit

vehicle and remove the cover plate which is beneath the brake pedal.

5   Clean the brake pedal and pivot and make sure that the brake pedal is pushed right back to the stop by the return spring. If it is not this must be rectified before anything else is done. There should be a really firm pressure.

6   With the pedal in this position the connecting rod should not exert pressure against the servo valve housing, but should commence to do so as the pedal is depressed.

7   Should adjustment be necessary remove the connecting rod from the brake lever, and adjust the length by screwing it in or out of the threaded part of the servo housing. Make the final adjustment by slackening the locknut and turn the connecting rod connection until the stirrup and pin can be reassembled to the brake pedal correctly with the rod the right length. Tighten the locknut and fit a new keep pin to the clevis pin.

8   Replace the coverplate.

---

14 Tandem master cylinder - removal and replacement

1   Remove the coverplate from under the brake pedal. This is done from under the vehicle. Clean the master cylinder and servo casing carefully.

2   Using a pump remove the brake fluid from the header tank of the brake system. **Do not** siphon it out by starting it with your mouth, the fluid is poisonous.

3   Prise the twin chamber reservoir away from the rear sealing plug of the master cylinder. Catch the brake fluid in a container as it drains from the reservoir. Now remove the front chamber in the same way. Disconnect the pipe from the header tank and remove the reservoir.

4   Label the electrical connections, and the brake pipes leading from the cylinder. Remove the electrical connections and tie them out of the way. Undo and remove the brake pipes, using bleed nipple caps to seal them as they are disconnected. It is most important that no dirt or grease gets into the pipes.

5   Now undo the two nuts holding the master cylinder to the brake servo and withdraw the master cylinder to the rear. It may be tight but do not bend or twist it.

6   Installation is the reverse of removal. Replace the sealing 'O' ring between the servo and the cylinder with a new one. Replace the cylinder and torque up the nuts on the servo studs correctly. Replace the wires and brake lines, refit the twin chamber reservoir (don't forget the pipe to the header tank), refill the header tank and reservoirs with **new** brake fluid, make sure the twin chambers are full and that no air bubble exists in the pipe and then bleed the brakes throughout. (Section 23).

15 Tandem master cylinder - dismantling, inspection and overhaul

1 The cylinder should have been cleaned before removal from the servo. However, it is most likely that some dirt remains so remove this before going any further.

2 It is unlikely that any fault will be apparent on the outside. It is also most important that no dirt or grease gets into the cylinder so arrange a clean receptacle in which to dismantle the cylinder, have a supply of non-fluffy rag and a number of small clean receptacles (eg; tobacco tins) to put the pieces in as they are removed. A plentiful supply of clean brake fluid is necessary.

3 Refer to Fig. 8.8. The rear brake piston protrudes from the end of the cylinder. Just inside is a circlip which may be removed if circlip pliers are available. The piston may now be removed after the stop screw from the centre of the cylinder has been taken out. With the rear brake circuit piston will come the stop washer, seal cups and plastic washers. Leave them on the piston.

4 The front circuit piston may come out easily, and it may not. Do not fish for it with wire - you will not hook it - and you will scratch the cylinder. Remove the residual pressure valves and seal the bores from which they came with wooden or rubber plugs. Now rig up a pressure line to the front reservoir hole in the casting and using a compressed air line or a foot pump blow the front piston out of the bore, with all its seals and springs.

5 The contents of the master cylinder may now be laid out in line as in Fig. 8.8. Wash everything carefully in **clean** brake fluid. Methylated spirits (denatured alcohol) may be used for cleaning but the parts must be washed in brake fluid before assembly so why use meths at all. **No** other cleaning fluid is permissible.

6 Having cleaned the bore of the cylinder and dried it examine it carefully for scoring. Any sign of scoring means a replacement cylinder. The VW agent may be able to hone slight scoring away but the maximum tolerance is 0.004 ins (0.10 mm) between the bore and the piston. This can be measured with a feeler gauge but remember the bore is only 0.874 ins diameter and the normal feeler is half an inch wide. To get accurate measurement a telescopic snap gauge and micrometer are required. It will be seen that machining other than with the proper tools and gauges is out of the question.

7 If it is decided that the cylinder is to be scrapped it may be possible to obtain a replacement part. An overhaul kit of seals and washers will also be required. It may well be better to reassemble the cylinder with the old parts and obtain a new or exchange rebuilt master cylinder from the VW agent.

8 However, the cylinder may well be in good condition and require only new seals. These come as a kit; use all the parts in the kit. There are two types of kit, ATE and SCHAFER; make sure you have the right one.

9 Clean all the parts in brake fluid. Check that all the ports of the cylinder are clear, in particular the compensating ports.

10 Ease off the seals from the pistons and replace them with new ones. They came off quite easily but the new ones are a problem. This can be made more simple by using a piece of tube the same diameter as the largest diameter of the piston and turning the tube or filing the tube into a cone. A piece of about 3 in (76 mm) long is sufficient and it may be metal or plastic, but it must be smooth. Lubricate it with brake fluid and ease the cup or seal onto the biggest diameter and then transfer it gently to the piston.

11 When all the seals and cups are in position lay the whole assembly in line as it will be in the cylinder (see Fig. 8.8), hold the cylinder vertically in a vice with its closed end down, lubricate the cylinder and pistons with clean brake fluid and assemble the components into the cylinder. The last parts to go in are the rear brake circuit piston with its sealing cups. Make sure that the lips of these cups are towards the master cylinder. In the kit a small packet of silicon grease is provided. This is to lubricate the annular grooves in the sealing cups and the shaft of the pushrod piston.

12 With all the parts installed push the rear brake circuit piston down until the circlip may be inserted. Make sure the rear piston is not blocking the stop screw hole and then insert the stop screw with its seal and tighten to the correct torque. If the hole is obscured by the piston push the piston in until the hole is clear.

13 Reinstall the stop/warning light switches and the plugs for the twin chamber reservoir. Fit a new 'O' ring to the front of the cylinder to seal between the cylinder and the servo and the cylinder is ready to be installed in the vehicle.

16 Testing the servo circuit

1 If the brakes seem to need more or less pressure than normal a check of the servo is indicated.

2 First of all trace the hoses and check their condition. There must be no leaks or obstructions.

3 Check the vacuum check valve. This is to be found in the vacuum line between the induction manifold and the servo. Remove it from the hose line and clean it carefully. There is an arrow on the valve. Blow into the valve in the direction of the arrow, the valve should open. Blow in the opposite direction and the valve must seat. The valve is there to stop pressure from the manifold eg; a backfire, arriving in the vacuum side of the servo, ie; it is a non-return valve, so that the induction suction can only suck, and not blow.

4 If all of the above are correct and the servo is still not assisting the brakes the trouble is either a leaky servo diaphragm or something wrong with the master cylinder. Check that the sealing ring between the master cylinder and the servo is not leaking.

5 If the pedal pressure increases only at a certain position each time then there may be wear in the master cylinder pushrod allowing air to get into the vacuum side of the servo. This will only be on elderly brake cylinders, and it is time the master cylinder was overhauled.

6 If none of the above checks clear the trouble remove the servo as in the next Section and replace the parts suggested. At the same time look at the master cylinder piston for scoring or leaky seals. Check the servo for obvious external damage.

7 If when the system is reassembled correctly the servo still refuses to function then a new servo is indicated.

17 Servo mechanism - removal, repair and replacement

1 Refer to Fig. 8.9. Thoroughly clean the servo and the master brake cylinder and then remove the master cylinder (see Section 14). This unfortunately involves removing the twin reservoirs and draining the brake fluid.

2 Remove the vacuum hoses (the ones that go to the manifold) from the same side as the master cylinder. Now remove the coverplate from under the brake pedal and take off the air hose from the servo.

3 Disconnect the connecting rod from the brake pedal, slacken the locknut and unscrew the connecting rod and remove it.

4 Remove the four nuts from the studs holding the servo to its bracket and withdraw the servo to the rear.

5 It is not possible to dismantle the servo to any great extent. Clean the exterior carefully but do not use solvents on interior parts.

6 The following action **must** be taken each time the servo is removed from the vehicle:

7 Remove the retaining ring from the rubber boot. Remove the circlip and pull off the 'T' shaped air connection from the pushrod connector. Remove the rubber boot. Prise the cap from the valve housing on the vacuum chamber and take the damping ring and filter out.

Replace these parts in the reverse order using a new filter, damping ring, rubber boot, and sealing ring for the air connector.

The slits in the new filter and damping ring must be 180° apart, when reassembled.

When the parts are reassembled with the circlip and retaining ring in place, reassemble the servo to its bracket.

8 When tightening the bolts do not exceed the corret torque or damage will occur to the servo casing.

9 Replace the connecting rod and adjust it as in Section 13.

10 Refit the master cylinder (new 'O' ring) switches and twin reservoirs as in Section 14 and bleed the brakes (Section 23).

18 Brake pressure regulator

1 On models fitted with front disc brakes a pressure regulator is installed which affects the operation of the rear brakes. This is because disc brakes have a more powerful braking action and accentuate the 'nose-dipping' attitude of the vehicle when sharp braking is used. This in turn lightens the load on the rear wheels and in certain circumstances when the vehicle is empty could cause the rear wheels to lock. The pressure regulation takes into account the rate of deceleration and the 'nose-dip' inclination and correspondingly reduces the pressure in the hydraulic system acting on the rear wheel cylinders if necessary.

2 The regulator consists of a ball in an inclined chamber and two spring loaded subsidiary pistons which act as pressure reducers. The angle of the inclined chamber depends on the position of the vehicle body. Consequently a loaded vehicle will not increase the angle so much as an empty one. When braking occurs the ball is thrown forward and depending on the rate of deceleration and the angle up which it has to roll it shuts off the direct fluid flow to the rear brake cylinders. Pressure is then applied to two intermediate pistons of different diameters, with a spring between them which effectively reduces the output pressure to rear brakes. Fig. 8.11 refers.

3 Malfunction of the unit will result in either locking of the rear wheels or, at the other extreme, ineffective braking. It is not possible to test the regulator accurately without having the suitable hoses and gauges up to 1500 p.s.i. to connect to the front and rear brake circuits. When the front circuit pressure is 1420 p.s.i. the regulated pressure at the rear should be 780 - 925 p.s.i.

4 The regulator is mounted on the left side frame (photo). It is not recommended that action should be taken to repair it. If it is suspected of malfunction then the vehicle should be taken to the VW agent for testing.

5 If you are certain it is not working properly it may be removed and exchanged for one which has been adjusted correctly. To do this disconnect the inlet and outlet pipes and remove the two bolts holding the unit to the frame. Do not lose the spacers installed between the unit and the frame.

6 A modified regulator was introduced in 1973. On the early type the output line is screwed into an adaptor. On the later type there is no need for an adapter but the routing of the pipe is altered slightly for the output to be taken from the top of the unit instead of the end. If you have to replace the old type with a new one remove the adapter; you may have to get a new pipe or modify the old pipe.

7 It is as well to consider renewing the piping anyway while the system is disconnected.

8 On the older type there is a bleeder valve, this has been discontinued on the new type but in any case **do not** open it when bleeding the brakes.

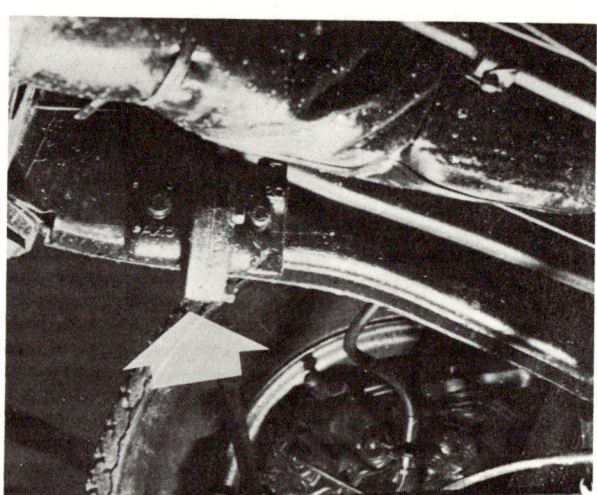

18.4 Brake pressure regulator (arrowed). It will be on the other side on L.H. drive vehicles

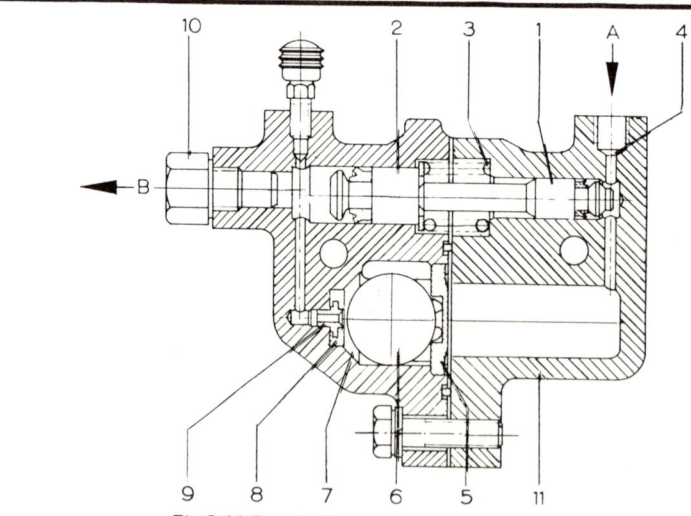

Fig 8.11 Rear brake pressure regulator - cross section

1 Primary piston
2 Secondary piston
3 Spring between pistons
   Note: The residual pressure valve was discarded in 1971 and an adapter fitted in its place

4 Fluid inlet passage
5 Spacer washer
6 Ball

7 Ball chamber
8 Valve seal
9 Valve seat

10 Residual pressure valve
11 Main housing
A   From master cylinder
B   To wheel cylinders

9 Replacement is the reverse of removal. The tapped holes in a replacement regulator are fitted with plastic screws. Leave these in until you are ready to fit the pipes to the regulator.

Bolt the unit in place (do not forget the spacers) and tighten to the correct torque. Install the pipes, for a replacement old type fit the adapter to the outlet pipe, for a new type discard it. Be careful to use the correct torque when tightening up.

10 It will now be necessary to bleed the rear brake circuit (see Section 23).

19 Brake stoplights and circuit failure warning lights

1 The 1972 version is fitted with lamps at the rear of the car which are illuminated when the brakes are applied. There is also a light on the dashboard which comes on if either of the brake circuits fail. In both cases the lights are operative only when the ignition is switched on.

2 The warning light comes on when the ignition is switched on and should go out, as do the charging circuit light and oil pressure lights when the engine is started. Failure to do so must be investigated right away.

3 There are two switches operated by the pressure in the master cylinder. Both are screwed into the body of the cylinder. A circuit diagram of the brake stop/warning light system is given at Fig. 8.12. One is for the rear circuit, the other for the front circuit.

4 The circuit includes a transistorised type of warning lamp incorporated in the dashboard layout. If the light does not come on when the ignition is switched on then probably the bulb is at fault. To replace the bulb prise out the little window with the symbol 'B' on it and then push a piece of insulation tube or plastic tube over the bulb and pull the bulb out. The tube should be 3/16 in (5 mm) diameter. Do not handle the bulb with bare fingers. Test the bulb and replace if necessary. If the bulb is not at fault check the wiring with a meter using the circuit given and the main wiring diagram.

If this does not cure the problem then proceed with the next test.

5 Open a bleeder valve in the front brake circuit. Put a tube on it and arrange to catch the fluid in a bottle. Start the engine and depress the brake pedal. The warning light should come on. If it does not the switch is not working. Repeat the test with the rear circuit. Remember to keep the reservoir topped-up.

If either of these tests fail the switch must be replaced.

6 Remove the wires from the switch, screw the switch out and install a new switch. Torque it to the correct pressure.

7 Equally important are the brake stoplights. These should be checked for operation regularly. If either light fails then remove the bulb (Chapter 10) and test it. Replace if necessary.

8 If the bulbs are in good order disconnect the red and black wires from the front pressure warning switch on the master cylinders. Start the engine and press the brake pedal.

9 The stoplights should go on. If they do then the disconnected switch is not working and should be replaced. If they do not go on reconnect and disconnect the other switch, wires '81' and '82a'. Try again and if they function then again it is the disconnected switch which is defective.

10 Replace it as in paragraph 6.

20 Hydraulic lines - inspection, maintenance and renewal

1 The magnitude of the pressure in the hydraulic lines is not generally realized. The test pressures are 1420 lbs per square inch (100 kg sq cm) for the front brakes, and the equalizing valve is set between 786 and 929 lbs per square inch (55 - 65 kg sq cm) for the rear brakes.

These pressures are with the braking system cold. The temperature rise in the drums and discs for an emergency stop from 60 mph is as much as 80°C (176°F), and during a long descent may reach 400°C (752°F). The pressure must be even

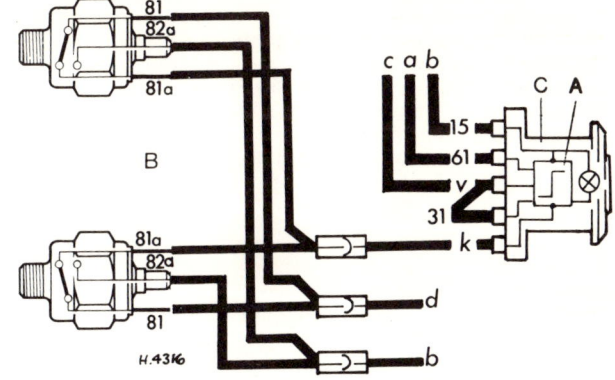

Fig. 8.12 Brake light/Brake pressure warning switches - circuit diagram (Sec 19)

A   Electric switch
B   Brake light switch
C   Dual circuit
    brake warning lamp

a   to switch terminal 6_1
b   to terminal 15
c   to ground
d   to brake lights

further raised as the temperature of the brake fluid in the cylinders rises.

The normal pressure in the hydraulic system when the brakes are not in use is negligible. The pressure builds up quickly when the brakes are applied and remains until the pedal is released. Each driver will know how quickly the build up is when equating it to the speed of his own reaction in an emergency brake application.

2 Recent research in the USA has shown that brake line corrosion may be expected to lead to failure after only 90 days exposure to salt spray such as is thrown up when salt is used to melt ice or snow. This in effect makes a four year old vehicle automatically suspect. It is possible to use pipe made of a copper alloy used in marine work called KUNIFER 10 as a replacement. This is much more resistant to salt corrosion, but as yet is not a standard fitting.

3 All this should by now have indicated that pipes need regular inspection. The obvious times are in the autumn before the winter conditions set in, and in the spring to see what damage has been done.

4 Trace the routes of all the rigid pipes and wash or brush away accumulated dirt. If the pipes are obviously covered with some sort of underseal compound do not disturb it. Examine for signs of kinks or dents which could have been caused by flying stones. Any instances of this mean that the pipe section should be renewed but before actually taking it out read the rest of this Section. Any unprotected sections of pipe which show signs of corrosion or pitting on the outer surface must also be considered for renewal.

5 Flexible hoses, running to each of the front wheels and from the underbody to each rear wheel should show no external signs of chafing or cracking. Move them about to see whether surface cracks appear. If they feel stiff and inflexible or are twisted they are nearing the end of their useful life. If in any doubt renew the hoses. Make sure also that they are not rubbing against the bodywork.

6 Before attempting to remove a pipe for renewal it is important to be sure that you have a replacement source of supply within reach if you do not wish to be kept off the road for too long. Pipes are often damaged on removal. If a Volkswagen agency is near you may be reasonably sure that the correct pipes and unions are available. If not, check first that your local garage has the necessary equipment for making up the pipes and has the correct metric thread pipe unions available. The same goes for flexible hoses.

7 Where the couplings from rigid to flexible pipes are made

there are support brackets and the flexible pipe is held in place by a 'U' clip which engages in a groove in the union (photo). The male union screws into it. Before getting the spanners on, soak the unions in penetrating fluid as there is always some rust or corrosion binding the threads. Whilst this is soaking in, place a piece of plastic film under the fluid reservoir cap to minimise loss of fluid from the disconnected pipes. Hold the hexagon on the flexible pipe coupling whilst the union on the rigid pipe is

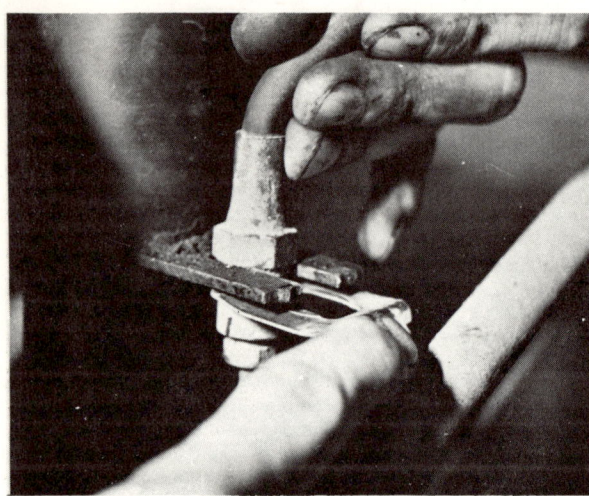

20.7 Flexible hose mounting bracket and clip

undone. Then pull out the clip to release both pipes from the bracket. For flexible hose removal this procedure will be needed at both ends. For a rigid pipe the other end will only involve unscrewing the union from a cylinder or connector. When you are renewing a flexible hose, take care not to damage the unions of the pipes that connect into it. If a union is particularly stubborn be prepared to renew the rigid pipe as well. This is quite often the case if you are forced to use open ended spanners. It may be worth spending a little money on a special pipe union spanner which is like a ring spanner with a piece cut out to enable it to go round the tube.

8 If you are having the new pipe made up, take the old one along to check that the unions and pipe flaring at the ends are identical.

9 Replacement of the hoses or pipes is a reversal of the removal procedure. Precautions and care are needed to make sure that the unions are correctly lined up to prevent cross threading. This may mean bending the pipe a little where a rigid pipe goes into a fixture. Such bending must not, under any circumstances, be too acute or the pipe will kink and weaken.

10 When fitting flexible hoses take care not to twist them. This can happen when the unions are finally tightened unless a spanner is used to hold the end of the flexible hose and prevent twisting.

11 If a pipe is removed or a union slackened so that air can get into the system then the system must be bled. This is discussed in Section 23, of this Chapter.

21 Brake pedal - removal and re-installation

1 It is most unlikely that the pedal assembly will give trouble, but if it does removal does not present many difficulties. Refer to Figs. 8.13 and 8.14.

2 Take off the cover plate under the pedal assembly from

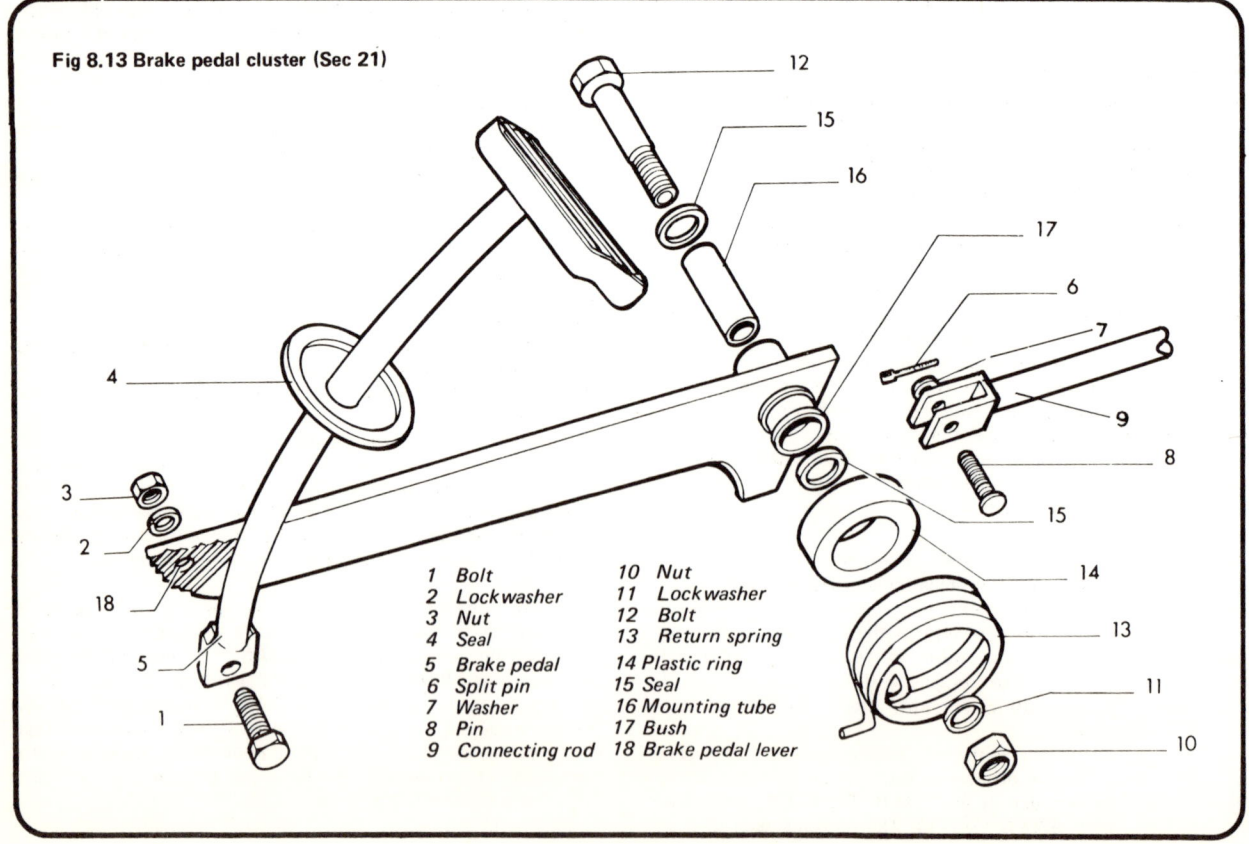

Fig 8.13 Brake pedal cluster (Sec 21)

1 Bolt	10 Nut
2 Lockwasher	11 Lockwasher
3 Nut	12 Bolt
4 Seal	13 Return spring
5 Brake pedal	14 Plastic ring
6 Split pin	15 Seal
7 Washer	16 Mounting tube
8 Pin	17 Bush
9 Connecting rod	18 Brake pedal lever

underneath the van. The pedal spindle is held to the pedal lever by a bolt which clamps the two together. Remove this bolt and the pedal may be pulled into the driving compartment.

3 Disconnect the servo connecting rod from the pedal lever. Now push a thin screwdriver in between the return spring and the tongue of the lever and prise the spring away. The pedal lever will now move freely on the pivot bolt, which may now be undone and the assembly removed.

4 The only repairs envisaged are rebushing the pedal lever, replacing the pin or possibly a broken spring. When rebushing make sure the new bush is flush with the shorter end of the mounting tube.

5 It is important that the spring holds the pedal against the stop or the servo will give trouble.

6 Replacement is the reverse of removal. Fit the mounting tube, seals, plastic ring and return spring on the lever and bolt the assembly to the mounting bracket. Refit the pedal, connecting rod and coverplate, making sure all bolts and nuts are correctly tightened.

7 On some RHD models the clutch pedal and brake pedal may be mounted differently, Fig. 8.14 refers. The clutch pedal rotates freely on the shaft, but the brake pedal is clamped to the shaft. The brake pedal lever is clamped and keyed to the other end of the shaft.

22 Parking brake, lever and cable - removal, repair and reassembly

1 The parking brake acts through a mechanical linkage to the rear drum brakes. The action at the brake end is explained in the Section on rear brakes.

2 The parking lever is secured to the dashboard frame (photo) and operates a vertical lever which pivots about a bracket in the

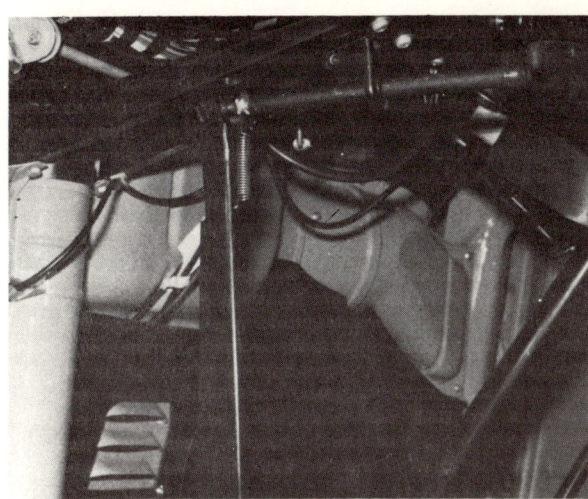

22.2 The parking brake assembly inside the cab

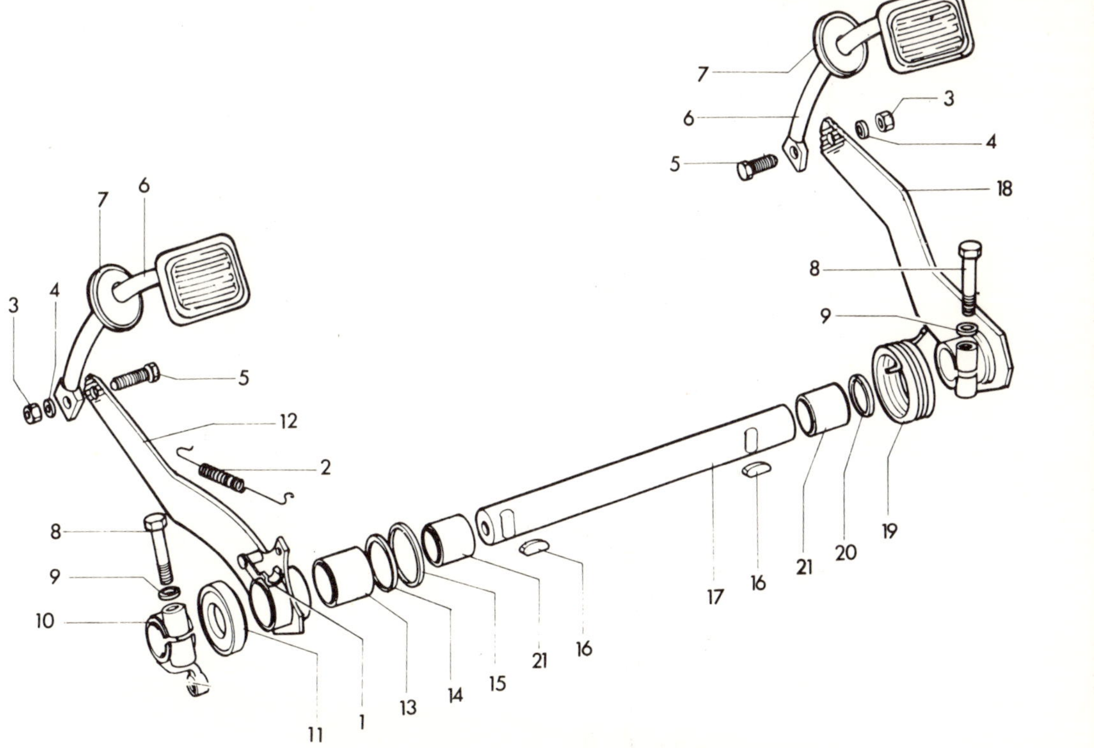

Fig 8.14 Brake (and clutch) pedal cluster - some versions R.H.D. (Sec 21)

1 Pin and clip	7 Seal	12 Clutch pedal lever	17 Shaft
2 Return spring	8 Clamp screw	13 Bush	18 Brake pedal lever
3 Nut	9 Lockwasher	14 Seal	19 Return spring
4 Lockwasher	10 Brake pedal lever	15 Thrust washer	20 Seal
5 Bolt	11 Seal	16 Woodruff key	21 Bush
6 Pedal			

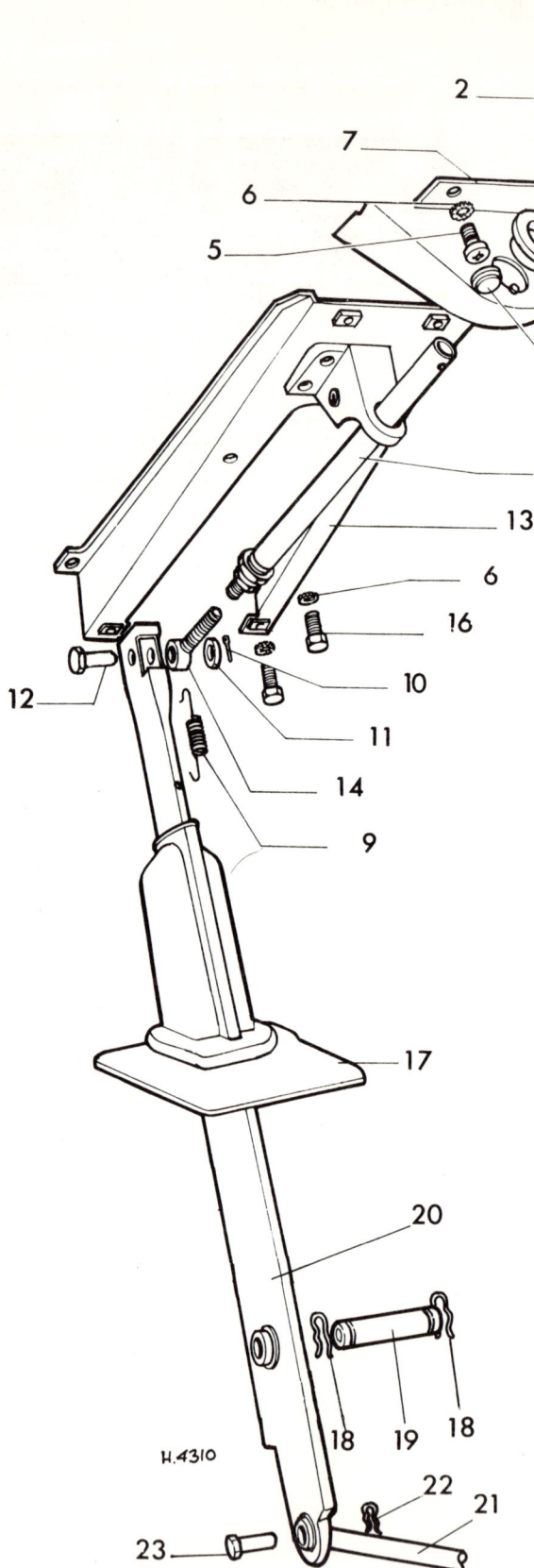

Fig 8.15 Parking brake lever assembly (Sec 22)

1   Roll pin
2   Handle
3   Ratchet bar stop
4   Cover
5   Screw
6   Lockwasher
7   Trim plate
8   Guide sleeve
9   Spring
10 Split pin
11 Washer
12 Pin
13 Ratchet bar
14 Eye bolt
15 Screw
16 Ratchet bar bracket
17 Boot
18 Spring clip (2)
19 Pin
20 Parking brake lever
21 Connecting rod
22 Spring clip
23 Connector rod pin

H.4310

floor of the cab. Details are shown in Fig. 8.15.

3 When the top of the lever is drawn to the rear the lower end moves forward pulling a connecting bar which is pivotted to the end of it and this in turn draws forward the equalizing bar.

4 The equalizing bar is pinned to the connecting rod at the centre and the brake cables are attached to the outer ends of it (photo).

5 When the brake is working correctly the handle should move out six clicks on the ratchet before the brakes engage and when fully on the equalizing bar should be at right-angles to the connecting bar.

6 To remove the lever assembly first go under the van and disconnect the connecting bar from the lever. There is a pin and spring clip. Now, inside the cab remove the ashtray and drive the pin out of the handle and remove the handle and ratchet bar stop. Take off the spring, take out the ratchet bar pin and remove the ratchet bar and trim plate.

7 If you wish to proceed further undo the bolts holding the ratchet bar bracket to the frame. To remove the lever first slide off the rubber sleeve, take the clip off the pivot pin and slide the lever out under the van.

8 Reassembly is the reverse of removal but be careful when fitting the ratchet bar that it does not foul the heater pipe in the 'off' position. This can be adjusted by screwing in the eye bolt.

9 To adjust the handbrake cables hold a screwdriver in the slot at the end of the cable and turn the nut until the correct tension is obtained. The threads will probably need some easing oil. Set the handle at six clicks on the ratchet and tighten the cables evenly until the brakes just come on. The equalizer bar should be at 90⁰ to the connecting bar.

10 If the equalizer bar is **not** at 90⁰ to the connecting bar when the brakes are correctly adjusted then one cable has stretched and should be replaced right away.

11 To remove the cable undo the adjusting nut and locknut and slip the cable out of the equalizing bar.

12 Jack-up the rear wheel and remove it. Take off the brake drum. Unhook the cable from the lever on the rearmost brake shoe. Soak the bolt holding the bracket to the cable with easing oil and undo it to remove the bracket. Be careful not to let the bracket turn or the flexible cable housing will require renewal. It is now possible to remove the cable and housing by pulling the cable to the rear.

13 The new cable should be greased before fitting. Assembly is the reverse of removal. Make sure no oil or grease are left in the drum. When the wheels are on the ground again adjust the cable properly. It will probably require readjustment again after 300 to 400 miles of running when it has stretched a little.

14 On RHD models the handbrake cable may foul the servo. To prevent this it is threaded through a plastic tube on the servo shoulder. This should be renewed if the cable is removed. The part No. is '214, 711, 494'.

23 Bleeding the hydraulic system

1 First locate the bleed nipples on all four brakes. The rear wheel bleed nipples are at the back of the drum at the centre of the hydraulic cylinder. A small dust cap covers the nipple. This will probably be covered with mud. Clean the mud from the back of the drum, wipe the dust cap and the area around it with a clean rag and the operation may start.

The front disc brake bleed nipples are on the inside surface of the caliper. Since 1971 two nipples are fitted to each caliper, one at the top for normal bleeding purposes, and one at the bottom to assist in draining the system when necessary. The bleed nipples should be cleaned carefully.

When all four wheels have been cleaned sufficiently sweep up the mud and then wash your hands, this is a job where cleanliness pays.

2 As fluid is to be pumped out of the system make sure you have plenty of new clean fluid. It must conform to SAE recommendation J1703, but better still, get the official VW fluid. If the wrong fluid is used the whole system may become

22.4 The brake cables are attached to the equalizer bar

useless through failure of piston seals. Top-up the header tank generously, and keep topping it up at intervals throughout the whole job.

3 Start with the front right-hand wheel. A piece of rubber or plastic hose 5/32 in. (4 mm) inside diameter and about two feet (600 mm) long is required. Fit this over the bleed nipple and immerse the other end in a jar or bottle with about 4 inches of clean brake fluid in it. Fix the hose so that the end of it cannot come out of the brake fluid, and stand the bottle on the ground in a secure place.

4 You will need a helper whose job is to depress the brake pedal when requested. It is as well to rehearse the operation before opening the bleed nipple valve. Open the valve about one turn and depress the pedal slowly to the floor of the vehicle. As soon as it is on the floor close the bleed valve **before** the pedal is released. Now release the pedal slowly. Brake fluid and air bubbles should have passed down the tube into the bottle. Repeat the operation until no further air bubbles are observed. Check the header tank level after every two strokes and top-up if necessary.

5 When you are satisfied that the front right-hand brake line is clear of air bubbles then wipe down the brake caliper and proceed to the next task; in order left front, right rear and left rear.

6 After each session clean down the brakes with care and wash your hands. Brake fluid is poisonous and it is a splendid paint remover. Use a soapy solution and wash any paintwork that has been splashed.

7 Finally, the brake fluid in the jar or bottle should be discarded. This is not too easy. I bury mine three spits deep - bubbles and all.

24 Renewal of brake fluid

1 The brake fluid is hygroscopic, which means that allowed to come into contact with the open air it will absorb moisture. If it does then when the brakes get hot the water will boil and the brakes will not work properly - at the moment they are needed most.

2 VW recommend that the fluid should be changed every two years - they give a variety of reasons - but the fact that they do recommend it should be reason enough.

3 The change over is simple to do. First of all clean the rear drums, particularly by the bleed nipples, and give the front calipers the same treatment.

4 Use two pieces of hose to connect the rear drum bleed

nipples to a suitable jar. The same hose as used for brake bleeding in Section 23 will be satisfactory. Now open the bleed nipple valves one turn and pump the brake pedal until the fluid ceases to flow out of the brakes.

5 Now repeat the operation on the front calipers. Use the lower bleed nipple. On some early models there may be only one bleed nipple which will be at the top. If so then use this one.

6 When no more fluid flows from the caliper close all the bleed nipples, front and rear, and refill the header tank until it is at the correct mark.

7 It can happen that an air bubble will form in the pipe between the header tank and the twin-chamber reservoir on the top of the master cylinder. This will cause the reservoirs to fill very slowly. They must be full before the next task can be done.

8 Again it is stressed that only new brake fluid supplied by VW should be used.

9 When you are satisfied that the system is full the brakes should be bled as detailed in Section 23.

10 One further caution. On some of the earlier models there is a bleed nipple on the pressure regulating valve. **Do not** open this either when refilling the system or when bleeding the system.

25 Roadwheels - description and maintenance

1 The wheels fitted are described as 5½J ·x 14. These are not the same as earlier models, having a different bolt hole (pitch) circle diameter and a different offset. Thus if you do damage a wheel and have to replace it be careful. Again, wheels sold by accessory dealers may fit the wheel studs but have a different offset. It is bad practice to fit these as they will affect the quality of the steering.

The offset is the distance from the centre of the rim width to the face which fits against the brake drum and should be 1 5/8 inch (41.00 mm). This may be measured by removing the tyre and laying the wheel on a flat surface with the mounting face downwards on a suitable block so that the rim is just clear of the flat surface. The thickness of the block will give the distance of the mounting face from the surface and the distance of the centre of the rim may be measured with a rule, being half the width of the rim added to the distance the lower lip of the rim is from the flat surface.

2 The wheels are safety pattern 'hump' rimmed type (see Fig. 8.16), so that on deflation the bead of the tyre does not go down into the centre of the rim but stays trapped between the hump and the outer flange of the rim. This does however raise problems when changing tyres as special tools are needed to exert enough force to lever the bead over the rim. This should be left to the man who sells you the tyre.

3 Damage to wheels is rare except by misuse. If the wheel nuts are loose the holes through which the studs go will become oval and the wheel is scrap.

A blow on the side of the wheel may damage the rim. The maximum runout permissible is 0.06 in. (1.5 mm). It is not possible to straighten rims and those with runout over the limit

must be replaced by new ones.

4 The hub cap has two small holes in the outer edge (photo). These are to take a hook through which a lever may be inserted in order to remove the hub cap from the wheel (photo).

5 Take a good look at the rim when the tyre is changed. If rust is present repaint the rim after cleaning off the rust and let the paint dry hard before the new tyre is installed.

6 Clean both sides of the wheel when it is taken off the vehicle and look carefully to see that there is no damage. In particular that the stud bolt holes are not damaged and that there are no cracks in the mounting face.

26 Tyres - selection, fitting, and maintenance

1 These can be an expensive problem if neglected. The most important matter is to keep them inflated at the correct pressure. A table of pressures is given at the start of the Chapter.

If the vehicle is driven over rough ground, or over glass in the road the tread should be inspected to see whether stones or glass fragments are lodged in the tread. These should be removed forthwith.

2 A careful study of the tread once a week will pay dividends. Tyres should wear evenly right across the tread but they rarely do, they are usually replaced because of misuse. A table is given showing some of the main troubles. Study it and watch your tyre treads.

Wear description	Probable cause
Rapid wear of the centre of the tread all round the circumference	*Tyre overinflated.*
Rapid wear at both edges of the tread, wear even all round the circumference	*Tyre underinflated.*
Wear on one edge of the tyre *(a) Front wheels only*	*Steering geometry needs checking.*
(b) Rear wheels only	*Check rear suspension for damage.*
Scalloped edges, wear at the edge at regular spacing around the tyre	*Maybe wheel out of balance, or more likely wear on the steering knuckle.*
Flat or rough patches on the tread	*Caused by harsh braking. Check the brake adjustment.*
Cuts and abrasions on the wall of the tyre	*Usually done by running into the kerbstone.*

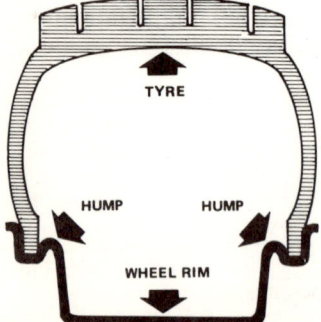

Fig 8.16 Diagram showing cross section of wheel rim with hump (Sec. 25)

25.4a Insert the hook from the tool kit in the nave plate holes and ...

25.4b ... put a bar through the hook and lever the plate away from the wheel

3 If the tyre wall is damaged it is a good idea to have the tyre removed from the wheel and study the inside of the wall as the inside plys may be affected. Such damage could lead to a 'blow-out' at speed which is best avoided. The tyre expert may be able to repair the wall, but if the tread is worn as well the casing should be discarded.

4 Tyres are best renewed in pairs, putting the new pair on the front and relegating the front ones to the rear. Take care of the spare wheel too. There is no point in carrying a badly worn spare tyre around; if you have had to use the spare to replace a damaged tyre then replace the damaged spare right away.

5 The much debated problem of radials as opposed to crossply tyres is partially solved for Transporter owners. The vehicle is fitted with radials when new. This policy started in 1971. The two types must never be mixed on one axle, and, equally important, if there are two radials and two crossplys the radials must be on the rear.

Crossplys are slightly cheaper and give a smoother ride at speeds below 50 mph. They are also quieter. Radials stand up to high speed, long distance driving better as the tyre does not get so hot. They do seem to last longer if well maintained and repay the extra cost. And, of course, radials provide for superior roadholding.

As you start with five radials it would seem sensible to stick to this type. Note that the tyres are described as 'reinforced', or for Delivery Vans and Station Wagons. They have the letter 'C' as a suffix.

If you are determined to change to crossply or bias-ply make sure that the tyre has an 8 ply rating. The recommended inflation pressures for crossplys are slightly less than for radials. Consult the VW agent to obtain these for the type selected.

27 Wheel balancing

1 It is most unlikely that a wheel fitted with a new tyre will be in correct balance, and it is most important that the wheel and tyre should be correctly balanced both statically and dynamically.

2 Such operations require expertise and special equipment, and the operation should be carried out whenever a new tyre is purchased. The out of balance is corrected by the addition of lead weights to the rim. Note how many and the position of fitting as they have been known to fly off.

3 If unbalance is suspected then a simple test of static balance is available for the front wheels. Jack the wheel from the ground so that it spins freely. With the wheel at rest mark the lowest point with a piece of chalk. Spin the wheel gently and allow it to rotate freely until it stops of its own accord. Repeat the operation two or three times noting the position of the chalk mark each time the wheel stops rotating. If it comes to rest at the bottom each time then the wheel is definitely out of balance.

The rear wheels will not rotate freely because of the dragging effect of the differential. If a rear wheel is suspect then transfer it to the front hub for testing.

4 This does not cover dynamic balance. Static imbalance will cause the wheel to vibrate in a vertical plane but dynamic imbalance will cause the wheel to vibrate in a sideways direction. It is caused by an unevenly moulded tyre which has a concentration of mass not in line with the vertical centreline of the wheel. When the front wheel is out of balance the effect is most unpleasant, making itself known by vibrations on the steering wheel. It will usually occur at a given speed and can, under the worst circumstances, cause loss of control of the car. If the wheel and tyre are balanced when new the problem will not arise.

5 Out of balance of the rear wheels does not affect the steering and unless it is very bad will not be detected until the tyre begins to wear unevenly - which is too late as the tyre will need replacement. Another good case for having the wheel balanced when a tyre is fitted.

6 If wheel wobble becomes apparent suddenly when driving along stop at the first convenient place. Check the wheel nuts for tightness, jack-up the wheel and check the rim for runout (max. 0.06 ins./0.15 mm) which may have been caused by rough roads or could be a defective front wheel bearing. Check the latter by testing the rim rock (see Chapter 11). Count the balance weights to check that one has not become dislodged. Check the tyre pressure.

If none of these tests indicate a fault, then there is something wrong with the steering mechanism on the front suspension and this must be diagnosed right away.

28 Fault diagnosis - braking system

Before diagnosing faults in the brake system check that irregularities are not caused by any of the following faults:
1. *Incorrect mix of Radial and Crossply tyres*
2. *Incorrect tyre pressures*
3. *Wear in the steering mechanism, suspension or shock absorbers.*
4. *Misalignment of the bodyframe.*

Symptom	Reason/s	Remedy
Pedal travels a long way before the brakes operate	Seized adjuster on rear shoes or shoes require adjustment Disc pads worn past limit	Check, repair, and adjust. Inspect and renew as necessary.
Stopping ability poor, pedal pressure firm	Linings, pads, discs or drums worn, contaminated, or wrong type One or more caliper piston or rear wheel hydraulic cylinder seized Loss of vacuum in servo	Renew pads, linings, discs and drums as necessary. Inspect and repair as necessary. Test servo.
Car veers to one side when brakes are applied	Brake pads on one side contaminated with oil Hydraulic pistons in calipers seized or sticking. Wrong pads fitted	Remove and renew. Repair source of oil leakage. Overhaul caliper. Install correct pads.
Pedal feels spongy when brakes are applied	Air in the hydraulic system Spring weak in master cylinder	Bleed brakes and check for signs of leakage. Top up header tank. Repair master cylinder.
Pedal travels right down with no resistance and brakes do not operate	Fluid reservoir empty Hydraulic lines fractured Seals in master cylinder have failed	Check refill and bleed all brakes. Trace through and replace as necessary. Dismantle cylinder and rebuild with new seals.
Brakes overheat or bind when car is in motion	Compensating port in master cylinder blocked Reservoir air vent blocked Connecting rod requires adjustment Brake shoe return springs broken or strained Caliper piston seals swollen Unsuitable brake fluid	Rebuild cylinder. Clean vent. Adjust. Replace. Replace. Drain and rebuild system.
Brakes judder or chatter and tend to grab	Linings worn Drums out of round Dirt in drums or calipers Discs runout of true excessive	Replace. Replace. Clean. Replace.
Brake shoes squeak (rear brakes)	Dirt in linings Back plates distorted Brake shoe return springs broken or distorted Brake linings badly worn	Clean. Fit new backplates. Fit new springs. Fit new linings.
Disc pads squeak (front broken)	Wrong type of pad fitted Pad guide surfaces dirty Spreader spring deficient or broken Pads glazed Lining on pad not secure	Fit new pads. Clean. Fit new spring. Fit new pads. Fit new pads.
Foot pedal must be pressed harder in one position only.	Groove in master cylinder pushrod due to wear at sealing cups. Air entering vacuum side of servo.	Rebuild master cylinder, new pushrod required.
Very high pedal pressure required to operate brakes, linings found to be in good condition and correctly adjusted	Servo has failed	Check hoses are tight and vacuum check valve is working, if so then remove and service Servo. If necessary fit a new one.

Chapter 9 Electrical system I: charging and starting systems

Contents

Specifications

Battery

Type	Lead acid, six cells with central terminal for computer connection. Negative terminal connected to earth strap. Voltage 12
Capacity	45 ampere hours

Alternator

Type	Rotating field with static windings for output current, built in rectification by diodes mounted in the end plate. VW part No. 021 903 023A	
Mean regulating voltage	14 V	
Nominal output speed rpm	2200	
Maximum current amps	55	
Maximum output watts	770	
	in.	mm
Maximum ovality - slip rings	0.001	0.03
Maximum ovality - rotor	0.002	0.05
Minimum length of brushes	0.5	14
Minimum diameter of slip rings	1.24	31.5
Pressure of springs on brushes	(300 - 400 grams) ¾ lb	
Stator winding resistance	0.13 ± 0.013 ohms	
Rotor winding resistance	4 ohms	
Cut in speed (rpm)	1000	
Ratio engine speed/alternator speed	1 : 2.26	

Voltage control

Type	Mechanical type single contact. ADN part number 021903803

Starter motor

Type	Solenoid operated pinion drive with over-run clutch

	Manual transmission	Automatic transmission
Part No.	311 911 023D	003911023A
Maker	BOSCH	BOSCH
Output HP	0.7	0.8
Voltage	12	12
Field coils	Aluminium	Copper
No. of brushes	4	2
No load test:		
Current amps	35/40	35/50
Volts	12	12
Starter shaft speed rpm	7000/9000	6400/8000

Load test:

Current amps	170/205	160/200
Volts	9	9
Starter shaft speed rpm	900/1300	1100/1400

Stall torque test:

Current amps	220/260	250/300
Volts	6	6

Note: A 12V 135 amp hour battery should be used when testing the starter motor (or a number in parallel). Test should be done at 20° C (68° F) or as near as possible.

Tightening torques	lbs ft	Kgm
Alternator pulley nut	29	4.0
Starter to clutch housing nuts	22	3.0

1 General description

1 Only one make of alternator is used, with a matched voltage regular. Drive for the alternator is taken from the fan by belt. The alternator may be adjusted to tighten the belt by moving the body of the alternator on a quadrant.

Two types of starter motor are employed. The manual transmission requiring slightly less power, has the latest type of starter with modern improvements such as aluminium field windings and four brushes instead of two. The automatic transmission requires a little more push to turn the torque converter and employs an older starter which has copper field coils and a slightly higher output.

The battery is a 12V 45 ampere hour type specially made to fit the VW computerized inspection system. A third small terminal in the middle has a gauge wire attached to it and is used to check the electrolyte level. This causes the battery to be expensive. At the time of writing such a battery will cost about £20 to £25 in UK so it is important to care for it properly.

If the special battery may not be obtained a standard battery of the correct shape may be substituted and will function just as well except that it will not respond to the computer diagnosis. It is imperative that the agent be informed if this substitution has been done **before** the computer diagnosis is attempted.

If the charging light does not go out when the engine is started the ignition should be switched off and the reason sought. Although on this engine the fan does not depend upon the fanbelt to keep it going the belt can very quickly become mixed up with the rotating parts if it breaks and will require a lot of work to remove it.

The system has a negative earth, and special safety precautions are necessary before work is done on the electrical system. These are discussed at length in a special paragraph.

The starter system is simple but the starter is inaccessible. It is important to keep the cables tight and well maintained. The pinion being engaged by the solenoid before the load current is switched on avoids the inevitable damage to the flywheel ring done by an inertia starter and the starter should not require overhaul more frequently than does the engine.

2 Battery - removal and replacement

1 The battery is mounted on the vehicle floor plate in the engine compartment on the right-hand side looking to the front. It is held in place by two clamps. One clamp is welded to the floor and the other one held by a bolt. (photo)

2 First remove the ground (earth) strap. This is the one which goes from the negative terminal post to the frame of the van. Then remove the positive cable. This goes to the starter solenoid, the supply of electricity to the vehicle being distributed from this solenoid terminal.

A word of warning, the battery is not all that accessible and although it is not fragile the case can be damaged quite easily.

2.1 The battery is on the right-hand side of the engine compartment

Do not use force either removing the lid or the terminals. The latter may be stuck and have to be prised off gently. On no account twist them or you may damage the seating of the terminal post.

3 Now remove the wire from the centre terminal. This goes to the computer diagnosis circuit.

4 The bolt may now be removed from the clamp and the battery taken out.

5 Before reinstallation check that no fluid leak has caused corrosion to the battery platform. If it has remove the corrosion until the metal is clean. It will be an acid substance and the metal should be swabbed with ammonia or baking powder (bicarbonate of soda) solution then dried and washed with clean water. Dry it again and apply a good undercoat of paint and then a good quality acid resisting paint on top. This may take time but it is worth doing well for once corrosion has started it is hard to stop and if allowed to continue will eat right through the metal.

6 The battery case should be clean and dry. Install it and fasten in the clamp. Make sure the battery is firmly held, if it can move even a little it will be damaged by road vibration and may need replacement.

7 Reconnect the terminals, centre one first, then the positive and finally the earth strap. The terminal posts must be clean and the cable connectors clean also. A small amount of dirt here will give a large volt drop and cause overheating when the starter current is drawn from the battery. Make sure the cable run does not put a strain on the terminal post, that the connections are tight and then coat the terminals with petroleum jelly (vaseline) to exclude corrosion. Do not use grease.

3 Battery - maintenance and inspection

1 Normal weekly battery maintenance consists of checking the electrolyte level of each cell to ensure that the separators are covered by ¼ inch of electrolyte. If the level has fallen, top up the battery using distilled water only. Do not overfill. If a battery is overfilled or any electrolyte spilled, immediately wipe away the excess as electrolyte attacks and corrodes any metal it comes into contact with very rapidly.

2 As well as keeping the terminals clean and covered with petroleum jelly, the top of the battery, and especially the top of the cells, should be kept clean and dry. This helps prevent corrosion and ensures that the battery does not become partially discharged by leakage through dampness and dirt. If topping up the battery becomes excessive and the case has been inspected for cracks that could cause leakage, but none are found, the battery is being over-charged and the regulator should be checked.

3 Because the battery is in a difficult position a special battery filler has been designed which will go into position easily. These are made by Matra-Werke of Frankfurt/Main and are known as: 'Battery filler bottle HERCO I V'. They are expensive but very convenient. If you cannot rig a filler bottle which will fill the battery without spilling distilled water it is better to take the battery out and do the job properly.

4 With the battery on the bench at the three monthly interval check, measure its specific gravity with a hydrometer to determine the state of charge and condition of electrolyte. There should be very little variation between the different cells and if a variation in excess of 0.025 is present it will be due to either;

a) *Loss of electrolyte from the battery at some time caused by spillage or a leak, resulting in a drop in the specific gravity of electrolyte when the deficiency was replaced with distilled water instead of fresh electrolyte.*

b) *An internal short circuit caused by buckling of the plates or a similar malady pointing to the likelihood of total battery failure in the near future.*

5 The correct readings for the electrolyte specific gravity at various states of charge and conditions are:

	Temperate	Tropical
Fully charged	*1.285*	*1.23*
Half charged	*1.20*	*1.14*
Discharged	*1.12*	*1.08*

6 The hydrometer is a glass tube tapered at one end and fitted with a rubber bulb at the other end. Inside it there is a float.

The tapered end of the tube is inserted into the filler hole of the cell to be tested and the bulb squeezed. When it is released acid is drawn into the tube. Enough must be drawn to allow the float to float freely.

The float has a scale on it and where the surface of the acid meets the float is the point to be read on the scale.

7 It is rare indeed for a battery to freeze but it can happen. If the battery is discharged and the specific gravity is low it may happen more easily. It will not happen while the engine is running so the first intimation will be a refusal to start, for a frozen battery will not supply current. Remembering that there is a solid lump of acid take care how it is handled. It must be thawed slowly. If it can be removed from the van so much the better but if it is frozen in any attempt to remove it by force will break the case. Indeed, the case may have split due to the expansion of the electrolyte so watch carefully as it does thaw or there may be an acid leak of considerable proportions which will do a lot of damage. If this happens take the battery out of the van as quickly as possible, but wear rubber gloves, to avoid being burned.

If the battery thaws out and no leaks appear then it will be of use again. However check the specific gravity and charge if necessary.

For interest value, acid at specific gravity 1.120 (ie; the battery is flat) will freeze at 12°F (−11°C), at 1.200 S.G. at −17°F (−27°C) and a fully charged battery at 1.285 is safe until −68°C (−90°F), so keep the battery well charged in cold weather, and if you do have to leave the van in a snowdrift get the battery out before it freezes.

8 If the battery looses its charge repeatedly then it is probably sulphated or damaged internally. First check the specific gravity of each cell. If some are high (1.285) and the odd one is lower then that is where the trouble lies. The S.G. throughout the six cells should not vary by more than 0.025.

The remaining test is a brutal one, which will probably kill an ageing battery anyway. It consists of short circuiting the battery through a "pair of tongs" equipped with a shunt and a voltmeter in such a way that a current of about 110 amps is passed for 5 to 10 seconds. The voltage between the terminals should not drop below 9.6 volts. Each cell may be tested in turn by putting one prong of the tester on the negative post and dipping the other prong into the electrolyte of each cell in turn. The voltage should read 2, 4, 6, 8, 10, 12 volts progressively. Do not keep the prong in the cell for more than 5 seconds, wear rubber gloves and goggles. Do not do this near a naked light as there will be quite a lot of hydrogen given off. You are advised to leave this test to a VW agent.

4 Battery - charging

1 In winter time when heavy demand is placed upon the battery such as when starting from cold and much electrical equipment is continually in use, it is a good idea occasionally to have the battery fully charged from an external source at the rate of 3.5 to 4 amps. Always disconnect it from the car electrical circuit when charging.

2 Continue to charge the battery at this rate until no further rise in specific gravity is noted over a four hour period.

3 Alternatively, a trickle charger, charging at the rate of 1.5 amps, can be safely used overnight. Disconnect the battery from the van electrical circuit before charging or you will damage the alternator.

4 Specially rapid 'boost' charges which are claimed to restore the power of the battery in 1 to 2 hours can cause damage to the battery plates through over-heating.

5 While charging the battery note that the temperature of the electrolyte should never exceed 100°F (37.8°C).

6 Make sure that your charging set and battery are set to the same voltage.

5 Electrolyte - replenishment

1 If the battery has been fully charged but one cell has a specific gravity of 0.025, or more, less than the others it is most likely that electrolyte has been lost from this cell at sometime and the acid over diluted with distilled water when topping-up.

2 In this case remove some of the electrolyte with a pipette and top up with fresh electrolyte. It is best to get this done at the Service Station, for making your own electrolyte is messy, dangerous, and expensive for the small amount you need. If you must do it yourself add 1 part of sulphuric acid (concentrated) to 2.5 parts of water. **Add the acid to the water,** not the other way round or the mixture will spit back as water is added to acid and you will be badly burnt. Add the acid a drop at a time to the water.

Having added fresh electrolyte recharge and recheck the readings. In all probability this will cure the problem. If it does not then there is a short circuit somewhere.

3 Electrolyte must always be stored away from other fluids and should be locked up, not left about. If you have children this is even more important.

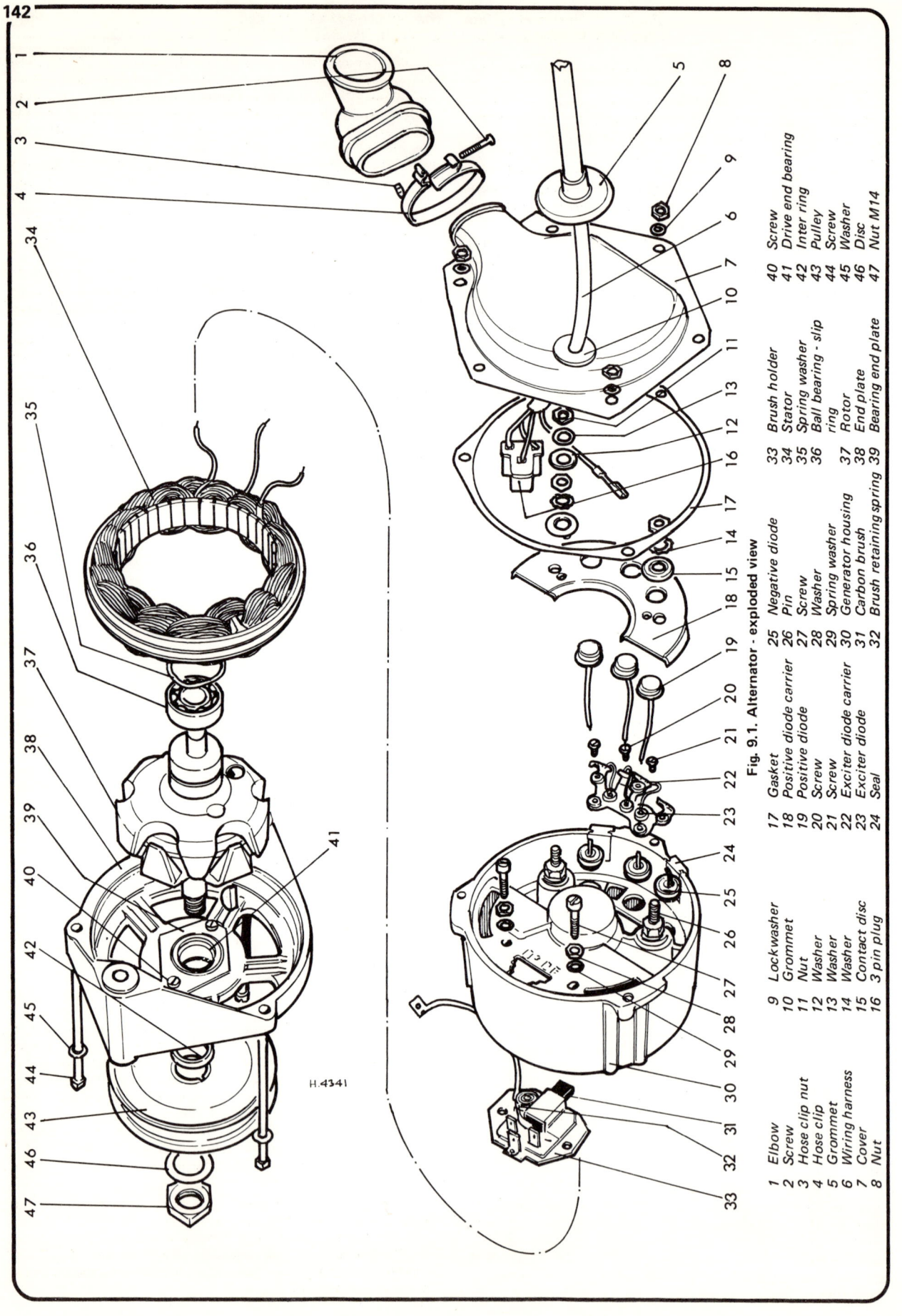

Fig. 9.1. Alternator - exploded view

1 Elbow	9 Lockwasher	17 Gasket	25 Negative diode	33 Brush holder	40 Screw
2 Screw	10 Grommet	18 Positive diode carrier	26 Pin	34 Stator	41 Drive end bearing
3 Hose clip nut	11 Nut	19 Positive diode	27 Screw	35 Spring washer	42 Inter ring
4 Hose clip	12 Washer	20 Screw	28 Washer	36 Ball bearing - slip	43 Pulley
5 Grommet	13 Washer	21 Spring washer	29 Spring washer	ring	44 Screw
6 Wiring harness	14 Washer	22 Exciter diode carrier	30 Generator housing	37 Rotor	45 Washer
7 Cover	15 Contact disc	23 Exciter diode	31 Carbon brush	38 End plate	46 Disc
8 Nut	16 3 pin plug	24 Seal	32 Brush retaining spring	39 Bearing end plate	47 Nut M14

H.4341

6 Alternator - general description

1   Refer to Fig. 9.1. The Bosch alternator has a stator wound with coils which are connected to 3 diodes in the endplate. A further three diodes are also in the circuit and these are for the supply of current to the rotor on which are the field windings. The current goes via the slip rings.

The rotor has the field winding surrounded by two iron claws, and the alternator is nearly self-exciting.

The rotor shaft is supported in a ball race at the slip ring end and a plain bush bearing at the other, the bearings being carried in the endplates. The drive pulley is fitted to the rotor shaft on the outside of the endplate with the plain bush and secured with a nut and washer.

The other endplate carries the diodes in two heat sinks, or holders, designed to conduct the heat away from the diodes.

Since the diodes allow the passage of electric current in one direction only the need for a ''cutout'' is obviated.

However, the unit requires a voltage regulator. Because the rotor is small there is not enough residual magnetism to excite the stator windings at first and a small current is supplied via the ignition switch and terminal 'B+/61', the regulator and terminal 'DF' on the generator from the battery. Once excitation starts the machine becomes self-exciting, current being supplied by the stator to the excitation diodes and thence rectified to the slip rings and field winding.

The unit is cooled by the engine fan. Because the weight of the rotor is small and the slip ring diameter and weight much less than that of a commutator of a comparable DC generator it is possible to run the machine at much higher speeds than the DC generator would allow. This is one of the inherent advantages for the alternator gives a high charging current at low engine speeds and so keeps the battery charged even when driving in city traffic.

7 Alternator - safety precautions

1   **All** alternator systems use a negative earth. Care must be taken not to reverse the battery connection or damage to the diodes will be extensive. Never run the alternator with the output wire disconnected.

2   **Always** disconnect the battery completely if an outside charging operation is contemplated (eg; trickle charge). Disconnect the battery and the alternator output wire if welding is being done to the car.

3   **Do not** use test connections which can 'short' accidentally. The fuses will not blow, the diodes will burn out.

4   When replacing a faulty alternator **clear external faults first**, or yet another alternator may be required.

8 Alternator - belt drive adjustment

1   The alternator is driven by a belt from the fan at the extreme rear of the engine (photo). The tension device is enclosed in the sheet metal covering of the engine. A small aperture is closed by a plastic seal. This is on the right side of the engine.

2   Remove this seal and the adjusting screw of the alternator drive belt is visible. This screw which is a socket head may be undone by use of a suitable key (photo). Undo also the alternator mounting bolt (see also Section 10.4). The alternator may now be moved about in the vertical plane; move it to the right or left until the belt can be depressed 9/16 ins. (15 mm), when pressed down with the thumb. Tighten the socket screw and the mounting bolt and replace the grommet.

3   A word of warning; the splined key necessary to undo this nut is not always available. A metric Allan key **may** undo it, but do not twist too hard. If the splines are sheared off the alternator is in such a position that it may be necessary to take the engine out to undo this nut. So much depends upon the belt driving the alternator efficiently, and the job can be done so quickly with the proper tools, that it seems a false economy not to go to the VW agent if the proper tools are unobtainable. (photo)

9 Alternator - testing in-situ

1   **Precaution - never run the alternator with the battery disconnected.**

2   The official method of testing involves the possession of a voltmeter (0-20v), ammeter (0-60 amps), a battery switch (recommended type SUN No. 7052 - 003), and adjustable electric load and a tachometer (0 - 2,500 rpm). If you are in possession of this kit then all that is needed is the following table. A circuit diagram is given with operating instructions. (Fig. 9.2)

Alternator VW part no.	Max current amps.	Mean regulating volts.	Nominal output
021903023A	55	14	2200

3   If the correct readings are not given, replace the voltage control. If that does not solve the problem the alternator must be removed and serviced. Do not prolong the test more than 30 seconds or the voltage regulator will overheat.

4   Although the charging warning lamp indicates failure to charge, the battery may be getting far less charge than it requires due to poor performance by the alternator. Thus trouble in the alternator will not be noticed until emergency action is required.

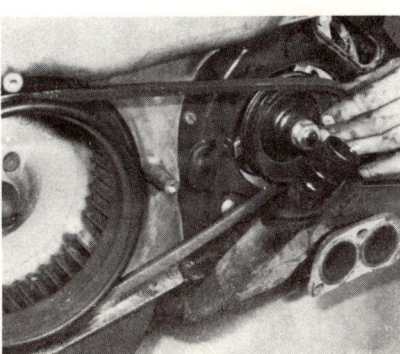

8.1 The generator drivebelt - this picture was taken with the engine removed

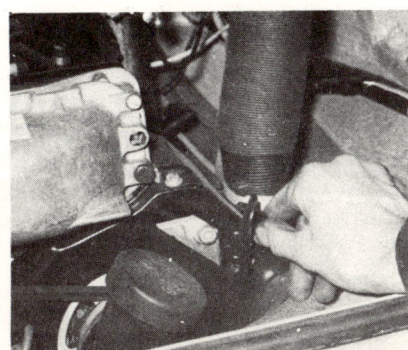

8.2 Removing the inspection plug from the sheet metal housing to get at the alternator adjusting screw

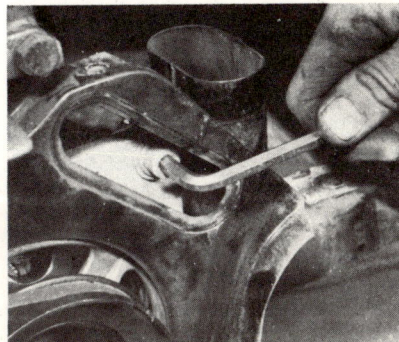

8.3 Undoing the adjusting screw. Be careful (see text)

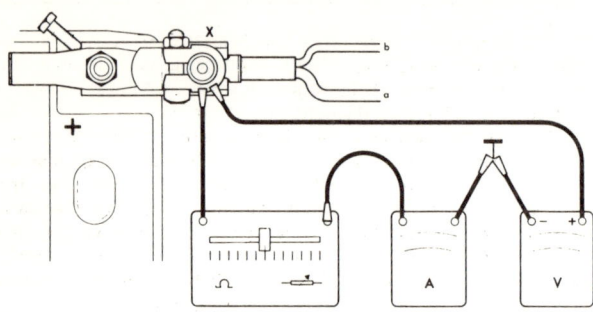

Fig 9.2 Circuit layout for testing charging circuit in situ

x   is the battery switch   a   to starter
(SUN electric No. 7052-003   b   to lighting switch terminal
Run up to 2000 rpm (with   30
switch on) adjust load to 25 amps, operate switch to cut battery
out and adjust to readings in the text Section 9.2*

If this happens at night when you have far to go the battery will
not keep the headlights and rear lights shining and supply the
ignition circuit for long, so you are unlikely to get home.

5   This state of affairs can be avoided by the purchase and
fitting of an ammeter in the charging circuit. The ammeter
showing charge and discharge should be installed on the facia
board and will tell you exactly what is happening in the charging
circuit, thus enabling action to be taken before the emergency
occurs.

Such an instrument may be obtained from dealers or Auto
shops in kit form quite inexpensively. They come complete with
installation instructions and should be installed as well as, not
instead of, the warning light.

10 Alternator - removal and replacement

1   Removing the alternator is no problem, but getting at it to
remove it is another matter. Disconnect the battery to avoid
accidents.

2   Take the clamp off the oil filler neck and remove the filler
neck. Now take out the dipstick and ease the grommet off the
dipstick tube. The object of this exercise is to allow the right
rear part of the engine cover plate (the piece that goes round the
dipstick tube) to be removed.

3   Take out the screws which clamp this plate to the engine. We
found them a bit tight and had to use an impact screwdriver on
two of them. Now slide the plate up and off the oil filler pipe.
The rubber grommet will come off with the plate. Clean it and
set it aside for reassembly or get a new one if it is perished or
damaged.

4   Remove the plastic insert from the cover plate (photo 8.2)
and slacken off the XZN screw. We spoke of this in Section 8.
The special tool required may be obtained through some VW
agents or Auto shops and is made by HAZET which is a German
firm. The part No. is '990 - 8LG' and it is for an M8 socket head
screw.

5   Undo the lower mounting bolt a little, move the alternator to
the left and take the belt off the alternator pulley. Now take the
lower mounting bolt right out and take off the alternator cover
plate.

6   The wiring from the alternator goes through the engine cover.
Ease this out and you will have enough slack to undo the wiring
harness from the alternator. Disconnect this, tagging the leads to
make assembly less difficult.

7   Remove the cooling air elbow from the fan housing.

8   The tensioning arm bracket is a slotted lever behind the

alternator. It is held by two screws. Remove these (one top, one
bottom) and the alternator complete with bracket will come
away. Mark the position of the tensioning arm on the alternator
housing if further work is contemplated.

9   Replacement is the reverse of removal. Position the alternator
on the engine and fit the tensioning arm bolts. The housing
should be in the same place on the tensioning arm as it was
before removal. Make sure the rubber grommet is on the wiring
harness and attach the wiring. It may be easier to connect the
wiring before finally tightening the tensioning arm screws.

10 Now fit the upper mounting bolt. Screw the lower mounting
bolt in a few turns and then fit the cooling air elbow. Take out
the lower bolt, fit the cover plate and then fit the lower bolt.

11 Move the alternator to the left, fit the belt and then move the
alternator to the right until the middle point of the belt may be
depressed only 5/8 in. (15 mm) with your thumb. This is the
correct tension so tighten both mounting bolts. Be careful again
with that Allan key if you do not have a proper XZN tool.

12 Fit the plastic plug into the inspection hole. Refit the cover
plate over the oil filler pipe. Do not forget the grommet. Tighten
the screws securing the plate to the engine and then fit the oil
filler neck and clip. Replace the dipstick. Reconnect the battery.

13 Run the engine for a little while and then recheck the belt
tension. Adjust again if necessary.

11 Alternator - overhaul

1   If either of the windings are faulty then a replacement unit is
required. It is possible to replace bearings and diodes. Brushes
may be renewed. However, unless you have the correct
equipment and knowledge it is recommended that you have the
unit overhauled by a reputable Auto Electrical Engineer or
obtain a replacement unit from the VW agent. **Read the whole
Section before starting work and then make up your mind.**

2   The tensioning bracket should be marked on the housing to
facilitate repair and then removed. Remove the nut from the
pulley and pull the pulley off with extractors. Clean the exterior
of the alternator, lay out a clean work place and work only with
clean hands.

3   Pull the carbon brushes out with a wire hook. If they are
pulled out far enough they can be held by the retaining spring.

4   Undo the housing screws (through bolts) ease the rubber
grommet along the wiring harness and the sections of the
alternator may be eased apart. The rotor will remain in the end
plate. Catch the nuts and washers off the housing screws and put
them in a safe place.

5   Having got so far, clean away any dust with a new paint
brush and a soft cloth, and have a good look round. Burnt out
windings are usually obvious by the distinctive smell and charred
wires, open circuits are not. Wear on the slip rings is obvious, the
diameter should not be less than 1.24 ins. (31.5 mm) and the
ovality should not exceed 0.001 ins. (0.03 mm).

The minimum length of the carbon brushes is 0.5 in. (14
mm). These unfortunately are not obtainable separately and if
renewal is required the complete brush holder must be purchased
with brush installed.

6   At this stage a decision as to whether to go further must be
made. The connections to the diodes must be unsoldered, unless
this is done by an experienced electrician, who knows how to
use long nosed pliers as a heat sink while unsoldering the wires,
damage will be done to the diodes and they will have to be
replaced.

7   When the positive and negative diodes and the stator
windings have been disconnected from the connecting strip of
the exciter diode carrier it will be possible to test the windings
and diodes.

8   Further cleaning may now be done. Use only trichlorethylene
or benzine and use it sparingly.

9   Check the diodes with a test lamp or meter and maximum
voltage of 24 volts. Current should flow only one way, if it flows
both ways the diode must be replaced. Keep the test current
down to 0.8 ma and do not allow the diode to heat up.

10 Check the stator and rotor windings with a resistance tester for short circuits, open circuits and shorts to earth. The resistance between slip rings of the rotor should be 4 ohms $\pm$ 0.4 ohms and of course there must be no circuit between the slip rings and the shaft or rotor core.

The resistance of the stator windings should be 0.13 ohms $\pm$ 0.013 ohms. This is measured between the stator leads in pairs. Check all three, they must be the same. Check the stator windings for short circuit to earth.

11 If the bearings are worn they should be renewed. It is necessary to press the rotor out of the end shield to renew the bush. Support the endplate carefully or it will distort. Having pressed the rotor out remove the screws holding the retaining plate, remove the plate and press the bush out of the endplate. You will probably have to turn up a mandrel on a lathe to do this. To replace the bush first grease it lightly and then press it in.

The ball race on the other end should not be touched unless a new one is to be fitted. Use a puller to draw it off and when pressing a new one on be sure to press only on the inner race. If you press on the outer race you will ruin the bearing.

12 If you intend to replace a diode first remove the screws holding the diode carrier for the positive diode and push the carrier to one side. Disconnect the wire from the brush holder to the exciter diode, and unsolder the wires from the other diodes. It will now be possible to press out the faulty diode. This should be done with a tubular mandrel. Press a new one in, grease it with a little silicone oil before insertion.

There is an art in this job. Use a pair of long-nosed pliers and a very small soldering iron. Draw as much heat away with the pliers as is possible and apply only enough to make the joint.

Any overheating will ruin the diode and you must do it again. The pressing job needs great care too for the diodes are fragile.
13 Once all this is done the alternator may be reassembled. This is the reverse of dismantling but be careful to re-route the brush connections in the same way as they were before.
14 The alternator should be tested either in, or out of, the vehicle. The method in Section 9 may be used if the test is done in-situ. The alternator should deliver 55 amps at 14 volts at 2200 rpm. It would be better to let an Auto electrical firm do an out of chassis test, and to get them to check the wave form too with an oscillograph.
15 At the start of this Section advice was offered. If after reading the Section you are confident you can do the job you may save a fair amount of money. If for instance only brushes or bearings need replacement the task is fairly simple. But unless you have the tools and knowhow the diode replacement is difficult. If the windings are faulty you need a new alternator anyway.

12 Voltage regulator

1 This is to be found fixed to the engine compartment floor by the battery. It is not repairable or adjustable. If faulty it must be replaced. Before working on it disconnect the battery earth strap.
2 To replace it remove the connector plug, undo the two screws holding it in position. Remove the old regulator and install the new one. Refit the connector plug and then reconnect the battery.

13 Fault diagnosis - generating circuit

Symptom		Reason/s	Remedy
Ignition switch on but not warning light	1	Battery flat or defective	Replace.
	2	Bulb requires replacement	Replace.
	3	Battery terminals loose or dirty	Clean and tighten.
	4	Broken or damaged wiring	Repair or replace.
	5	Ignition switch not working	Replace.
	6	Alternator brushes open circuit	Overhaul alternator.
	7	Regulator faulty	Replace.
Light glows when engine is running	1	Fan belt broken or slipping	Adjust.
	2	Regulator faulty	Replace.
	3	Alternator not delivering charge	Test and repair.
Light remains on when engine switched off		Regulator points closed, probably burnt and stuck	Replace.

14 Starter motor - general description

1 The two types of starter to be found are identical in operation and the procedure for removal, dismantling and overhaul is the same. All manual transmission vehicles have starter part No. '311 911 023D', and all automatic transmission part No. '003911023A'.
2 When the ignition is turned on and the key turned still further the winding of the solenoid on the starter is energised. This causes the solenoid core to operate the solenoid lever which pivots and moves the pinion along a coarse pitched thread until it contacts the starter ring on the flywheel. If its teeth are opposite the teeth gaps in the starter ring it continues into mesh.
3 Just before the pinion reaches the starter ring, contacts in the solenoid are closed which complete the armature circuit and the starter commences to rotate, and the pinion is pushed into mesh with the starter ring completely at a very low speed.
4 Should the pinion not have meshed immediately, the operating lever compresses a spring behind the pinion and as the starter begins to turn this spring forces the pinion into mesh as

the teeth come opposite to the gaps in the starter ring.
5 The current then builds up in the starter winding and the starter increases in speed until the maximum speed is reached. When the engine fires the ignition key is released and current is cut-off from the solenoid, the return spring works, and the pinion is withdrawn from mesh.
6 The overrun clutch prevents the pinion from driving the starter armature should the starter key not be released, or the pinion jam in mesh.

The ignition switch has a "no repeat" device which means that the starter may not be energised when the engine is running, and the key must be returned to the 'OFF' position before the starting cycle can be repeated.

15 Starter - testing in car, removal and replacement

1 On the Volkswagen the starter is an inaccessible article and short of checking that the mounting bolts are tight and the electrical connections properly made to the solenoid, there is nothing else to be done except take it out if it malfunctions. If

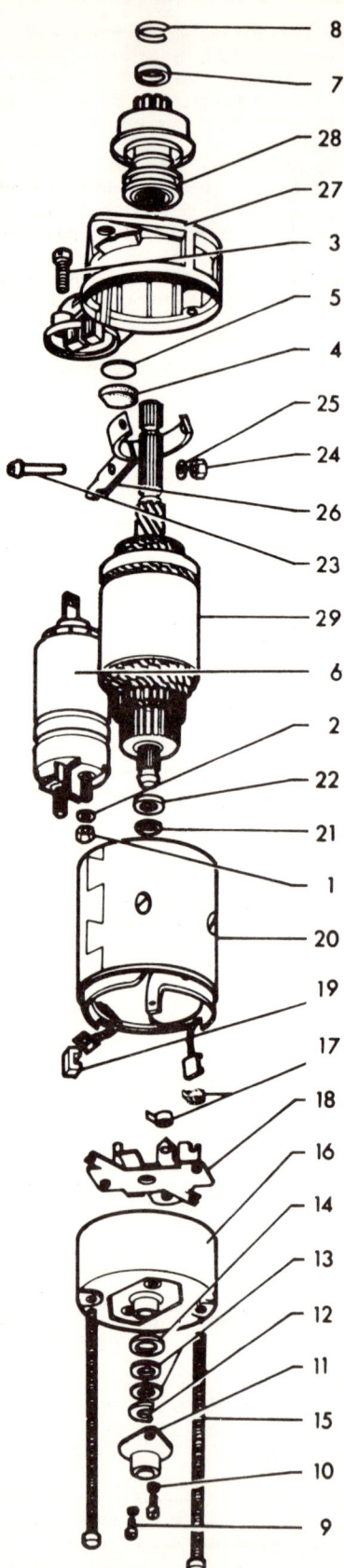

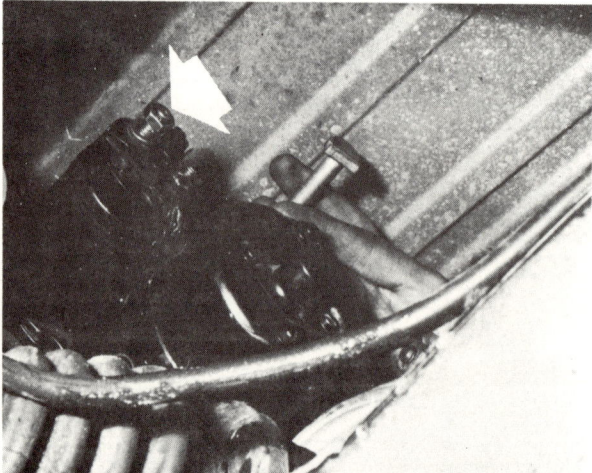

15.2a Removing the starter top bolt head and the terminal for the main starter cable connector (arrowed)

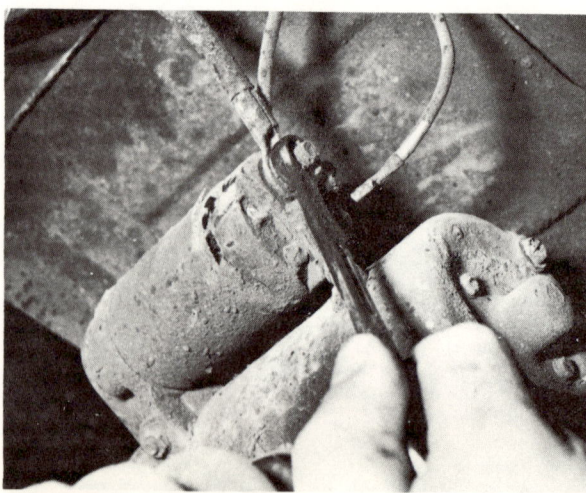

15.2b Do not confuse the two nuts on the solenoid

Fig 9.3 Starter motor components (Bosch)

1	Nut	16	End plate
2	Lockwasher	17	Spring
3	Screw	18	Brush holder
4	Rubber seal	19	Grommet
5	Disc	20	Housing
6	Solenoid switch	21	Insulating washer
7	Stop ring	22	Thrust washer
8	Circlip	23	Pin
9	Screw	24	Nut
10	Washer	25	Lockwasher
11	End cap	26	Operating lever
12	C washer	27	Mounting bracket
13	Shim	28	Drive pinion
14	Sealing ring	29	Armature
15	Housing screw		

the starter fails to kick at all ascertain that current is being fed from the starter switch to the solenoid. This can be done by connecting a suitable long lead to test each of the terminals on the solenoid in turn. Connect the other end via a voltmeter or bulb to earth. When connected to the smaller terminal (the lead from the ignition switch), there should be an indication on the bulb or voltmeter when the starter switch is operated. If there is not then check the other end of the wire at the starter switch terminal in the same way. If there is no voltage then the fault is not with the starter. Then connect the lead to the larger terminal on the solenoid.

Normally the solenoid can be heard to move but this does not necessarily mean that it is switching the main current to the starter. If the solenoid plunger can be heard to move yet no voltage is recorded at the large terminal then the solenoid is defective.

2   Before attempting to remove the starter disconnect the earth strap from the battery. The starter is held by a bolt at the top and a stud and nut at the bottom. You may have to get someone to hold the bolt head from within the engine compartment. The lower nut is accessible from under the van. (photos)

3   From underneath the van disconnect the small lead at the connection and then undo the nut securing the large cable. There may be a plastic strap type clip holding the cable to the solenoid housing. This must be undone, or you may even have to cut it. The cable should be clipped to the floor of the cab. Do not disturb this clip. Be careful not to confuse the two large terminal nuts on the solenoid. The lower one connects the strap between the solenoid and starter.

4   With the cables disconnected remove the large upper bolt and then the nut off the stud and the starter may be withdrawn.

5   Replacement is the reversal of removal. Install the starter and reconnect it. It is most important that the bolts and nuts are tight. Even more important that the big terminal is connected tightly and is clean and the cable routed correctly. The solenoid is close to the warm air control box and the warm air hose. Make sure the cable terminal points vertically down when tightened. If the plastic clip was damaged either replace it with a new one or make up a satisfactory substitute.

The load test current is 170/205 amps so with a cold engine there may well be 170 amps or more flowing through the connection of the large terminal. A simple ohms law calculation shows that a resistance of 0.02 ohms will cause a volts drop of nearly 4 volts at the connection. The voltage expected due to load on the battery etc is only 9, so a bad connection may drop that to 5 volts, and the engine will not start because the starter does not develop enough power.

If this trouble does develop then a voltmeter connected to the stud and to earth should show the drop in volts when the starter is activated and you will know the fault and remedy.

16 Starter motor - overhaul

1   Although there are two types of starter, depending on the type of transmission, the overhaul procedure is the same. Refer to Fig. 9.3 which is a typical Bosch starter.

2   Clean the exterior of the starter carefully and arrange to hold it in a vice. Remove the cover plate to give access to the brushes. If these do not protrude beyond their holders renewal is necessary which calls for further dismantling.

Undo the nut connecting the strap between the solenoid and the starter and then the two screws holding the solenoid to the end frame. (photos)

3   The solenoid can now be unhooked from the operating lever inside the end frame. (photo)

4   If the solenoid only is faulty this is as far as it is necessary to go. A new solenoid unit can be fitted now.

5   Remove the two screws holding the end cover cap. (photo)

6   Slide out the 'U' clip and remove the shims from the end of the shaft. These shims control the endfloat. (photos)

7   Remove the two through bolts from the end cover and the

16.2a Undoing the connection strap terminal nut

16.2b Removing the solenoid retaining screws

16.3 Unhook the solenoid from the operating lever

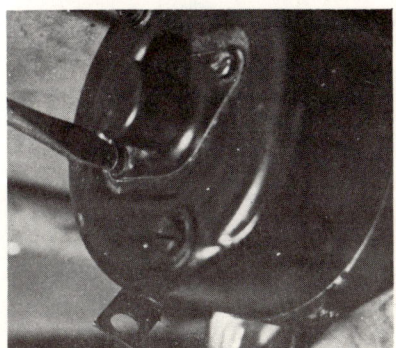
16.5 Remove the end cover cap screws

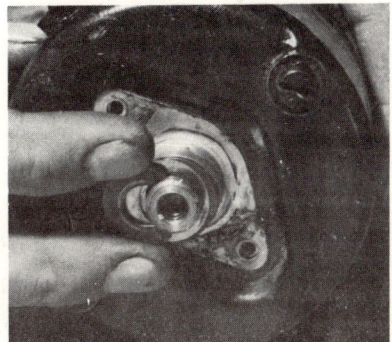
16.6a Remove the 'U' clip from the end

16.6b ... and the shim washers.

end cover may then be taken off giving access to the commutator brushes. (photos)

8 Hook up the springs holding the carbon brushes in the holders and push them to one side so that the pressure is relieved. The yoke complete with the brush holder mounting plate may then be drawn off with the armature. Watch out for the washers on the end of the shaft. (photo)

9 To renew the brushes, two may be detached by simply removing the screws whilst the other two need to be cut off and new ones soldered to the braided leads. Leave sufficient length to solder the new ones onto easily.

10 To remove the end frame from the drive end of the shaft first push back the stop ring with a suitable tube so that the jump ring underneath can be released from its groove. The end cover assembly complete with the pinion may then be drawn off.

11 The pinion drive should turn one-way only inside the clutch easily. If it does not the whole unit needs renewing. The pinion teeth should not be badly worn or chipped. The yoke of the pinion operating lever should be a good fit in the groove of the pinion sleeve.

12 Reassembly is a reversal of the dismantling procedure. Thoroughly grease the moving parts of the pinion operating lever first. When replacing the yoke engage the cut-out and tongue correctly. (photo)

13 The carbon brushes should all be held up in their holders and this can be achieved if the springs are jammed against the sides of the brushes. The armature has two washers, on the end of these, which must be fitted so that the thrust washer goes on first and the insulating washer after that.

14 When the pinion stop ring is refitted stake it into position over the jump ring after the latter has been fitted in its groove.

15 When refitting the solenoid ensure the plunger hooked end is securely placed over the operating lever.

16 The screw heads and joint faces of the commutator end cover, the solenoid and end frame should all be treated with sealing compound to keep water out. Use the Volkswagen product specially for this if possible. It is important that it is not applied too thickly, otherwise clearance distances may be upset. If, after reassembly, the endfloat of the shaft exceeds 0.012 inch (0.30 mm) it should be reduced by adding shim washers under the 'U' retaining clip on the end of the armature shaft under the small cover.

17 Testing the starter on the bench

1 Before reinstalling the motor it is well worthwhile checking that it works first. Clamp the starter body firmly in a vice and

16.7a Remove the through bolts (housing screws)

16.7b Take off the end cover

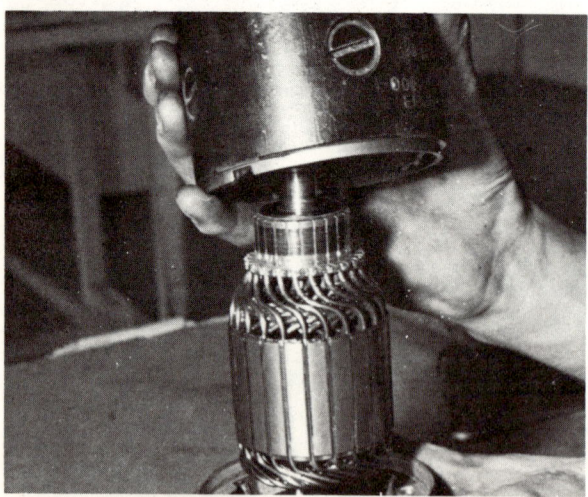
16.8 Lift the yoke and brush holder off the armature

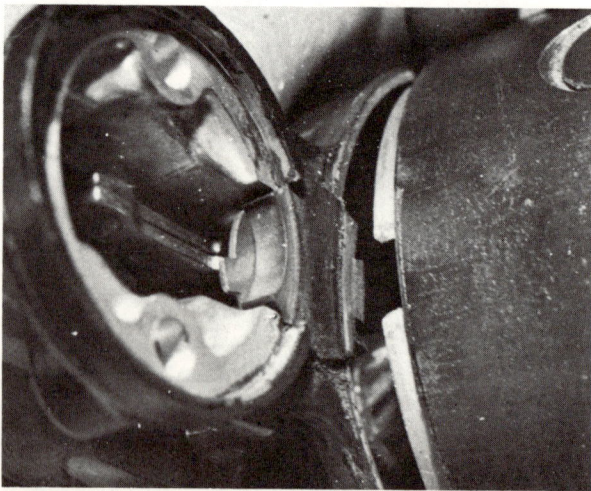
16.12 Refit the yoke so that the tongue and cut out fit together

take the battery out of the car. Connect a heavy cable from the large solenoid terminal to the '+' terminal of the battery and an equally heavy one from the body of the starter to the negative terminal on the battery. Then use a piece of smaller wire to connect the '+' terminal of the battery to the small blade terminal on the solenoid. When this is done the pinion should shoot forward and the motor revolve. Note: Although the wires in this test do not need to be as heavy as those used in the car, if they are too small they will heat up.

2   The above test should suffice to show that the starter is functioning correctly. If however, you have access to a suitable test bed it is quite simple to test the starter accurately. The correct figures for the "no load" "full load" and "stall torque" tests are given in the Specifications.

18 Fault diagnosis - starting system

Symptom	Test and possible reason	Remedy
1 Starter does not operate when key is turned to "start" position	Turn on the lights for this test 1 Lights go out - loose connections, corroded terminals, flat battery 2 Lights go dim - battery run down 3 Connect a cable between terminals 30 and 50. If starter now turns either cables or ignition switch is faulty 4 Lights stay bright. Connect cable from terminal 30 to connector strip terminal - starter now turns	Check circuit and replace battery. Recharge or replace battery. Replace cables, starter to ignition switch and/or ignition switch. Solenoid needs service or replacement.
2 Drive pinion sticks in mesh with starter ring	1 Coarse thread damaged 2 Solenoid not working	Overhaul starter. Replace solenoid.
3 Starter turns slowly and will not start engine	1 Battery run down 2 Loose connections 3 Brushes not making proper contact 4 Commutator dirty, burnt or damaged 5 Windings damaged	Charge or replace. Check circuit. Overhaul or replace starter. Overhaul or replace starter. Overhaul or replace starter.
4 Erratic starting i.e. sometimes it will and sometimes it will not, particularly from cold	1 Battery has internal fault. Load test battery with tongs	Replace battery if necessary.

Chapter 10 Electrical system II: Lighting system, fascia board and electrical accessories

Contents

Specifications

Battery ... ...   Lead acid with special sensor wire. 12v - 45 amp hour - BOSCH

Bulbs

	DIN Designation	VW pt no.	Type
Headlight normal	A 12v 45/50W	N 177053	Twin filament ball
Headlight Halogen	YD 12v 60/55W	N 177632	Halogen H 4.
Parking light	HL 12v 4W	N 177172	Tubular
Turn signal	RL 12v 21W	N 177322	Ball
Brake/Tail	SL 12v 21/5W	N 177382	Twin filament ball.
License (number) plate	G 12v 10W	N 177192	Ball
Interior light	K 12v 10W	N 177232	Festoon
Back-up light and Ambulance sign interior light	RL 12v 21W	N 177322	Ball
		N 176981	Neon tube
Spot light	12v 35W	211941 253	Ball

Sealed beam:

Headlight	6012 (US)	111 941 261A	Sealed beam
Turn signal front with parking light	SL 12v 21/5W	N 177382	Twin filament ball

U.S. equipment only:

Headlight	6014 (US)	111 941 261B/C	Sealed beam
Sidemarker lights	HL 12v 4W	N 177172	Ball

Fuse box layout

The fuse box layout varies without warning. The tables given are typical, but see Section 17.

Circuit	1972	1973	1974
Auxiliary heater (switch current)	9/10	9/10	9/10
Back-up lights (automatic transmission only)		11	11
Emergency flasher system	8	8	8
Fuel gauge	11	11	11
High beam headlight and warning light	6	5	5
High beam (right)	5	6	6
Horn	12	12	12
Interior light (front)	8	8	8
Interior light (rear)	9	9	9

Circuit						1972	1973	1974
'Kick-down' (automatic transmission)	...	...	...	...			11	11
License plate (number plate)	...	...	...	...	...	2	2	2
Low beam headlight (left)	...	...	...	...	...	4	3	3
Low beam headlight (right)	...	...	...	...	...	3	4	4
Parking lights	...	...	...	...	...	2	2	2
Heated rear window (switch current)	...	...	...	...	10	10	10
Side lights (front)	...	...	...	...	...		2	2
Side lights (rear left)	...	...	...	...	...	1	1	1
Side lights (rear right)	...	...	...	...	...	2	2	2
Stop (brake) lights	...	...	...	...	...	12	12	12
Tail light (left)	...	...	...	...	...	1	1	1
Tail light (right)	...	...	...	...	...	2	2	2
Turn signals (direction indicators)	...	...	...	...	11	11	11
Fresh air fan	...	...	...	...	...	...		7	7
Charging system warning light	...	...	...	...	11	11	11
Oil pressure warning light	...	...	...	...	...	11	11	11
Windscreen wipers	...	...	...	...	...	10	10	10

Note (i): 9 and 11 are 16 ampere the remainder 8 ampere rating

Note (ii): In line fuses - In the engine compartment - back-up lights and (16 amp) warm air blower

Wiper motor

Type	...	...	...	...	...	...	...	2 speed - worm drive - permanent magnet field

Current consumption:

low speed	...	...	...	...	...	...	...	2.5 amps
high speed	...	...	...	...	...	...	...	3.5 amps

Relay panel

Relays are located behind the fuse panel (see Section 7) Numbers from left to right

1	...	...	...	...	...	...	...	...	...	Turn signal - emergency flasher
2	...	...	...	...	...	...	...	...	...	Combi relay - headlamp and dimmer
3	...	...	...	...	...	...	...	...	...	Intermittant wiper relay (optional extra)
4	...	...	...	...	...	...	...	...	...	Buzzer relay (Ambulance)
5	...	...	...	...	...	...	...	...	...	Fog light relay (optional extra)
6	...	...	...	...	...	...	...	...	...	Transistor light relay (brake system warning light)

1 Lighting system - general description

1 The 12 volt system has a negative earth. It is important therefore that water, and consequent rust, be excluded from all fittings. Regular inspection of grommets and lens to see that no damage has occurred is recommended.

2 A diagram of the fascia board is included showing which switch works which light. (Fig. 10.1) A bulb chart is included in the Specification.

3 The basic exterior layout is the minimum legal requirement, head, tail, license plate and parking lights plus brake stop and turn signals. To this may be added emergency stop (mandatory in some Countries), back-up or reversing lights, fog and spot lamps, and for the ambulance and fire truck an illuminated sign.

4 Two interior lights are provided on some models, one in the cab and one in the body. In certain areas the fresh air ventilation and heater controls must be illuminated, and on automatic transmission models the gear lever console so that you can see where the lever is at night. This latter idea is a very good one for it can avoid an element of surprise should the lever have been moved accidentally.

5 The fascia board has five warning lights (oil, charging, indicators, high beam and brake circuit). The first four are set in the fuel gauge and the last one adjacent to the speedometer. Add to this illuminating lights for the speedometer dial, fuel gauge and clock and it will be realized that no mean electrical circuit exists behind the fascia board.

6 Control of lighting is by rotary or push pull switches and the cab interior light by an additional switch operated by the opening and closing of the door. Headlamps and indicator lights are controlled by a lever on the steering column switch box.

7 Fuses for all lighting circuits are provided, and those requiring heavier current (eg headlamps and fog lamps) are operated through relays. Most of the circuits are routed through the fuse box but one or more may be fitted with in-line fuses which are located in the engine compartment.

8 Over the period covered various types of light have been fitted to the headlamp circuit. These are discussed in the next Section.

2 Headlights - description, replacement and adjustment

1 Three types may be found on the vehicle. Sealed beam types are fitted to USA models. Another type is the replacable bulb with a lens permanently cemented to the reflector. The latter type may be fitted with a normal twin filament bulb 45/50W or with a Halogen H.4 bulb 60/55 watt. The bulb holders differ slightly so that the bulbs are not interchangable.

2 All three types use the same method of fixing and aiming, the essential difference being in the replacement of the lighting element.

Sealed beam pattern

3 The sealed beam pattern has a seven inch lens with a twin filament bulb. To remove it undo the screw in the plated ring and remove the ring. The screw is in the edge of the ring and stays in the ring even when unscrewed. (photo)

Underneath the plated ring is the retaining ring. An illustration of the unit with an exploded view is provided. The retaining ring is fastened in with three short screws. Remove these and the whole unit may be pulled forward. **Do not** alter the position of the beam adjusting screws, these fasten the sealed beam unit contained in the retaining ring to the securing ring (the one screwed to the vehicle body). (Fig. 10.2)

4   The terminal block may now be pulled off its terminals and the sealed beam unit removed.

5   Replacement is the reverse of removal. Be sure that the three glass lugs of the sealed beam unit engage snugly in the aiming ring, fit the retaining ring and hook the chromium plated trim ring over the lug on the body recess, check that the rubber sealing ring is correctly positioned and then tighten the turn ring mounting screw.

Replacable bulb pattern and Halogen bulb pattern

6   An exploded view of this lamp is illustrated (Fig. 10.3). Remove the trim ring as in paragraph 3. Undo and remove the screws holding the retaining ring to the body. (photo)

7   The unit may now be lifted out of the body and the wires detached. There are two spade terminals which go on one way only. Mark which wire, grey and brown, goes to which terminal or you may try to operate the side lamp with the headlamp

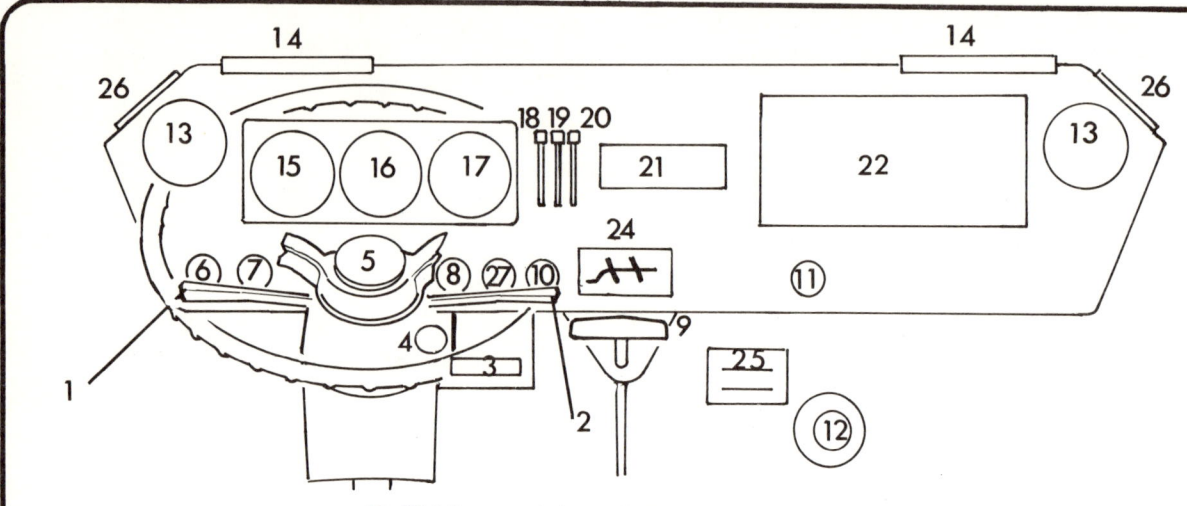

Fig 10.1 Key to switches and instruments on the dashboard

1 Turn signal and dimmer switch
2 Lever for windscreen wiper and washer
3 Fuses and relays
4 Ignition/steering lock switch
5 Horn button
6 Lighting switch
7 Rotary switch for

fresh air fan
8 Rear interior light switch
9 Handbrake lever
10 Emergency light switch
11 Heated rear window switch
12 Windscreen washer tank filling. aperture
13 Adjustable fresh

air beats
14 Defroster vents
15 Fuel gauge with warning lamps
16 Speedometer
17 Clock
18 Warm air distribution lever
19 Heater lever
20 Fresh air ventilation

lever
21 Cover plate for radio aperture
22 Glove box
23 Brake warning lamp
24 Ashtray
25 Warm air vents
26 Fresh air vents
27 Interior light switch fan cab

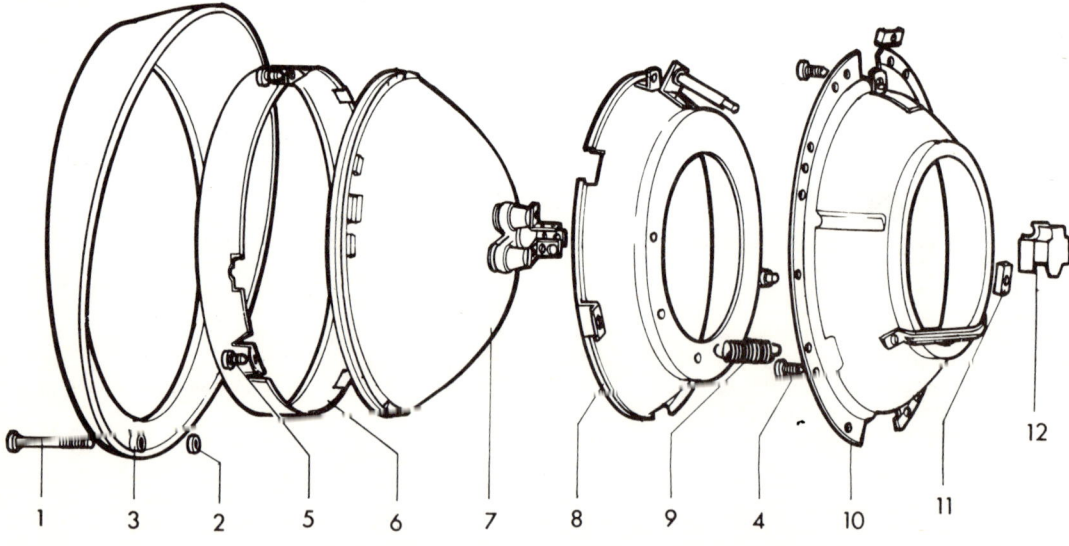

Fig 10.2 Sealed beam headlamps - components (Sec 2)

1 Rim securing screw
2 Rubber washer
3 Rim
4 Securing ring screw

5 Retaining ring screw
6 Retaining ring
7 Sealed beam unit

8 Aiming ring with 2 aiming Screws
9 Retaining ring spring

10 Securing ring
11 Tapped plates
12 Terminal block

switch (photo).

8 The rubber cover may now be removed (photo) and the side lamp bulb extracted (photo) from its nylon holder.

9 The headlight bulb may now be removed by turning the

spring and holder in an anticlockwise direction and pulling the bulb out. (photo)

10 Replacement is the reverse of removal. **Do not** touch the glass part of the bulb with naked fingers or your finger prints will

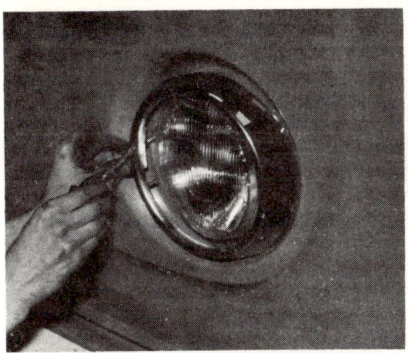

2.3 Removing the screw securing the trim ring

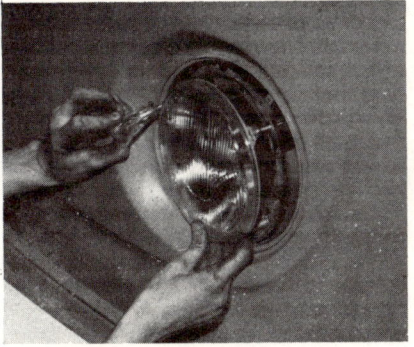

2.6 Undoing the screws holding the retaining ring to the body

2.7 Lifting the lamp away from the body to disconnect the wires. Tag the wires to ensure correct replacement

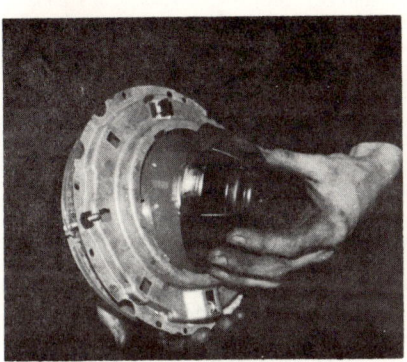

2.8a Removing the rubber cap

2.8b Take out the sidelamp bulb from the nylon holder

2.9 Turn the bulb holder and spring in an anticlockwise direction

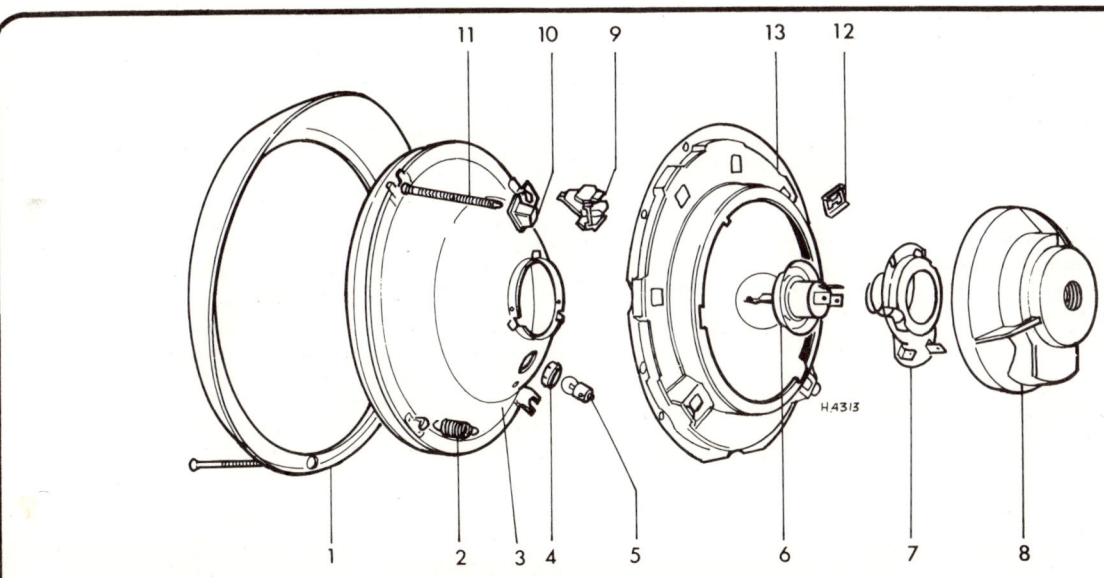

Fig. 10.3 Round headlight (replaceable bulb) (Sec 2)

1 Rim	5 Sidelight bulb	8 Cover for bulb	11 Adjuster screw
2 Spring	(4 watt)	holder	12 Clip
3 Headlight unit	6 Bulb for head light	9 Retainer	13 Retaining ring
4 Sidelight bulb holder	7 Bulb holder	10 Adjuster screw nut	

appear on the bulb when it gets hot. Hold the bulb in a duster. It goes in only one way as the bayonet pins are offset.

11 The copper wire of the main bulb holder must contact the base of the sidelight bulb properly. If you have removed the side lamp bulb holder the tab must point downwards on reassembly.

12 Do not alter the adjusting screw, but should this be done inadvertantly make sure the nut seats properly in the retainer ring. If you have to fit a new lens unit make sure the glass is the right way up.

13 The halogen bulb pattern is similar to the standard bulb but the headlight unit (see illustration) differs in detail so that conversion entails more than changing the bulb.

14 Adjustment of the unit can be done only with the correct equipment accurately. However a rough setting may be done until the time when accurate setting is possible with a beammaster or similar test equipment.

15 The accompanying diagrams show the setting dimensions for lamps with replaceable bulbs and sealed beam units for vehicles with lamps which dip to the right (ie; drive on the right of the road). For vehicles which drive on the left and dip to the left both diagrams should be mirrored. The adjusting screws for the vertical adjustment of the beams are at the top of the rim and those for the lateral adjustment at the side. (Figs. 10.4 and 10.5).

16 The vehicle should be standing on level ground with tyre pressures correct and the equivalent of the driver's weight in the driving seat. It should face a vertical screen which should be 16.4 ft (5 metres) away for conventional bulb units and 25 ft (7.6 metres) away for sealed beam units.

17 The vehicle should be settled on the suspension by rolling backwards and forwards and each light should be checked with the other covered up. All settings are made with the beams dipped. The high beams will be correct automatically if this is done.

18 Check the dimensions given with your local agent because regulations vary from time-to-time and in some countries are more stringent.

3 Front turn signals - bulb replacement

1 The flashers have been moved to above the headlight. Access is gained by removing the crosshead screws, (photo) when the bulb may be removed and replaced. Remember not to handle it with bare fingers but hold it in a duster when inserting a new one.

Flasher signals are particularly sensitive to poor earth return so make sure the lens fits snugly into the gasket when replaced. If it is necessary to replace the whole unit drill out the pop rivets with a 3.5 mm drill and install a complete new unit.

4 Rear light cluster - bulb replacement

1 Three bulb holders are located in this cluster. The cover is held on by crosshead screws. Remove these, and ease the cover away (photo).

2 The top bulb is the turn signal. The centre bulb has twin filaments and acts as brake/tail light. At the bottom is the back-up (reversing) light.

3 Remove these bulbs by pressing in and turning to the left. When refitting the twin filament bulb the pin nearest the glass on the bayonet fitting must be downwards. (photo)

4 Make sure the assembly is watertight when refitting the lens , but do not tighten too much, or the lens may crack.

5 License plate (rear number plate) light

1 Loosen the screws securing the lens, remove it from the body and the bulb may be removed from its holder and replaced as necessary.

2 Be careful with the gasket.

6 Interior lights - removal and replacement

1 To remove these insert a flat screwdriver between the lamp rim and the head lining on the switch side and lever the assembly out. Replace the festoon lamp and replace the light in the lining, insert the retaining lug first and then press the lamp in until the spring engages.

7 Fog lamps - guidelines for fitting

1 These are not standard equipment but provision is made for fitting them as an optional extra. If you live in a country where fog is a prevalent feature at certain times of the year then the addition of a powerful fog lamp fitted as low down as the law allows and directed on the near side kerb or road edge about ten to fifteen yards ahead of the vehicle may prove a very well worthwhile addition, that is if you must go out. VW kits provide for two fog lamps and a rear fog lamp. However, you may wish to fit only one.

2 There are two ways of fitting such a lamp. One, using the VW option is neat, efficient and will improve the vehicle. A standard switch fitted to the dashboard should be connected to the relay which will fit in the relay rack at the back of the fuse board, No 5 from the left. The wiring circuit should be obtained from the Agent, and a 16 amp fuse will be necessary in the circuit.

Consult also the local regulations as to the placement of the lamp, how far it must be from the ground, and when it can be used, and in conjunction with what (ie; dipped headlamps or side lamps). The VW wiring arrangements allow it with dipped head and sidelights only.

3 It may be that an admirer has given you a different pattern lamp for Christmas and for diplomatic reasons you must fit it. The same rules about placement pertain but the problem of how is not so easy. Try to fit it so that it protrudes as little as possible in front of the line of the bumper, and as low as the law and the shape of the vehicle will allow. It is normal for such a lamp to come with fitting instructions but if it did not then bear the following in mind. The lamp will have a powerful bulb so the current will be of the order of 5 amps. This will need a heavy duty switch unless a relay is used, and it may get hot anyway. There **must** be a fuse in the circuit, unless it can be built into the existing circuit properly attaching it to existing wiring will cause overload, blown fuses, or even a fire.

4 You can run a cable back to the battery and tap off from the battery terminals but that will not be very efficient as there will be a long cable run, an ugly switch, and, although you are not likely to leave the lamp on when the vehicle is parked, the light will not go out when the ignition is switched off. This method is not recommended and should be used only in an emergency. It is much better to go to the agent and discuss the problem and then take his advice. If you have the slightest idea that someone is going to give you a fog lamp make sure it is a VW standard kit.

8 Direction indicators and emergency flashers

1 The direction indicator system is operated by the column switch and is accompanied by a warning light when the indicator is working. The indicators do not work when the ignition is switched off.

2 A switch on the fascia board (number 10 Fig. 10.1) next to the ashtray may be pulled out to set all four indicators flashing if you have to pull up in a dangerous place to remedy a defect. The flashers do not in this case go out when the ignition is turned off. A small bulb in the switch flashes as well. On USA vehicles switches are of the rocker type (see Figs. 10.6 and 10.7).

3 The direction indicators and emergency system share the same relay (no 1 - reading from left to right on the relay rack). It is the largest one in the rack and has a number 'FAR 9202'

4 If the indicators do not function properly a series of tests may be carried out to ascertain which part of the circuit is

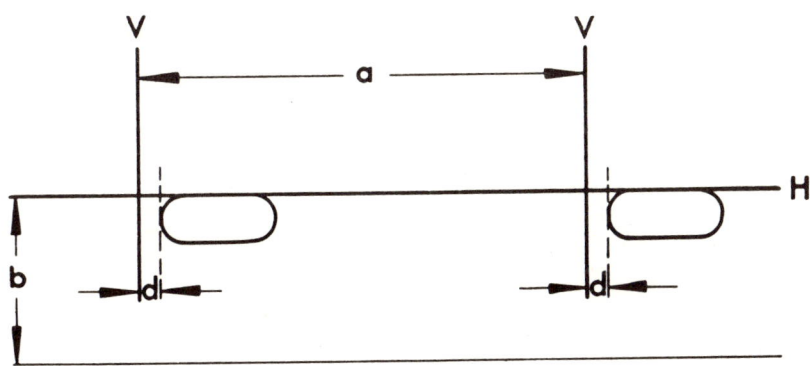

Fig 10.4 Headlamp beam aiming dimensions sealed beam units, right side dip (Sec 3)

     a   Distance between lamp centres (1080 mm & 42.5 ins)
     b   Height of lamp centre above ground (measure on vehicle)
     d   2.0 ins/50 mm
     H   Lamp horizontal centre line
     V   Lamp vertical centre lines

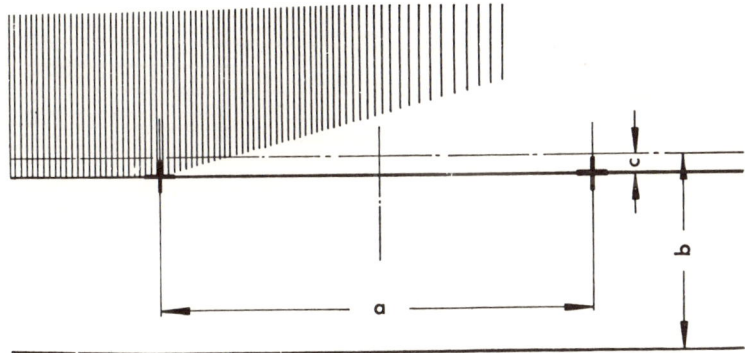

Fig 10.5 Headlamp beam aiming dimensions, replaceable bulbs, right side dip (Sec 3)

     a   Distance between lamp centres (1080 mm/42.5 ins)
     b   Height of lamp centre above ground (measure on vehicle)
     c   Dip angle height (1%) for distance i.e. 50 mm/2 ins.
     N.B. Mirror diagram for left dip

3.1 Removing the front flasher lens

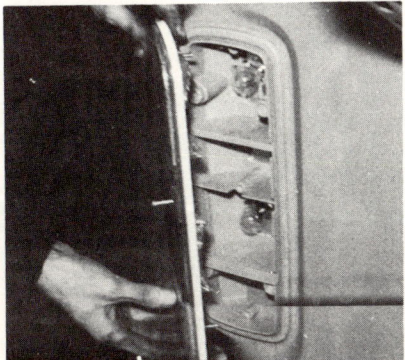

4.1 Removing the rear light cluster lens

4.3 Removing a bulb from the rear light cluster

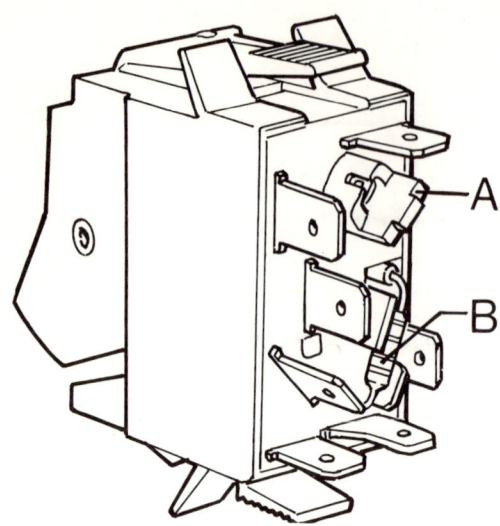

Fig 10.6 Rear view of emergency switch as fitted to vehicles in U.S.A. (Sec 8)

A *Warning lamp*
B *Resistance which dims the fascia warning light when the main lights are switched on. When the emergency signal is operated the warning light is bright*

Fig. 10.7 On U.S.A. vehicles the switches are of the rocker type (Sec 8)

faulty, checking in turn, bulb installations, emergency flasher switch, turn signal switch, and finally the relay.

5 By far the most common cause of trouble is defective bulbs, dirty or corroded contacts or poor earth contacts. Before checking anything else test all four lamps and be sure the bulbs are in good order and making proper contact. If this is the case then next proceed to test the emergency flasher switch, turn signal switch and the relay.

6 If the flashers work when either of the switches is closed then the relay is working properly. Switch off the ignition and disconnect the earth (ground) strap of the battery. Unscrew the emergency switch from the fascia board and take it out from the board. Turn the switch to 'ON'. Measure the resistance between (a) terminals '30' and '+' and (b) terminals '49a' and terminals

'R' and 'L'. The resistance in each case should be zero. If it is greater than zero replace the switch with a new one, replace in the board and reconnect the battery. Turn on the ignition and check the system. If it still does not work disconnect the battery and test the turn signal switch.

7 Pull out the black/green/white wire to the turn signal switch at the plug guide. Check continuity of circuit between terminal '54 BL' and terminals 'R' and 'L' of the turn signal switch. Resistance greater than zero ohms indicates that a new turn signal switch is required (see Section 16 for fitting instructions).

8 Replacement of the relay is described at Section 17. This should be done only after the switches have been tested and the flasher lamp installations checked.

9 Instrument panel warning lights - removal and replacement

1 It is possible with patience to get at the bulbs in the warning lights without removing the fascia board. Each bulb is housed in a holder which slides into the back of the instrument cluster housing and may be removed by pulling out the holder, replacing the bulb and fitting it back in the panel. Bulb values are given in the table in the Specification.

2 If however the job gets too difficult it is not a long job to take out the fascia board so that you can see clearly where things go. (see Section 12).

10 Instrument panel switches - removal and replacement

1 There are a possible total of seven switches on the fascia board. They are either push/pull or rotary, but fit into the board in the same way.

2 To remove a switch, first disconnect the battery. Unscrew the knob from the switch, remove the ring which holds the case to the fascia and extract the switch to the rear (oddly enough forwards). It should then be possible to lower the switch enough to get at the connections. **Do not** pull off the wires until you have tagged them. Freezer tape of different colours, or sellotape with bits of paper with numbers attached and a diagram showing which wire fits onto which terminal tag will save a lot of trouble when reconnecting time comes.

3 The connections are all pull off type which push on to reconnect. No heavy current wiring is located behind the fascia board as the switches controlling such current (emergency flasher, fog, headlight and heated rear window) switches are connected to relays.

The lighting switch has two positions (side tail and fascia lights, and head, tail and fascia light) so pulls out in two stages. The cab interior light has three positions: on, off, and door switch controlled. The fresh air fan switch is a rotary one with three positions:

0 = stop, 1 = slow speed, 2 = fast speed

The remainder are single position push/pull but two of them, emergency flasher and heated rear window, have small bulbs in them which light up when the switch is in the 'ON' position.

4 Replacement is the reverse of removal. Check that all spade push on terminals are secure and not touching. Be careful to engage the tongue of the hole in the fascia board with the slot in the switch when reassembling. Switches are not repairable and must be replaced if faulty.

11 Door contact switches - removal and replacement

This switch is mounted in the door jamb in such a way that when the door is closed a plunger is pressed, compressing a spring and making a contact inside to complete the cab light circuit. To remove one simply undo the crosshead screw and lever the switch away, the seal comes away with it. If the switch is faulty remove the wire (disconnect the battery first) and fit a new switch.

12 Instrument panel - removal and replacement

1   The instrument panel is secured to the fascia board by four screws. Early models had these screws fitting into brackets on the dashboard, but later (1973 onwards) models have them screwing into spring clips.

2   First disconnect the battery earth lead (ground strap). It is then necessary to remove the knobs of the heater control levers. This can be done by pushing out the pins that hold them to the levers and then pulling off the knobs. If this is not possible then the levers must be removed. On earlier models this may be done by removing the radio (if installed) and through the aperture removing the plastic plugs which hold the two parts of the lever together (photo).

3   With the knobs removed from the heater controls it is possible to slide the instrument panel away from the fascia board once the four screws are removed. (photo) On models 1973 onwards be careful to catch the spring clips, or better still try to turn them on the screws so that they will remain on the end of the thread.

4   From underneath undo the speedo cable outer cover nut and pull the cable out of the back of the speedometer. If you cannot reach the nut from underneath it may be possible to ease the

instrument panel out pulling the speedo cable with it and then undo the nut. We managed to do this but be careful not to strain the cable. (photo)

5   It is now possible to inspect the back of the panel (photo). **Do not disconnect the wires until you have read Section 13.1 of this Chapter.**

6   Replacement is the reverse of removal. A typical instrument panel is illustrated. Later models are fitted with three spaces for instruments the third space being for an electric clock which is an optional extra. (Fig. 10.8)

13 Instrument panel - dismantling and reassembly

1   Before pulling all the wires away tag them and note to which location each one goes. If you do not mark them clearly it will be almost impossible to reconnect them properly unless you trace each circuit individually. It takes about ten minutes to fix a marking tag on each wire and draw a diagram. Trial and error reconnection can take a whole morning.

Once tagged the connections may be pulled off and the instrument panel may be taken out of the vehicle.

2   If you are going to dismantle the panel clear a space on the bench and cover it with a sheet of clean paper and wash your

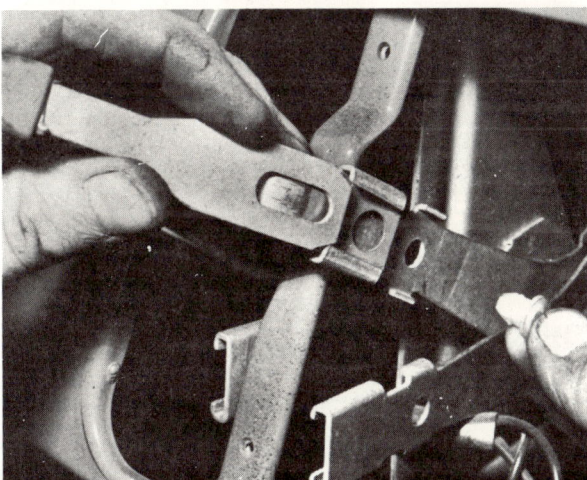

12.2 On the early models, it may be necessary to remove the plastic plug from the lever and withdraw the lever from the fascia board

12.3 Remove the screws from the instrument panel. From 1973 onwards they fasten into spring clips

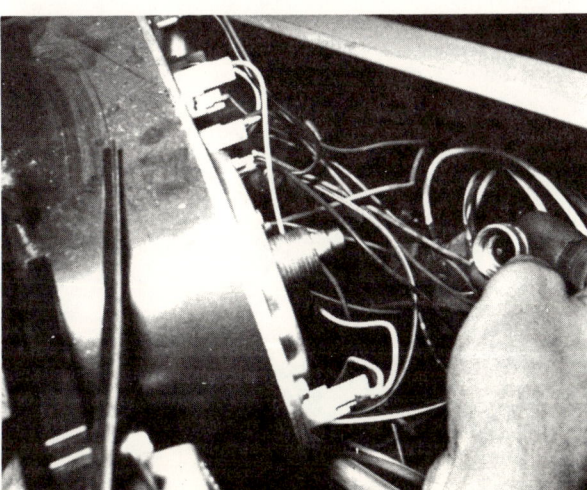

12.4 Ease the panel forward and disconnect the speedometer cable nut

12.5 The connections at the rear of the panel

hands. Have receptacles to put small screws and washers in, and you will need a small screwdriver.

3   There are two long screws which fix the instrument case to the panel. Remove these, they are shown on the illustration, and the case with the instruments. The speedometer, fuel gauge, warning light console and clock are fixed to the metal casing by small screws and may be removed separately for repair. (Fig. 10.8)

4   Testing and repair of the fuel guage system is discussed in Chapter 3. There is no repair possible to the gauge, if it is faulty a replacement is required.

5   The speedometer may be exchanged if faulty. If only the speedometer cable is giving trouble it is not necessary to remove the speedometer (proceed as in Section 14).

6   Reassembly is the reverse of removal. Be careful to locate the instrument cluster accurately or the various light bulb holders will not fit.

---

14 Speedometer and speedometer cable - removal, replacement and overhaul

1   If the speedometer trip mechanism does not work, or pieces are broken away the speedometer must be removed, as in Section 13.3, and either exchanged or a new one fitted. Do not attempt to set the mileage recorder of the new one but enter the mileage of the old one and the commencement mileage of the new one (probably 00000) in the log book.

2   If however the problem is no reading or a noisy drive, or a needle which oscillates steadily the problem lies with the cable and the instrument panel need not be removed.

3   Undo the knurled nut from behind the instrument panel and remove the cable from the speedometer head: If you cannot get it undone then proceed as in Section 12.4.

4   Now remove the hub cap from the left-hand front wheel. Protruding through the wheel bearing dust cover is the end of the speedometer cable held in place by a circlip or by a split pin. Remove the circlip or pin.

5   From behind pull the cable out of the steering knuckle. Watch which way the cable is routed to the fascia board. Remove the grommet in the bulkhead and extract the cable and cover.

6   If the cable has stretched or broken it must be replaced. There is always a temptation to replace the cable only and not the cover. If a broken or damaged cable has rotated in the cover it will probably have damaged it. Anyway what broke the cable will probably break another one so pull the cable out of the cover and find where the break was. An inspection of the outside of the cover at this point may offer a clue such as a kink, dent,

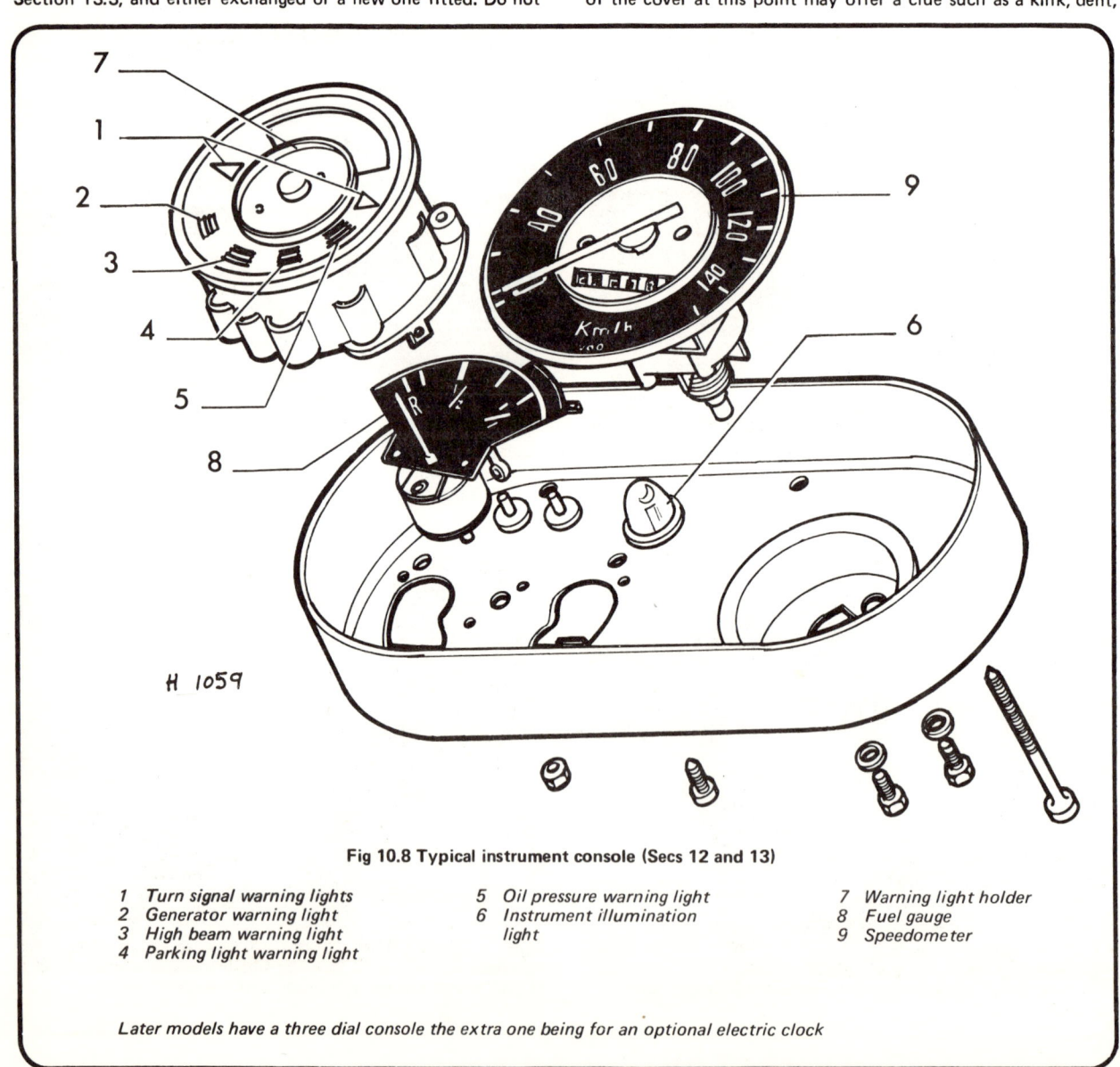

H 1059

Fig 10.8 Typical instrument console (Secs 12 and 13)

1 Turn signal warning lights	*5 Oil pressure warning light*	*7 Warning light holder*
2 Generator warning light	*6 Instrument illumination*	*8 Fuel gauge*
3 High beam warning light	* light*	*9 Speedometer*
4 Parking light warning light		

Later models have a three dial console the extra one being for an optional electric clock

or sharp bend. Any such damage must reject the cover.

If you cannot find a reason insert the head of the cable into the back of the speedo and see that the cable will turn the speedo head. It could be that the drive bearing in the head has seized or is very stiff. If so remove the speedometer, as in Section 13, and carry on from there with easing oil and patience.

7   If you decide the cover is in good order and you can obtain a cable only, then insert the cable into the cover covered with a thin layer of grease from the hub drive end. Do not grease the speedometer end or grease will penetrate into the head and cause the mechanism to stick. Fit a new rubber sleeve. Now refit the cable to the vehicle. Feed the lower end of the cable and cover through the grommet from inside the cab. Do this a little at a time and guide the end in such a way that it does not foul any part of the steering damper or side frame. There is a plastic tube which protects it in the proximity of these parts.

Re-install the cable into the speedometer head.

Feed the other end into the stub axle, coax the cable through the hub and refit the pin or circlip on the outside of the dust cap.

8   It is most important that bends in the cable are greater than 6 inches radius. Sharper bends will cause broken cables.

15 Clock - removal and replacement

1   The clock is secured to the panel cluster in the same way as the speedometer.

2   To remove it proceed as in Section 12, easing the board out until the wires may be disconnected and the two screws undone to allow the clock to come out of the cluster.

3   If you are contemplating fitting a clock for the first time then the obvious choice is the VW type supplied as an optional extra. It will be easy to install and will fit the fascia board. However whichever type of electric clock is fitted it must be wired so that it is permanently in circuit and is not switched off by the ignition switch.

In addition there must be provision for the clock light, which should be connected in series with the speedometer light.

On the official diagram the clock mechanism wire is connected to terminal '30' of the lighting switch and the light is interposed in the instrument lighting circuit between and terminal '58b' on the lighting switch.

4   Should the electric clock installed in the vehicle give trouble apart from checking the wiring and insulation there is little that can be done except return it to the maker for servicing.

16 Steering column switches - general description, removal and replacement

1   The column switch has grown steadily from a simple direction indicator control to the present multiple purpose switch box which sprouts levers on both sides and also contains the ignition switch/steering lock. The horn circuit is also carried on the steering wheel so that there is a multiplicity of wiring around the column. This Section does not deal with all the circuits carried on the column. The horn circuit, steering/ignition lock and windscreen wiper/washer controls are dealt with under separate headings. However the dismantling of one involves disturbing the others so that this Section should be read in conjunction with those Sections. Before any work is done on the steering column electrical switches disconnect the battery earth strap.

2   The switch has to be dismantled completely to deal with each of the pieces separately. However, once it is reduced to its component parts each part may be replaced without interfering with the others.

3   Fig. 10.9 is an exploded view of the combined turn signal, wiper/washer part of the assembly which shows how the two controls each masked in a plastic cover are clamped to the steering column. There are two clamps, the upper one has a lug which fits

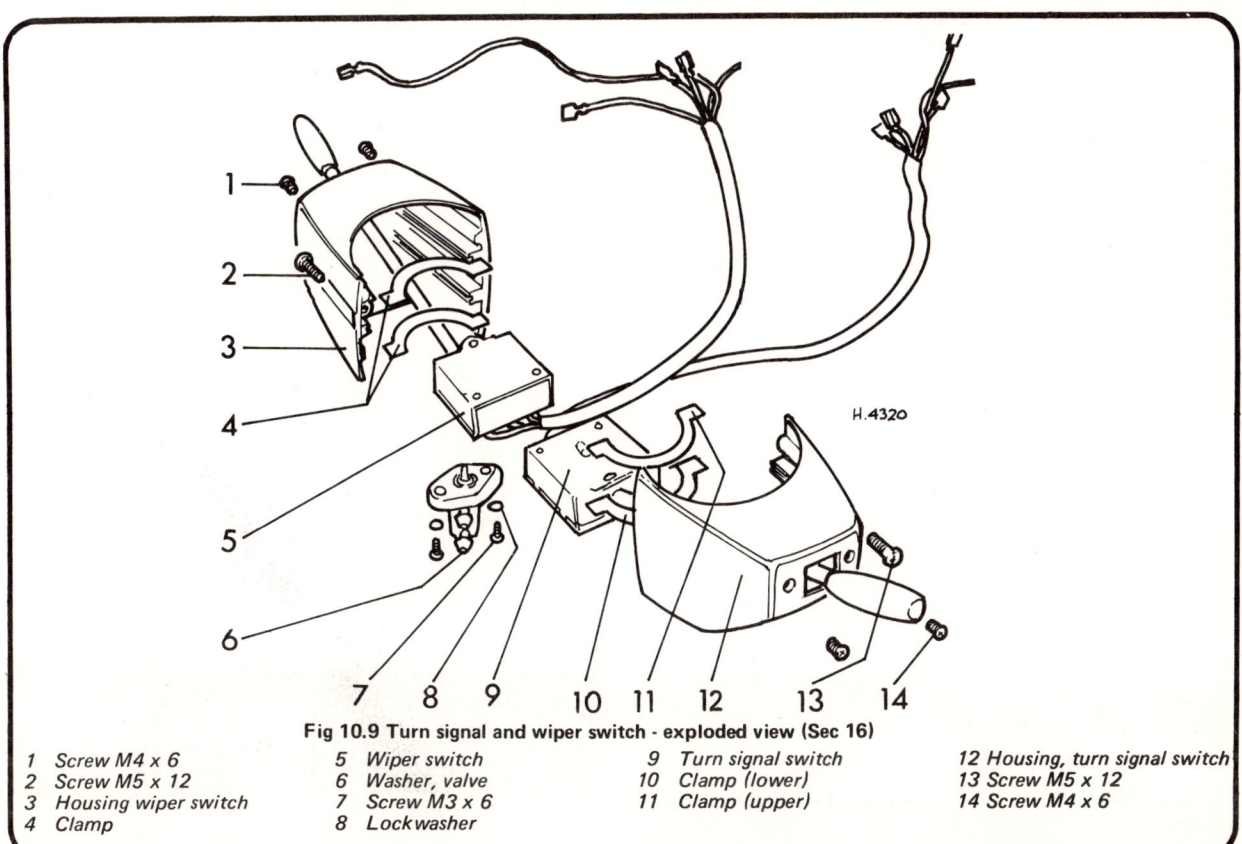

Fig 10.9 Turn signal and wiper switch - exploded view (Sec 16)

1 Screw M4 x 6	5 Wiper switch	9 Turn signal switch	12 Housing, turn signal switch
2 Screw M5 x 12	6 Washer, valve	10 Clamp (lower)	13 Screw M5 x 12
3 Housing wiper switch	7 Screw M3 x 6	11 Clamp (upper)	14 Screw M4 x 6
4 Clamp	8 Lockwasher		

into the steering column to prevent the lug rotating, and so locates the assembly.

The washer valve is fixed to the underside of the wiper switch and may be removed separately. There is no electricity about this, the lever which operates the wiper switch is also pivotted in the vertical plane and when it is pulled up towards the steering wheel the other end of it depresses the stem of the washer valve allowing the water under pressure in the washer tank to squirt out onto the screen. If you intend to replace the valve assembly then the pressure must be let out of the washer tank or there will be a spray of water in the cab when the hoses are disconnected.

4   It will be seen that each switch has its own cable harness. If it is necessary to replace either of the switches the cable connections must be traced and the new assembly connected correctly.

5   Although the washer/wiper/turn signal switch may be removed without much trouble the removal of the ignition/steering lock involves quite a lot of problems. First remove the turn signal/wiper switch assembly and let them hang loose away from the column. Pry off the horn button and then undo the steering wheel nut. Now undo the screws which hold the turn signal cancelling ring to the underside of the steering wheel and let the ring slide down the column. The steering wheel may now be pulled off. This may need an extractor as it is tight on the splines.

6   A 'G' clamp with a forked end is the ideal tool but if this is not available get someone to pull the steering wheel upwards while you give a series of taps with a soft drift on the steering column. This will usually jar it sufficiently to pull the wheel off a bit at a time. Be careful not to damage the thread on the shaft.

7   Remove the insulating ring, circlip and washer which lie between the wheel and the rubber bushing which is fitted between the column tube and the ignition/steering lock housing. Turn the ignition key into the drive position. It is now possible to remove the rubber bushing by putting two screwdrivers under it and levering it out of the column tube and lock. A little talcum powder will ease the strain if it is tight.

8   Now undo the screws holding the ignition/steering lock assembly to the bracket which is bolted to the fascia (there are four of them) disconnect the wires from the steering/ignition lock from the back of the fascia board and slide the assembly up, and off the column.

9   To remove the ignition/steering lock from its housing turn the housing upside down and undo the two screws holding the lock in the housing.

10   Reassembly is the reverse of removal. Refit the lock in the **housing**, assemble the lock housing to the column and reconnect the wires, install the rubber bush, washer, circlip, and insulating

ring. Refit the cancelling ring to the steering wheel, install the steering wheel and tighten the nut correctly and then reconnect the horn and install the horn button.

11   Finally re-install the wiper/washer and turn signal switches. When these are correctly fitted, there must be a clearance between the switch housing and the streering wheel of 0.080 inches or the wheel will foul the housing when turned. (see Fig 10.10).

---

17   Fuse panel and relays

---

1   The fuse and relay panel is situated in the cab underneath the fascia board (photo). To replace a fuse remove the plastic cover, it lifts off, and ease the fuse from its clips.

2   A selection of fuse layouts is given in the Specification but the safest way to check the layout is to consult the excellent handbook supplied with the vehicle.

3   It will be seen that fuses '9' and '11' are 16 ampere fuses and the remainder 8 ampere fuses. '9' carries the buzzer alarm and '11' the turn signal although each may carry other circuits as well.

4   Always replace a fuse with one of identical value and **never** put a fuse of higher value in the 8 amp station. If a fuse blows the circuit should be tested with a meter to find where the fault has occurred. It may be chafed wiring, particularly where wires pass through metal bulkheads, or water may have caused a short. If you cannot find a short then replace the fuse and try again. If the fuse blows again then isolate the circuit and the next port of call is an auto-electrican.

5   It cannot be over emphasised that fuses are warning signals. Faulty wiring causes fires. It is best to sort out the fuse circuits at home in peace and quiet. Note which circuit each fuse should serve, switch those circuits on to see that they work, switch off, remove the fuse, switch on again and check that they do not work. Switch off, replace the fuse and then check that the circuits work again. This will give you confidence and knowhow for there seems to be a natural law that fuses always blow when it is snowing or you are in a traffic jam on a hot day. Mark well which one controls the horn circuit and that will save pulling off wires if the horn starts to blow without being asked. Keep a set of spare fuses, say three of each denomination, with a chart of fuse numbers in the cab of the vehicle.

6   In addition to the fuses in the console there are in-line fuses in the engine compartment for the back up lights, warm air blower and auxilliary air heater (photo). These are listed in the driver's handbook. They are red (16 amp) fuses. The case unscrews to give access to the fuse. (photo)

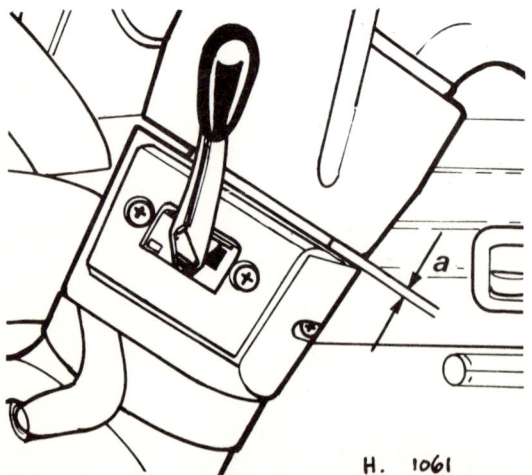

H. 1061

Fig. 10.10 Turn signal switch mounting (Sec 16) (gap 'a' is 2 mm/0.08 ins

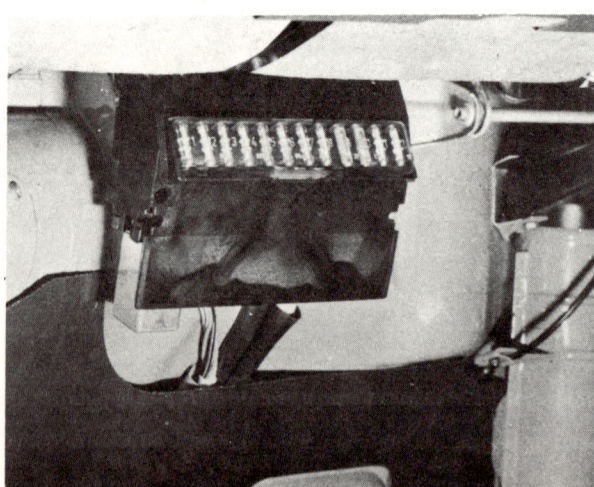

17.1 The fuses are in a console under the fascia board

7   The relays are mounted at the rear of the fuse rack. Access is obtained by unscrewing the two crosshead screws which hold the rack to the van body and lowering the rack. (photo)

There will always be two relays, the combi relay for the headlights and the larger one for the turn signal/emergency flasher.

There may be others. A table is given in the Specification enumerating these. They are removed by pulling out from the rack.

8   The tests involving relays are given in the Sections which deal with the circuit in which the relay is situated.

18 Horn

1   The horn is under the front of the vehicle bolted to the frame.

2   Two wires connected to it are the brown earth wire, which is connected, via the steering column, to the horn button and thence to earth when the button is pressed, and the yellow and black wire which is connected directly to the fuse box (fuse 12).

3   If the horn refuses to function at all then check the earth circuit testing first from the horn earth terminal, then from the flexible coupling on the steering column, and finally prise out the horn button and disconnect the wire from it and check continuity back to the horn earth terminal. The horn button contacts may be dirty or bent. Check these and clean if necessary. Check the potential at the positive terminal. It should be nearly 12 volts. If the two circuits are correct then the horn itself is at fault.

4   As a last resort the sealing compound on the back which covers the adjusting screw should be chipped away and the adjusting screw turned clockwise ¼ turn at a time. If this produces no noise then the horn should be removed and checked separately. (photo)

5   Undo the battery earth strap, disconnect the wires from the horn and remove the horn from the vehicle. Using an ohmmeter check resistance between the horn terminals. If this is infinity then there is an open circuit and the horn winding is burned out. The horn must be replaced. If there is a circuit with high resistance, then either the horn points are burned or dirty, or the condenser is at fault.

6   At this stage there is nothing to lose so dismantle the horn and have a look. It may be possible to clean the points or replace the condenser and all will be well. It may ever work if it is sealed carefully and tuned correctly.

To tune the horn connect it in series with an ammeter and turn the adjusting screw until the horn note is clear and at the

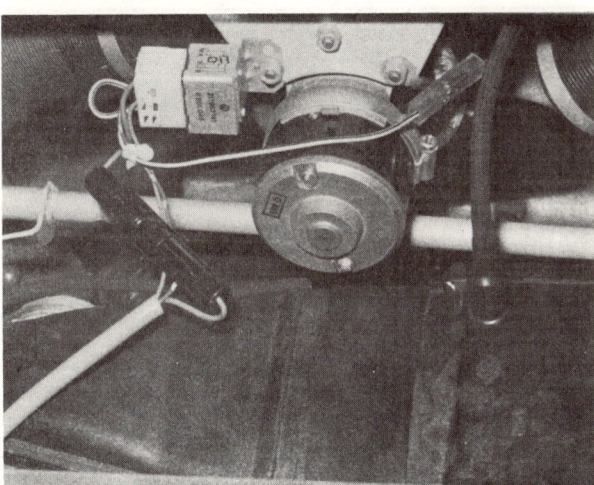

17.6a The in-line fuse for the blower motor ...

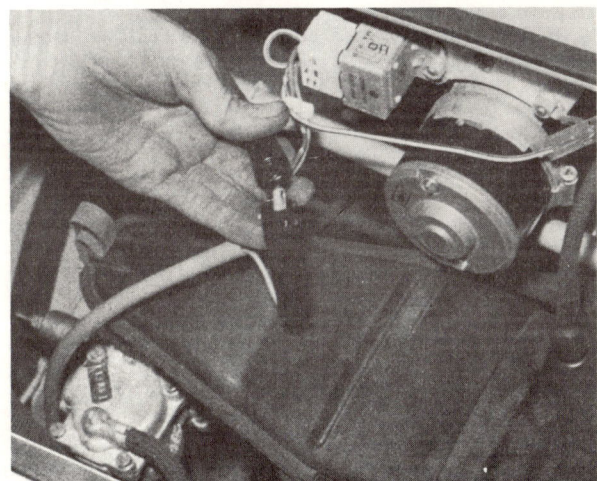

17.6b .... unscrews to expose the fuse

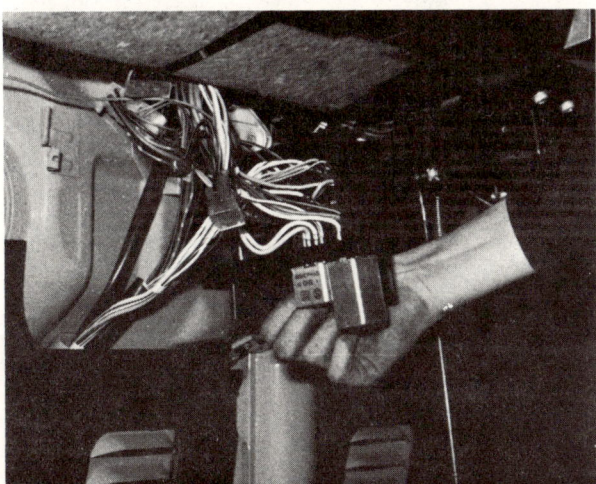

17.7 Lower the fuse console and turn it carefully to get at the relays

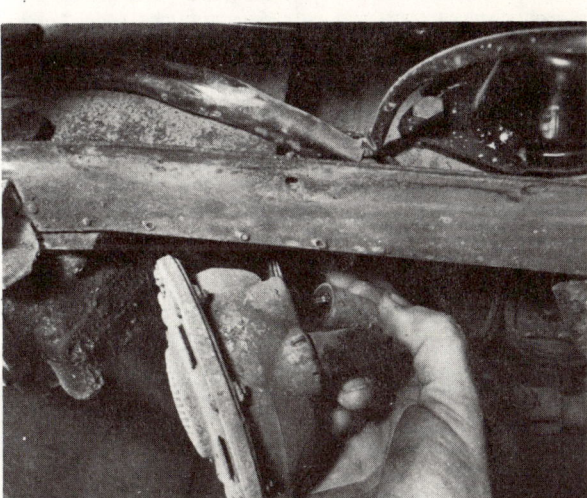

18.4 As a last resort try moving the adjusting screw

same time the horn uses minimum current. **Do not** turn the screw while the current is flowing or you will burn out the winding.

7   When re-installing the horn to the vehicle make sure the case of the horn does not touch the body. If it does the horn will not function correctly.

19   Heated rear window

1   The heated rear window consumes a fairly high current and the heater should be switched off once the window is clear of misting.

2   The control on the fascia board is a push/pull switch which has a green light in it. The system works only when the ignition is switched on.

3   The switch activates a relay in the engine compartment which may be seen in photo 17.6b next to the fresh air heater relay. Switch current goes through the fuse box on fuse 10. The relay controls the temperature of the window heater.

4   If only the window grid is damaged repair materials are available from VW agents. It is not necessary to remove the window. Apply a strip of masking tape along each side of the broken heater wire and then apply the repair material evenly over the broken part. Leave it for an hour to dry, remove the tape and all should be well.

5   If the window is fractured then disconnect the battery, disconnect the window terminals, remove and replace the window as shown in Chapter 12, reconnect the terminals and reconnect the battery.

6   The earth (ground) cable is connected by a tapping screw to the side panel and the positive cable to the relay.

20   Radio - fitting guidelines

1   Although a radio is not a standard fitting it is obtainable as an optional extra. There are several sets from which to choose and they fit into the space in the fascia by the side of the instrument panel. A wiring diagram may be obtained from the agent to show how to connect the set.
    The kit is supplied in three boxes.

2   The aerial should be fitted in front of the near side door pillar. A template for drilling the body is provided. Cutting the hole presents problems. It is probably better to drill a number of 1/8 in (3.17 mm) holes round the edge of the template and then join them using a hacksaw and finishing off with a file.
    The aerial is fitted from inside, a job requiring a lot of patience to get it into place and then secured by gasket, dome shaped distance piece and nut. Make sure the aerial body is earthed to the van body, by scraping a little of the paint from the underside of the hole. Also make sure the gasket is watertight or there will be rust trouble later.

3   Installation of the speaker and set in the centre of the fascia is only a matter of sorting out how best to fit the set to the existing metal work. If a VW Blaupunkt set is installed all the necessary bits are there. The power supply comes from the adjacent fuse box. Cable is supplied with a push on tag. It is necessary to undo the screws of the fuse pack to connect the radio. There is an extra 2 amp in-line fuse supplied with the set. Advice should be sought from the agent as to which fuse box terminal to use but if that is not forthcoming use the headlamp fuse.

4   Suppressors must be fitted to the coil and alternator. There may also be a problem to fit a suppressor to the wiper motor. The newer types of wiper motor should not present this problem.

5   The amount of work is not great if the VW set is used and the job can well be done over a weekend, or even shorter time if the owner has the tools and skill.

6   If it is decided to fit a different type then the difference in cost should be weighed up against the additional problems of fitting but in any case consult the experts of the shop from

which you get the set and make sure you have a clean circuit diagram and layout before you pay out your hard earned cash.

21   Tape player - fitting guidelines

1   The fitting of a tape player presents less problems than that of fitting a radio. Since the normal recorder is self-contained it remains only to select a spot to secure the recorder to and the provision of a power supply.

2   The choice of recorder is very wide and the price range is equally wide.

3   Depending upon how the set you have choosen is loaded and controlled the tape player may be fitted under the fascia board, in the centre hole of the fascia board, or even clamped to the bulkhead in the case of a delivery van.

4   If it is intended to supply the recorder with power from the vehicle battery it is essential to fit an in-line fuse. It will also be necessary to suppress the alternator and coil, if this has not been done.

5   Finally a suitable provision should be made for storing cassettes/cartridges and for illuminating the recorder control buttons or knobs.

22   Windscreen wiper and washer - general description and re-charging washer

1   The two speed windscreen wiper is self-parking when switched off. It is controlled by the lever on the column. Moving the lever forward to position one gives a slow speed wipe, and even further forward a fast speed wipe. Raising the lever opens the pressure valve for the washer.
    The liquid for the washer is in a tank fastened to the body by a bracket and behind the right front trim panel. A cap and pressurizing tube are all that can be seen. To recharge the tank mix one pint VW antifreeze window cleaner with three parts clean water. Remove the cap. There is up to 40 lbs per square inch pressure in the tank so allow it to seep out gently. Fill the tank to the top of the neck, replace the cap and screw it home tightly.
    Now connect the charging tube to the footpump or air hose and pressurize the tank to 43 lbs/sq inch. (3 bar). The tank holds 2.4 imperial pints (2.9 pints US, or 1.5 litres).
    If a headlight washer is fitted the tank is much bigger (17 pints US or 14 pints imperial) and is not pressurized.

2   The wiper motor is bolted to a frame, which in turn is bolted to the body underneath the fascia board. The motor shaft is extended to finish with a worm gear. This engages with a gear which turns a crank. The whole contraption is contained in one case as shown in the illustration.

3   A system of levers transforms the rotational movement of the tank into an oscillatory movement. The wiper arm cranks are fastened to a flat bar which oscillates in a horizontal plane and as the lower end of the wiper crank moves back and forth a rotary motion is transmitted to the wiper blade shaft. As the flat bar reverses direction so the rotation of the wiper blade shaft is reversed and the sweeping action is transmitted to the wiper blade. This all sounds very complicated but is in fact a simple link motion which seldom gives trouble.

4   Since 1972 the wiring to the motor has terminated in a plug so that the motor may easily be removed with the frame without undoing any wiring. Just disconnect the plug from the wiring harness. Prior to this it was necessary to disconnect the wiring from the wiper switch and each lead had to be labelled to facilitate reconnection.

23   Wiper motor and frame - removal and replacement

1   Disconnect the battery earth strap (ground strap).

2   Remove the wiper arm cap and the M.6 nut. Prior to 1973

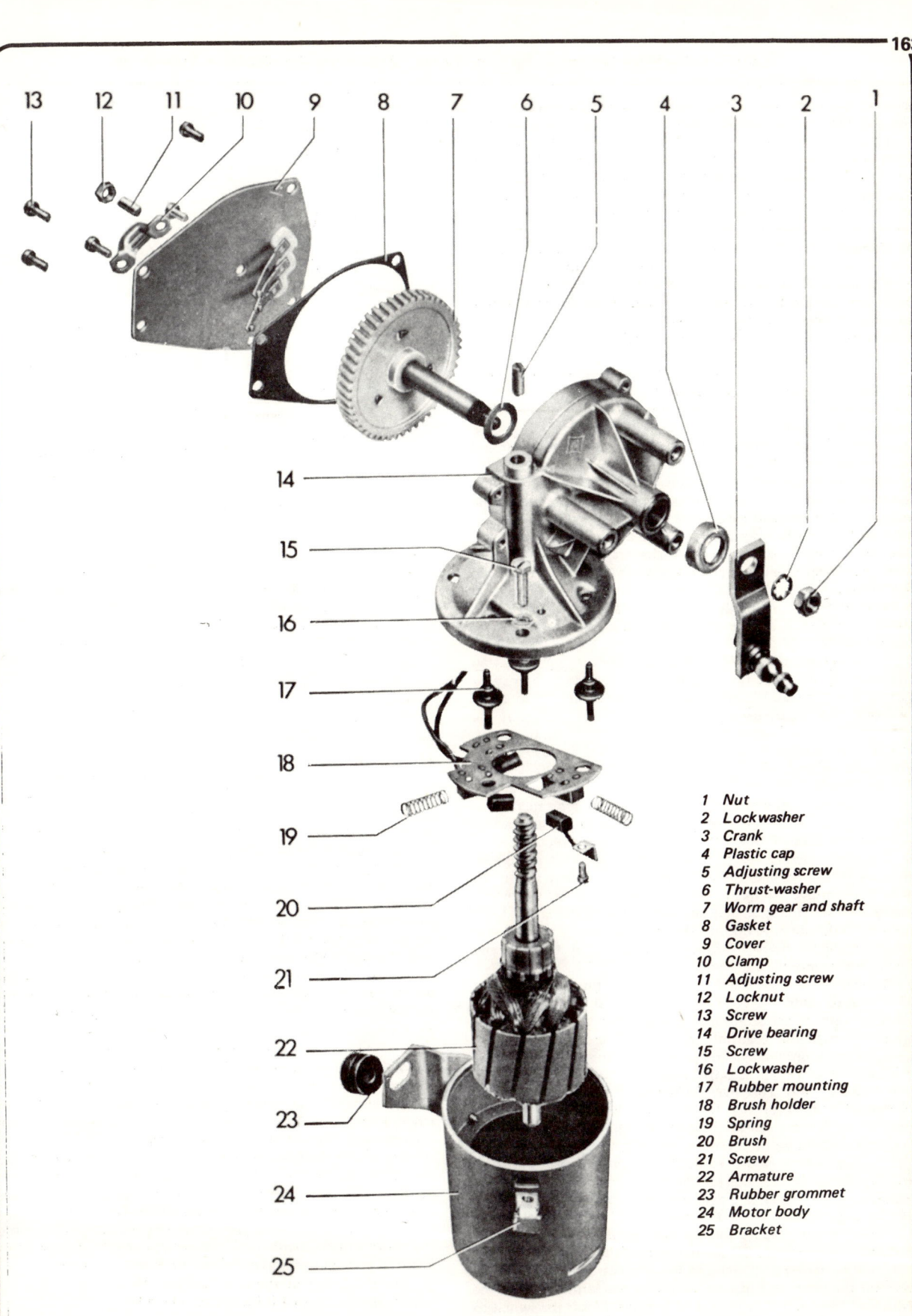

1 Nut
2 Lockwasher
3 Crank
4 Plastic cap
5 Adjusting screw
6 Thrust-washer
7 Worm gear and shaft
8 Gasket
9 Cover
10 Clamp
11 Adjusting screw
12 Locknut
13 Screw
14 Drive bearing
15 Screw
16 Lockwasher
17 Rubber mounting
18 Brush holder
19 Spring
20 Brush
21 Screw
22 Armature
23 Rubber grommet
24 Motor body
25 Bracket

Fig 10.11 Windscreen wiper motor - exploded view

the arm was held with a plated cap nut. Take off the wiper arms. Refer to Fig. 10.13. Remove the nuts, washers, and outer seals.

3 Now go inside the vehicle. From under the fascia board remove the flexible heater connections and unplug the motor wiring from the main cable harness. If your vehicle does not have this refinement disconnect the wires from the wiper switch on the column. Label each wire carefully to ease reconnection. (For removal of switch, see Section 16).

4 Remove the mounting bolt from the wiper motor housing bracket and take the motor and frame out downwards. The wiper blade shafts must be eased out of their housings.

5 It is now possible to check all the joints of the mechanism, adjust them and lubricate where necessary.

6 Replacement is the reverse of removal.

24 Windscreen wiper motor - overhaul

1 Refer to Fig. 10.11.

2 Disconnect the battery earth lead and remove the wiper and frame as detailed in Section 23.

3 Mark the position of the motor on the frame. Remove the connecting rods from the crankpin, undo the bolts holding the motor to the frame and remove the motor.

4 Two hexagon headed screws bolt the drive unit to the motor. Remove these screws. Rotate the drive crank to disengage the worm gear from the worm and the drive unit may be lifted from the motor casing.

5 The brush gear may only be replaced as a set. If the brushes are worn down or the springs weak then a new set should be fitted.

6 The commutator should be clean and smooth. Wipe it clean and examine it for burns. If it is rough or grooved it may be turned down to 0.846 inches diameter. Below this it must be replaced. The maximum out of round is 0.001 inches. If the commutator is turned then the insulation must be undercut. Unless you are experienced in this work it is best to leave it to an expert auto-electrician.

7 Test the armature for short and open circuits. There are no field windings. If the armature and brush gear are satisfactory the next check is the drive gear. It is unlikely that the bearings will have worn, but if they are then a new motor is required.

8 The drive gear cover plate is fastened on by five screws. Remove these and take off the cover and the gasket. From the other end remove the nut holding the crank, take off the plastic spacer cap and the gear may be withdrawn. Examine the teeth for wear. This will have occured if the end play adjustments were incorrect. Small burrs may be removed but if there is any significant wear replace the gear.

9 Reassembly is the reverse of removal but there are a number of things to watch for. Smear lightly the shafts and bearing surfaces with a light universal grease. The endplay of both armature shaft and gearshaft is critical. There is a small grub screw bearing on the end of each of the shafts. The endplay allowable in each case is 0.010 inches $\pm$ 0.002 inches (0.25 mm + 0.05 mm). This may be measured with a feeler gauge in the case of the gear shaft but is not so easily done for the armature shaft. Set the gearshaft correctly, screw the armature grub screw in until the worm is binding on the gear and then slacken it off until the shafts revolve easily. Take some care over this for if the adjustment is not correct the current consumption of the motor will be too high and overheating will occur.

10 The angular position of the drive crank is also critical. If it is not right then the blades will not park correctly when the wiper is switched off. Before bolting the motor to the frame reconnect it to the wiring system, replace the earth strap to the battery, connect the earth terminal on the motor and terminal 31 on the switch to the battery negative and terminal 30 on the switch to the battery positive. This needs a long piece of flex and some crocodile clips. Switch on and see that the motor is running correctly for twenty seconds. Switch off and the motor will stop in the park position. Now fit the crank arm to the motor so that its centre line is parallel to the motor casing and the crank points

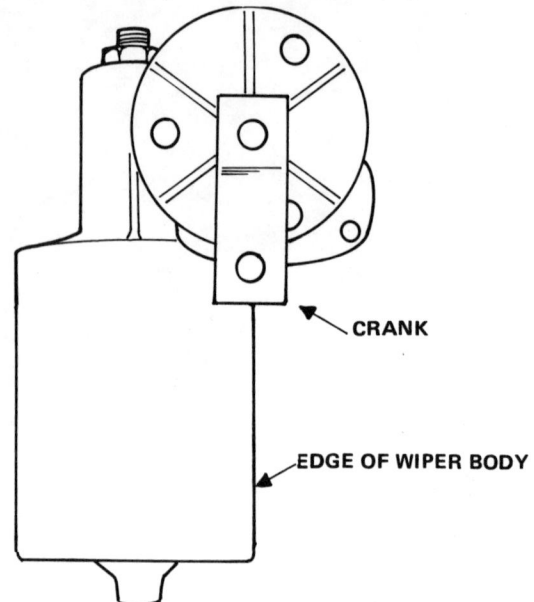

Fig 10.12 Position of drive crank in the correct parking position - diagram showing end view of drive gear shaft. Centre line of crank parallel with armature shaft, tolerence $\pm$ 5°

downwards. (see Fig. 10.12).

11 The motor may now be installed in the frame and refitted to the vehicle.

25 Windscreen wiper spindles - renewal of bearings

1 The spindle bearings have a hard life and do tend to wear. This will affect the operation and should be put right.

2 Remove the motor and frame as detailed in Section 23.

3 Refer to Fig. 10.13. Take the connecting rod off the balljoint of the wiper shaft, remove the circlip and pull the shaft out of the bearing. The bearing is held in position in the frame by the brass nut. Remove this and the bearing may be pressed out of the frame. Be careful not to lose the spring washer when withdrawing the shaft, it may stick to the brass nut. Also note how the large spring washers are fitted.

4 Reassembly is the reverse of removal. There is a small keyway on the bearing which fits into a projection on the frame. Grease the ball joints.

26 Windscreen wiper blades - fitting

1 These should be renewed each year. Notice that they are marked Left and Right. Check which is which before you take them off and fit the new ones accordingly.

2 The blades must be positioned correctly on the splines. To do this the blades should, when looking at the screen from in front of the vehicle, park so that the tip of the passenger's (left-hand drive) wiper almost touches the side of the screen and the other end of it is 4 inches from the bottom of the screen. The tip of the driver's blade should be 3 1/8 inches from the bottom of the screen. For right-hand drive the mirror of this is correct.

3 The tightening of the nuts holding the arms is also critical and should be 3½ to 4 ft lbs (42 to 60 cm kg).

27 Windscreen washer

1 The washer is operated by a valve incorporated in the wiper

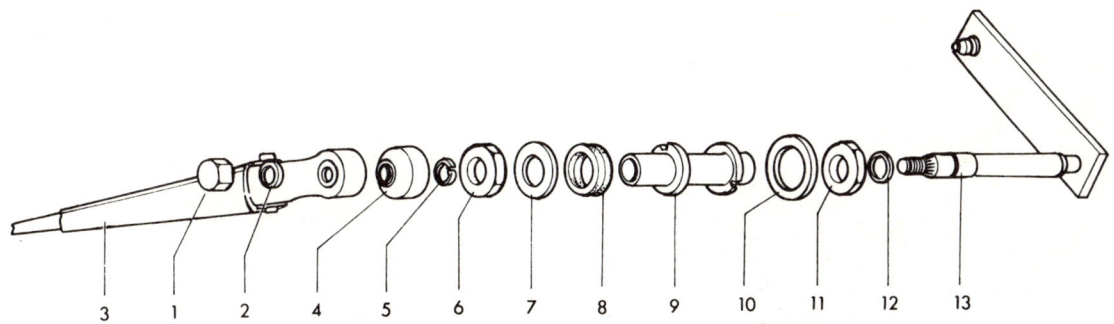

Fig 10.13 Windscreen wiper spindle and bearing assembly (Secs 23 and 25)

1 Cap nut	5 Circlip	8 Seal	11 Brass nut
2 Lockwasher	6 Nut	9 Shaft bearing	12 Spring washer
3 Wiper arm	7 Washer	10 Spring washer	13 Wiper shaft
4 Bearing cover			

Note. on later models the cap nut is replaced by an M6 nut and a plastic cap

switch. The water reservoir tank is mounted on the front panel in the driver's compartment and a detachable cover gives access to the filler cap and pressure hose. The container is filled and then pressurized from an ordinary air pump to 42 p.s.i.

When the wiper switch button is depressed the valve opens and fluid under pressure passes through the jets onto the screen.
2 If no water issues from the jets, first check that all pipes are connected and intact and that the reservoir is pressurised correctly.
3 Then check that the nozzles of the jets are clear. Use a piece of fine wire to poke them out if necessary.
4 If it becomes obvious that the valve is not working, then it must be renewed.
5 To renew the switch remove the steering column cluster (Section 16) and remove the washer valve. Make sure there is no pressure in the tank, remove the hoses and replace the valve. Make sure the hoses are located in the metal clip at the foot of the column bracket. Do not use any lubricant other than water when installing the hoses.
6 The tank is hidden behind the trim panel. Remove this and the tank may be removed by undoing the large plastic nut and the three bolts which hold the bracket supporting the filler neck. The hose is secured to the tank with a plastic ferrule nut.

28 Fault diagnosis - Windscreen wipers and washers

Symptom	Probable fault	Remedy
1 Motor does not start, runs slowly, cuts out or stops	(a) Brushes worn, stuck in holders or weak brush spring	(a) Clean and if necessary replace brush gear Sec 24.5.
	(b) Commutator dirty, worn or grooved	(b) Clean and if necessary skim commutator. If too worn replace armature. See Sec 24.6.
	(c) Armature open circuit or short circuit	(c) Replace armature
	(d) Linkage or spindle bearings seized	(d) Free, lubricate and if necessary replace.
	(e) Loose connections in motor or switch	(e) Locate and reconnect.
	(f) Battery run down	(f) Charge battery.
2 Motor runs when switched off, or will not park blades in the correct position	(a) Contacts in cover faulty	(a) Clean and adjust. Replace cover if necessary
	(b) Ground wire from terminal 31b to switch and earth faulty	(b) Reconnect. Replace if necessary
3 Wiper works slowly with squeaky noise*	(a) Spindle bearings faulty	(a) Remove and service See Sec. 25.
	(b) End clearances in gear shaft and armature shafts incorrect	(b) Adjust. See Sec. 24.9.
	(c) Drive housing not correctly assembled to motor body	(c) Dismantle and assemble correctly.

Note: If the symptom 3 is allowed to continue the motor will overheat and the commutator will be damaged

29 Computer diagnosis

1 In 1970 VW introduced the computer diagnosis system. It is a truely immense step forward in preventative maintenance. The system is devised to assess the state of maintenance of all the major and many minor components of the vehicle. Over 80 points are checked, many of them automatically.
2 A multi-pin plug is installed in the engine compartment (photo). The operator at the VW agency will check the correct pressures of your tyres and then plug in a large cable to the diagnosis plug. He selects the correct master card for your

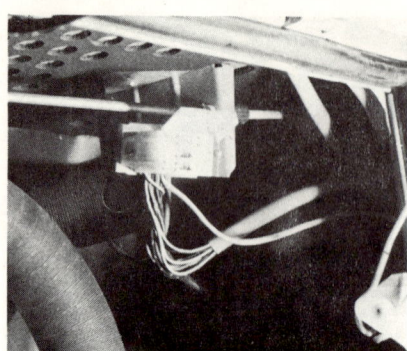

29.2 The computer diagnosis connector plug bolted to the top of the engine compartment

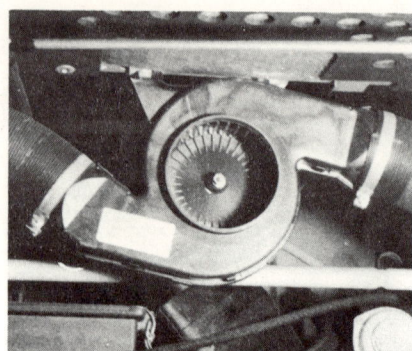

30.3 The motor and fan in the engine compartment

vehicle, installs it, and from there on a computer takes over. The operator has a hand set connected to the computer which has a small window showing the number of the test to be carried out. As each check is done the print out is marked '+' if the measurement agrees with the vehicle specification or - where it is beyond tolerance.

3   The items which are not measured automatically are checked by the operator, where all is well he presses a button marked '+' on the hand set, where all is not well the '− ve' button is pressed.

4   The items which are measured by the equipment automatically are the steering geometry, ignition and charging systems and cylinder compression. Lights and battery condition are checked automatically.

The steering geometry is checked by photo electric beams and mirrors as the steering wheel is turned through 180°, 90° each side of the straight ahead position. This is done within a 20 second period and measures toe and camber and prints out the answer in degrees and minutes. The ignition and charging systems are measured by the resistances of the various circuits. It is important that all connections are clean and that cable sizes are standard.

The cylinder compression is measured by calculating the load on the starter motor when the engine is turned over. The state of the battery and the temperature of the engine oil is measured and taken into account for this check.

There is no doubt that the system is quick, accurate and calculated to tell the unhappy customer all the awful things wrong with his vehicle in the shortest possible time.

5   If the vehicle is used a lot then this system is without doubt the finest way to take care of its working parts. The system does not repair, it diagnoses only, but a record such as the computer gives is worth many hours of hard work inspecting all these things manually, and of course it measures accurately items which the owner of the van cannot measure without expertise and a lot of expensive equipment.

6   Finally, it does away with opinion. It measures and compares with the vehicle specification. After that it is up to the owner what repairs he does, and which he leaves to the VW agent to do. What more could you want, you are not dependant on the opinion of an operator who wants some work for his mechanics, or worse still doesn't want the job. The computer gives you the facts and you can investigate further and decide the economics of the matter.

30 Warm air heating and fresh air ventilation

1   Since September 1973 a supplementary heater has been available as an optional extra. It is fitted in conjunction with the standard heating system.

2   The BA6 heater is installed in the space between the van floor and the underfloor (see Fig. 10.14).

3   A motor and fan are installed in the engine compartment (photo). The ducting system is connected to the heater ducts of the normal heater system of the engine. The air is directed by moving the control levers on the fascia board, directing warm air into the cab, onto the screen and into the van body in some cases. Refer to Fig. 10.1. The middle lever controls the flow of air, "up" is off, "down" is on. The left-hand one distributes warm air "up" is foot wells all heated, "down" is foot wells not heated, screen heated. Both these levers have red knobs.

The right-hand knob, blue, admits fresh cool air, "up" - closed "down" - open.

4   The control switch is on the fascia board on the left of and next to the steering column (L.H.D.). It has three positions: 'O' is stop, '1' is slow speed, and '2' fast speed. It is a rotary switch. To remove the switch read Section 10, of this Chapter. There is a main 16 amp fuse in an in-line holder behind the fascia panel, and another in the engine compartment. A relay is incorporated in the circuit and an overheating switch.

5   The temperature may be further raised by starting up a supplementary heater which consumes fuel from the fuel system. The liquid is forced into the combustion chamber by a metering pump. Air is supplied by yet another blower which operates when the engine is not running, and cuts out when the engine runs, air then being supplied through the normal system.

To start the system press the engine heating lever (the middle one with a red knob) down, press the temperature regulating switch in and turn it 90° clockwise. Set the switch to the heat required. The heater turns itself off after about 10 minutes running time.

6   Combustion is started by a glow heater plug and coil which uses a suprisingly low current of 1 amp and causes the plug to spark at the rate of 100 sparks per second.

7   A temperature sensor is incorporated in the system located on top of the combustion chamber of the supplementary heater.

8   In the USA the illumination of the heater control levers is legally mandatory. The lettering and arrows showing which way the levers move are illuminated by two spot lamps.

9   We do not recommend that the owner driver should attempt to service the supplementary heater. If it is not serviced correctly the result will be unfortunate. This does not mean that the system is dangerous, but that it requires an experienced technician to adjust it corrrectly, and there is no room for trial and error.

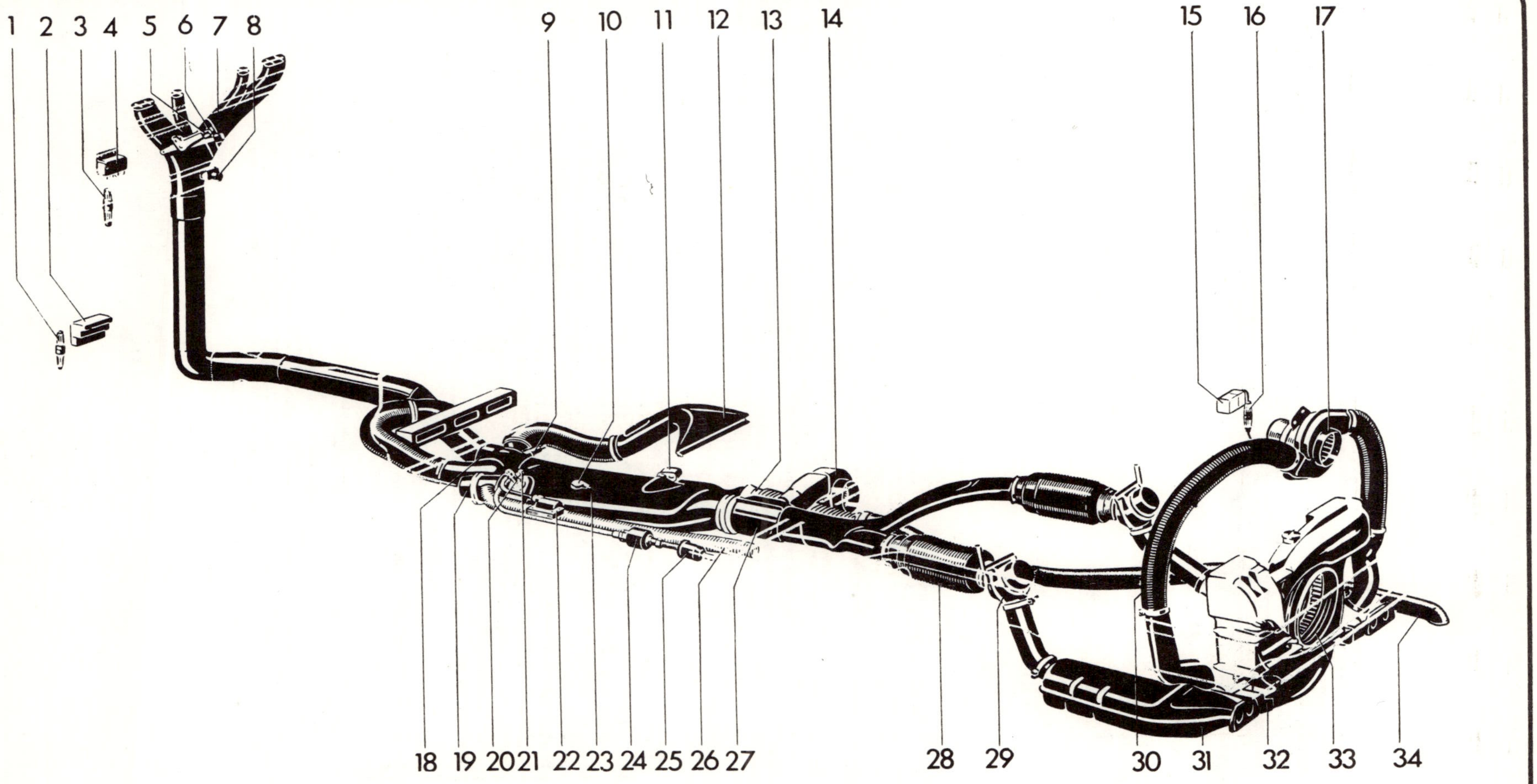

Fig. 10.14 The BA 6 Heater (Sec 30)

1 Overheating switch (8 amp)
2 Relay
3 Fuse
4 Safety switch
5 Warm air lever
6 Heater flap lever

7 Fresh air lever
8 Temperature regulating switch
9 Temperature sensor
10 Overheating switch
11 Thermoswitch
12 Heater

13 Injector
14 Blower
15 Relay (Warm air blower)
16 Fuse (Warm air blower)
17 Warm air blower
18 Warm air distributor

19 Combustion air blower
20 Glow spark plug
21 Fuel connection
22 Coil
23 Heater body
24 Metering pump

25 Filter
26 Air hose
27 Flap valve housing
28 Heat exchanger
29 Warm air flap

30 Warm air hose
31 Heat exchanger
32 Non-return flap
33 Engine fan
34 Exhaust tailpipe

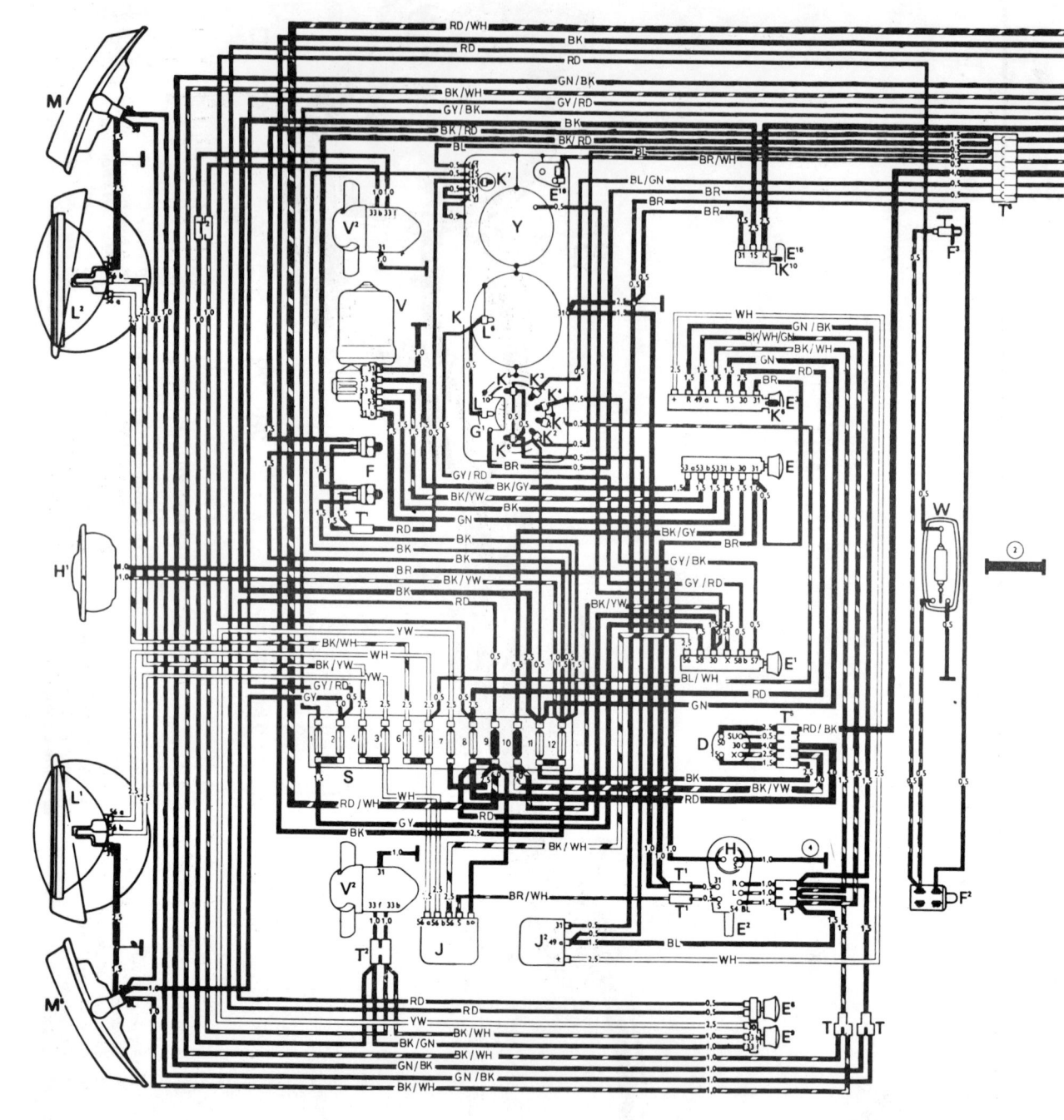

Key to Wiring Diagram – UK models 1972 on

A	Battery
B	Starter
C	Generator
C1	Regulator
D	Ignition/starter switch
E	Windshield wiper
E1	Lighting switch
E2	Turn signal and headlight dimmer switch
E3	Emergency flasher switch
E6	Switch for interior light, rear
E9	Fan motor switch
E15	Heated rear window switch
E16	Switch for warm air fan
F	Brake light swich
F1	Oil pressure switch
F2	Door contact switch, left
F3	Door contact switch, right
F4	Switch for back up lights
G	Fuel gauge sender unit
G1	Fuel gauge
H	Horn button
H1	Horn
J	Relay for dimmer
J2	Emergency flasher relay
J14	Relay for warm air fan
K1	High beam warning lamp
K2	Generator charging warning lamp
K3	Oil pressure warning lamp
K4	Parking light warning lamp
K5	Turn signal warning lamp
K6	Emergency flasher warning lamp
K7	Dual circuit brake system warning lamp
K10	Heated rear window warning lamp
L1	Sealed beam insert, left
L2	Sealed beam insert, right
L6	Speedometer light
L10	Instrument panel light
M2	Brake/tail light right
M4	Brake/tail left
M5	Turn signal and parking light, front, left
M6	Turn signal, rear, left
M7	Turn signal and parking light, front, right
M8	Turn signal, rear, right
M16	Back-up light, left
M17	Back-up light, right
N	Ignition coil
N1	Automatic choke left
N2	Automatic choke right
N3	Electro-magnetic cut-off valve left
N4	Electro-magnetic cut-off valve right
O	Distributor
P1	Spark plug connector, cylinder no. 1
P2	Spark plug connector, cylinder no. 2
P3	Spark plug connector, cylinder no. 3
P4	Spark plug connector, cylinder no. 4
Q1	Spark plug, cylinder no. 1
Q2	Spark plug, cylinder no. 2
Q3	Spark plug, cylinder no. 3
Q4	Spark plug, cylinder no. 4
S	Fuse box
S1	Fuse for back-up lights, warm air fan
T	Cable distributor
T1	Cable connector, single
T2	Cable connector, double
T3	Push-on connector, 3 point
T6	Push-on connector, 8 point
T20	Test socket
V	Wiper motor
V2	Fan motor
V4	Heater fan
W	Interior light, front
W1	Interior light, rear
X	License plate light
Y	Clock
Z1	Heated rear window
1	Ground strap from battery to frame
2	Ground strap from transmission to frame
4	Ground cable from horn button to steering coupling

Wiring colour code

BK	=	Black
BN	=	Brown
RD	=	Red
GN	=	Green
GY	=	Grey
BL	=	Blue
YW	=	Yellow
WH	=	White

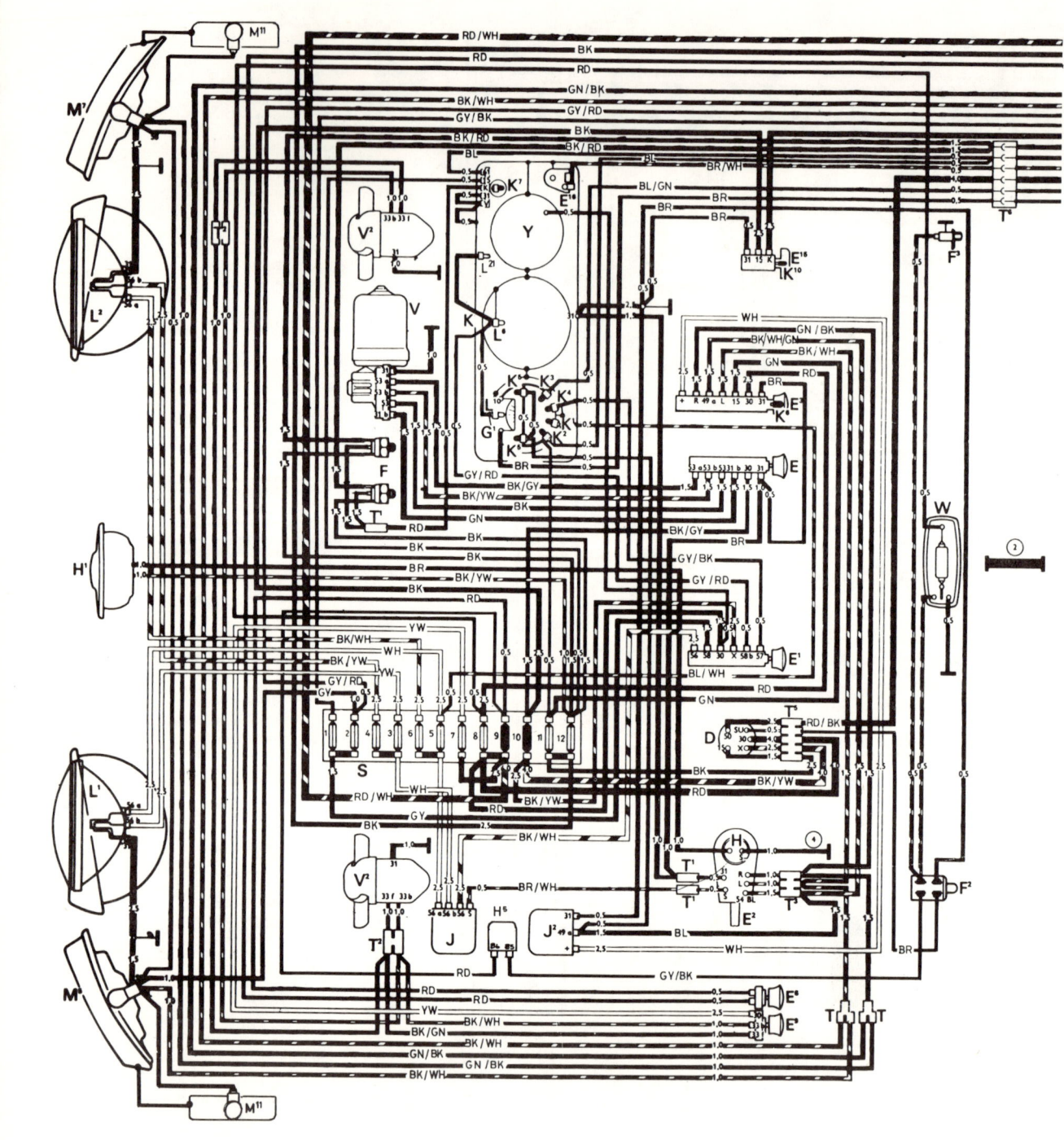

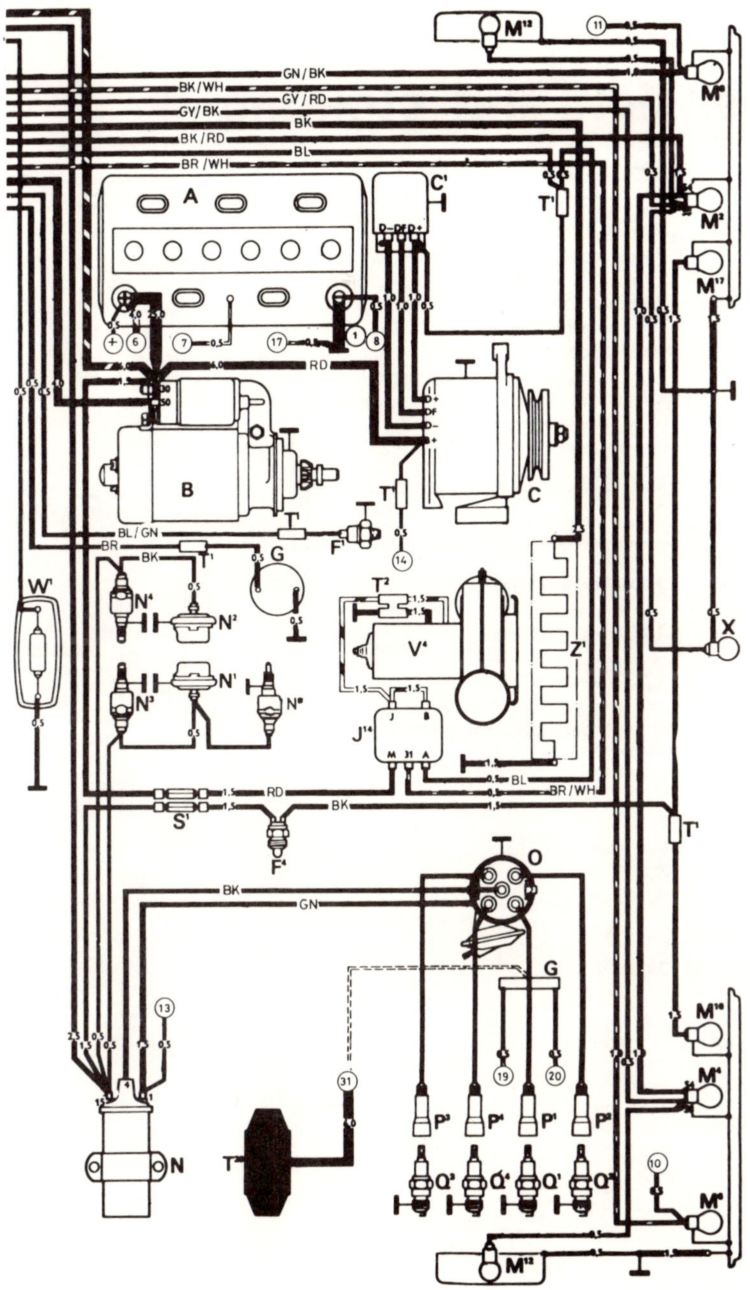

Key to Wiring diagram – US models 1972 on

A — Battery
B — Starter
C — Alternator
C1 — Regulator
D — Ignition/starter switch
E — Windshield wiper
E1 — Lighting switch
E2 — Turn signal and headlight dimmer switch
E3 — Emergency flasher switch
E6 — Switch for interior light, rear
E9 — Fan motor switch
E15 — Heated rear window switch
E16 — Switch for warm air fan
F — Brake light switch
F1 — Oil pressure switch
F2 — Door contact switch, left with contact for buzzer H5
F3 — Door contact switch right
F4 — Switch for back up lights
G — Fuel gauge sender unit
G1 — Fuel gauge
G4 — Ignition timing sender unit
H — Horn button
H1 — Horn
H5 — Buzzer for ignition key warning device
J — Relay for dimmer
J2 — Emergency flasher relay
J14 — Relay for warm air fan
K1 — High beam warning lamp
K2 — Alternator charging warning lamp
K3 — Oil pressure warning lamp
K5 — Turn signal warning lamp
K6 — Emergency flasher warning lamp
K7 — Dual circuit brake system warning lamp
K10 — Heated rear window warning lamp
L1 — Sealed beam insert, left
L2 — Sealed beam insert, right
L6 — Speedometer light
L10 — Instrument panel light
L21 — Light for heater lever illumination
M2 — Brake/tail light right
M4 — Brake/tail light left
M5 — Turn signal and parking light, front, left
M6 — Turn signal, rear, left
M7 — Turn signal and parking light, front, right
M8 — Turn signal, rear, right
M11 — Side marker light, front
M12 — Side marker lights, rear
M16 — Back-up light, left
M17 — Back-up light, right
N — Ignition coil
N1 — Automatic choke left
N2 — Automatic choke right
N3 — Electro-magnetic cut-off valve left
N4 — Electro-magnetic cut-off valve right
N8 — Cut-off valve for central idling
O — Distributor
P1 — Spark plug connector, cylinder no. 1
P2 — Spark plug connector, cylinder no. 2
P3 — Spark plug connector, cylinder no. 3
P4 — Spark plug connector, cylinder no. 4
Q1 — Spark plug, cylinder no. 1
Q2 — Spark plug, cylinder no. 2
Q3 — Spark plug, cylinder no. 3
Q4 — Spark plug, cylinder no. 4
S — Fuse box
S1 — Fuse for back-up lights, warm air fan
T — Cable distributor
T1 — Cable connector, single
T2 — Cable connector, double
T3 — Push-on connector, 3 point
T6 — Push-on connector, 8 point
T20 — Test socket
V — Wiper motor
V2 — Fan motor
V4 — Heater fan
W — Interior light, front
W1 — Interior light, rear
X — License plate light
Y — Clock
Z1 — Heated rear window

1 — Ground strap from battery to frame
2 — Ground strap from transmission to frame
4 — Grand cable from horn button to steering coupling

Wiring colour code

BK	=	Black
BN	=	Brown
RD	=	Red
GN	=	Green
GY	=	Grey
BL	=	Blue
YW	=	Yellow
WH	=	White

Chapter 11 Front suspension and steering

Contents

Specifications

Wheel base	2400 mm (94.5 ins.)
Front track	1395 mm (54.9 ins.)
Turning circle	12.3 metres (40 ft 4 inches)
Front suspension	Independent, twin transverse leaf torsion bars with trailing arms to steering knuckles

Torsion bars

Number of leaves	9
Length of bar	980 mm (38.6 ins.)
Setting angle	60º $\pm$ 1º
Wear limit for torsion arm bushes	43.4 mm (1.709 ins.)

Steering ball joints

Maximum play (vertical)	2 mm (0.08 in.)

Steering

Type (August 1972 onwards)	Worm and roller
Steering gear ratio	15
Overall steering ratio	15.7
Steering wheel turns (lock-to-lock)	2¾

Steering geometry

Total toe-in (wheels not pressed)	+ 15' $\pm$ 15' (0.0 to 3.3 mm or 1/8'')
Total toe-in (wheels pressed 15 kg/33 lbs)	+ 5' $\pm$ 15'
Maximum permissible difference between toe (with wheels pressed or unpressed)	25'
Camber angle	30'
Castor angle	3º $\pm$ 40'

Shock absorbers (dampers) ... ...   Hydraulic, telescopic, double acting

Torque wrench settings	ft lbs	Kgm
Axle to frame	90	12.5
Shock absorber mounting (upper)	36	5
Shock absorber mounting (lower)	25	3.5
Ball joints to steering knuckles *	72	10
Stabilizer bar to torsion arm	36	5
Setscrew locknut	29	4
Torsion bar setscrew	29	4
Steering damper to axle tube	32	4.5

	ft lbs	Kgm
Steering damper to relay lever	32	4.5
Tie rod and drag link clamps	11	1.5
Tie rods and drag link (M12 castellated nut)	22	3
Tie rods and drag link (M10 castellated nut)	18	2.5
Wheel bearing clamp nut clamp screw	14	2
Splash plate to steering knuckle	7	1
Brake caliper to steering knuckle (M14)	116	16
Brake caliper to steering knuckle (M12)	72	10
Steering gear to side member	36	5.0
Drop arm to shaft	101	14
Swing lever to shaft	58	8
Steering wheel to column (nut)	22	3
Steering gear end cover bolts	11	1.5
Steering gear case cover bolts	18	2.5
Steering gear to floor (screws)	3.5	0.5
Coupling disc to flange (nut)	11	1.5
Flange to steering worm (nut)	14	2
Locknut for adjuster	43	6

* When replacing ball joints to steering knuckles always use new self-locking nuts.

1 General description

1 The front suspension and steering system has three tasks, to carry the weight of the vehicle, to provide a method of steering the vehicle and of course to incorporate the front brakes. The braking system has been dealt with in Chapter 8; this Chapter discusses the arrangements for steering and suspension.

2 Fig. 11.1 shows an exploded view of one side of the system. Two large parallel steel tubes are welded to endplates and the endplates are bolted to the bodyframe. Each tube carries a multileaved torsion bar fixed at the centre and mounted in needle roller bearings at the outer end for each side of the suspension (two in each tube).

3 Splined on to the outer end of each torsion bar are metal forgings respectively known as the upper and lower torsion arms. (photo) At the outer end of each arm is a ball joint. These balljoints fit into the upper and lower bores of the steering knuckle (photo); protruding from the steering knuckle is the stub axle which carries the wheel and its bearings. The brake caliper is bolted to the steering knuckle. Thus the wheel can move in a vertical plane to overcome road shocks, resistance to its movement being provided by the twisting of the torsion bars. The force required to resist the braking effort is also supplied by the torsion bars (plus the weight of the vehicle). So much for the problems of braking and suspension; each wheel is independent.

4 To provide the necessary movement to steer the vehicle the steering knuckles may rotate in a horizontal plane (hence the top and bottom balljoints). A horn on the bottom of the steering knuckle (photo), extends at right angles to the stub axle. Attached to this is the tie-rod (see Fig. 11.1). The other end of the tie-rod is jointed to the swing lever which pivots about a pin fixed to the lower axle beam. The swing lever is moved about its axis by the draglink and the drop arm from the steering box. Thus as the steering wheel is rotated the drop arm moves backwards and forwards and the linkage transmits the motion to the knuckle joint causing it to rotate about its vertical axis and so steer the vehicle.

5 Since 1972, the worm and peg steering box has been replaced by a worm and roller box which is adjustable but not repairable.

6 The steering column tube is fastened to the floor of the cab and the fascia board in such a way that in the event of an accident and the driver being flung against the wheel the bolts holding the bracket to the fascia board will shear and the column will move forward.

Because of the position of the steering wheel it is not thought necessary to fit plastic sections in the steering column (which would crumple on impact).

The steering column is joined to the steering box by a spider joint just under the floor of the vehicle.

A revised version of the steering column appeared in June 1974, together with revised column switches (Chapter 10).

7 The suspension is fitted with telescopic hydraulic shock absorbers and an anti-roll stabilizer bar.

8 A hydraulicc, telescopic, damper is also fitted to the steering linkage. It is attached to the swing lever and anchored on the lower axle beam.

2 Maintenance and fault finding

1 This is mainly a matter of crawling under the van and checking the rubber seals on the balljoints. If they are not in proper order then the joints must be taken to pieces and the seals renewed after the joints have been checked.

2 Study the tyre treads weekly. If uneven wear is showing then

1.3a The fitter is pointing to the upper and lower torsion arms. The tip of the screwdriver and his finger are on the locknuts and screws which must be removed to dismantle the arm from the bar

1.3b The upper and lower torsion arms fixed into the steering knuckle with ball joints, the tips of the screwdrivers are on the eccentric bushing used to adjust camber

1.4 The horn on the bottom of the steering knuckle jointed to the tie-rod

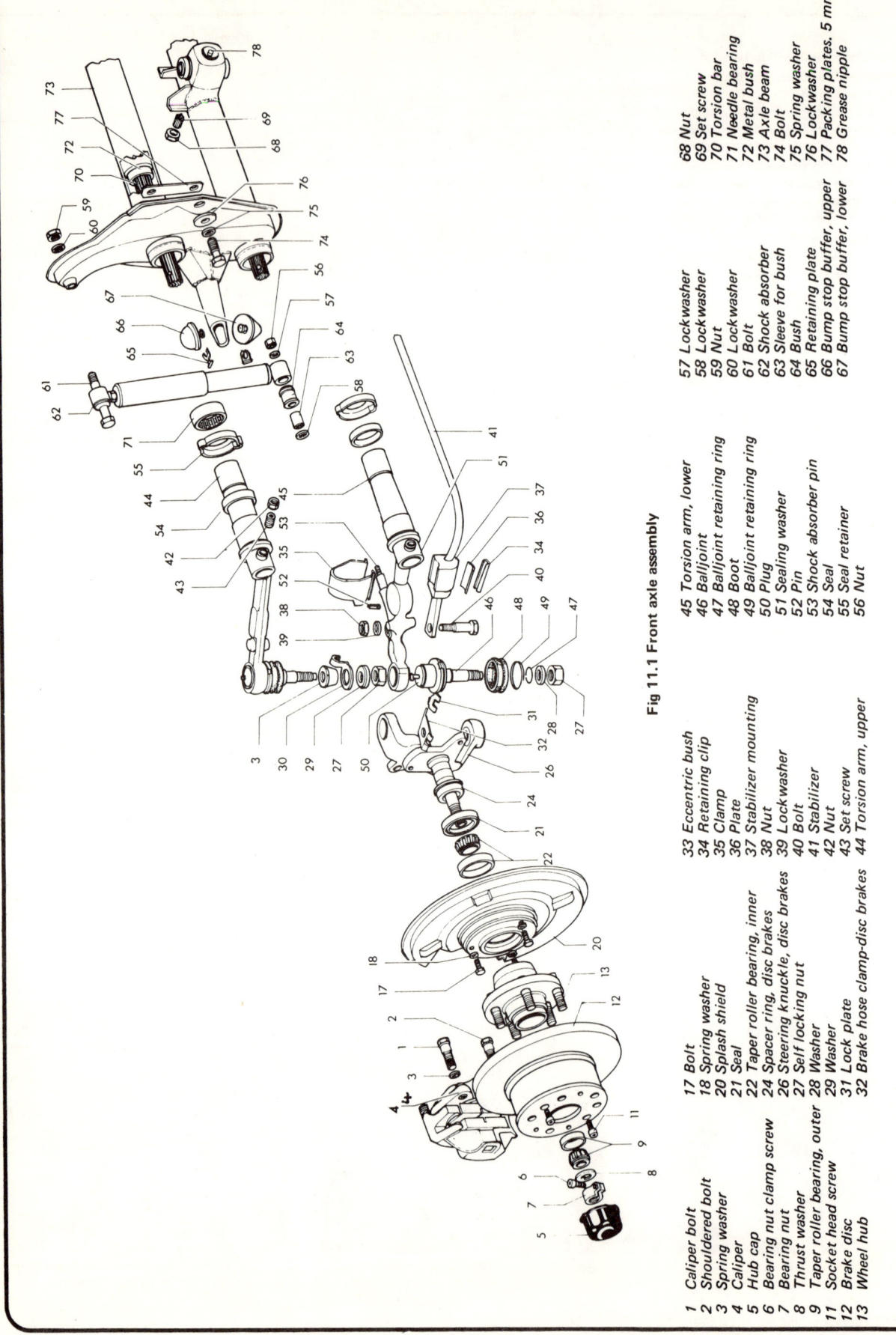

Fig 11.1 Front axle assembly

1 Caliper bolt
2 Shouldered bolt
3 Spring washer
4 Caliper
5 Hub cap
6 Bearing nut clamp screw
7 Bearing nut
8 Thrust washer
9 Taper roller bearing, outer
11 Socket head screw
12 Brake disc
13 Wheel hub

17 Bolt
18 Spring washer
20 Splash shield
21 Seal
22 Taper roller bearing, inner
24 Spacer ring, disc brakes
26 Steering knuckle, disc brakes
27 Self locking nut
28 Washer
29 Washer
31 Lock plate
32 Brake hose clamp-disc brakes

33 Eccentric bush
34 Retaining clip
35 Clamp
36 Plate
37 Stabilizer mounting
38 Nut
39 Lockwasher
40 Bolt
41 Stabilizer
42 Nut
43 Set screw
44 Torsion arm, upper

45 Torsion arm, lower
46 Balljoint
47 Balljoint retaining ring
48 Boot
49 Balljoint retaining ring
50 Plug
51 Sealing washer
52 Pin
53 Shock absorber pin
54 Seal
55 Seal retainer
56 Nut

57 Lockwasher
58 Lockwasher
59 Nut
60 Lockwasher
61 Bolt
62 Shock absorber
63 Sleeve for bush
64 Bush
65 Retaining plate
66 Bump stop buffer, upper
67 Bump stop buffer, lower

68 Nut
69 Set screw
70 Torsion bar
71 Needle bearing
72 Metal bush
73 Axle beam
74 Bolt
75 Spring washer
76 Lockwasher
77 Packing plates, 5 mm
78 Grease nipple

the steering linkage needs attention, or the steering knuckle balljoints are at fault. Since the tyre wear is rapid once it starts, this is a matter of some urgency.

3   If the response at the steering wheel changes and the familiar feel of the steering alters then this must be sorted out. It could be a soft front tyre if the steering is pulling one way. A defective steering damper will cause vibrations and harsh steering. Again vibrations or harsh steering may be due to mal-adjustment of the steering box. A defective shock absorber will affect the steering; and of course a broken torsion arm will cause all sorts of steering problems.

4   The lubrication maintenance is minimal. Three grease nipples on the axle beam to be serviced every 6,000 miles (photos) and the front wheel bearings should be taken down and repacked with grease every 18,000 miles.

5   The wheel bearings are taper roller, prestressed, races, and the rock at the wheel rim may seem excessive but consult the Section on front wheel bearings before deciding that the steering problems are due to slack bearings.

6   Vibration on the steering wheel may be due to out of balance of one of the front wheels. This is discussed in Chapter 8.

7   The steering geometry is checked during the computer diagnosis and compared with the specification. Adjustments are simple, but measurement is not, unless the necessary special equipment is available. The owner is advised to have the steering geometry checked periodically to assess wear, and always when new parts are fitted.

---

3   Front wheel bearings - removal, replacement and adjustment

1   The front wheel hubs each run on two taper roller bearings. Adjustment is effected by a clamp nut which is locked into position by a socket head screw incorporated into it.

2   The left-hand front hub has a left-hand thread. The axle is hollow to permit the speedometer drive cable to go through it. This cable is driven by a square hole in the bearing dust cover. Jack up the wheel and remove the securing bolts and wheel.

3   To remove the bearing dust cover, first take out the circlip securing the speedometer cable and tap the dust cover from side to side until it comes free. (photo)

4   Undo the socket head screw and undo the wheel bearing clamp nut (photo)

5   If the thrust washer is now taken off the hub may be removed. There will be the outer races of each bearing left in the hub and the inner race of the inner bearing left on the axle. These should be drifted out of the hub from the inside if the bearings are to be renewed. If the same bearings are being replaced, they may be left in position and merely flushed out. The race on the shaft should be drifted off also. Note that if the races are renewed then the oil seal on the inner part of the hub will be driven out at the same time as the race. This must be renewed as well. (photo)

6   It is possible that the bearing race is a loose fit on the shaft. If this is so, which would tend to let it turn, a few centre punch marks around the axle where it fits will give it some grip once again when fitted.

7   Refitting new bearings means that the outer races will first have to be driven into the hub and the new oil seal fitted on the inside. Coat the bearings and the space between them in the hub with liberal quantities of Castrol LM Grease and place the hub back on the shaft. Fit the outer bearing followed by the thrust washer and screw on the clamp nut.

8   To adjust the bearing endfloat correctly the nut should be tightened up firmly to make sure the bearings are properly located, spinning the wheel at the same time to ensure the bearings are not overtightened. Then the nut should be backed off until the axial play is between 0.03 - 0.12 mm (0.001 - 0.005 inch) at the spindle. This seems quite a lot and can result in some

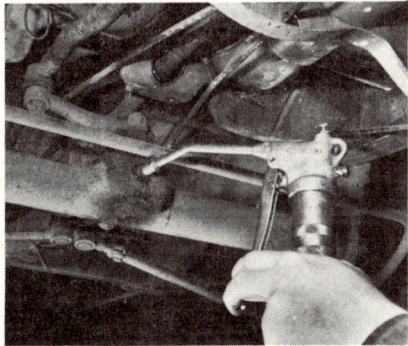
2.4a Grease point in the centre of the axle beam and ...

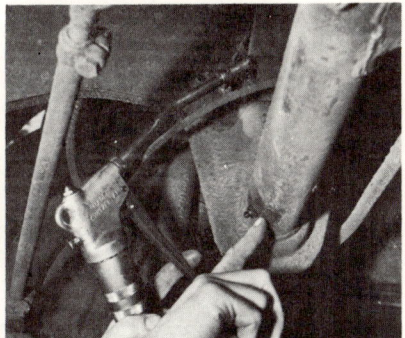
2.4b ... one at each end

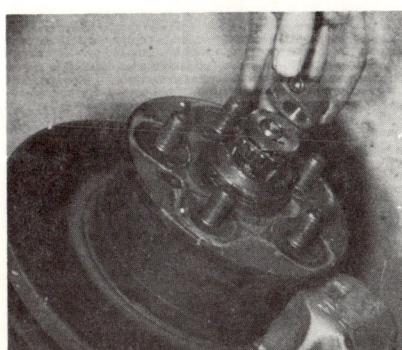
3.3 Tap off the hub cap, this is the right-hand one, the other has the speedo drive

3.4 Undo the socket head screw with an allen key

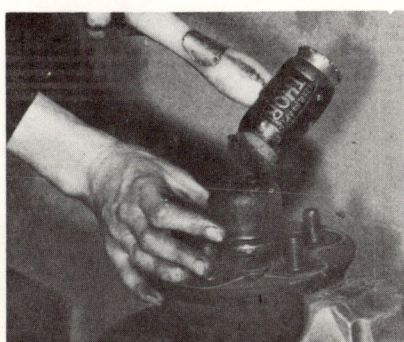
3.5 Unscrew the nut and the thrust-washer and race may be removed

quite noticeable rock at the outer rim of the wheel. It is never-theless correct although the axial play should be kept to the lower limit where possible. When correct tighten the socket screw.

9 Replace the hub cover and re-secure the speedometer drive cable where appropriate.

4 Front suspension balljoints - inspection and renewal

1 With the exception of the correct setting of the camber adjusting bush on the upper joint pin there are no adjustments which can be made (photo 1.3b). When the joints are worn beyond specification limits they must be renewed. Each joint has a removable plug (photo). When removed, a grease nipple can be fitted to add more grease if the joint should squeak. Regular greasing is not necessary. These plugs are not fitted for this reason. They merely cover a special recess which is used in conjunction with a special jig for checking that the arm is not bent. Later models do not have the plugs. A special recess is machined to the body of the joint.

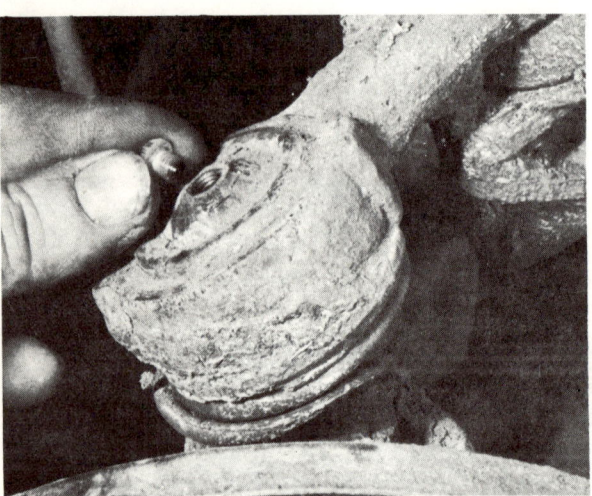

4.1 On earlier models the plug may be replaced by a grease nipple. This is discontinued on later models

2 Testing of the play in the suspension balljoints cannot be carried out as on some vehicles by the accepted method of jacking up the vehicle and then lifting the wheel independently. This is because the lower halves of the balljoint bearing cups are strongly spring loaded. The play is therefore measured by drawing the pins of the balljoints downwards to see how far they move. As the pins are attached to the steering knuckle this means that the wheel has to be moved downwards in relation to the torsion arms. This is done by means of a lever with a pivoting hooked section attached. To check the lower joint play hook the swinging section under the lower torsion arm and lever the upper torsion arm down. To check the upper joint put the hook and arm between the torsion arms to lever the upper arm up. A diagram of a suitable lever is given (Fig. 11.2).

3 In order to renew the balljoints they have first to be removed from the knuckle by unscrewing the taper pin nuts and pressing them out of the knuckle eyes with a claw clamp. This may be done without removing the hub or splash plate but care must be taken to avoid damaging the hydraulic pipe. If a claw clamp is not available and it is known that the balljoints are going to be renewed anyway it is possible to loosen the tapers by striking the sides of the eyes in the steering knuckle. Such striking should be firm and smart. Excessive striking could distort the knuckle.

4 The balljoints then have to be removed from the torsion arms. As they are a splined press fit into the torsion arms the torsion arms will have to be removed. This is not difficult (see next Section).

5 With the torsion arms removed the best thing to do is to take them along to a VW agent and get him to fit the new balljoint to them. Without the proper press tools the greatest difficulty will be encountered in removing the old joints and installing the new ones. If the torsion arm should get damaged it could be very expensive.

6 The eccentric bush on the upper joint pin will have to be removed and fitted to the new joint.

7 Replace the torsion arms and then refit the balljoint pins into the steering knuckle. Note that the eccentric bush of the top joint pin has a notch which normally faces forward. If the notch did not face forward on the joint you took off then it would be as well to have the steering geometry checked out completely. This is a wise precaution in any case.

5 Torsion arms - removal and replacement

1 If indications show that a torsion arm is damaged then it

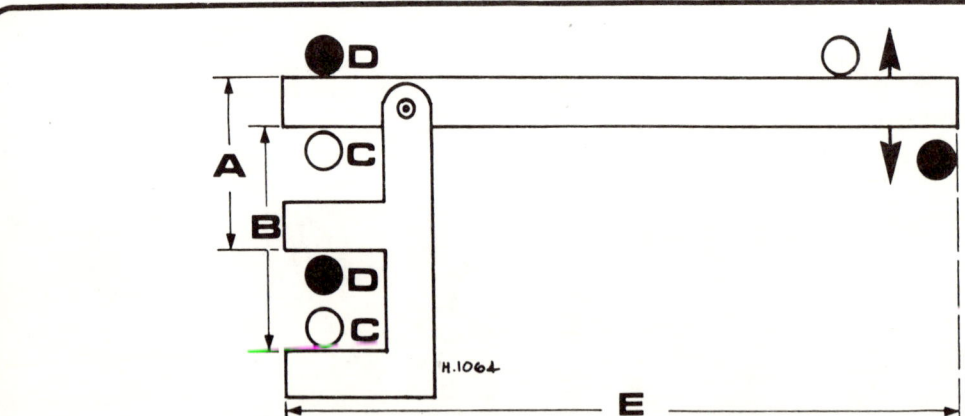

Fig 11.2 Dimensions of special lever required to check play in the front suspension balljoints (Sec 4)

A=   6''/15 cm approx   lever for checking play   D= Position of torsion arms/   in upper joint
B= 8''/23 cm approx   in lower joint   lever for checking play   E= 2.5 ft/75 cm
C= Position of torsion arms/

must be renewed.

2   First remove the wheel hub assembly. If a lower torsion arm is being removed the stabiliser bar must also be taken off (see Section 7).

3   Loosen the locknuts on the ends of the torsion arm securing and then screw the pins right out (photo 1.3a). The torsion arm can then be pulled out of the axle tube. The torsion arm tube is positioned in two bearings - an inner bush and outer needle roller. If either of these is seriously worn causing radial movement of the torsion arm they should be renewed by a specialist with the correct tools. If you have already carried the dismantling of the front axle a considerable way it may be simplest to disconnect the brakes and steering gear as well and detach the whole assembly from the car. This can be done by removing the four securing screws (see Section 12 for complete procedure).

6   Torsion bars - removal and replacement

1   One would normally only need to remove a torsion bar if it broke and this is a rare occurrence.

2   First remove the hub and steering knuckle and torsion arm from one end of the torsion bar concerned. Then detach the steering knuckle from the torsion arm on the opposite side but do not remove the other arm from the torsion bar.

3   If the upper bar is to be removed it will be necessary to detach the gearshift rod at the coupling and push it to one side. For the lower bar the shock absorber will have to be removed.

4   In the centre of the torsion bar tube slacken the locating screw locknut and remove the screw. The bar and the attached torsion arm may then be drawn out.

5   The torsion bar is composed of a number of leaves. Make sure that any replacement is of the correct type.

6   When refitting a torsion bar make sure first it is liberally coated with grease and position it so that the recesses for the locating screws will line up. Fix the centre screw and locknut and then reassemble the torsion arm and steering assemblies in the reverse order of dismantling.

7   Stabiliser bar - removal and replacement

1   The stabiliser bar is fixed to the lower torsion arms on each side of the vehicle and is clamped in position. The bar is held by clamps secured by sliding clips. Drive off the clips against the taper having bent down the securing tab and then remove the clamp, plate and buffer blocks. Remove the bolts securing the ends of the bar to the torsion arms.

2   When refitting the clamps make sure they are the correct way round - cut out portion towards the wheel - and then fit the plate and sliding clip. A good pair of long handled pliers will be needed to squeeze the clamp so that the clip can be engaged. Bend up the lock tab on the clip when it is in position.

8   Steering knuckles - removal, inspection and replacement

1   A modified steering knuckle was introduced in August 1972 at the same time as the larger brake caliper so be careful when obtaining spares. **Read the whole of the Section before commencing work.**

2   Jack-up the vehicle and remove the front wheel. Secure the front axle beam on an axle stand.

3   If the vehicle has been driven and the brake calipers are hot then the operation must stop until they are at room temperature. Now remove the bolts holding the calipers to the steering knuckle (Chapter 8) and hang the caliper with a sling from the frame. **Do not** let it dangle on the brake hose. The hose clip on the knuckle must also be removed.

4   Refer to Section 3, remove the wheel bearing and draw off the brake disc and wheel hub. Undo the bolts (3) holding the splash plate to the knuckle and remove the splash plate. Disconnect the tie-rod from the steering knuckle using an extractor

(Do not hammer the thread).

5   Remove the nuts from the balljoints and disconnect the balljoints from the knuckle arm. If you have the right tool the upper joint may be split by turning the camber eccentric bush (photo 1.3b) but be careful to put it back to the previous setting if you use this method. The lower joint must now be disconnected and the knuckle may be removed from the car.

6   A word about the disconnection of balljoints. The obvious way is to take off the nut, support the female part of the joint and bash the stud with a soft hammer. Only it doesn't work, the joint does not come apart, and the threaded portion is distorted beyond further use.

Experienced fitters can get these joints apart in an almost magical fashion. Using a lever to put pressure on the joint to force it apart they then tap the joint smartly with a hammer on the side and the joint springs apart. The only trouble is that they know just where to tap and how hard to tap (that is why they are master craftsmen). Unfortunately this knowledge is not for sale. The owner driver must resort to extractors. A little outlay on suitable extractors will save a lot of money in the long run.

7   Inspection of the steering knuckle is quite a business. The machined diameters on which the bearings fit should be 0.7495 in $\pm$ 0.0004 and 1.2495 $\pm$ 0.004 in respectively. The spacer ring bearing surface should be 1.4984 in $\pm$ 0.0008 in.

To check whether the axle is bent is simple enough. Hold the knuckle in a vice so that the stub axle points upwards. Using a machinist's square (trisquare) on the machined surface that supports the splash plate measure (with an inside vernier) the distance from the outer bearing seat to the blade of the trisquare when the corner of the trisquare butts against joint of the axle and machined surface.

Repeat this measurement in three different spots. The difference (measured with feelers from the smallest setting) should not be greater than 0.010 in (0.25 mm).

If you suspect that the knuckle is bent or distorted it should be taken to the agent for checking in his special jigs. Under no circumstances try to straighten it. If it is damaged replace it with a new one.

8   Replacement is the reverse of removal. Put the lower balljoint in position and fit the nut. Raise the lower arm using a lever or a jack until the upper balljoint stud enters the steering knuckle. Fit the nut a few turns onto the thread. The eccentric bush for adjusting camber should be positioned so that the notch points forward (photo 1.3b). Fit new self-locking nuts and tighten them to Specification. Connect the tie-rod and torque it correctly. Install the splash shield and refit the hub, brake caliper and wheel.

9   The steering geometry should now be checked and adjusted if necessary.

9   Shock absorbers - removal, testing and re-installation

1   Front shock absorbers are removed by undoing the nut and bolt holding the upper end to the front axle beam and then the nut holding the lower end in position on the stud in the lower torsion arm.

2   The shock absorber may then be removed and exercised. It should give a steady smooth resistance throughout the whole stroke in both directions. Small leaks are unimportant as the unit is overfilled to allow for this but large leaks indicate that the seals have ruptured. There is no repair; the unit must be replaced if it is faulty. If you are not sure ask the VW agent to compare it with a new one.

3   If the rubber bushes have perished they may be replaced (see Chapter 7 Section 5.8); a photograph of a badly worn bush is shown. Should this stage of affairs have occurred then it is most likely that the nut will be rusted on the stud and the stud may snap when the nut is turned. It is possible to obtain an oversize pin as a replacement but the old pin must be cut off flush and the broken part drilled out of the torsion arm. There is a small dowel pin which locates the stud in the torsion arm. It is about 5/32 in (3.96 mm) diameter, drive it out and try to remove the

9.3 Inspect the shock absorber bushes. These need renewal

10.4 The balljoint between the drag link and the drop arm. Note the number of threads visible before undoing the clamp

broken stud with a mole wrench or similar tool before cutting the stud. If it will not come out you may be able to drill it out without removing the torsion arm but it is an awkward job and it may be better to take the arm off. Centre punch the broken stud and use a pilot drill 1/8 in, then follow that with a 7/16 in drill. It is now necessary to enlarge the hole with a 31/64 in drill and finally ream it out with a 0.4904 to 0.4914 inch reamer.

The new oversize stud must then be pushed in until the amount it projects from the arm is 1.78 in $\pm$ 0.009 in. Finally drill the dowel hole out with a 5/32'' drill and fit the dowel. If you do not have all the tools then the arm must be removed and taken with the stud to a machine shop that does have them.

4   There is a lot to be said for making sure these nuts do not get rusty, and even more for taking care not to break the stud. If you can get the old stud out without damaging the hole it could be an idea to try a standard size new stud but make sure it is a tight fit.

10 Steering mechanism - checking the linkage

1   The steering wheel transmits the movement to the wheels via the steering column, then the steering gear and finally from the steering gear drop arm along a drag link to the relay lever and thence by a tie rod to the steering arm on each front wheel. The drag link and tie rods each have a balljoint at both ends, a total of 6, which are subject to wear. If any of the rods are bent or incorrectly adjusted the wheel alignment will be upset causing incorrect handling and abnormaal tyre wear. In the case of worn joints the wheels will be able to move independently of the steering gear. This will cause 'wander' and imprecise steering or, in extreme situations, wheel wobble (Refer to Fig. 11.3).

Only 3 to 6 balljoints are separately renewable and this is because they have to be adjustable. They are fitted to the right-hand tie rod (left on RHD vehicles) and the front end of the drag link. If any of the other joints wears out then the tie rod or drag link as appropriate must be renewed as well.

2   Wear in the steering balljoints can be detected by observation. With the front wheels on the ground the steering wheel should be moved from side to side. Wherever there is any lost motion between two rods connected by a balljoint then the joint is worn out and must be renewed.

3   The balljoint pins are a taper fit into their locations and are usually very tight. After removing the split pin and castellated nut if you have no extractor tool, strike one side of the eye through which the pin goes whilst holding another hammer against the opposite side, but do not hit it too hard and if it does

not have the desired effect stop and go and buy or borrow an extractor.

4   When renewing a tie rod end that is adjustable mark its position carefully in relation to the tie rod before undoing the clamp and screwing it out. This will help to ensure that the overall length of the tie rod is not altered and thus minimise any upset of the wheel alignment. Note that one of the balljoints on the adjustable tie rod has a left-hand thread. This one is normally fitted at the inside end. The same principle applies to the fitting of the balljoint on the drag link. (photo)

5   All the balljoints have grease retaining seals and these must be in good condition. It is possible to renew them if they split; and where the balljoint also has a removal plug fitted it is possible to put some more grease in to replace any that may have escaped (use Castrol MS3).

6   When fitting the new joint make sure that it is screwed in as near as possible to the position of the one removed. Also it should line up with the joint at the other end of the tie rod. Then tighten the clamp.

7   When refitting the taper pin make sure that both surfaces of the taper are perfectly clean. If the threads for the nut do not 'run' easily clean them up, otherwise difficulty may be experienced because the pin rotates as the nut is tightened. If this happens anyway try levering another spanner or blade behind the nut to draw the taper tight as the nut is screwed further on. Tighten the nuts to the correct torque and move them on a little more if necessary to line up the split pin holes. Always use new split pins.

8   Wheel alignment must always be checked when steering balljoints are renewed. The adjustment on the tie rod so that the correct wheel toe can be set. The adjustment on the drag link is to centre the steering gear when the wheels are straight ahead. These two adjustments are interdependent to some extent and alignment is done quickly and accurately if carried out by a VW agency with the proper optical alignment equipment.

11 Steering damper - removal, checking and replacement

1   The steering damper is a double acting piston which serves to smooth out vibration and shocks through the steering. One end is fixed to the steering swing lever and the other to a bracket welded to the axle tube. Each fixing bolt is rubber bushed.

2   If the bushes are worn allowing play the damper should be removed and new bushes fitted. New bushes comprise a rubber bush with a steel central sleeve. Old ones can be cut or driven out and new ones pressed in between the jaws of a vice.

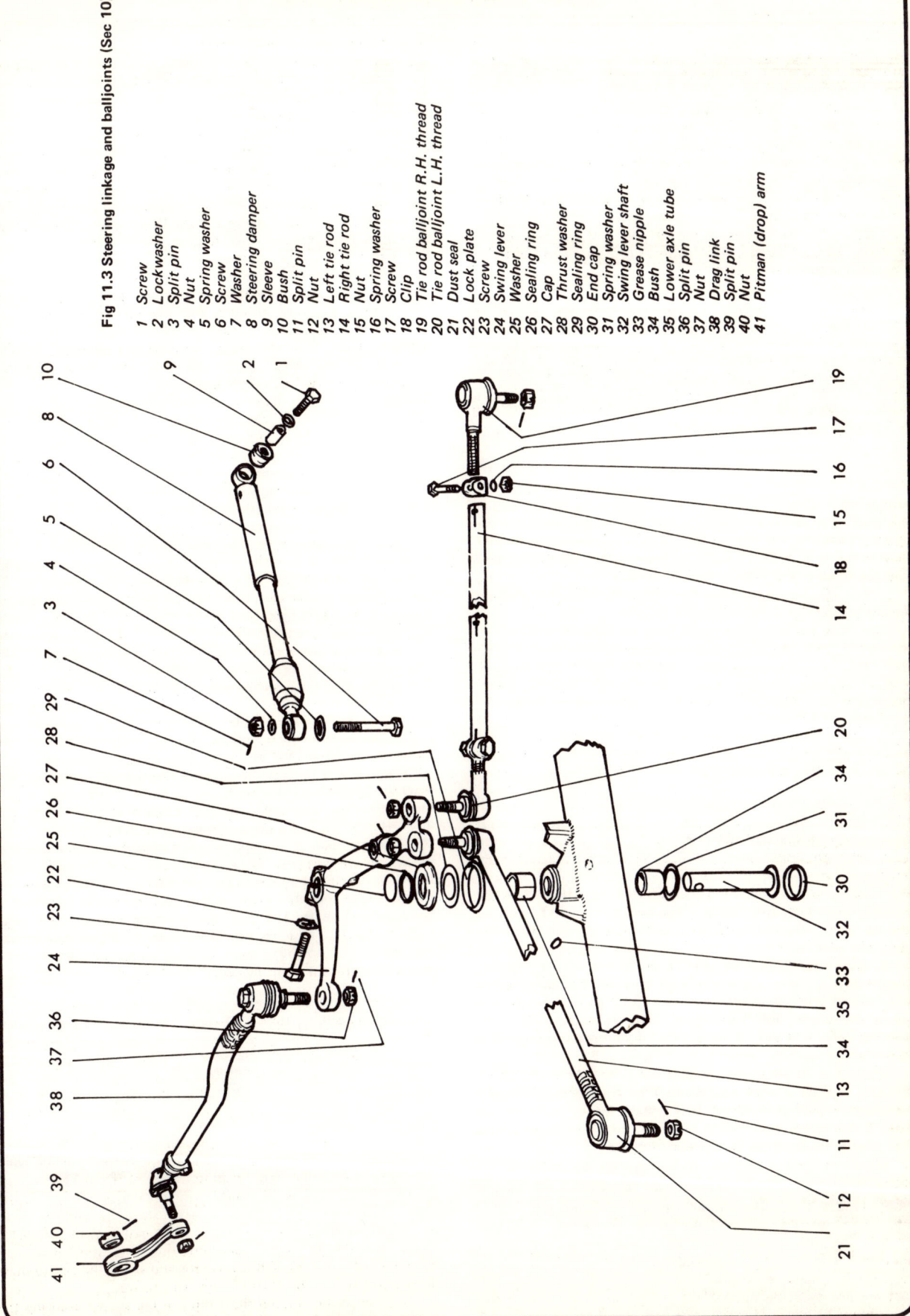

Fig 11.3 Steering linkage and balljoints (Sec 10)

1 Screw
2 Lockwasher
3 Split pin
4 Nut
5 Spring washer
6 Screw
7 Washer
8 Steering damper
9 Sleeve
10 Bush
11 Split pin
12 Nut
13 Left tie rod
14 Right tie rod
15 Nut
16 Spring washer
17 Screw
18 Clip
19 Tie rod balljoint R.H. thread
20 Tie rod balljoint L.H. thread
21 Dust seal
22 Lock plate
23 Screw
24 Swing lever
25 Washer
26 Sealing ring
27 Cap
28 Thrust washer
29 Sealing ring
30 End cap
31 Spring washer
32 Swing lever shaft
33 Grease nipple
34 Bush
35 Lower axle tube
36 Split pin
37 Nut
38 Drag link
39 Split pin
40 Nut
41 Pitman (drop) arm

179

3   To remove the damper take out the split pin from the M10 nut which holds the damper to the bolt through the swing lever and then remove the bolt which anchors the other end to the axle beam bracket.

4   If the damper is leaking fluid badly and there is inadequate action in either direction it should be renewed. To test the action of the damper push and pull the piston throughout its full travel. There should be no roughness or variations in resistance anywhere along the travel of the piston. Note that dampers fitted to right-hand drive vehicles are not the same as for those fitted to left-hand drive.

5   Replace the damper (with the cylinder end mounted on the axle tube) by fitting the securing bolts and nuts and tightening them to the specified torques.

12 Drag link and drop arm - removal and re-installation

1   Take out the cover plate under the pedal cluster. This is done from underneath.

2   Remove the split pins from the nuts on the drag link ends and take off the nuts.

3   Using a heavy duty extractor press the drag link ends out of the drop arm and the swing lever.

4   Remove the split pin and nut from the roller shaft of the steering box and using a heavy duty extractor pull the drop arm off the shaft.

5   Reassembly is the reverse of removal. There are two marks on the drop arm one marked 'L' for left-hand drive vehicles and the other 'R' for right-hand drive vehicles. The appropriate mark should be aligned with the notch on the steering box shaft. Tighten the nut to the correct torque and then turn it further until the split pin will go in; always fit a new split pin.

13 Swing lever, shaft and bush - removal, repair and re-installation

1   If there is play in the bush of the swing lever the lever must be removed and a new bush fitted, or a new shaft.

2   Take the cover plate under the pedal cluster off and disconnect the tie rods, steering damper and drag link from the swing lever.

3   There is a spring washer under the head of the shaft which will force the lever up as you undo the nut on the top. This must be prevented or damage may occur to the shaft so fix a clamp to hold the lever down onto the shaft head until the nut is removed.

4   Remove the nut and the clamp, pry the cap off the head of the shaft and pull the shaft out downwards. It may be stiff so feel round the top to see whether there are any burrs. The lever may now be removed.

5   If the bush in the axle arm is worn it must be removed downwards. A home made extractor of a suitable bolt washer and a bit of tube can be arranged. When fitting the new bush the top of the bush should protrude about 0.050 in (1.27 mm) above the mounting or the lever will rub on the mounting when refitted.

6   There is a grease nipple for this joint. Remove it before removing the bush, refit it after the new bush is in place and make sure grease is getting to the pin before installing the lever.

7   The spring washer will give trouble again so fit the clamp to pull the lever down onto the shaft before installing the nut. Torque all the nuts correctly.

14 Steering box - adjustment, removal and replacement

1   All the models covered by this manual are fitted with a worm and roller steering box. It is possible to adjust the box but not to overhaul it. Overhaul requires a number of gauges and fixtures that are not available outside the VW organization. This if the box cannot be adjusted to conform with specification it must be

removed and the new one obtained.

2   A new box will not be filled with oil so this must be done right away 8 ounces (imperial), 9 2/3 oz (USA), or 284 millilitres of hypoid oil are required. When installed it may be checked and topped up by removing the plug at the top.

3   A sectional view of the steering box is given. (Fig. 11.4)

4   To adjust the idler to the worm means eliminating any clearance. This clearance is measured by turning the steering wheel from side to side around the straight ahead position with the front wheels raised from the ground. Assuming there is no play in the steering linkage there should be no more than 15 mm peripheral movement of the steering wheel before resistance is felt at each side (wheels start to turn).

5   To adjust this the drag link should be first separated from the drop arm. This will make it easier to judge the clearance at the drop arm rather than through the steering column. Turn the steering wheel just over ½ turn to left or right of the central position. The central position is indicated on the steering gear by a pointer on the worm spindle dust cap which lines up with a raised lug on the worm spindle cap.

6   Slacken off the adjusting screw locknut and back off the screw one turn. Then carefully screw the adjuster in, all the while rocking the drop arm until no further backlash can be felt. (photo) If after making this adjustment there is still an excess of play in the central position further slight adjustment may be made to compensate but it indicates that wear is developing. Once the wear in any part of the roller type steering gear becomes excessive the whole unit has to be replaced. Parts for overhaul and repair are not available.

7   In order to remove the steering box it is necessary that the steering column can be moved upwards away from the coupling.

8   Remove the turn signal and wiper switches from the steering column (Chapter 10).

9   Separate the drag link from the drop arm. This is best done with a suitable puller if damage to either is to be avoided. The drop arm has then to be pulled off the steering shaft with a two arm puller once the securing nut is removed. Any method other than a puller is likely to cause damage to the arm. Damage to the steering gear will also result but of course this does not matter if you are going to renew it anyway.

10 Bend back the tabs of the lockplate which lock the single securing nut and bolt of the steering column coupling and withdraw the bolt after removing the nut.

11 Remove the four bolts holding the steering gear case to the side member, and the bolts holding the coupling. (photo)

12 Push the steering coupling together with the column upwards so that the steering gear can be taken out.

13 When refitting the steering gear make sure it is filled with oil.

14 Make sure that the notch on the drop arm lines up with the notch on the shaft. The drop arm has two notches marked 'L' and 'R' for left and right-hand vehicles as appropriate. When fitting the drop arm it must not be hammered but drawn on to the splines with the securing nut.

15 Steering column, tube and wheel - removal and replacement

1   The forward drive design of the vehicle means that the steering column shaft is mounted much nearer the vertical than in a conventional car. For this reason no special safety features are incorporated because in the event of a collision there is no danger of the shaft impaling the driver. A new type of column is installed from June 1974; both types are illustrated. There are no complications in removal and replacement; before starting work disconnect the battery ground strap. (Figs. 11.5 and 11.6)

2   To remove the steering wheel prise out the centre cap for the horn button and remove the turn switch from the column. Undo the wheel securing nut and take it off together with the spring washer and the turn signal cancelling ring. The wheel may be pulled off. If tight pull it upwards and strike the centre shaft downwards with a soft drift of some sort to free it.

3   To remove the column shaft remove the screws securing the cap at the base of the tube inside the driving compartment and

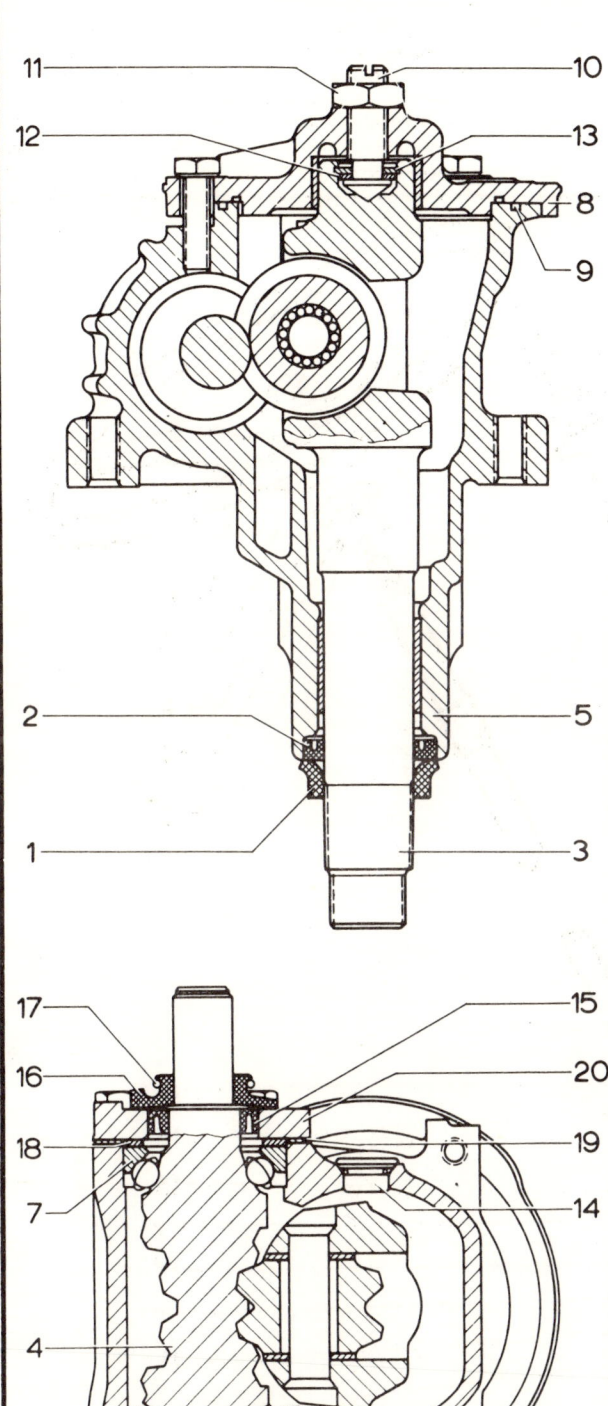

Fig. 11.4 Worm and roller steering gear - cross sections (Sec. 14)

1 Roller shaft dust seal
2 Oil seal
3 Roller shaft
4 Worm shaft
5 Housing
6 Lower ball thrust bearing
7 Upper ball thrust bearing
8 Housing cover
9 Housing cover seal
10 Roller shaft adjusting screw
11 Adjusting screw lock nut
12 Guide washer
13 Circlip
14 Oil filler plug
15 Oil seal
16 Dust cap, worm shaft
17 Circlip
18 Dished washer
19 Shims
20 Worm spindle cap

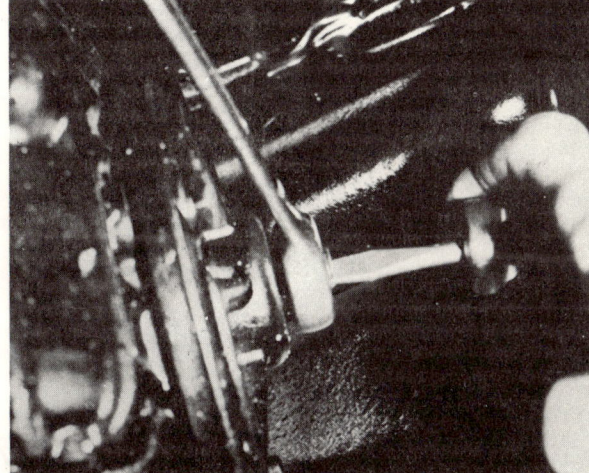

14.6 Adjusting the play between the worm and roller. You will need a stubby screwdriver

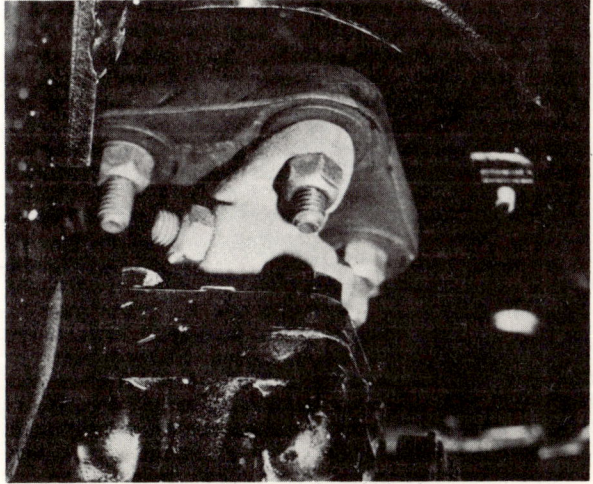

14.11 The coupling at the top of the steering box

make sure the ignition key is not in the locked position. Then remove the undertray at the front and remove the steering gear as described in Section 11. The column shaft may then be drawn out from underneath.

4 The column tube can be removed without removing the shaft if required. First take off the steering wheel as described already and ensure the column is not locked.

5 Remove the securing screws from the tube base cap and then the circlip holding the rubber bush at the top of the tube.

6 Lift the tube a little so that the horn earth cable may be disconnected at the bottom and then straighten out the connection tag. Pull the cap and plastic clamping ring off the bottom of the tube and then remove the tube upwards.

7 When replacing the tube make sure that the enlongated holes in the tube and the insulating ring line up. The procedure is a reversal of the removal operation. Remember to bend back the tag at the bottom at right angles after the base cap is refitted. When the tube is finally in position see that the hole is in line with the locking pin. Turn the ignition key to see that it engages. The column upper bearing spring support ring goes in shoulder

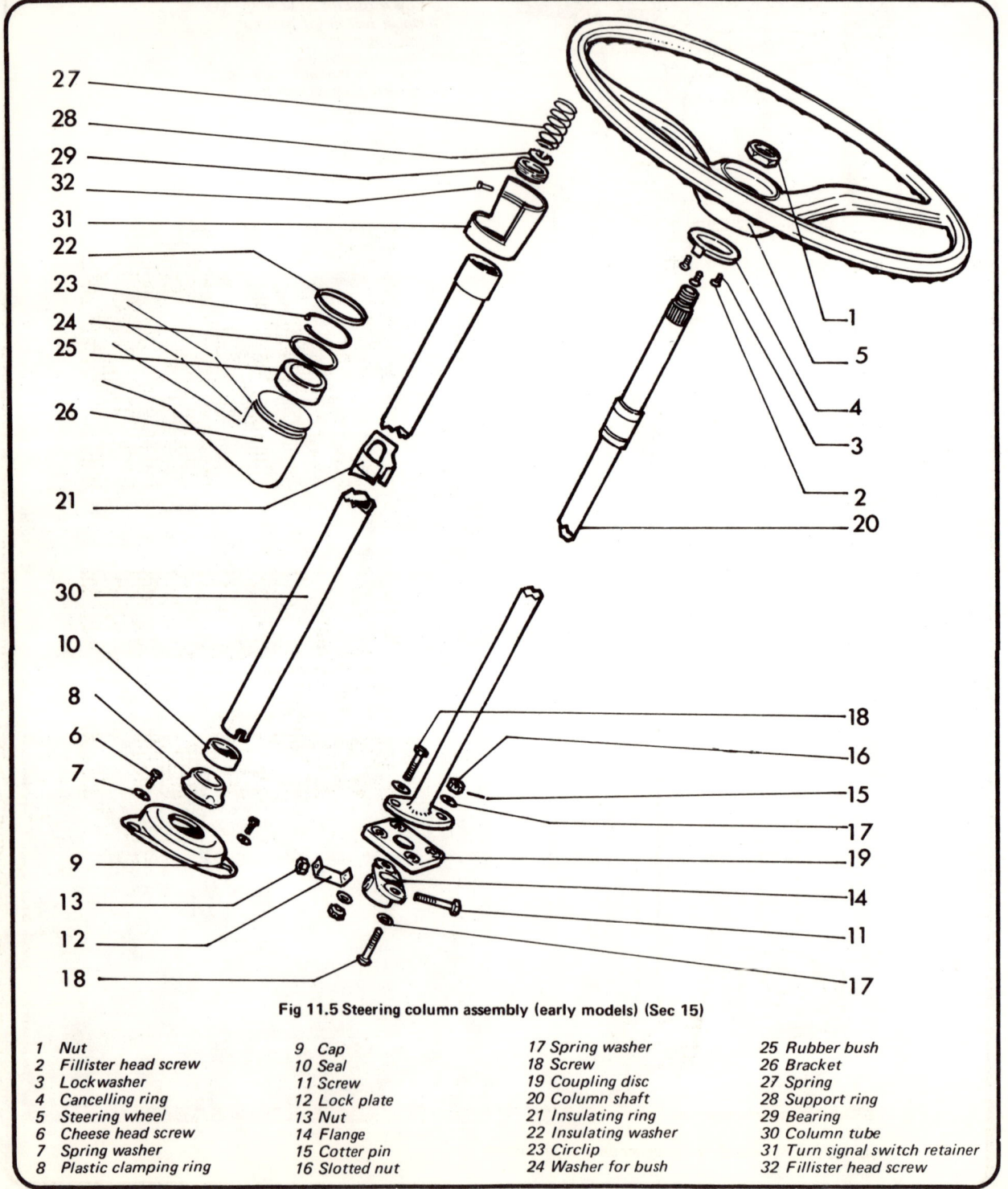

Fig 11.5 Steering column assembly (early models) (Sec 15)

1 Nut	9 Cap	17 Spring washer	25 Rubber bush
2 Fillister head screw	10 Seal	18 Screw	26 Bracket
3 Lockwasher	11 Screw	19 Coupling disc	27 Spring
4 Cancelling ring	12 Lock plate	20 Column shaft	28 Support ring
5 Steering wheel	13 Nut	21 Insulating ring	29 Bearing
6 Cheese head screw	14 Flange	22 Insulating washer	30 Column tube
7 Spring washer	15 Cotter pin	23 Circlip	31 Turn signal switch retainer
8 Plastic clamping ring	16 Slotted nut	24 Washer for bush	32 Fillister head screw

upwards. (photos)

It must be remembered that the column tube acts as part of the earth return for the horn circuit and so must be effectively insulated from the body and steering shaft. If it is not the horn will operate as soon as the ignition is switched on.

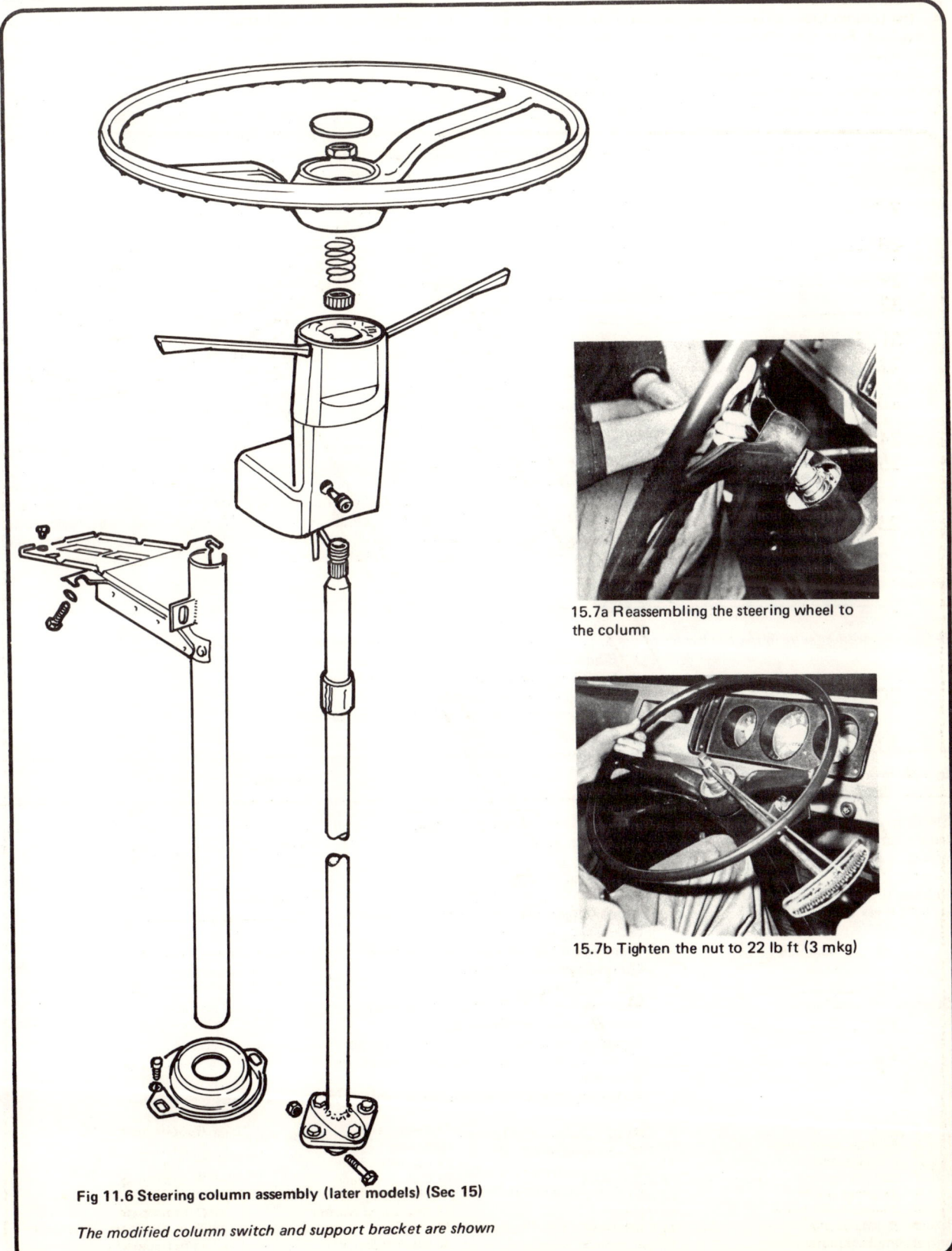

15.7a Reassembling the steering wheel to the column

15.7b Tighten the nut to 22 lb ft (3 mkg)

Fig 11.6 Steering column assembly (later models) (Sec 15)

The modified column switch and support bracket are shown

16 Front axle beam - removal and re-installation

1   If the front axle assembly is badly worn or damaged requiring a considerable amount of repair (or total replacement) it can be readily removed.

2   Disconnect the brake hoses at the brackets and plug the ends - use the bleeder valve dust caps if they are still there.

3   Disconnect the speedometer cable from the left front wheel bearing dust cover and pull it through from behind the steering knuckle.

4   Remove the cover plate under the foot pedal cluster underneath.

5   Engage 1st or 3rd gear so that the muff coupling and screw which join the front and rear gear change rods is accessible. The screw is locked with wire. Remove the screw and disengage and remove the front section.

6   From inside the driving compartment remove the gear change lever assembly (see Chapter 6).

7   Disconnect the clutch cable at the pedal end and the handbrake cables from the handbrake lever.

8   Disconnect the drag link from the swing lever in the steering linkage.

9   Remove the bolt securing the steering damper at the axle bracket end and turn it downwards.

10 Now raise the vehicle and support it securely on stands at each side under the floor frame members. Raise it so that the wheels are just clear of the floor.

11 Support the front axle assembly under the lower tube with a trolley jack and remove the bolts holding the side plates to the frame side member, two bolts at each side.

12 The axle assembly may then be lowered and wheeled out.

13 Replacement is a reversal of the removal procedure bearing the following points in mind. Any gap between the side plates and side members should be taken up by packing pieces of suitable thickness. When the axle is in position and before the bolts are tightened the assembly should be turned forward to take up any slack between the bolts and the holes. This prevents movement under braking forces. Then tighten the bolts to the correct torque.

17 Steering geometry and wheel alignment

1   The correct alignment of the front wheels does not normally alter and the need for checking and realigning occurs only after certain conditions, namely:

a) *Renewal of track rod joints.*

b) *Damage to front suspension or steering linkage.*

Theoretically, if worn balljoints, wheel bearings and so on, are all renewed the steering geometry will automatically be correct. This, of course, presumes that no adjustment has been made in the misguided attempt to compensate for wear. If adjustments have been made then of course, when the various parts are renewed the steering will have to be realigned.

2   The only adjustments which can be made are to the adjustable tie rod (wheel toe), the drag link (centering) and upper balljoint eccentric bush (camber). The alteration of camber automatically alters the king pin inclination at the same time. King pin inclination is the old term for steering pivot angle and recalls the times when the steering pivoted on pins rather the balljoints.

3   Adjustments of steering geometry should never be made in a haphazard manner. In order to check all the angles correctly proper equipment is needed. Furthermore, it is quite pointless trying to realign the steering if one or more of the components is worn. A reputable garage would not normally undertake to readjust steering which had significant wear - although they may be prepared to inform you of the state of the alignment.

18 Fault diagnosis - front suspension and steering

Before diagnosing faults in the mechanics of the suspension and steering itself, check that any irregularities are not caused by:

1   *Binding brakes*
2   *Incorrect 'mix' of radial and crossply tyres*
3   *Incorrect tyre pressures*
4   *Misalignment of the body frame and suspension due to accident damage*

Symptom	Reason/s	Remedy
Steering wheel can be moved considerably before any sign of movement of the wheels is apparent	Wear in the steering linkage, gear and column coupling	Check movement in all joints and steering gear and adjust, overhaul and renew as required.
Vehicle difficult to steer in a consistent straight line - wandering	As above	As above
	Wheel alignment incorrect (indicated by excessive or uneven tyre wear)	Check wheel alignment.
	Front wheel hub bearings loose or worn	Adjust or renew as necessary.
	Worn suspension ball joints	Renew as necessary.
Steering stiff and heavy	Incorrect wheel alignment (indicated by excessive or uneven tyre wear)	Check wheel alignment.
	Excessive wear or seizure in one or more of the joints in the steering linkage or suspension	Repair as necessary.
	Excessive wear in the steering gear unit	Adjust if possible, or renew.
Wheel wobble and vibration	Road wheels out of balance	Balance wheels.
	Road wheels buckled	Check for damage.
	Wheel alignment incorrect	Check wheel alignment.
	Wear in the steering linkage or suspension	Check and renew as necessary.
Excessive pitching and rolling on corners and during braking	Ineffective steering damper	Check and renew as necessary.
	Defective dampers and/or broken torsion bar springs	Check and renew as necessary.

Chapter 12 Body and fittings

Contents

Specifications   *Dimensions in millimetres; weights in kilograms.*

Vehicle code	221	241	231/235
Vehicle type	Microbus Std	Microbus de luxe	Kombi (g)
Length	4505	4545	4505
Width	1720	1760	1720
Height unladen	1955	1955	1955
Ground clearance laden	200	200	200
Kerb weight unladen	1380 *(a)*	1425 *(a)*	1305 *(b)*
Payload	870	855	995
Total permissible weight	2250	2280	2300
Max. front axle load	1010	1010	1010
Max. rear axle load	1270	1270	1300
Max. roof rack weight	100	100	100
Max. trailer weight with trailer braked	800	800	800
Max. trailer weight, no trailer brakes	600	600	600
Trailer nose weight	25/50	25/50	25/50

Vehicle code	211/215		261/264	
Vehicle type	Delivery Van	Delivery Van, high roof	Without cover	Pick-up With cover
Length	4505	4505	4505	4505
Width	1720	1720	1720	1720
Height unladen	1960	2290	1960	2245
Ground clearance laden	200	200	200	200
Kerb weight unladen	1300 *(c)*	1350	1300 *(c)*	1335 *(c)*
Payload	1000	950	1000 *(c)*	965 *(c)*
Total permissible weight	2300	2300	2300	2300
Max. front axle load	1010	1010	1010	1010
Max. rear axle load	1300	1300	1300	1300
Max. roof rack weight	100	Nil	Nil	Nil
Max. trailer weight with trailer braked	800	800	800	800
Max. trailer weight, no trailer brakes	600	600	600	600
Trailer nose weight	25/50	25/50	25/50	25/50

Vehicle code	265/268			215	271/274
Vehicle type	Double cab pick-up Without cover	With cover	Pick-up Large platform	Fire Truck	Ambulance
Length	4505	4505	4525	4460	4505
Width	1720	1720	1980	1720	1720
Height unladen	1960	2220	1960	2250(d)	2250(d)
Ground clearance laden	200	200	200	200	200
Kerb weight unladen	1350 *(c)*	1375 *(c)*	1380 *(c)*	1440 *(e)*	1515 *(a) (e)*
Payload	950 *(f)*	975 *(f)*	920	955	565
Total permissible weight	2300	2300	2300	2395	2100
Max. front axle load	1010	1010	1010	1045	1010
Max. rear axle load	1300	1300	—	1350	1090
Max. roof rack weight	75	75	Nil	Nil	Nil
Max. trailer weight with trailer braked	800	800	800	800	800
Max. trailer weight, no trailer brakes	600	600	600	600	600
Trailer nose weight	25/50	25/50	25/50	25/50	25/50

(a) Without driver
(b) Less driver but including seats
(c) With driver
(d) With emergency light

(e) Local regulations may be different
(f) Allow for passengers. Do not exceed max. axle loading (ie; deduct weight of passengers).
(g) The KOMBI has several versions including the FIRE CREW Truck.

1 General description

Although there are several models of body type the transporter range has the same basic structure for all diagrammatic layouts and seating plans as shown at the end of the Chapter. The Van and Kombi models are the most basic. The Kombi is a van with windows and seats. The seats are readily removable to provide the same freight capacity as the van if necessary. Both models have either one or two sliding doors to the main load area behind the driver's compartment.

The Micro Bus is a vehicle permanently equipped as a passenger carrying vehicle having up to 12 seats. It is supplied in varying degrees of luxury with options such as sun roof.

The 'Campmobile' is the travelling home version fitted with an elevating roof and kitted out with most of the necessities of living; with tents and seats for external use included in some instances. These models are referred to as the Caravette - 2 to 4 berth or the Continental - 4 to 5 berth. The style of the roof lift differs - one being telescopic and the other hinged at the front.

Various specialist coach building firms have produced other versions but the principles are much the same. In all those models with two sliding doors and where the roof panel is modified to provide an opening additional strengthening is provided in the floor frame.

The pick-up versions and the high roof van are almost exclusively for commercial applications. The load area of the pick-up is flat at the level of the top of the engine compartment

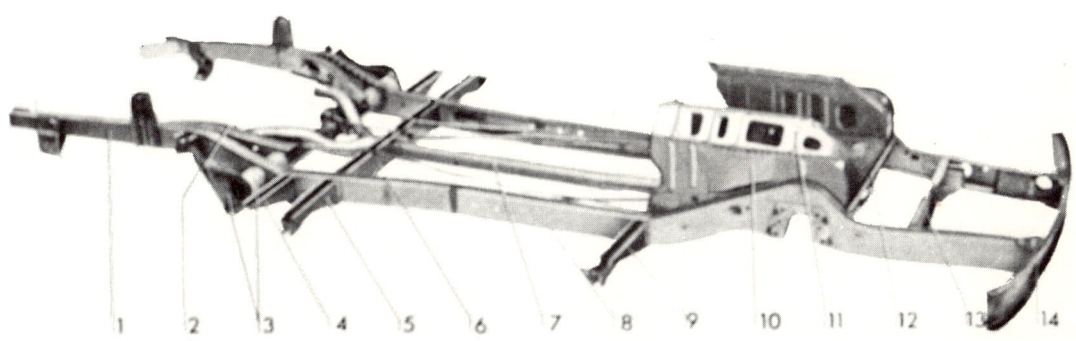

Fig 12.1 Typical floor frame layout (Sec 1)

This shows the frame for the 1600 cc engine. To accommodate the 1700/1800 engine several modifications have taken place. The frame is wider at the back; the rear cross tube has been moved; there is an additional cross member; and the engine mounting brackets are bolted on

1 Side member, rear	5 Outrigger, centre	9 Outrigger, front	member inserts
2 Side member insert, rear	6 Support, rear member	10 Side member insert	13 Cross member, front
3 Cross tube with flange	7 Heater tube	11 Seat box	14 Front cross support
4 Outrigger, rear	8 Side member, front	12 Stiffener between side	

Fig 12.2 Bodyshell

Note This shell has now been considerably modified. The side lights have been moved and a deformation element is welded to the front cross member. The photograph is included to show the principle as the main structure is still the same

and the locker space underneath is accessible through a side panel door. The fuel tank is also mounted in this under floor space.

There have been several modifications in the last three years but the structure is basically the same.

The body is of unitary construction and is reinforced on the floor plates by a frame of side and crossmembers.

The floor plates are welded to the reinforcing frame together with the seat box, wheel housings, cab rear panel and the jack brackets. The extra strengthening for those models requiring it is by means of additional plates in the centre section of the frame.

The front suspension assembly bolts to the side frame members which loop over it. The rear part of the frame bears the cross tube for the torsion bars of the rear suspension and the flanges to which the diagonal suspension arms are attached.

All models are treated with a wax based under seal which protects the body underneath. Exposed areas will need inspection about every 6 months as the protective coating will be abraded away by mud, stones and slurry. It does not last indefinitely.

2 Maintenance - bodywork and underframe

1 The general condition of vehicle's bodywork is the one thing that significantly affects its value. Maintenance is easy but needs to be regular and particular. Neglect, particularly after minor damage, can lead quickly to further deterioration and costly repair bills. It is important also to keep watch on those parts of the car not immediately visible, for instance, the underside and inside all the wheel arches.

2 The basic maintenance routine for the bodywork is washing - preferably with a lot of water, from a hose. This will remove all the solids which may have stuck to the car. It is important to flush these off in such a way as to prevent grit from scratching the finish. The wheel arches and underbody need washing in the same way to remove any accumulated mud which will retain moisture and tend to encourage rust. Paradoxically enough, the best time to clean the underbody and wheel arches is in wet weather when the mud is thoroughly wet and soft. In very wet weather, the underbody is usually cleaned of large accumulations automatically and this is a good time for inspection.

3 Periodically it is a good idea to have the whole of the underside of the vehicle steam cleaned, so that a thorough inspection can be carried out to see what minor repairs and renovations are necessary. Steam cleaning is availabe at many garages and is necessary for removal of accumulations of oily grime which sometimes cakes thick in certain areas near the engine and transmission. The facilities are usually available at commercial vehicle garages but if not there are one or two excellent grease solvents available which can be brush applied. The dirt can then be hosed off.

4 After washing paintwork, wipe it with a chamois leather to give an unspotted clear finish. A coat of clear protective wax polish will give added protection against chemical pollutants in the air. If the paintwork sheen has dulled or oxidised, use a cleaner/polisher combination to restore the brilliance of the shine. This requires a little more effort, but is usually caused because regular washing has been neglected. Always check that drain holes are completely clear so that water can drain out. Brightwork should be treated the same way as paintwork. Windscreens and windows can be kept clear of the smeary film which often appears if a little ammonia is added to the water. If they are scratched, a good rub with a proprietary metal polish will often clear them. Do not use any form of wax or chromium polish on glass.

3 Maintenance - upholstery and floor coverings

1 Mats and carpets should be brushed or vacuum cleaned regularly to keep them free of grit. If they are badly stained remove them for scrubbing or sponging and make quite sure they are dry before replacement. Seats and interior trim panels can be kept clean by a wipe over with a damp cloth. If they do become stained (which can be more apparent on light coloured unholstery) use a little liquid detergent and a soft nailbrush to scour the grime out of the grain of the material. Do not forget to keep the head lining clean in the same way as the upholstery. When using liquid cleaners inside the car do not over-wet the surfaces being cleaned. Excessive damp could get into the seams and padded interior causing stains, offensive odours or even rot. If the inside of the car gets wet accidentally, it is worthwhile taking some trouble to dry it out properly, particularly where carpets are involved. **Do not** leave heaters inside for this purpose.

4 Minor body damage - repair

See also the photo sequences on pages 189, 190 and 191.

Repair of minor scratches in the bodywork

If the scratch is very superficial, and does not penetrate to the metal of the bodywork, repair is very simple. Lightly rub the area of the scratch with a paintwork renovator (eg; T-Cut), or a very fine cutting paste, to remove loose paint from the scratch and to clear the surrounding bodywork of wax polish. Rinse the area with clean water.

Apply touch-up paint to the scratch using a thin paint brush, continue to apply thin layers of paint until the surface of the paint in the scratch is level with the surrounding paintwork. Allow the new paint at least two weeks to harden; then, blend it into the surrounding paintwork by rubbing the paintwork in the scratch area with a paintwork renovation (eg; T-Cut), or a very fine cutting paste. Finally apply wax polish.

An alternative to painting over the scratch is to use Holts "Scratch-Patch". Use the same preparation for the affected area; then simply, pick a patch of a suitable size to cover the scratch completely. Hold the patch against the scratch and burnish its backing paper; the patch will adhere to the paintwork, freeing itself from the backing paper at the same time. Polish the affected area to blend the patch into the surrounding paintwork. Where a scratch has penetrated right through to the metal of the bodywork, causing the metal to rust, a different repair technique is required. Remove any loose rust from the bottom of the scratch with a penknife; then apply rust inhibiting paint (eg; Kurust) to prevent the formation of rust in the future. Using a rubber or nylon applicator fill the scratch with bodystopper paste. If required, this paste can be mixed with cellulose thinners to provide a very thin paste which is ideal for filling narrow scratches. Before the stopper-paste in the scratch hardens wrap a piece of smooth cotton rag around the tip of a finger. Dip the finger in cellulose thinners and then quickly sweep it across the surface of the stopper-paste in the scratch; this will ensure that the surface of the stopper-paste is slightly hollowed. The scratch can now be painted over as described earlier in this Section.

Repair of dents in the bodywork

When deep denting of the car's bodywork has taken place, the first task is to pull the dent out, until the affected bodywork almost attains its original shape. There is little point in trying to restore the original shape completely, as the metal in the damaged area will have stretched on impact and cannot be reshaped fully to its original contour. It is better to bring the level of the dent up to a point which is about 1/8 inch (3 mm) below the level of the surrounding bodywork. In cases where the dent is very shallow anyway, it is not worth trying to pull it out at all.

If the underside of the dent is accessible, it can be hammered out gently from behind, using a mallet with a wooden or plastic head. Whilst doing this, hold a suitable block of wood firmly against the impact from the hammer blows and thus prevent a large area of bodywork from being 'belled-out'.

Should the dent be in a section of the bodywork which has a double skin or some other factor making it inaccessible from behind, a different technique is called for. Drill several small

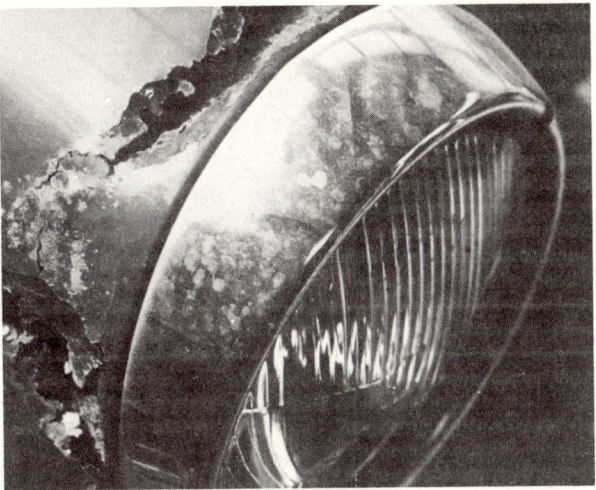

Preparation for filling
Typical example of rust damage to a body panel. Before starting ensure that you have all of the materials required to hand. The first task is to ...

... remove body fittings from the affected area, except those which can act as a guide to the original shape of the damaged bodywork - the headlamp shell in this case.

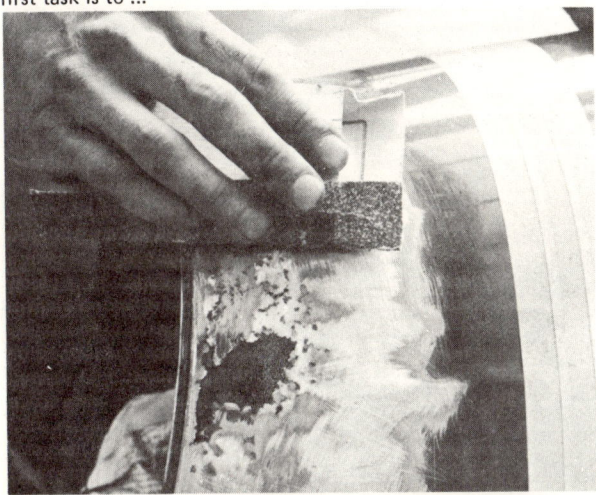

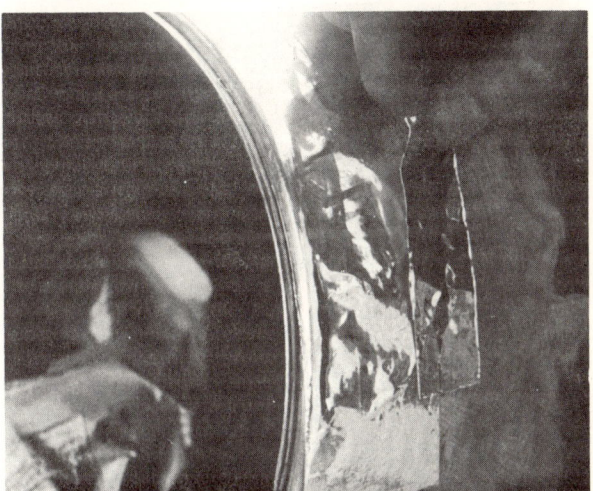

Remove all paint from the rusted area and from an inch or so of the adjoining 'sound' bodywork - use coarse abrasive paper or a power drill fitted with a wire brush or abrasive pad. Gently hammer in the edges of the hole to provide a hollow for the filler.

Before filling, the larger holes must be blocked off. Adhesive aluminium tape is one method; cut the tape to the required shape and size, peel off the backing strip (where used), position the tape over the hole and burnish to ensure adhesion.

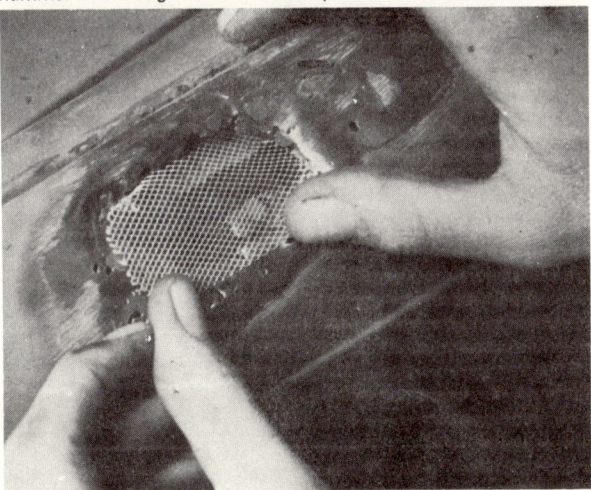

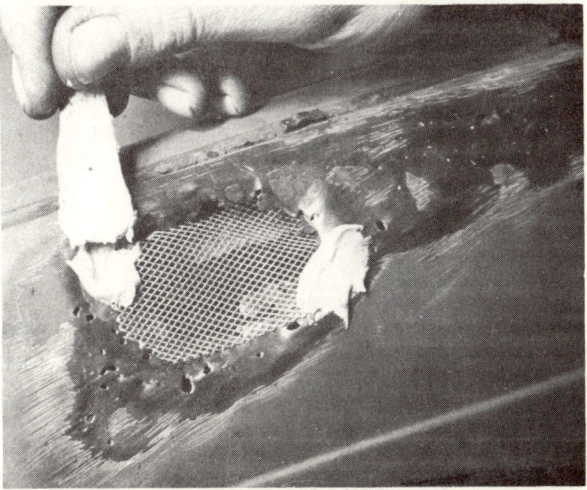

Alternatively, zinc gauze can be used. Cut a piece of the gauze to the required shape and size; position it in the hole below the level of the surrounding bodywork; then ...

... secure in position by placing a few blobs of filler paste around its periphery. Alternatively, pop rivets or self-tapping screws can be used. Preparation for filling is now complete.

Filling and shaping
Mix filler and hardener according to manufacturer's instructions -
avoid using too much hardener otherwise the filler will harden
before you have a chance to work it.

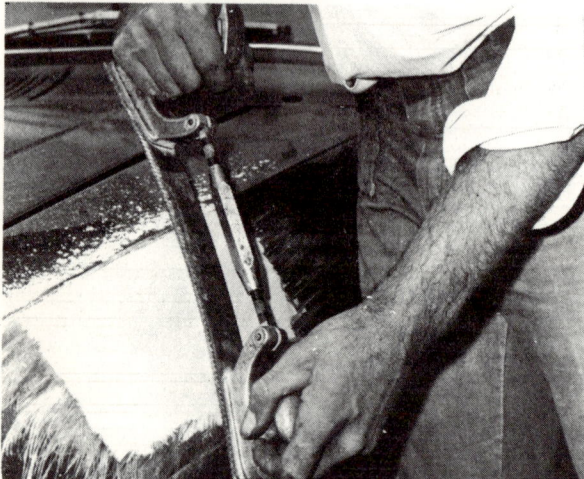

... remove excess filler and start shaping with a Surform plane or
a dreadnought file. Once an approximate contour has been
obtained and the surface is relatively smooth, start using ...

40 grit production paper is best to start with, then use progressively finer abrasive paper, finishing with 400 grade 'wet-and-dry'
When using 'wet-and-dry' paper, periodically rinse it in water
ensuring also, that the work area is kept wet continuously.

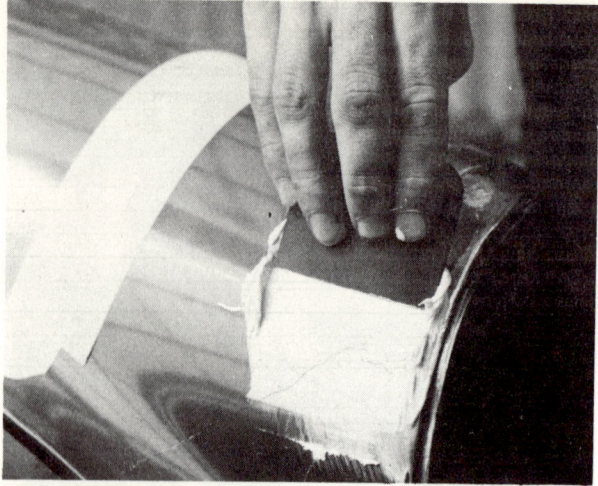

Apply the filler to the affected area with a flexible applicator -
this will ensure a smooth finish. Apply thin layers of filler at 20
minute intervals, until the surface of the filler is just 'proud' of
the surrounding bodywork. Then ...

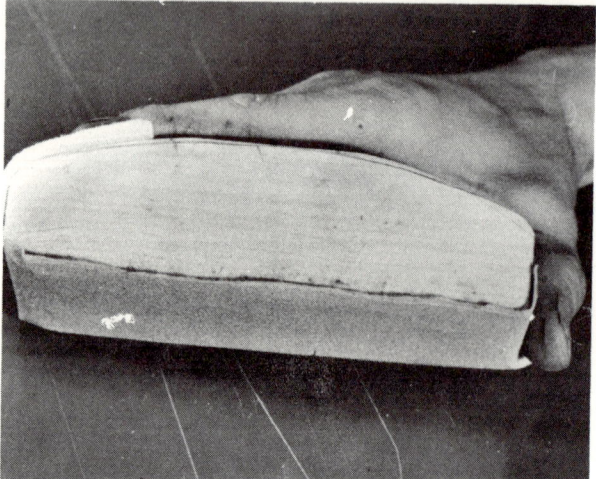

... abrasive paper. The paper should be wrapped around a flat
wood, cork or rubber block - this will ensure that it imparts a
smooth surface to the filler.

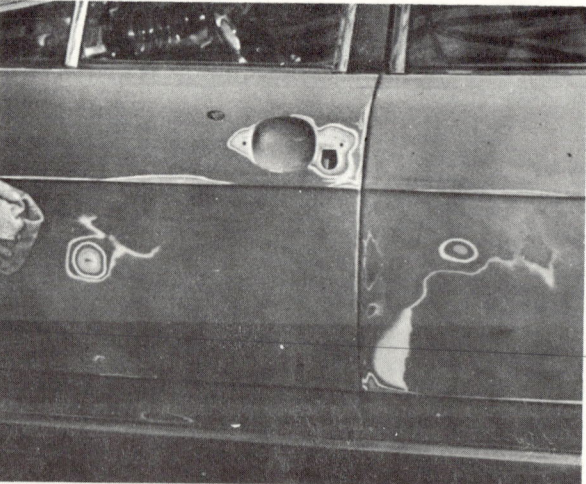

Rubbing-down is complete when the surface of the filler is
really smooth and flat, and the edges of the surrounding paintwork are finely 'feathered'. Wash the area thoroughly with clean
water and allow to dry before commencing re-spray.

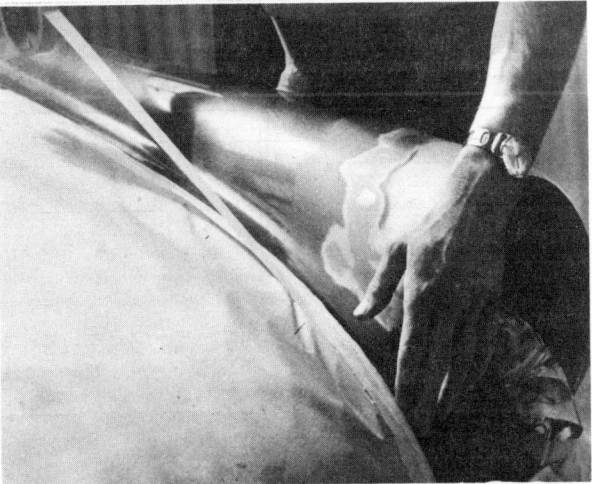

Masking and spraying
Firstly, mask off all adjoining panels and the fittings in the spray area. Ensure that the area to be sprayed is completely free of dust. Practice using an aerosol on a piece of waste metal sheet until the technique is mastered.

Spray the affected area with primer - apply several thin coats rather than one thick one. Start spraying in the centre of the repair area and then work outwards using a circular motion - in this way the paint will be evenly distributed.

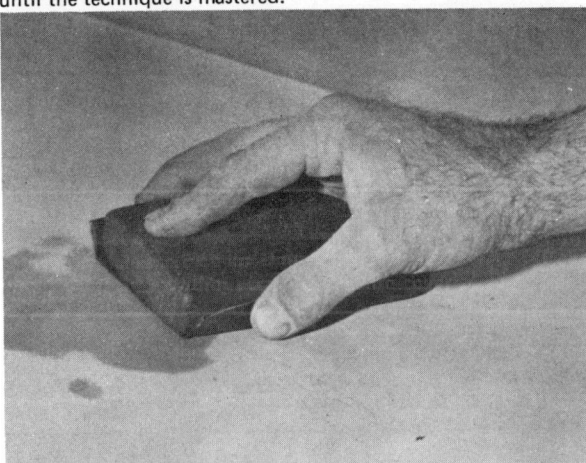

When the primer has dried inspect its surface for imperfections. Holes can be filled with filler paste or body-stopper, and lumps can be sanded smooth. Apply a further coat of primer, then 'flat' its surface with 400 grade 'wet-and-dry' paper.

Spray on the top coat, again building up the thickness with several thin coats of paint. Overspray onto the surrounding original paintwork to a depth of about five inches, applying a very thin coat at the outer edges.

Allow the new paint two weeks, at least, to harden fully, then blend it into the surrounding original paintwork with a paint restorative compound or very fine cutting paste. Use wax polish to finish off.

The finished job should look like this. Remember, the quality of the completed work is directly proportional to the amount of time and effort expended at each stage of the preparation.

holes through the metal inside the dent area - particularly in the deeper sections. Then screw long self-tapping screws into the holes just sufficiently for them to gain a good purchase in the metal. Now the dent can be pulled out by pulling on the protruding heads of the screws with a pair of pliers.

The next stage of the repair is the removal of the paint from the damaged area, and from an inch or so of the surrounding 'sound' bodywork. This is accomplished most easily by using a wire brush or abrasive pad on a power drill, although it can be done just as effectively by hand using sheets of abrasive paper. To complete the preparations for filling, score the surface of the bare metal with a screwdriver or the tang of a file, or alternatively, drill small holes in the affected area. This will provide a really good 'key' for the filler paste.

To complete the repair see the Section on filling and re-spraying.

Repair of rust holes or gashes in the bodywork

Remove all paint from the affected area and from an inch or so of the surrounding 'sound' bodywork, using an abrasive pad or wire   brush on a power drill. If these are not available a few sheets of abrasive paper will do the job just as effectively. With the paint removed you will be able to gauge the severity of the corrosion and therefore decide whether to replace the whole panel (if this is possible) or to repair the affected area. Replacement body panels are not as expensive as most people think and it is often quicker and more satisfactory to fit a new panel than to attempt to repair large areas of corrosion.

Remove all fittings from the affected area except those which will act as a guide to the original shape of the damaged bodywork (eg. headlamp shells etc.,). Then, using tin snips or a hacksaw blade, remove all loose metal and any other metal badly affected by corrosion. Hammer the edges of the hole inwards in order to create a slight depression for the filler paste.

Wire brush the affected area to remove the powdery rust from the surface of the remaining metal. Paint the affected area with rust inhibiting paint (eg; Kurust); if the back of the rusted area is accessible treat this also.

Before filling can take place it will be necessary to block the hole in some way. This can be achieved by the use of one of the following materials: Zinc gauze, Aluminium tape or Polyurethane foam.

Zinc gauze is probably the best material to use for a large hole. Cut a piece to the approximate size and shape of the hole to be filled, then position it in the hole so that its edges are below the level of the surrounding bodywork. It can be retained in position by several blobs of filler paste around its periphery.

Aluminium tape should be used for small or very narrow holes. Pull a piece off the roll and trim it to the approximate size and shape required, then pull off the backing paper (if used) and stick the tape over the hole; it can be overlapped if the thickness of one piece is insufficient. Burnish down the edges of the tape with the handle of a screwdriver or similar, to ensure that the tape is securely attached to the metal underneath.

Polyurethane foam is best used where the hole is situated in a section of bodywork of complex shape, backed by a small box section (eg; where the sill panel meets the rear wheel arch - most cars). The unusual mixing procedure for this foam is as follows: Put equal amounts of fluid from each of the two cans provided in the kit, into one container. Stir until the mixture begins to thicken, then quickly pour this mixture into the hole, and hold a piece of cardboard over the larger apertures. Almost immediately the polyurethane will begin to expand, gushing frantically out of any small holes left unblocked. When the foam hardens it can be cut back to just below the level of the surrounding bodywork with a hacksaw blade.

Bodywork repairs - filling and re-spraying

Before using this Section, see the Sections on dent, deep scratch, rust hole, and gash repairs.

Many types of bodyfiller are available, but generally speaking those proprietary kits which contain a tin of filler paste and a tube of resin hardener (eg; Holts Cataloy) are best for this type

of repair. A wide, flexible plastic or nylon applicator will be found invaluable for imparting a smooth and well contoured finish to the surface of the filler.

Mix up a little filler on a clean piece of card or board - use the hardener sparingly (follow the .maker's instructions on the packet), otherwise the filler will set very rapidly.

Using the applicator, apply the filler paste to the prepared area; draw the applicator across the surface of the filler to achieve the correct contour and to level the filler surface. As soon as a contour that approximates the correct one is achieved, stop working the paste - if you carry on too long the paste will become sticky and begin to 'pick-up' on the applicator. Continue to add thin layers of filler paste at twenty-minute intervals until the level of the filler is just 'proud' of the surrounding body-work.

Once the filler has hardened, excess can be removed using a Surform plane or Dreadnought file. From then on, progressively finer grades of abrasive paper should be used, starting with a 40 grade production paper and finishing with 400 grade 'wet-and-dry' paper. Always wrap the abrasive paper around a flat rubber, cork, or wooden block - otherwise the surface of the filler will not be completely flat. During the smoothing of the filler surface the 'wet-and-dry' paper should be periodically rinsed in water. This will ensure that a very smooth finish is imparted to the filler at the final stage.

At this stage the 'dent' should be surrounded by a ring of bare metal, which in turn should be encircled by the finely 'feathered' edge of the good paintwork. Rinse the repair area with clean water, until all of the dust produced by the rubbing-down operation is gone.

Spray the whole repair area with a light coat of grey primer - this will show up any imperfections in the surface of the filler. Repair these imperfections with fresh filler paste or body-stopper, and once more smooth the surface with abrasive paper. If bodystopper is used, it can be mixed with cellulose thinners to form a really thin paste which is ideal for filling small holes. Repeat this spray and repair procedure until you are satisfied that the surface of the filler, and the feathered edge of the paintwork are perfect. Clean the repair area with clean water and allow to dry fully.

The repair area is now ready for spraying. Paint spraying must be carried out in a warm, dry, windless and dust free atmosphere. This condition can be created artificially if you have access to a large indoor working area, but if you are forced to work in the open, you will have to pick your day very carefully. If you are working indoors, dousing the floor in the work area with water will 'lay' the dust which would otherwise be in the atmosphere. If the repair area is confined to one body panel, mask off the surrounding panels; this will help to minimise the effects of a slight mis-match in paint colours. Bodywork fittings (eg; chrome strips, door handles etc) will also need to be masked off. Use genuine masking tape and several thicknesses of newspaper for the masking operation.

Before commencing to spray, agitate the aerosol can thoroughly, then spray a test area (an old tin, or similar) until the technique is mastered. Cover the repair area with a thick coat of primer; the thickness should be built up using several thin layers of paint rather than one thick one. Using 400 grade 'wet-and-dry' paper, rub down the surface of the primer until it is really smooth. While doing this, the work area should be thoroughly doused with water, and the 'wet-and-dry' paper periodically rinsed in water. Allow to dry .before spraying on more paint.

Spray on the top coat, again building up the thickness by using several thin layers of paint. Start spraying in the centre of the repair area and then, using a circular motion, work outwards until the whole repair area and about 2 inches of the surrounding original paintwork is covered. Remove all masking material 10 to 15 minutes after spraying on the final coat of paint.

Allow the new paint at least 2 weeks to harden fully; then, using a paintwork renovator (eg. T-Cut) or a very fine cutting paste, blend the edges of the new paint into the existing paintwork. Finally, apply wax polish.

5 Major body damage - repair

1 Where serious damage has occurred or large areas need renewal due to neglect it means certainly that completely new sections or panels will need welding in and this is best left to professionals. If the damage is due to impact it will also be necessary to check the alignment of the body structure. In such instances the services of a Volkswagen agent with specialist checking jigs are essential. If a body is left misaligned it is first of all dangerous as the car will not handle properly - and secondly, uneven stresses will be imposed on the steering, engine and transmission, causing abnormal wear or complete failure. Tyre wear will also be excessive.

6 Bumpers - general description

Up to model year 1973 all vehicles were fitted with bumpers attached to the bodyframe by brackets. The front bumpers were also secured to the frame at the side. Rear bumpers had side cover plates and brackets.

In 1973 the front bumper was redesigned and is simply a metal section covering a deformation element, which is welded to the front end crossmember (Fig. 12.3). The rear bumper is a stronger section and is attached to the frame by two brackets.

7 Bumpers (early models) - removal and replacement

1 When removing the fixed front bumper either have someone to hold the bumper once you have undone one side or arrange a support. The bumper is fixed in four places. There are two bolts holding each of its side supports to the body just in front of the front wheel on either side and four bolts which hold the brackets supporting the centre of the bumper to each side frame. It is best to remove the brackets with the bumper. These bolts may be rusty and need soaking with easing oil. Take off the centre bracket bolts first, then loosen the bolts on one side, leave them in place and undo the side bracket on the other side. Support this with an axle stand or get someone to hold it and then take the bolts from the other end. The brackets will come away with the bumper, and may be removed if necessary.

2 If the bumper has been deformed it is probable that the brackets will be bent as well so that when refitting a new or straightened bumper the brackets will not line up and will need attention. This can be difficult. If you can, make a paper template showing the positions of the holes through which the eight bolts go to fasten the brackets to the frame. Otherwise refitting the bumper will be largely a matter of trial-and-error. Brackets which have been badly bent should be annealed after straightening by a competent blacksmith.

3 Bolt the bracket loosely to the bumper and offer up the assembly to the frame. Fit as many bolts as will go and check that the space between the body and bumper is uniform. Slide the brackets about on the elongated holes until the remainder of the bolts will enter and torque the bolts to 25 lbs ft (3.5 mkg) all round.

4 The rear bumper is removed and replaced in the same way. It has a gravel guard (a piece of angle) held to it with nuts and bolts. This may be removed without taking the bumper off.

5 The rear bumper is then disconnected by undoing the nuts and bolts which hold the cover plates to the frame on each side and then by unbolting the main brackets from the frame. Do not lose the rubber spacers. Installation is the reverse of removal.

8 Bumpers (1973 onwards) - removal and replacement

1 The front bumper is removed by taking out the four bolts which hold it to the buffer. Installation is the reverse.
2 The buffer (or deformation element) is welded to the front

Fig 12.3 Front bumper (later models) (Sec 6)

A   Front panel   C   Deformation unit

end crossmember. If this is damaged the job becomes a major repair and must be done in a properly equipped body repair shop.

3 The rear bumper is removed by unbolting the brackets from the frame. There are two bolts on each side. Remove the brackets with the bumper. The brackets are secured to the bumper with nuts and bolts and may be removed if necessary.

4 Replacement is the reverse of removal. Slide the brackets with the bolts loosely installed in the elongated holes until the space between the body and the bumper is uniform and then torque the bolts to 25 lbs ft.

9 Doors and flaps - general description and maintenance

1 There are several combinations of doors and flaps according to the year and model. Most models have two hinged cab doors fitted with windows and a sliding door on the side. This may or may not have a window. At the rear a full width door, hinged at the top opens to give entrance, and a flap also hinged at the top opens to give access to the engine compartment. There is also a flap in the floor just inside the rear door which may be removed to give improved access to the engine compartment. It has open end hinges and turn buckles.

The pick-up has either a single cab with two cab doors or a double cab with two larger doors and two smaller doors for access to the extra compartment.

2 The hinges, locks and window gear are the same on all models and the problems arising from them the same. Hinges need oil at regular intervals **before** the pins become rusty, striker plates should be adjusted as soon as a slight rattle is heard, and locks require lubrication regularly.

3 Door rattles are due either to loose hinges, worn or maladjusted catches, or loose components inside the door. Loose hinges can be detected by opening the door and trying to lift it. Any play will be felt. Worn or badly adjusted catches can be found by pushing and pulling on the outside handle when the door is closed. Once again any play will be felt. To check the window mechanism open the door and shake it with the window first open and then closed. Rattles will normally be heard.

10 Cab doors - removal, replacement and hinge lubrication

1 This is a job for two people, and strong ones at that for the door is heavy. It must not be unsupported while the hinges are unscrewed.
2 The hinges are welded to the door and fastened to the body by crosshead screws. There is also a check strap to stop the door opening too far.
3 If it is intended to replace the same door then the exact position of the hinges on the door pillar should be marked by

scribed lines.

4   Removal of the crosshead screws is difficult unless you have an impact screwdriver. We have not met anyone who could undo them with an ordinary screwdriver and although they can be tapped round with a punch the screwheads become so distorted that new screws are required. If you do not have access to an impact screwdriver it is suggested that you go to a garage and ask them to loosen the screws, retighted them with an ordinary screwdriver and then go home and get on with the job.

5   Once the screws are started remove the check stray hinge pin, there is a circlip on it to take off first, and then with a helper holding the door remove the screws from the lower hinge and then the top hinge and take the door away.

6   If the old door is being put in again inspect the weather strip around it. If it is hard, cracked, or deformed then a new one should be fitted. To do this cut away the old strip, clean the adhesive away with a solvent and when the whole area is smooth and dry fix the new strip with adhesive (trim cement).

7   If the hinges were marked then refitting the old door is simple. With the aid of a helper install the screws in the hinges line up the marks and tighten the screws with an impact screwdriver. Reconnect the check strap, close the door and check the fit of the seal, and if necessary, adjust the striker plate.

8   If a new door is being fitted it makes things easier if the striker plate is removed before fitting the door. With the aid of a helper install the door as in paragraph 6 but do not tighten the screws finally. Check that the weather strip is sealing the door all round and that the door trim moulding matches up with that on the body.

The rear edge of the door should present an even gap and the top and bottom edges of the door must not foul the body. The hinges are serewed into plates which are in turn moveable so that it is possible to adjust the hinge to reset the door. When the door is seated correctly tighten the crosshead screws finally and then refit the striker plate.

9   It is important to see that the hinge pins are lubricated. On the top of the hinge there is a small plastic cap. Remove this and you will see a small reservoir which should be filled with oil. (photo) Do not forget to oil the pin in the check strap. (photo)

11 Cab door latch striker plate - adjustment

1   If the door latch striker plate is the cause of rattles first check that it is not worn out. This can be done by taking it off completely and fitting it over the latch hook with the latch in the vertical position.

There should be no up and down movement between the

two. If the rubber wedge is obviously worn renew it. Otherwise it is possible to put some packing under the wedge to reduce the clearance to zero.

2   Check that the door fits the aperture properly by seeing that the gaps are more or less equal all round and that it fits flush with the side panel of the bodywork. There should be no rubbing and all the weatherstrip should show signs of equal compression.

3   Refit the striker plate leaving the screws just tight enough to hold it in position.

4   If the door will shut and latch only when slammed it means that the rubber wedge at the top of the striker plate is too far out thus preventing the corresponding wedge on the door from moving right in. If the door can be rattled in and out when latched the wedge on the striker plate is too far in. To remedy either of these conditions move the upper end of the striker plate in or out as necessary. (Fig 12.4) (photo).

12 Cab door trim panels - removal and replacement

1   Various types of trim panels have been fitted, modified to suit the ventilation ducts. Two illustrations are given and it will be seen that the variation is considerable. It is recommended that if you need a replacement panel the advice of the VW agent should be sought. However, the type of panel does not affect the removal and assembly greatly. If there is an external air duct then looking at the hinge end of the door push back the air duct sealing rubber and remove the two crosshead screws which hold the air duct in place. (Figs 12.5 and 12.6) (photo).

2   Next remove the window winder, door latch lever and door pull strap. The winder handle has a plastic cover which should be prised off at the spindle end. A crosshead screw is then accessible and should be removed. (photo) The recessed finger plate behind the inner door handle lever can be prized out also with a screwdriver (photo). The crosshead screw behind it can then be removed to release the assembly (photo). Then use a piece of wood and pry off the twin panel all round the edge. There may be a hook at the back of it which holds it to the door in the middle so when the edges are free lift the panel slightly to remove it. Underneath there is a sheet of plastic. Do not remove this entirely unless absolutely necessary.

3   Reassembly is the reverse of removal. If the plastic has been removed use the opportunity to clear the drain vents and to remove and make good any rust spots. The window winder should point forward when the window is closed. Do not forget the rubbing washer behind the window winder handle. (photo)

10.9a Lubricating the door hinge

10.9b Lubricating the check strap pin

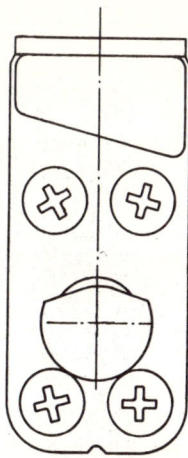

Fig 12.4 Diagram of the striker plate (early types) (Sec 12)

Slacken screws to move the plate

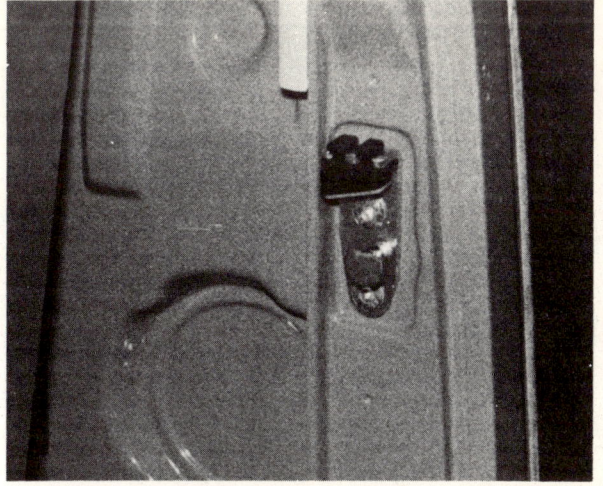

11.4 Striker plate 1975 pattern - cab door pillar - note revised stop and only two screws. But the adjustment is the same

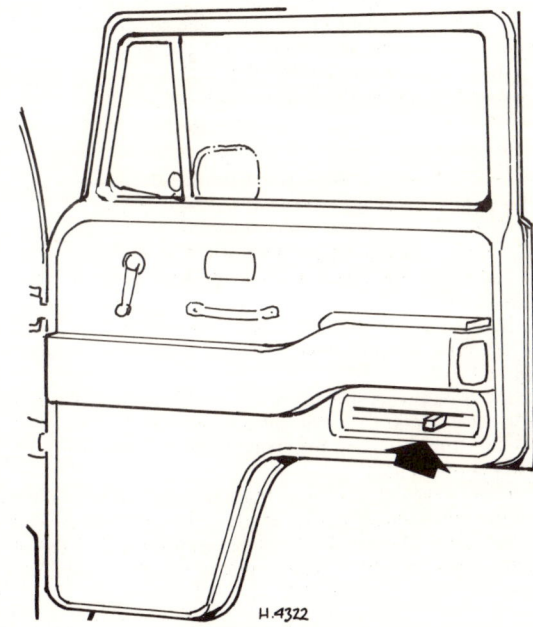

Fig 12.5 1972 pattern door - note the large trunking (Sec 12)

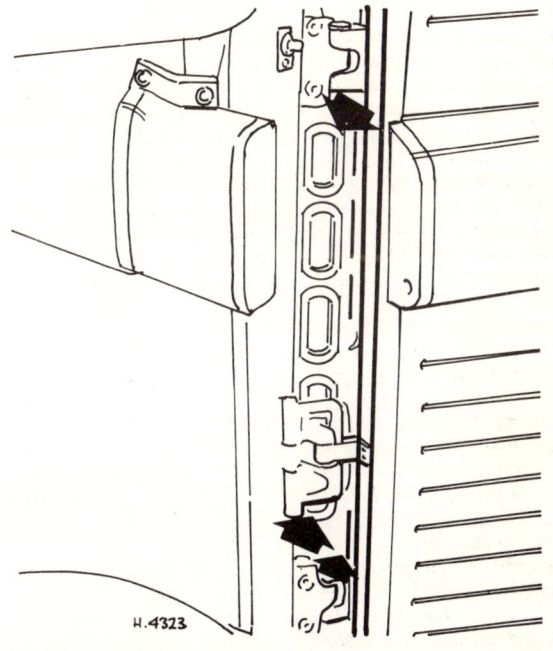

Fig 12.6 The trunking on the door fits into a similar tube when the door is closed (Sec 12)

12.1 1975 pattern door. The works are all inside now

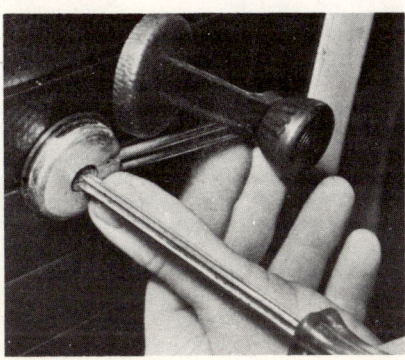

12.2a Remove the window winder handle

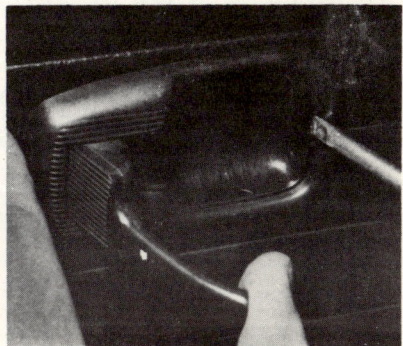

12.2b Prise out the door latch finger plate

 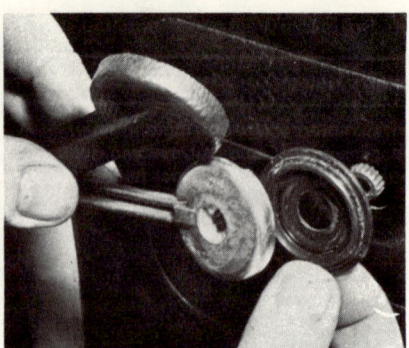 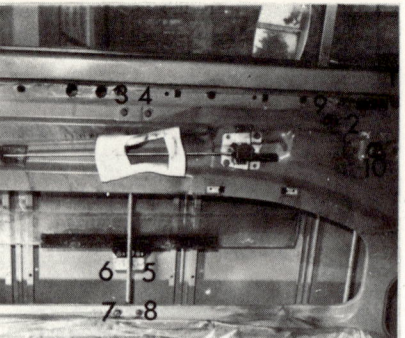

12.2c Remove the escutcheon retaining screw

12.3 Do not forget the rubbing washer window winder handle

13.4 There are eight screws to remove 1 & 2 hold the winder shaft 10 to the door 3.4.7.8 hold the cable winder mechanism to the door and 5.6. hold the glass support channel to the winder mechanism

13 Cab door window lifter mechanism - removal and replacement

1 The cable type window lifter is attached to the door at four points. On early models it was necessary to replace it entirely if any part of it was faulty but recently replacement cables have been made available so consult the VW spares agent if only the cable is faulty.
2 Remove the door trim panel and take off the PVC sheet.
3 Take out one screw holding the upper end of the front window guide channel, and then undo and remove the two screws holding the window lifter channel to the lifter mechanism. Push the window up and make sure it is jammed in position.
4 Remove the six screws holding the complete assembly to the door panel and unclip the bottom end of the transparent plastic cable tube from the door. (photo)
5 Press the front window guide channel off its bracket and then take the whole assembly out of the door.
6 When refitting, which is done in the reverse order first make sure that the mechanism works freely and that the cable does not rattle in any of the tubes. The tubes may be squeezed a little to prevent this if necessary. See that the foam strips at the top of the lifter are secure.
7 When the lifter mechanism is once more fixed to the door attach the window lifter plate and run the window up and down several times before finally tightening the front window channel screw and the two lifter channel screws.
8 The drive cable may be replaced if only that part is required without the remainder. Dismantle the door as far as paragraph 5, but do not remove the window. Make sure the window cannot slip down and push the shaft to which the crank is attached (the cable drive) out of the inner door panel. Now tilt the window lifter assembly and lower it until the cable bracket comes down far enough for the cable drive to be got at through the opening in the door panel.
  Put the crank in place again and wind the old cable out as far as you can, bend the sheet metal tabs on the guide tube at the point where the cable comes out at the bottom and pull the old cable out of the guide tube.
9 Grease the new cable with molybdenum grease and feed it into the guide tube until it engages in the cable drive. Now turn the crank and pull the cable fully into the cover. Bend the tabs at the bottom back into place. Refit the winder mechanism back into the door, test the lifter mechanism and reinstall the trim and handles.

14 Cab door window glass - removal and replacement

1 Before the glass can be removed the lifter mechanism must be

taken out as described in the previous Section. In addition the screw holding the window rear guide channel must be undone and the channel pushed to one side. The window may then be lowered and taken out of the bottom of the door.
2 If the lifter channel is separated from the glass it should be refitted so that the centre hole is equidistant from the front and rear edge of the glass.

15 Cab door quarterlight - removal and replacement

1 To remove glass grind off the bottom of the rivet at the top pivot and punch the rest out. (It is too hard to drill). The glass can then be tilted out and lifted out of the bottom clamp.
2 It is important to renew the upper pivot rivet with the proper hardened type suitably spread. The security of the vehicle may depend on it.
3 If the glass pivots too freely or too stiffly then it is possible to alter the friction on the bottom pivot clamp. Remove the door inner trim panel and the clamp screw is accessible through a hole in the door panel.
4 For other repairs the frame must be removed from the door. This entails removing the trim, window glass, front guide channel and rear guide channel. It is not recommended that the owner attempts such extensive repairs unless he has a good deal of experience in this type of work.

16 Cab door latch mechanism - removal and replacement

1 Remove the door trim panel and wind the window up. The rear guide channel is removed by taking out the bolt at the bottom and disengaging the clip at the top.
2 Undo the two screws holding the interior latch release lever to the door panel. Then unhook the pull rod at both ends and take it out.
3 Remove the two hexagon socket head cap screws holding the door handle to the panel and take the handle off.
4 Unscrew the locking button from the locking rod and then unhook the rod spring from the lock and take out the pull rod.
5 Put the latch in a vertical position, undo the three crosshead screws holding the latch mechanism to the inner panel and then take it out downwards complete with its plastic cover.
6 Replacement is the reverse of this procedure except that the locking rod should be attached to the lock before it is put up in position. When refitting the rear window guide channel difficulty may be experienced in refastening the top clip. This can be seen if the run channel is raised a little in the window slot at the top with the window in the raised position. Make sure the top run channel is firmly engaged afterwards.

17 Front door lock cylinder - replacement

1 Dismantle the front door, as in Section 16, to remove the door handle.
2 Inside the handle is the operating pin (see Fig. 12.7). Remove the crosshead screw holding this and the lock cylinder may be pushed out to the outside.

3 When reassembling make sure the 'O' ring and the gasket are in good order or water will seep into the latch.

18 Sliding door mechanism - description and adjustment

1 The sliding door runs in three channels. At the bottom, a roller bracket fitted at the front corner supports weight and guides the door in a channel fitted along the bottom of the door

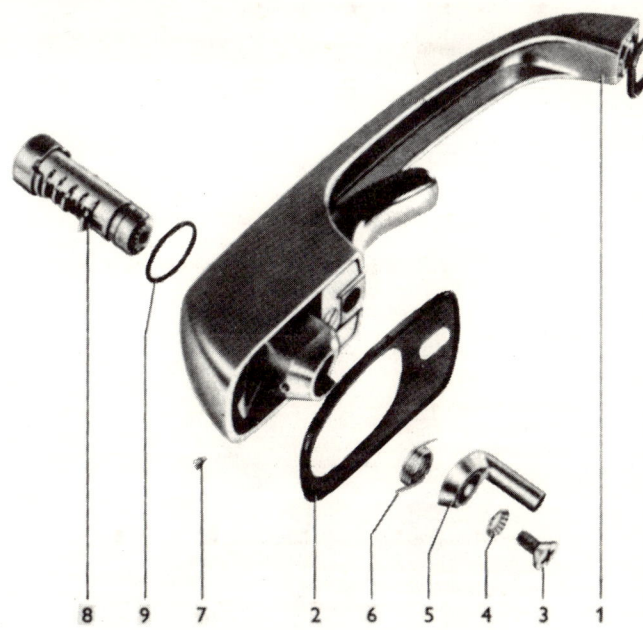

Fig 12.7 Cab door handle and lock cylinder later models (Secs 16 and 17)

1 Door handle
2 Gasket
3 Crosshead screw
4 Lockwasher
5 Operating pin
6 Spring
7 Setscrew
8 Lock cylinder
9 O-ring

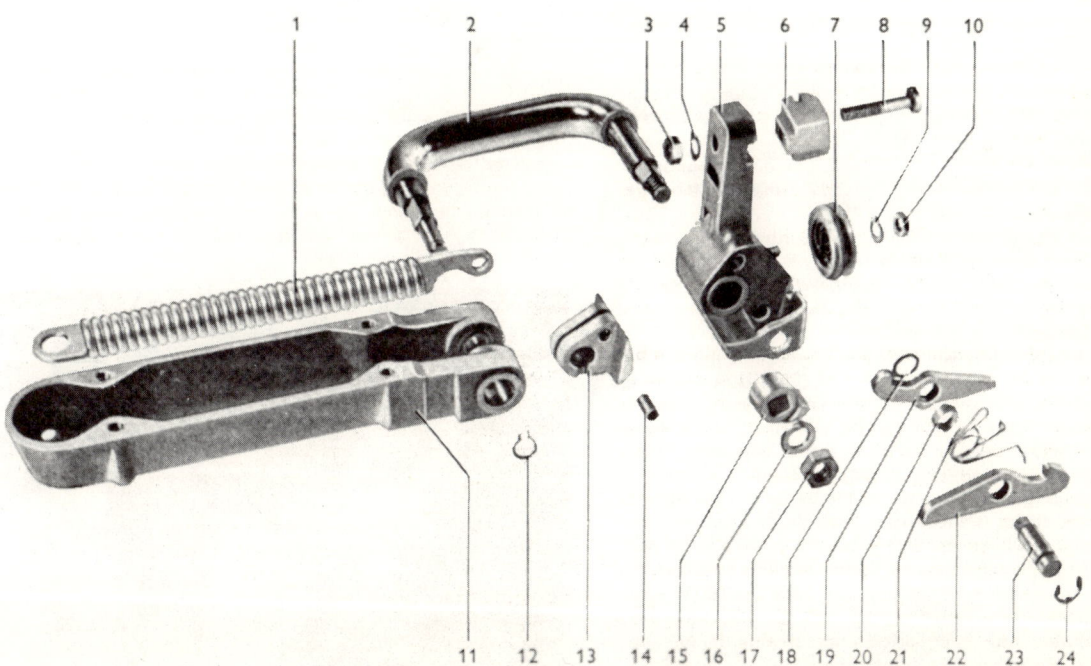

Fig 12.8 Sliding door - hinge link assembly components (Secs 18 and 19)

1 Return spring	7 Roller and bearing	13 Pivot	19 Lower locking lever
2 Hinge link	8 Phillips screw	14 Pin	20 Spacer
3 M6 nut	9 Spring washer	15 Operating cam	21 Spring
4 Lockwasher	10 M6 nut (thin)	16 Spring washer	22 Upper locking lever
5 Roller bracket	11 Housing	17 M8 nut	23 Pin
6 Guide block	12 Circlip	18 Washer	24 Circlip

opening. In the centre a roller bracket combined with a throw-out hinge is fitted on the rear edge and thus takes weight and runs in a channel fitted to the outside of the vehicle under a cover. At the top edge a bracket with a guide roller runs in a channel along the top edge of the door opening. The door slides back on the outside of the bodywork. The rear runner hinge bracket throws the rear edge of the door out and once the front edge of the door is clear of the front latch the top and bottom channels guide the front of the door outwards, thus enabling it to slide back parallel with the body.

There are three latch devices. At the front there is a remote control lock to which the operating handles are attached. From this latch a connecting rod and a cable run to the rear centre lock. When the operating handle is moved upwards the rear latch engages. When the handle is moved down the rear latch disengages, and the spring loaded hinge bracket moves the rear edge of the door outwards. Further downward movement of the handle disengages the front latch and the door may then be pushed back. A retainer catch mounted above the remote control latch engages with a pin on the rear buffer bracket mounted at the front end of the central runner. This prevents the door from sliding shut under its own weight on forward slopes. A connecting lever from the remote control latch releases the retainer catch when the door is to be closed.

2 Adjustments are necessary if the door does not run freely or does not line up in the body aperture. When closed the gap should be equal around the edges of the door. The door should also line up flush with the body panels.

3 To adjust the vertical position of the door the lower roller is moved. It is secured by a crosshead screw on the door front face and two socket head cap screws underneath. If the door needs raising, then additional shims will be needed between the horizontal part of the mounting and the door. If the door is not flush with the body panels it can be moved in or out in relation to the roller bracket. (Fig. 12.9)

4 If the top of the door is not flush the roller may be moved on its bracket as necessary. The top roller should also be as high up into the track as possible without binding. This can be adjusted on the bracket which has slotted holes for vertical adjustment. (Fig. 12.10) (photo)

5 The gap at the front and rear vertical edges is adjusted by moving the hinge link. Slacken the four bolts holding it to the door (when the door is shut) and move the door forward or backward as required. (Fig. 12.11)

6 The door retainer should line up with the locking pin on the buffer bracket and can be moved up and down when the three retaining screws are slackened. (Fig. 12.12)

7 The proper engagement of the remote control lock into the locking plate is dependent on the fore and aft adjustment of the door by the hinge link already mentioned. This plate can be adjusted vertically as required to accept the tongue of the latch. (Fig. 12.13) (photo)

8 The rear of the door, when closed, should not move when pressed from outside near the hinge link. If it does move, or conversely, if the engagement of the centre latch seems to require excessive force on the handle, the striker plate needs adjustment. Slacken the two securing screws and move it up, down, in or out as required. (Fig. 12.14) (photo)

9 The connecting rod and the cable between the remote control and the centre lock are adjustable. Remove the door trim and the locks will be visible. The rear latch has a 4 mm hole in the front of it. Insert a screw or rod in this hole to secure the lock and tighten cable with the adjuster until the cable is just taut and then lock the adjuster with the locknut. Now adjust the connecting rod and lock it in position by screwing the threaded sleeve as far as the stop on the lock pushrod.

Finally remove the screw or rod from the hole and replace the trim.

---

19 Sliding door - removal, overhaul and replacement

1 Before the door may be removed the outside runner cover

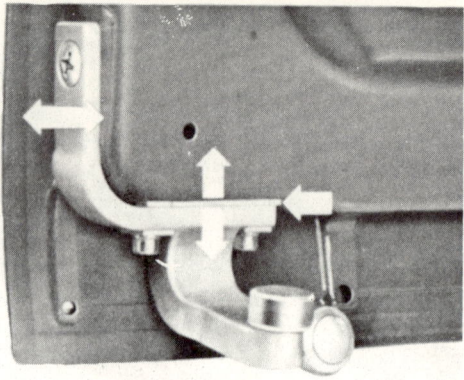

Fig 12.9 Sliding door lower rollers and bracket (Sec 18)

Arrows indicate movement and shim

Fig 12.10 Sliding door top guide roller and bracket (Sec 18)

Arrows indicate adjustment of roller

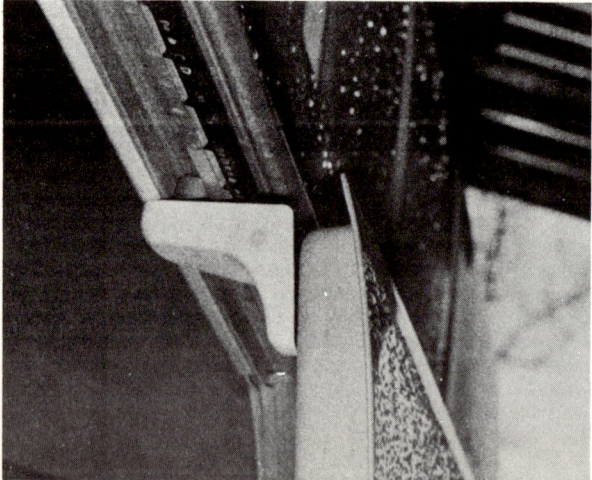

18.4 Sliding door top guide roller 1975 high roof van.

Fig 12.11 Sliding door hinge link showing mounting screws (Sec 18)

On later models the inner screws are covered with caps and can be undone without moving the trim

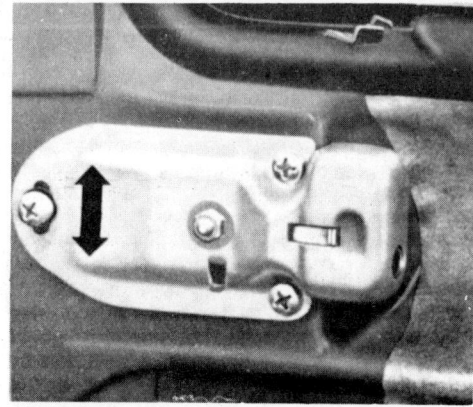

Fig 12.12 Sliding door retainer latch showing direction of adjustment (Sec 18)

Fig. 12.13 Sliding door remote control latch lock plate indicating vertical adjustment (Sec 18)

18.7 1975 pattern sliding door remote control latch. Adjustment still the same

Fig 12.14 Sliding door centre latch striker plate indicating adjustment directions (Sec 18)

18.8 1975 pattern centre latch striker plate and remote control lock. Note introduction of plastic. Adjustment is still the same

must be taken off. The cover consists of three components, beading, cover and retaining strip. The retaining strip is held in tension by a crosshead screw. (Figs. 12.15 and 12.16)

The cover is held in place by two crosshead screws at the front one at the rear and a cover securing nut and bolt accessible from inside the passenger compartment. There may be a combination of these fixings. When these have been removed open the door fully and undo the tensioning screw about 15 turns (photo) (from inside the front end of the cover). Using a drift tap the screw smartly to the rear. The cover may be lifted up and out. Now take the crosshead retaining screws out of the retaining strip and remove the strip.

2 Move the door back until the guide piece and roller on the hinge link may be disengaged from the channel. Next push the door to the rear until the upper roller clears the top channel. Now swing the rear of the door out a little so that the lower rollers can be moved out of the gap in the bottom channel.

3 It all sounds very complicated but it isn't if there are two people doing the job. Unless you have had a lot of practice do not tackle the job on your own, it is quite easy to damage the running gear if the heavy door is not controlled carefully.

4 Inspect the runners, if they are damaged you may be able to straighten them but be careful. If you are not sure it is best to go to the expert; unless the runners are true the door cannot be fitted correctly.

5 The retaining latch may be removed without disturbing the

trim (Fig. 12.17). Replacement of the other locks will require the removal of the trim. It is not necessary to replace the bracket if the top guide roller is worn. The roller may be removed and replaced from the bracket once the door is out of the body.

6 The hinge is held to the door by four bolts. These must be extracted from the inside of the door. Depending on which type of door is being repaired remove the trim and the four bolts are easily removed. However, it may not be necessary to take the hinge off the door to repair it. An illustration is given of an exploded view of the hinge. Unless the return spring is broken or the bearing between the housing and the hinge link worn, the remainder of the parts may be removed from the link. If you are wise you will push a piece of rod slightly smaller in diameter

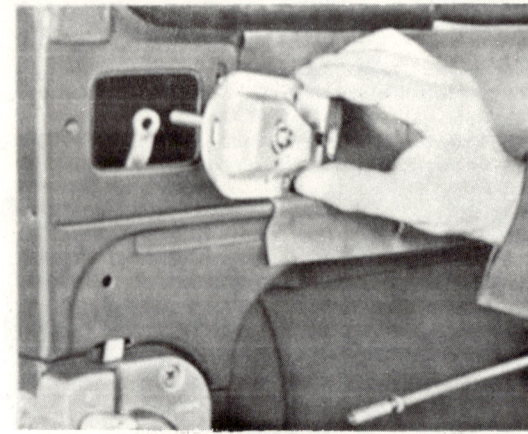

Fig. 12.17 Removing the sliding door retainer catch (Sec 19)

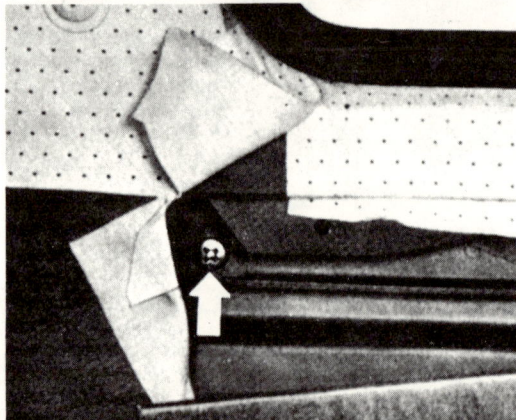

Fig 12.18 Removing the trim to get at the crosshead screw for the retainer rear bracket (Sec 19)

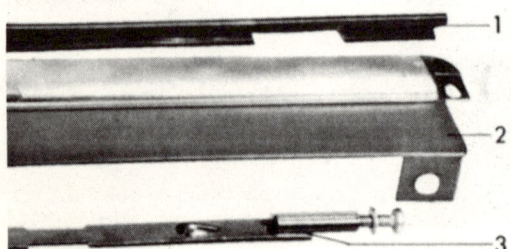

Fig 12.15 The components of the centre runner cover strip (Sec 19)

1 Beading   2 Cover   3 Retaining strip

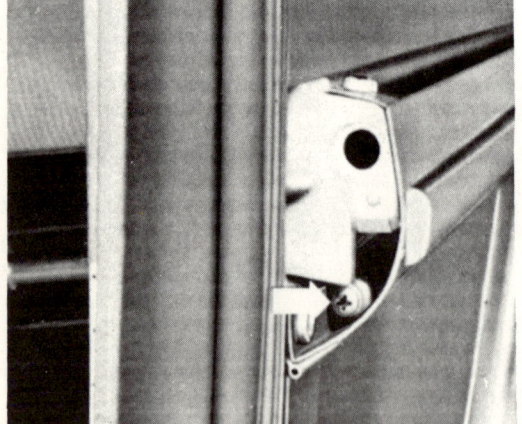

Fig 12.16 Centre runner cover strip tensioning screw (arrowed) (Sec 19)

Fig 12.19 Retainer rear bracket A - spring B - buffers. Having taken the screw out of the inside, undo the bolts to remove the bracket (Sec 19)

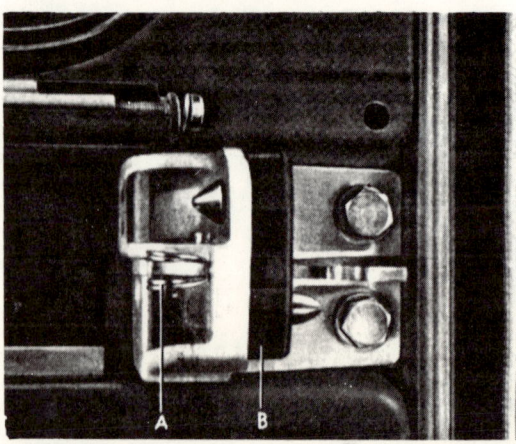

than the link spindle against the end of the link after the M8 nut has been removed and pull the whole of the roller bracket assembly on to the rod. You can then take the roller bracket away and sort it out with the rod held in the vice. The guide link and roller may be removed without taking the roller bracket off the link. If the locking levers or springs are worn or broken then they may be replaced but unless you drew them off onto a rod you will have no idea of which goes where. (Fig. 12.8)

7 The sliding door retainer rear bracket (the part that the retainer latches onto when the door is fully open) is located at the back end of the centre runner. It may be serviced only when the sliding door is removed, so this is the time to do it if it is necessary. Depending on the model it may be necessary to remove a piece of the trim at the bottom corner of the window to get at the crosshead screw from inside; the other two bolts are removed from outside. If the spring or rubber buffer is damaged it should be replaced. If the bracket is removed then it may be necessary after re-installation of the door to adjust the door retainer latch (see Section 18.6). (Figs. 12.18 and 12.19)

8 Before re-installing the door check the condition of the weatherstrip round the door opening in the body. If this is hard, torn or deformed it should be replaced.

9 Lubricate the guide rail with grease (photo) and put some grease on the rollers. Now with the aid of a helper insert the door first into the bottom runner and then into the top runner, keeping it level to avoid straining anything, ease the door forwards until the roller and guide of the hinge can be fitted into the break in the centre runner.

The door is now back in place. Move it cautiously to the shut position and then to the fully open position. If all is well install the outside runner cover and oil the hinge link assembly. (photo)

10 To install the runner cover first fit the retaining strip but do not tighten the screws. Insert the cover between the body and the retaining strips - start at the back and ease it in gently, put in the two crosshead screws from below and tension the retaining strip by turning the screw on the end of it until the cover is correctly fitted. Now tighten the remaining screws and fit the nut and bolt from inside the vehicle.

11 Do not be discouraged if it does not come right first time. It is a large weight to carry on such bearings and the latch settings are critical. The main thing is to proceed gently and not to force things. It is as well to be sure what you are going to do before you start, a little time in rehearsal is well spent.

---

20 Windscreen and windows - removal and replacement

1 The Transporter windscreen is a large, heavy and expensive

article. If you are unfortunate enough to have to obtain a new one you would be well advised to let the supplier fit it. If you acquire one removed from a wrecked vehicle you will still be paying a reasonably high price for it. Unless you are experienced and have competent assistance it is recommended that it be professionally fitted. Other fixed windows are similarly fitted and the procedure is the same.

First loosen the rubber sealing strip on the inside where it fits over the edge of the window frame. Use a piece of wood for this. Anything sharp may rip the rubber weatherstrip. The glass can be pushed out, weatherstrip attached, if pressure is applied at the top corners. Two people are needed on this to prevent the glass falling out. Push evenly and protect your hands to avoid accidents. Remove the finisher strip from the weatherstrip.

2 When fitting glass first make sure that the window frame edges are even and smooth. Examine the edges of the glass to see that it is ground smooth and no chips or cracks are visible. Any such cracks could be the start of a much bigger one. The rubber weatherstrip should be perfectly clean. No traces of sealing compound should remain or rubber, glass or metal. If the sealing strip is old, brittle or hard, it is advisable to fit a new one even though they are not cheap.

3 Fit the weatherstrip to the glass first so that the joint comes midway along the top edge.

4 Next fit any decorative moulding into the weatherstrip. This is done by first feeding fine cord into the slot (use a piece of thin tubing as a guide and time saver) and leave the ends overlapping long enough to be able to grip later. The two halves of the moulding are then put in place and the cord drawn out so that the edge of the strip locks them into place.

5 Apply suitable sealing compound to the weatherstrip where it will seat onto the metal window frame and also onto the outside faces of the frame at the lower corners.

6 Fit a piece of really strong thin cord into the frame channel of the weatherstrip as already described and then offer up the glass to the aperture. This operation requires two people.

7 When you are sure that the glass is centrally positioned, pull the cord out so that the lip of the weatherstrip is drawn over the inner edge of the frame flange. One of the most frequent difficulties in this job is that the cord breaks. This is often because of sharp or uneven edges on the frame flange so a little extra time in preparation will pay off.

---

21 Seats - removal and replacement

1 The driver's seat is removed by lifting the fore and aft adjustment lever and sliding it forward out of its runners.

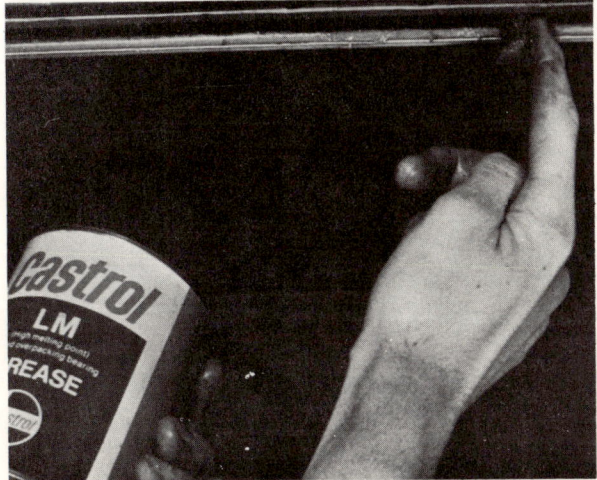
19.9a Lubricate the guide rail

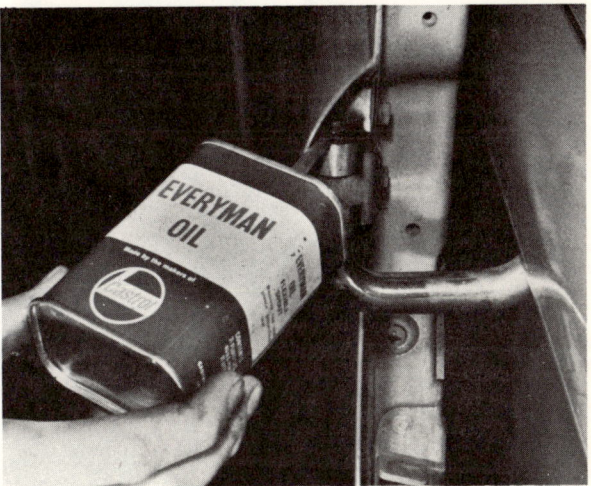
19.9b Oil the link assembly

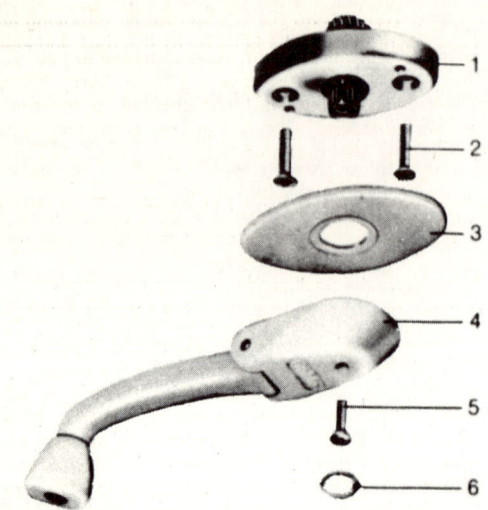

Fig 12.20 Sliding roof crank handle and gear components (Sec 22)

1	*Drive gear*	4	*Handle*
2	*Gear retaining screw*	5	*Screw*
3	*Escutcheon*	6	*Cap*

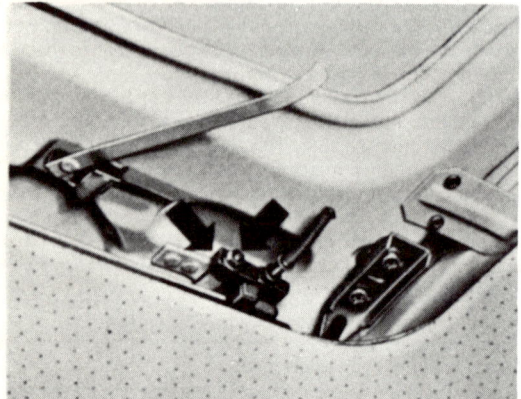

Fig. 12.21 Sliding roof rear lifter showing leaf spring moved away, locknut and lifter pin. (Sec 22)

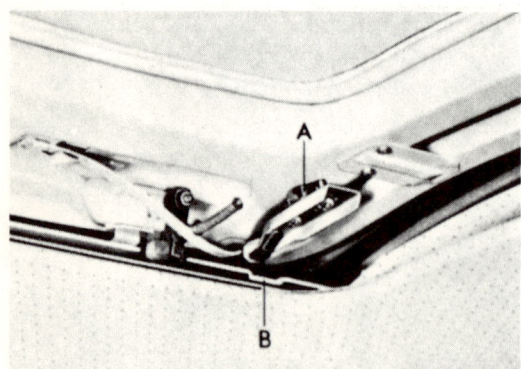

Fig. 12.22 Sliding roof rear guide height adjuster screw (A) and recess in Channel (B) (Sec 22)

2   To remove the front passenger's seat lift up the front of the squab. This draws the back rest downwards so that it disengages from a retainer loop behind. The seat and back rest together are then lifted out. The retainer loop behind the backrest is adjustable to make the seat secure properly.

3   Cargo space seats are removed by unbolting from the floor; unclip the side trim to make it easier to get at the bolts, unscrew the nuts and remove the clips. To remove the bolts take off the mounting plates and remove the bolts by turning them 90° in either direction.

4   On later models the mounting plate has been discontinued and the holes in the floor are a different shape to accommodate 'T' headed bolts.

22 Sliding roof - operation and adjustment

1   The movement of the sliding roof is controlled by special flexible cables, a sort of flexible rack, which engage with a pinion drive gear revolved by a crank handle.

2   Any tendency for the sliding roof to jam must be investigated without delay otherwise damage or excessive wear of the components may result. Generally speaking adjustments are confined to ensuring that it runs parallel and is maintained at the correct height.

3   To adjust the roof to ensure that it slides parallel first unclip the front edge of the trim panel with the roof open a little way. Then push the trim panel as far back as it will go (it is not possible to remove the trim panel without taking the roof off completely). Close the roof again. Remove the crank handle retaining screw and pull off the handle and escutcheon. Then slacken the drive gear retaining screws 6 turns so that the gear can be drawn down far enough to disengage from the cables. (Fig. 12.20)

4   Check the height of the rear end of the roof. This is done by swinging the leaf springs out to one side and then slackening the hexagon lock nut and screw. Move the lifter pin in the elongated hole to correct the height, (Fig. 12.21), at the same time the rear guides can be adjusted for height so that they run in the recesses in the runners. This prevents the roof bouncing about when open on rough surfaced roads. (Fig. 12.22)

5   Set the sliding roof panel exactly square in the aperture. Turn the cable drive gear shaft clockwise as far as it will go and come back ½ turn. Then push the gear back into mesh with the cables and secure it and replace the handle.

6   Pull forward the trim panel and clip it back in position.

7   If the front of the roof is set at the wrong height, the front guide screws should be loosened and the adjusting screw turned as required. (Fig. 12.23)

8   Water which may enter the roof opening is collected in channels in the roof frame and drains out through hoses fitted at

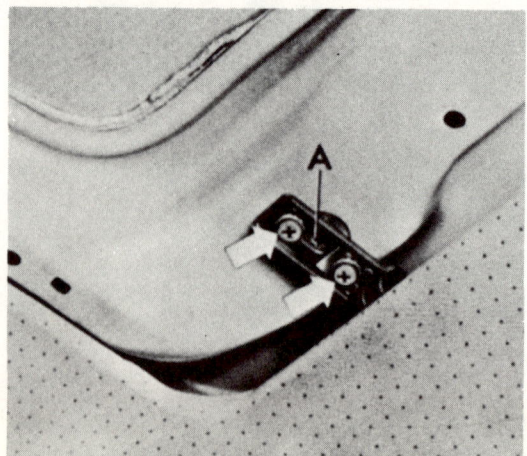

Fig 12.23 Sliding roof front guide height adjustment showing securing screws and adjusting screw (A) (Sec 22)

the front centre and rear of the channels. Make sure the hoses are not blocked. The front ones can be cleared from above with some flexible wire. The centre and rear ones can be cleared from below after removing the non-return valves on the ends.

23 Sliding roof - removal of trim panel

1   Remove the sliding roof, as in Section 22. The trim panel remains behind. Working through the roof opening from above remove the eight crosshead screws and the single countersunk head screw which hold the left runner to the body. See Fig. 12.24.
2   Remove the runner with its retainer forward out of the bracket and lift it clear of the roof. It is now possible to ease the trim panel out sideways to the left.
3   Replacement is the reverse.

24 Pop-up and hinged roofs - checking, maintenance and repair

1   The most important points to check on the opening type roof are the condition of the special weather seal strips and the security of the mounting bracket screws. If any sealing strip comes adrift get it fixed before it is trapped and damaged. The main roof seal strip incorporates steel clips which may have lost some of their tension. Pull the strip clear, squeeze the clips together and then push the seal back on. See that all the pivot pins of the support brackets are lightly oiled and the slotted runners thinly greased.
2   The fabric parts should be wiped clean without the use of detergents and should never be folded and left damp. Whenever conditions require the roof to be closed whilst wet be sure to open it and dry it out at the first opportunity.

3   Removal of the hinged roof is simple. Lift the roof into the raised position. Work round the bellows inside removing all the screws and strips that hold the bellows to the roof and ease the bellows material clear of the roof. Have someone to help you by holding the roof while you remove the hinge bolts. There are three on each side holding the hinge channel to the roof and then the two crosshead screws holding each roof support retaining plate (the ones that hold the stays - they are in the roof channel). It is the reverse of removal. (Figs. 12.25 and 12.26)
4   It is not necessary to remove the hinged roof to renew the bellows material (so we are told) but we recommend that the frame is taken off if a proper job is to be done by the d-i-y enthusiast. The bellows is fixed to the wooden frame with staples which must be carefully removed. If you are going to fit a new bellows (and it is actually in your posession and it fits) then cut the old cover away near to the frame and it will be much easier to remove the staples without damaging the wood.

   When refitting a new bellows, tack or staple it in all four corners first and then work from one end to the other. When the material is securely fixed tack the plastic strips in place over it.

   The lower edge is fixed by first glueing the plastic moulding to the roof (if there isn't one there already) and then screwing the bellows securing strips in the following order (1) front (2) rear (3) left side (4) right side.

25 Interior trim - removal and replacement

1   It is difficult to be specific on this point as this manual would need to be very long indeed if every piece of interior trim was dealt with separately.
2   For the Combi or campmobile the passenger rear side trim arm rest is fastened by screws underneath. These screws have small plastic caps. Once the arm rest is off the panel is prised away, being held by clips.

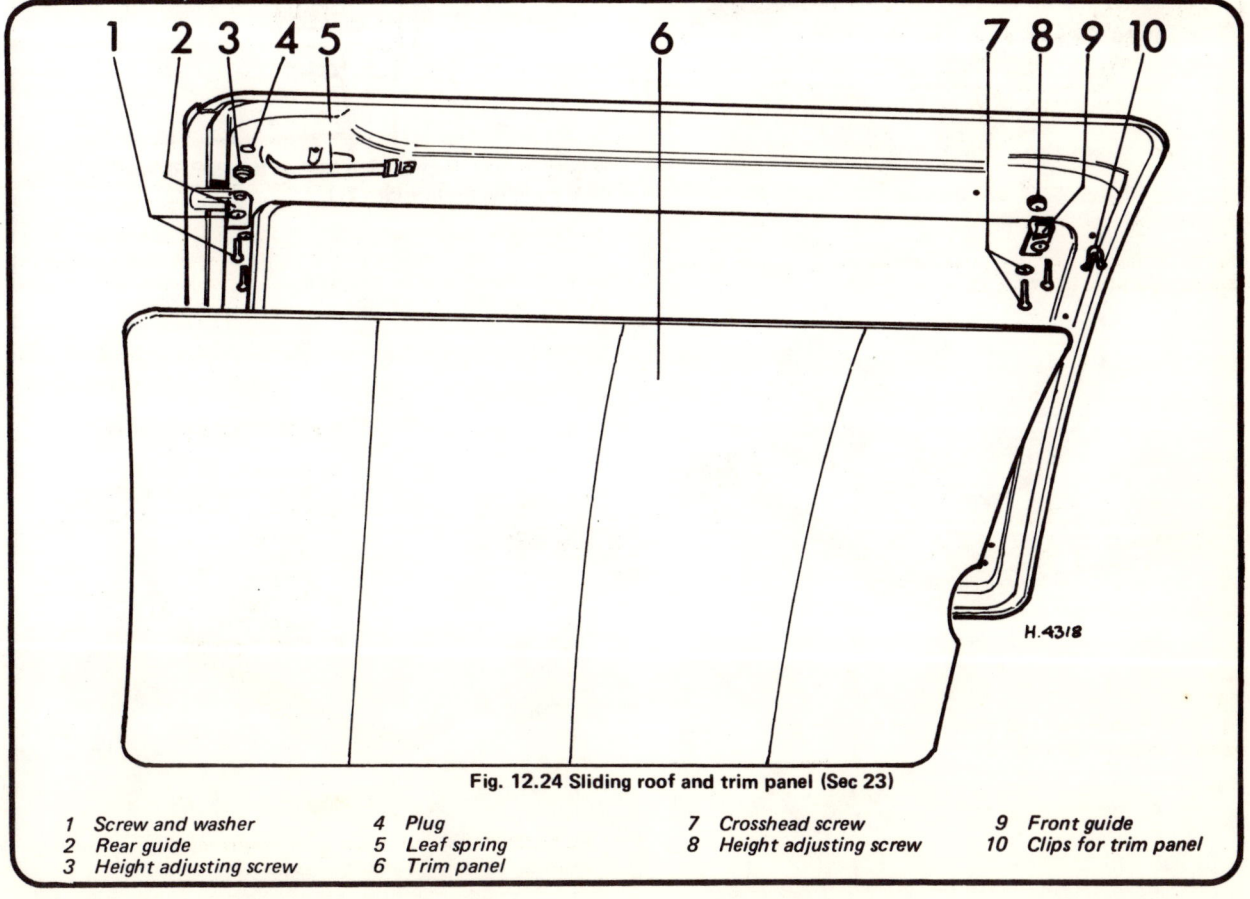

H.43/8

Fig. 12.24 Sliding roof and trim panel (Sec 23)

1	Screw and washer	4	Plug	7	Crosshead screw
2	Rear guide	5	Leaf spring	8	Height adjusting screw
3	Height adjusting screw	6	Trim panel		

9	Front guide
10	Clips for trim panel

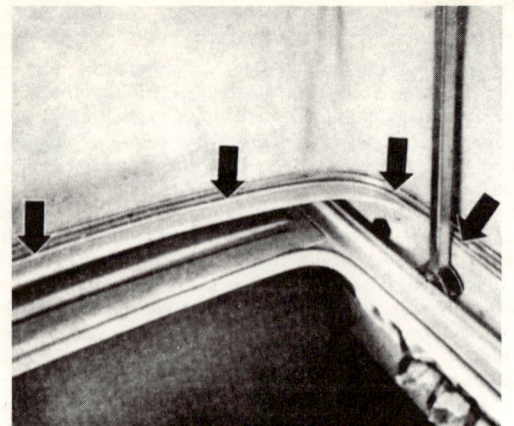

Fig 12.25 The plastic strips holding the bellows to the frame (Sec 24)

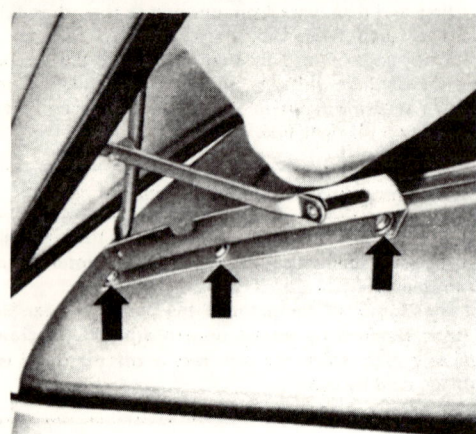

Fig 12.26 The bolts holding the hinge to the roof (Sec 24)

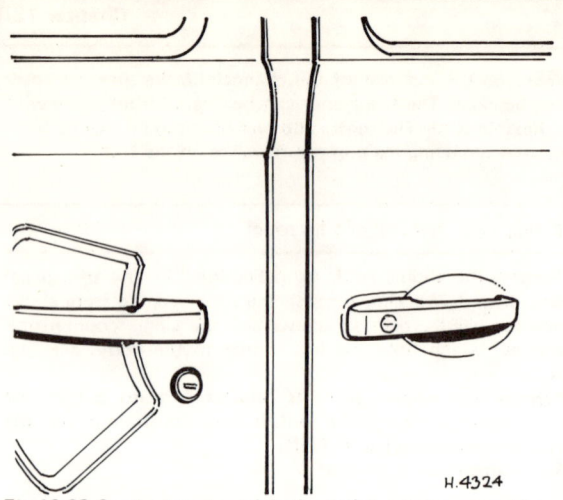

Fig 12.28 On the latest models the lock has been moved from the sliding door handle and is now situated just below it (Sec 27)

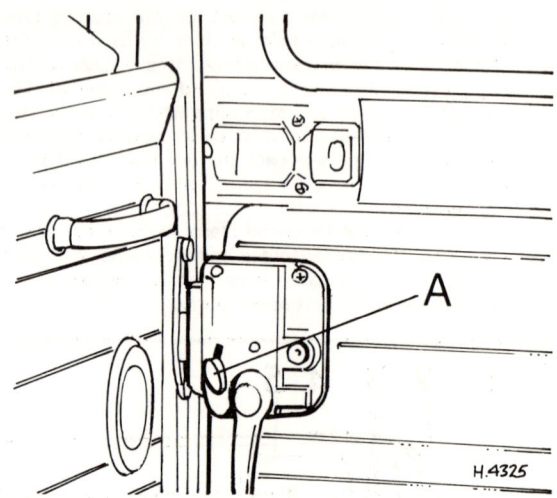

Fig 12.29 The locking knob (A) can be released from the outside by using the key (Sec 27)

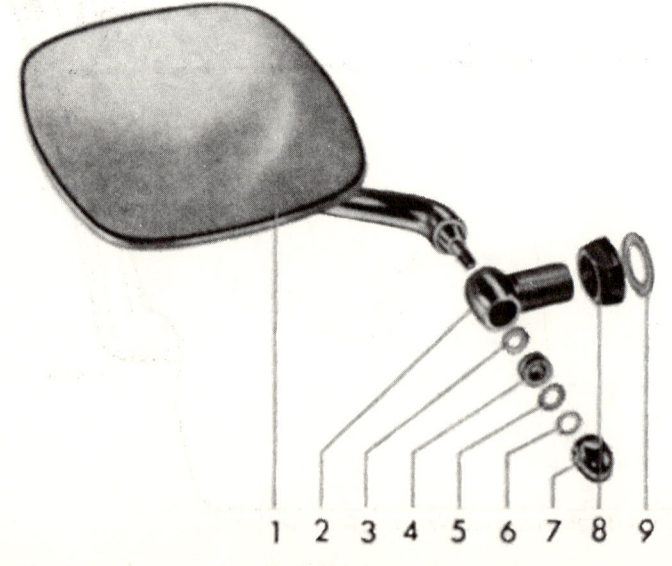

Fig. 12.27 Exterior mirror

1 Mirror
2 Mirror bracket (tee piece)
3 Washer with hexagonal hole
4 Spring
5 Washer
6 Washer
7 Dome nut
8 Union nut
9 Plastic washer

3 The luggage compartment trim is held in place by screws covered by plastic caps.

4 The trim panels are usually held by clips and any fixture is screwed on after the trim is in its clips. The important thing to remember when removing trim is not to use too much force. If it will not come away then stop and look to see why.

26 Exterior mirrors

1 The exterior mirrors are not fitted at the factory, they come separately boxed (so do the screen wipers). They may, or may not, have been adjusted to suit the owner (see Fig. 12.27).

2 There are two pivots so that the mirror may be set at any angle. The 'T' piece is screwed into the body and held with a 19 mm locknut (¾ in AF spanner). To fit the mirror remove the plug which is by the gap in the body trim just in front of the edge of the quarter light in the front door.

3 Dismantle the mirror by removing the self locking cap nut and taking the mirror arm out of the 'T' piece, then screw the 'T' piece with locknut in place into the hole in the body where a thread is provided to receive it. Do not forget the plastic washer which should be between the locknut and the body. When the 'T' piece will not go in another complete turn, rotate it back to the horizontal and fix it with the locknut.

4 Re-install the mirror arm washers and spring (first the washer with the hexagon hole, then the coil spring, then the lock washer and plain washer) and screw on the self-locking cap nut.

5 The mirror frame is held to the arm by a split clamp with another locking screw.

6 By loosening the two pivots so that they allow the mirror to move stiffly it is possible to adjust the mirror to your own personal requirements.

7 It is advisable to have a helper to move the mirror while you sit in the driving seat, but tighten the mirror yourself when it is set, to save a lot of argument.

8 Provision is made for mirrors on both sides and two mirrors should be supplied with the vehicle.

27 Modifications

Each year there is a crop of minor modifications to the bodywork. At the moment a new method of locking the sliding door by means of a lock below the handle, (not in it) has been introduced. (Figs. 12.28 and 12.29)

On the 1975 model we were priviliged to examine there were a number of minor modifications, mainly in the use of plastics where metal had been used before. However, we must stop somewhere if this book is to go to print; even this excellent vehicle can be improved and VW are constantly trying to do just that.

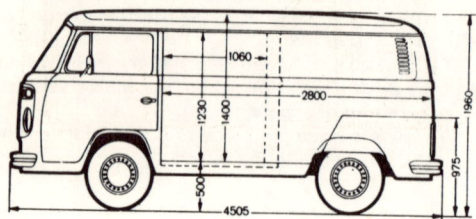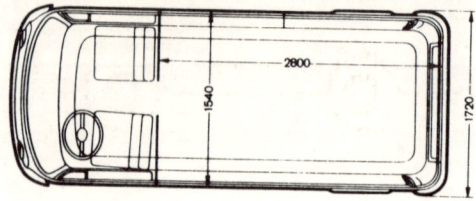

VAN

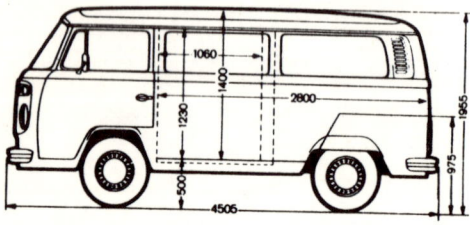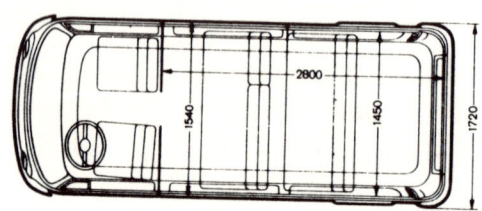

COMBI

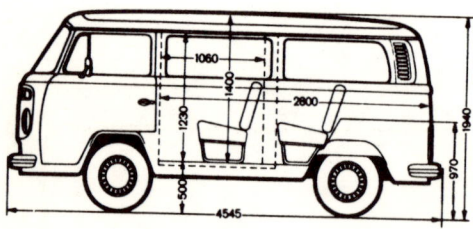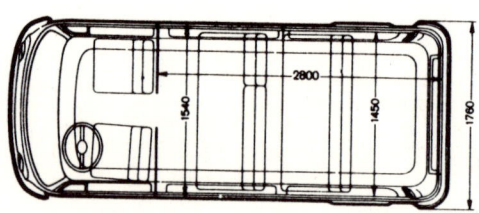

MICROBUS

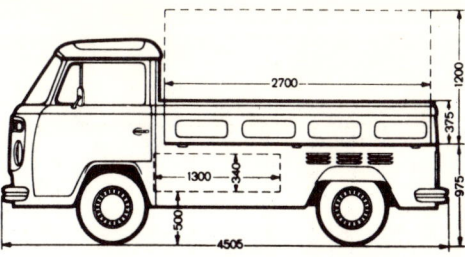
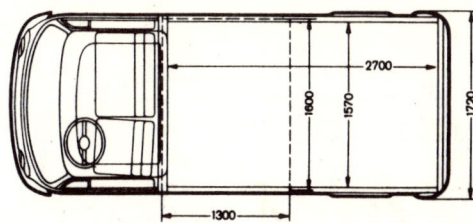

PICK—UP

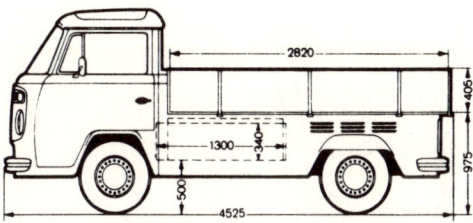
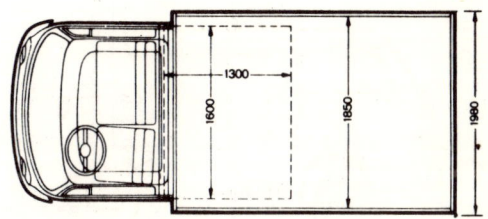

PICK—UP — WIDE PLATFORM

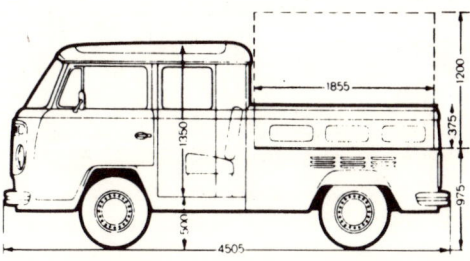
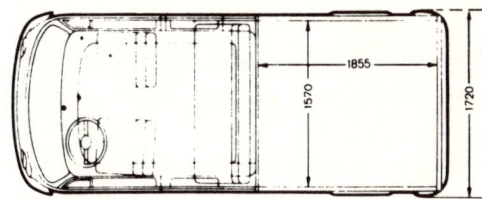

PICK—UP — DOUBLE CAB

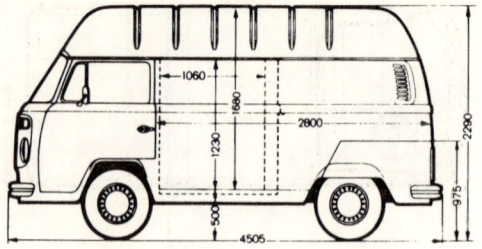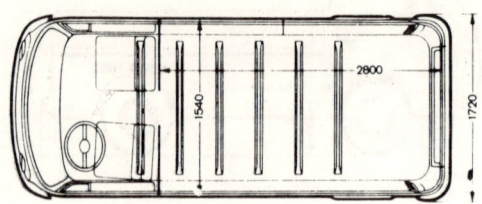

HIGH ROOF VAN

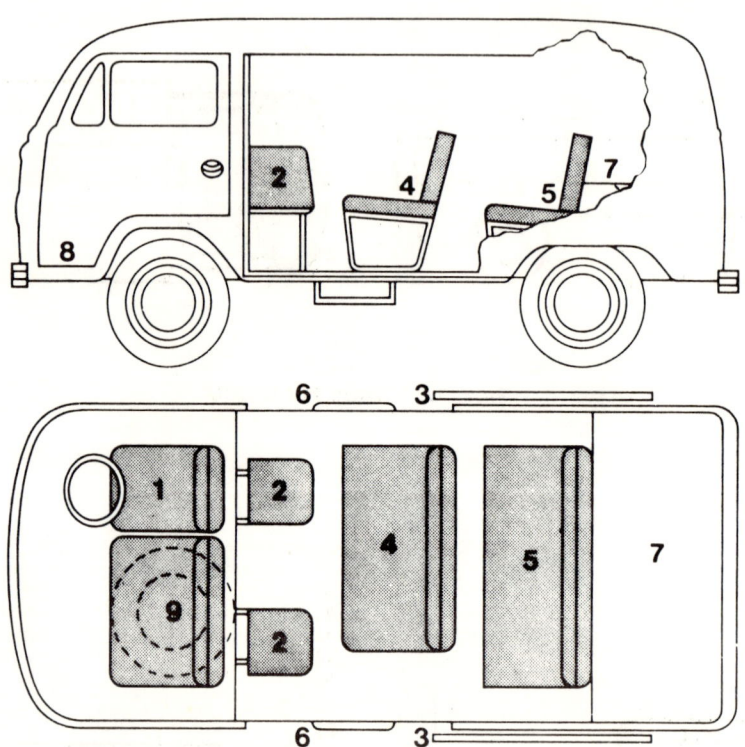

12 SEATER BUS

1 Driver
2 In facing foldaway seats
3 Sliding doors (one each side)
4 3 place bench seat
5 4 place bench seat

6 Entry step. 1 each side
7 Baggage space
    35 cubic feet/1 cubic metre
8 Cab access step
9 Spare wheel under 2 place bench seat

CAMPMOBILE — CARAVETTE

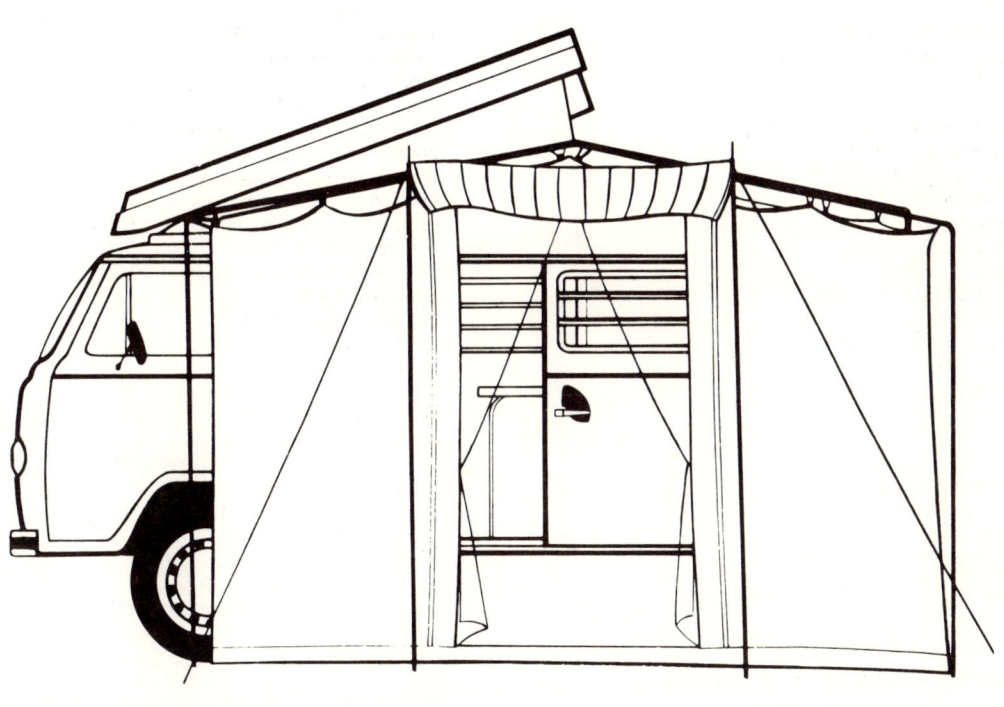

CAMPMOBILE — CONTINENTAL

Index

Metric conversion tables

Inches	Decimals	Millimetres	Millimetres to Inches		Inches to Millimetres	
			mm	Inches	Inches	mm
1/64	0.015625	0.3969	0.01	0.00039	0.001	0.0254
1/32	0.03125	0.7937	0.02	0.00079	0.002	0.0508
3/64	0.046875	1.1906	0.03	0.00118	0.003	0.0762
1/16	0.0625	1.5875	0.04	0.00157	0.004	0.1016
5/64	0.078125	1.9844	0.05	0.00197	0.005	0.1270
3/32	0.09375	2.3812	0.06	0.00236	0.006	0.1524
7/64	0.109375	2.7781	0.07	0.00276	0.007	0.1778
1/8	0.125	3.1750	0.08	0.00315	0.008	0.2032
9/64	0.140625	3.5719	0.09	0.00354	0.009	0.2286
5/32	0.15625	3.9687	0.1	0.00394	0.01	0.254
11/64	0.171875	4.3656	0.2	0.00787	0.02	0.508
3/16	0.1875	4.7625	0.3	0.01181	0.03	0.762
13/64	0.203125	5.1594	0.4	0.01575	0.04	1.016
7/32	0.21875	5.5562	0.5	0.01969	0.05	1.270
15/64	0.234375	5.9531	0.6	0.02362	0.06	1.524
1/4	0.25	6.3500	0.7	0.02756	0.07	1.778
17/64	0.265625	6.7469	0.8	0.03150	0.08	2.032
9/32	0.28125	7.1437	0.9	0.03543	0.09	2.286
19/64	0.296875	7.5406	1	0.03937	0.1	2.54
5, 16	0.3125	7.9375	2	0.07874	0.2	5.08
21/64	0.328125	8.3344	3	0.11811	0.3	7.62
11/32	0.34375	8.7312	4	0.15748	0.4	10.16
23/64	0.359375	9.1281	5	0.19685	0.5	12.70
3/8	0.375	9.5250	6	0.23622	0.6	15.24
25/64	0.390625	9.9219	7	0.27559	0.7	17.78
13/32	0.40625	10.3187	8	0.31496	0.8	20.32
27/64	0.421875	10.7156	9	0.35433	0.9	22.86
7/16	0.4375	11.1125	10	0.39370	1	25.4
29/64	0.453125	11.5094	11	0.43307	2	50.8
15/32	0.46875	11.9062	12	0.47244	3	76.2
31/64	0.484375	12.3031	13	0.51181	4	101.6
1/2	0.5	12.7000	14	0.55118	5	127.0
33/64	0.515625	13.0969	15	0.59055	6	152.4
17/32	0.53125	13.4937	16	0.62992	7	177.8
35/64	0.546875	13.8906	17	0.66929	8	203.2
9/16	0.5625	14.2875	18	0.70866	9	228.6
37/64	0.578125	14.6844	19	0.74803	10	254.0
19/32	0.59375	15.0812	20	0.78740	11	279.4
39/64	0.609375	15.4781	21	0.82677	12	304.8
5/8	0.625	15.8750	22	0.86614	13	330.2
41/64	0.640625	16.2719	23	0.90551	14	355.6
21/32	0.65625	16.6687	24	0.94488	15	381.0
43/64	0.671875	17.0656	25	0.98425	16	406.4
11/16	0.6875	17.4625	26	1.02362	17	431.8
45/64	0.703125	17.8594	27	1.06299	18	457.2
23/32	0.71875	18.2562	28	1.10236	19	482.6
47/64	0.734375	18.6531	29	1.14173	20	508.0
3/4	0.75	19.0500	30	1.18110	21	533.4
49/64	0.765625	19.4469	31	1.22047	22	558.8
25/32	0.78125	19.8437	32	1.25984	23	584.2
51/64	0.796875	20.2406	33	1.29921	24	609.6
13/16	0.8125	20.6375	34	1.33858	25	635.0
53/64	0.828125	21.0344	35	1.37795	26	660.4
27/32	0.84375	21.4312	36	1.41732	27	685.8
55/64	0.859375	21.8281	37	1.4567	28	711.2
7/8	0.875	22.2250	38	1.4961	29	736.6
57/64	0.890625	22.6219	39	1.5354	30	762.0
29/32	0.90625	23.0187	40	1.5748	31	787.4
59/64	0.921875	23.4156	41	1.6142	32	812.8
15/16	0.9375	23.8125	42	1.6535	33	838.2
61/64	0.953125	24.2094	43	1.6929	34	863.6
31/32	0.96875	24.6062	44	1.7323	35	889.0
63/64	0.984375	25.0031	45	1.7717	36	914.4

1   Imperial gallon = 8 Imp pints = 1.16 US gallons = 277.42 cu in = 4.5459 litres

1   US gallon = 4 US quarts = 0.862 Imp gallon = 231 cu in = 3.785 litres

1   Litre = 0.2199 Imp gallon = 0.2642 US gallon = 61.0253 cu in = 1000 cc

Miles to Kilometres		Kilometres to Miles	
1	1.61	1	0.62
2	3.22	2	1.24
3	4.83	3	1.86
4	6.44	4	2.49
5	8.05	5	3.11
6	9.66	6	3.73
7	11.27	7	4.35
8	12.88	8	4.97
9	14.48	9	5.59
10	16.09	10	6.21
20	32.19	20	12.43
30	48.28	30	18.64
40	64.37	40	24.85
50	80.47	50	31.07
60	96.56	60	37.28
70	112.65	70	43.50
80	128.75	80	49.71
90	144.84	90	55.92
100	160.93	100	62.14

lb f ft to Kg f m		Kg f m to lb f ft		lb f/in^2 : Kg f/cm^2		Kg f/cm^2 : lb f/in^2	
1	0.138	1	7.233	1	0.07	1	14.22
2	0.276	2	14.466	2	0.14	2	28.50
3	0.414	3	21.699	3	0.21	3	42.67
4	0.553	4	28.932	4	0.28	4	56.89
5	0.691	5	36.165	5	0.35	5	71.12
6	0.829	6	43.398	6	0.42	6	85.34
7	0.967	7	50.631	7	0.49	7	99.56
8	1.106	8	57.864	8	0.56	8	113.79
9	1.244	9	65.097	9	0.63	9	128.00
10	1.382	10	72.330	10	0.70	10	142.23
20	2.765	20	144.660	20	1.41	20	284.47
30	4.147	30	216.990	30	2.11	30	426.70

Printed by
J. H. HAYNES & Co. Ltd
Sparkford Yeovil Somerset
ENGLAND